The Law Office Reference Manual

McGraw-Hill Business Careers Paralegal Titles

MCGRAW-HILL PARALEGAL TITLES: WHERE EDUCATIONAL SUPPORT GOES BEYOND EXPECTATIONS

Building a solid foundation for a successful paralegal career is becoming more challenging as the needs of students and instructors continue to grow. The McGraw-Hill paralegal texts offer the solution to this ever-changing environment. Integrated real-world applications in each chapter teach students the practical skills needed for a thriving career in the field. A common vocabulary among all McGraw-Hill titles ensures consistency in learning. Up-to-date coverage of the available technology used in a legal setting and a purposefully designed set of pedagogical features with shared goals across the list provide the systems needed for students to fully grasp the material and apply it in a paralegal setting. With a thorough set of ancillaries and dedicated publisher support, these texts will facilitate active learning in the classroom and give students the skills sets desired by employers.

Introduction to Law & Paralegal Studies
Connie Farrell Scuderi
ISBN: 0073524638
© 2008

Introduction to Law for Paralegals
Deborah Benton
ISBN: 007351179X
© 2008

Basic Legal Research, Second Edition
Edward Nolfi
ISBN: 0073520519
© 2008

Basic Legal Writing, Second Edition
Pamela Tepper
ISBN: 0073403032
© 2008

Legal Research and Writing for Paralegals
Neal Bevans
ISBN: 007352462X
© 2008

Contract Law for Paralegals
Linda Spagnola
ISBN: 0073511765
© 2008

Civil Law and Litigation for Paralegals
Neal Bevans
ISBN: 0073524611
© 2008

Wills, Trusts, and Estates for Paralegals
George Kent
ISBN: 0073403067
© 2008

Legal Terminology Explained for Paralegals
Edward Nolfi
ISBN: 0073511846
© 2008

The Law Office Reference Manual
Jo Ann Lee & Marilyn L. Satterwhite
ISBN: 0073511838
© 2008

The Paralegal Reference Manual
Charles Nemeth
ISBN: 0073403075
© 2008

The Professional Paralegal
Allan Tow
ISBN: 0073403091
© 2008

Titles to come:
Ethics for Paralegals
Linda Spagnola
© 2009

Real Estate Law for Paralegals
George Kent
© 2009

The Law Office Reference Manual

Second Edition

Jo Ann Lee
Professor Emeritus of Business
Pasadena City College, CA

Marilyn L. Satterwhite
Danville Area Community College, IL

 **McGraw-Hill Irwin**

Boston   Burr Ridge, IL   Dubuque, IA   Madison, WI   New York
San Francisco   St. Louis   Bangkok   Bogotá   Caracas   Kuala Lumpur
Lisbon   London   Madrid   Mexico City   Milan   Montreal   New Delhi
Santiago   Seoul   Singapore   Sydney   Taipei   Toronto

 **McGraw-Hill**
Irwin

THE LAW OFFICE REFERENCE MANUAL

Published by McGraw-Hill/Irwin, a business unit of The McGraw-Hill Companies, Inc., 1221 Avenue of the Americas, New York, NY, 10020. Copyright © 2008 by The McGraw-Hill Companies, Inc. All rights reserved. No part of this publication may be reproduced or distributed in any form or by any means, or stored in a database or retrieval system, without the prior written consent of The McGraw-Hill Companies, Inc., including, but not limited to, in any network or other electronic storage or transmission, or broadcast for distance learning.

Some ancillaries, including electronic and print components, may not be available to customers outside the United States.

This book is printed on acid-free paper.

1 2 3 4 5 6 7 8 9 0 DOC/DOC 0 9 8 7 6

ISBN 978-0-07-351183-2
MHID 0-07-351183-8

Editorial director: *John E. Biernat*
Publisher: *Linda Schreiber*
Developmental editor: *Tammy Higham*
Marketing manager: *Keari Bedford*
Media producer: *Benjamin Curless*
Lead project manager: *Pat Frederickson*
Production supervisor: *Gina Hangos*
Lead designer: *Matthew Baldwin*
Media project manager: *Rose Range*
Typeface: *11/13 Times New Roman*
Compositor: *GTS—New Delhi, India Campus*
Printer: *R. R. Donnelley*

LIBRARY OF CONGRESS CATALOGING-IN-PUBLICATION DATA
Lee, Jo Ann, 1942-
    The law office reference manual / Jo Ann Lee, Marilyn L. Satterwhite. — 2nd ed.
      p. cm. — (McGraw-Hill business careers paralegal titles)
    Rev. ed. of: The Irwin law office reference manual. 1996.
    Includes bibliographical references and index.
    ISBN-13: 978-0-07-351183-2 (alk. paper)
    ISBN-10: 0-07-351183-8 (alk. paper)
    1. Legal secretaries—United States—Handbooks, manuals, etc. 2. Legal assistants—United States—Handbooks, manuals, etc. 3. Law offices—United States—Handbooks, manuals, etc. I. Satterwhite, Marilyn L. II. Lee, Jo Ann, 1942- Irwin law office reference manual. III. Title.
KF319.L338   2008
651'.934—dc22

                                          2006029583

www.mhhe.com

Table of Contents

v

How to Use the Law Office Reference Manual

Law office personnel—paralegals or legal assistants, legal secretaries, law clerks, librarians, and attorneys—complete a variety of tasks throughout the day. Some of the questions that may come up include:

- What is the correct form of pronoun to use?

- How do I address a letter to a client?

- How do I format a business report?

- How do I cite Supreme Court decisions?

- What is the proper sequence of filing business names?

The Law Office Reference Manual is an easy-to-use tool with several ways to find helpful information and guidelines. First, look in the index, which contains an alphabetic listing of all topics covered. When you have located the unit and the specific reference number for the desired entry, scan the upper corners of the pages in that unit to locate the appropriate section.

Second, refer to the opening-page tabs for each unit. Scan the listing of topics to locate the range of reference numbers for each topic.

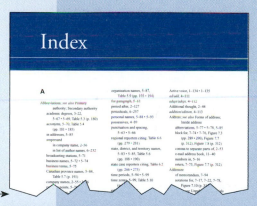

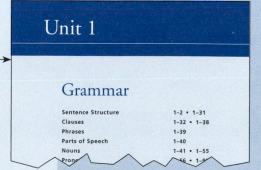

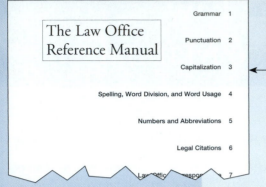

Third, refer to the titles of the units contained on the back cover and on the first page of the manual to locate a particular unit.

For more resources on how to apply the information found in *The Law Office Reference Manual*, please visit http://www.mhhe.com/paralegal.

Preface

THE NEED FOR A LAW OFFICE MANUAL

Law offices require a high standard of performance of its employees: precise use of words, correct citations to primary and secondary sources of information, knowledge of law office and court rules and procedures, and a specialized—although varied—type of work. Because of the variety of information required in the law office, we felt the need to compile information from business, law, and office management into one useful reference source. Thus, this manual contains information and resources that both students and on-the-job law office employees can use. Our conviction is that an office reference manual should be accurate, comprehensive, easy to access, and a pleasure to use.

THE FOUNDATIONS

Unit 1, Grammar, explains and illustrates the basic rules of English grammar and usage and serves as a guide to clear writing style. Samples of correct and incorrect writing are included to clarify grammar rules and concepts. Units 2, 3, 4, and 5 support the grammar unit with comprehensive coverage of punctuation, capitalization, spelling and word division, and abbreviations, respectively.

FOCUS ON THE LAW

Unit 6, Legal Citations, contains rules and guidelines for citing primary authority—court decisions, constitutions, statutes, and administrative materials—and secondary authority—treatises, encyclopedias, books, and periodicals. The rules presented conform to *The Bluebook: A Uniform System of Citation* published by The Harvard Law Review Association. The unit includes information and examples on citing quoted and paraphrased material, placement of footnotes, use of shortened references, and abbreviations. Tables list the accepted abbreviations used when citing state and federal courts and their respective court reporters.

FOCUS ON WRITING

Unit 7, Law Office Correspondence, and Unit 8, Reports and Legal Writing, offer concise, practical guidance on planning, writing, and formatting letters, memorandums, and reports as well as memorandums of law. Checklists serve as guidelines to help users develop clear, well-written, and well-organized correspondence and reports.

OFFICE TECHNOLOGY AND PROCEDURES

Unit 9, Law Office Procedures, provides reliable guidelines for organizing work, maintaining office calendars, scheduling and planning meetings and conferences, and filing various types of records. The section on information processing reflects technological advances in the electronic office. Updated coverage includes the guidelines for using the latest computer technologies for information processing, such as voice- and handwriting-recognition programs.

Unit 10, Numerical Data, includes guidelines for basic calculations such as discounts and percentages and units of measure. Information includes methods of visually presenting data such as tables, charts, and graphs.

OFFICE SERVICES

Unit 11, Communication Services, contains guidelines for using telecommunications tools including telephone services, facsimile (fax) services, and electronic mail. Guidelines for efficient use of the World Wide Web and Internet services are included as important means of worldwide communications. Updated procedures and information are also provided for traditional postal services.

Unit 12, Law Office References, contains an annotated listing of the most frequently used legal and business references and resources available from private organizations and public libraries. A separate listing of selected research and information resources available on the World Wide Web and the Internet is also included.

ACKNOWLEDGMENTS

We want to thank the many individuals who offered their encouragement and assistance through the development of this project. First, we'd like to offer thanks to the reviewers of *The Law Office Reference Manual* 2d Edition:

Elizabeth Eiesland	Sheila M. Huber
Katherine A. Greenwood	Carol D. Kellogg
Carol Halley	R. Eileen Mitchell
Sydnie Harrington	Kathleen M. Reed

Special thanks go to the following professional colleagues for their guidance and encouragement in shaping this project:

Stanley A. Hutchinson, J.D., Fountain Valley, CA
Carol D. Kellogg, J.D., Burbank, CA
L. Edmund Kellogg, J.D., Burbank, CA
Mark Leicester, CPA, J.D., Burlington, MA
Kathleen M. Meehan, CPA, J.D., Pasadena, CA

Jo Ann Lee
Marilyn L. Satterwhite

Unit 1

Grammar

-1 Grammar is the study of the structure of a language—the forms of words and their arrangement in sentences. Sentence structure refers to the sequence of words in the sentence, the length of the sentence, and the kinds of words contained in the sentence (parts of speech).

SENTENCE STRUCTURE

-2 A sentence is a unit of speech: a word or group of words arranged to convey a complete idea.

Sentence Parts

-3 Each word in a sentence has a specific function depending on its arrangement in the sentence. The basic parts of a sentence are a subject, a verb or predicate, a direct object, an indirect object, and a complement.

Subject

-4 The subject of a sentence is a word or group of words about which the sentence is written. The subject may be singular (one person, place, object, or idea) or plural (two or more persons, places, objects, or ideas). A compound subject consists of two or more equally ranked persons, places, or objects.

> **Joan Lauricella** is a practicing attorney.   **[singular subject]**
>
> The **cases** are being docketed in Superior Court.   **[plural subject]**
>
> The **Pacific Rim** and the **Middle East** cover the greatest territory. **[compound subject]**

Verb

-5 The verb expresses the action, condition, or state of being of the subject of the sentence.

> Professor Elaine Fong **teaches** family law.   **[describes action]**
>
> Do the District Attorney's Office and the Public Defender's Office **feel** the effects of decreased staffing?   **[describes a condition]**
>
> Rodrigo **is** a dedicated paralegal.   **[describes a state of being]**

Direct Object

-6 The direct object of a sentence receives the action of the verb. The direct object generally answers the question "who" or "what."

> The marshal served the **subpoena**.   **[served what?]**
>
> The clerk passed the **photographs**.   **[passed what?]**
>
> Did the client receive the **interrogatories**?   **[receive what?]**

Indirect Object

-7 The indirect object of a sentence identifies the person or object that receives the action of the verb and the direct object. An indirect object generally answers the question "to whom" or "for whom" (or "to what" or "for what").

> The marshal served the **defendant** with the subpoena.   [**served the subpoena to whom?**]
>
> The clerk passed the **jury** the photographs.   [**passed the photographs to whom?**]

1–8   The indirect object may be written with a preposition, such as *in*, *of*, *on*, *to*, *by*, or *at*. The noun following the prepositional phrase is the object of the preposition.

> She addressed her concerns **to Karen Luchsinger.**   [**addressed her concerns to whom?**]
>
> Did the mayor give the awards **to the outstanding citizens?**   [**give the awards to whom?**]

Complement

1–9   A complement is a noun, pronoun, or adjective that follows the various forms of the verbs *am*, *appear*, *are*, *become*, *is*, *look*, *seem*, *was*, and *were*. The complement refers to, identifies, or describes the subject or direct object.

> That writer was the **author** of a well-known series of children's books.   [**noun describing writer**]
>
> Were **they** the top-selling Realtors? [**pronoun identifying Realtors**]
>
> The surgeons appeared **optimistic** about the patient's recovery. [**adjective describing surgeons**]

Sentence Patterns

1–10   The words in sentences are arranged in various sequences or patterns to express an idea. Sentences are most commonly written in either a normal-order pattern or an inverted-order pattern.

Normal-Order Sentence Pattern

1–11   A normal-order sentence consists of words arranged in one of the following patterns: (1) subject–verb, (2) subject–verb–direct object, (3) subject–verb–indirect object, or (4) subject–verb–complement. These sentence patterns convey ideas directly; they show who is doing what, to whom or for whom, or how.

> She teaches.   [**subject–verb**]
>
> She teaches constitutional law.   [**subject–direct object**]
>
> She teaches law students constitutional law.   [**subject–verb–indirect object–direct object**]
>
> Ms. Santiago is a law professor.   [**subject–verb complement**]

Inverted-Order Sentence Pattern

1–12   When sentences are written in inverted order, the subject does not appear at the beginning of the sentence. These sentence patterns generally convey ideas indirectly. Questions are usually inverted-order sentences. (See also 1–102.)

> Does **she** teach?
>
> Is **she** a law professor?
>
> What does **she** teach?
>
> Does **she** teach law students constitutional law?

Sentence Purpose

1–13 Sentences are classified according to their purpose and include statements, questions, commands or requests, and exclamations.

Statements

1–14 A statement is a declarative sentence.

> Suprio Banerjee was asked to attend the meeting.
>
> We asked Suprio Banerjee to attend the meeting.

Questions

1–15 A question is an interrogative sentence. (See also 1–12.)

> Was Suprio Banerjee asked to attend the meeting?

Commands or Requests

1–16 A command or a request is an imperative sentence.

> You and Chuck Harrington must attend the meeting.
>
> Ask Chuck Harrington to attend the meeting.

Exclamations

1–17 Strong emotion is expressed in an exclamatory sentence.

> How fortunate we are to have Chuck Harrington at our meeting!

Sentence Length and Type

1–18 Vary sentence length to avoid monotony. Short sentences are generally more direct, while longer sentences provide continuity to writing. Sentences are classified as simple, compound, complex, or compound-complex.

Simple Sentences

1–19 A simple sentence contains a single independent clause—a complete idea containing a subject and a verb.

> Louise Peebles is the owner of The Main Event Planners.

Compound Sentences

1–20 A compound sentence contains two or more independent clauses joined by a comma and a conjunction *(and*, *or*, *nor*, or *but)* or by a semicolon.

> Louise Peebles is the owner of The Main Event Planners, and Linda Hawkins is the owner of L'Menu Caterers.
>
> Louise Peebles is the owner of The Main Event Planners; Linda Hawkins is the owner of L'Menu Caterers.

Omitting a conjunction after the comma creates a grammatically incorrect run-on sentence.

> Louise Peebles is the owner of The Main Event Planners, Linda Hawkins is the owner of L'Menu Caterers.

Complex Sentences

1–21 A complex sentence contains one independent clause and one or more dependent clauses.

> Louise Peebles is the owner of The Main Event Planners, although she is also a corporate planning consultant.

Compound-Complex Sentences

1–22 A compound-complex sentence contains two or more independent clauses and one or more dependent clauses.

> As the owner of The Main Events Planners, Louise Peebles consults with corporate planners; she often works with L'Menu Caterers.

Sentence Fragments

1–23 A sentence fragment is an incomplete thought. It occurs when words necessary to complete the thought are missing or when a punctuation mark is used incorrectly and chops the sentence into phrases.

Fragment:	Regardless of who the programmer may be.
Correct:	Regardless of who the programmer may be, he or she must verify the accuracy of the new program.
Fragment:	Thank you for your order; requesting shipment for November 13.
Correct:	Thank you for your order requesting shipment for November 13.

Parallel Structure

1–24 Related ideas should be stated in parallel grammatical style, whether in a series of words, clauses, or phrases; in comparisons; within linking verbs; or with connecting (or correlative) expressions.

Inconsistent:	Staff members received Employee Personnel Manuals, training manuals, and where to report for orientation.
Consistent:	Staff members received Employee Personnel **Manuals,** training **manuals,** and the **location** for orientation.
Inconsistent:	Johanna will go to the meeting, make her presentation to the group, and is leaving at 2 p.m.

Consistent: Johanna will **go** to the meeting, **make** her presentation
                 to the group, and **leave** at 2 p.m.

Point of View

1–25

Each sentence—regardless of length or complexity—should be written
using the same point of view for the subject, verb tense, person, number, or emphasis throughout. Inconsistency from either the reader's or the
writer's point of view results when a shift in any of these elements occurs
within the sentence.

Incorrect: **You** should write sentences from only one point of view;
               otherwise, *one* can confuse the reader.

Correct: **You** should write sentences from only one point of view;
               otherwise, **you** can create confusion for the reader.

Incorrect: **We** appreciate your assistance in this matter, and *I* look
               forward to meeting with you soon.

Correct: **We** appreciate your assistance in this matter, and **we** look
               forward to meeting with you soon.

Incorrect: She lectures in a way that **anyone** *will be able* to
               understand.

Correct: She lectures in a way that **anyone is able** to understand.

Connectives

1–26

Connectives—words used to connect ideas—should be used carefully so
that the meaning of a sentence is clear. Some common connectives are
and, *or*, *as*, *when*, *because*, *since*, and *while*.

Confusing: Dr. Paul Wilkinson was appointed to the board and is
               employed by CompTech, Inc.

Better: Dr. Paul Wilkinson, who was appointed to the board, is
               employed by CompTech, Inc.

Confusing: *While* our "efficiency expert" resigned, staff morale has
               improved dramatically.

Better: **Since** our "efficiency expert" resigned, staff morale has
               improved dramatically.

Correlative Expressions

1–27

Certain expressions are written in pairs because they convey a related
thought. Examples of such expressions are both . . . and, either . . . or,
neither . . . nor, not . . . but, and not only . . . but also. Be consistent in the
form and the tense of words used with these expressions.

Incorrect: *Neither* Christine Allen *or* Felipe Gonzalez would qualify for
               the treasurer's job.

Correct: **Neither** Christine Allen **nor** Felipe Gonzalez would qualify
               for the treasurer's job.

Incorrect: *Not only* the administrative assistant *but* his supervisor admits the error.

Correct: **Not only** the administrative assistant **but also** his supervisor admits the error.

Appositives

1–28 Appositives are descriptive or explanatory expressions that follow and further explain a word or idea. Use correct punctuation—generally a comma or a dash—to create a complete sentence. An incorrectly punctuated appositive is a sentence fragment. (See also Nonrestrictive Clauses, 1–36.)

Incorrect: Marion Graff, who will be celebrating a milestone birthday soon.

Correct: Marion Graff, who will be celebrating a milestone birthday soon, is being honored at a special luncheon.

Incorrect: Dr. Sandra Rittman was credited with establishing the management programs. Programs that incorporate innovations in systems and procedures.

Correct: Dr. Sandra Rittman was credited with establishing the management programs—programs that incorporate innovations in systems and procedures.

1–29 Some appositives are not set off from the rest of the sentence. Generally, if an appositive is short or is closely related to the noun or pronoun preceding it, a comma is not necessary.

July 4, **2076,** will be our country's tricentennial.   **[commas set off the appositive 2076]**

Our country will celebrate our tricentennial in July 2076.   **[no comma before the appositive 2076]**

Please contact our regional manager, **Carol Mitzner.**   **[a comma sets off the appositive]**

My friend **Carol** is the regional manager.   **[no commas]**

Modifiers

1–30 A modifier is a word or group of words that limits, describes, or explains the meaning of another word. Place words or groups of words close to their related thoughts, or rearrange words to form a sentence that is logical in thought. A misplaced modifier may convey an unclear meaning to the reader.

Unclear: Byron *almost* practiced two hours on his trombone.

Clear: Byron practiced **almost** two hours on his trombone.

Dangling Modifiers

1–31 A dangling modifier is a phrase describing a condition or an action that does not correctly relate to the subject of the sentence.

Dangling: While walking down the hall, the computers were being delivered.   **[Were the computers walking down the hall?]**

Correct: While walking down the hall, I noticed that the computers were being delivered.

Correct: As I was walking down the hall, I noticed that the computers were being delivered.

CLAUSES

1–32 A clause is a group of words containing a subject and a verb. Clauses may be independent or dependent (subordinate).

Independent Clauses

1–33 An independent clause can stand alone as a complete sentence.

Betty Lou Collier manages her schedule well, although she travels to Oregon frequently.

Dependent Clauses

1–34 A dependent clause cannot stand alone as a single idea even though the clause contains a subject and a verb. A dependent clause depends on the independent clause for its meaning.

Although she travels to Oregon frequently, Betty Lou Collier manages her schedule well.

Dependent clauses that contain such words as *although*, *as*, *because*, *since*, *if*, and *when* should be followed by a comma if they appear at the beginning of a sentence. Incorrect punctuation produces a sentence fragment.

Fragment: As soon as we receive your financial statement.

Sentence: As soon as we receive your financial statement, we will be able to evaluate your loan application.

Sentence: We will be able to evaluate your loan application as soon as we receive your financial statement.

Dependent clauses that begin with a verb form are often incorrectly punctuated as sentences. They are sentence fragments.

Fragment: Thanking the shareholders for their participation.

Sentence: Thanking the shareholders for their participation, the chairperson adjourned the annual meeting.

A dependent clause appearing at the end of a sentence may or may not be preceded by a comma. If the clause is essential to the meaning of the sentence, no comma is used. (See 1–35.) If the clause is nonessential to the meaning of the sentence, use a comma. (See 1–36.)

Restrictive (Essential) Clauses

1–35 A restrictive dependent clause describes or explains the word or idea immediately preceding it. These clauses are essential to the meaning of the sentence and should not be set off by commas.

> Books **that are out of date** will be sold at a discount.
>
> Everyone **who enters the competition** will receive a souvenir pin.

Nonrestrictive (Nonessential) Clauses

1–36 A nonrestrictive dependent clause provides an explanation or additional information but can be omitted from the sentence without affecting its meaning. Use commas to set off these nonessential clauses. (See also Appositives, 1–28 • 1–29.)

> These books, **which will be sold at a discount,** are outdated publications.
>
> Eduardo, **who produced and directed the play,** received a standing ovation on opening night.

That *and* Which *Clauses*

1–37 Use the relative pronoun *that* to introduce an idea that is essential to the meaning of the sentence and thus cannot be omitted without affecting the meaning or correctness of the sentence. To test whether the clause is essential, omit it. Any change in the correctness, completeness, or meaning indicates the clause is essential. Use *that* and do not set off the clause with commas.

> Books **that are out of date** will be sold at a discount.
>
> Books . . . will be sold at a discount. **[sentence meaning changes]**

1–38 Use the relative pronoun *which* to introduce an idea that is nonessential to the sentence and could be omitted without affecting its meaning or correctness. To test whether the clause is nonessential, omit it. If there is no change in meaning or correctness, the clause is nonessential. Use *which* and set the clause off with commas.

> These books, **which will be sold at a discount,** are outdated publications.
>
> These books . . . are outdated publications. **[sentence meaning has not changed]**

PHRASES

1–39 A phrase is a group of words that explains or describes an idea. A phrase does not have a subject and a verb and cannot stand alone as a complete idea or a complete sentence.

> A new representative **with 20 years'** experience has been selected. **[restrictive phrase]**

The common stock, **currently selling for $20 per share,** will split 3 for 1. **[nonrestrictive phrase]**

The Robbins Building is a **five-story structure.** **[adjective phrase]**

Were the speeches **organized and logically presented?** **[adverbial phrase]**

I found some errors **in analyzing the data.** **[prepositional phrase]**

To learn a foreign language, one should work and live in the country where the language is spoken. **[infinitive phrase]**

Having completed their work, the auditors left. **[participial phrase]**

PARTS OF SPEECH

1–40 Words are classified into eight parts of speech (or categories) according to their functions and relationships in a sentence. Each word in a sentence has a specific function or use—as a subject, a verb, an object, and so forth. A particular word may have different functions in different sentences, depending on the relationship of that word to the other words in the sentences. The eight parts of speech are noun, pronoun, verb, adverb, adjective, preposition, conjunction, and interjection.

Nouns

1–41 A noun is the name of a person, place, object, idea, or quality. Nouns are classified as common or proper; singular, plural, collective, or compound; and possessive.

Common Nouns

1–42 A common noun identifies a class of persons, places, objects, ideas, or qualities.

Consumers [persons] need to be taught **self-reliance [quality]** and **financial management [skill].**

The **bystanders [persons]** watched the **commotion [object or idea]** at the **scene [place]** of the **accident [idea].**

Everyone needs to display **courage [quality]** and a **sense [quality]** of **optimism [idea]** to be successful in **life [object].**

Proper Nouns

1–43 A proper noun identifies a particular person, place, or object. A proper noun is always capitalized.

Southern California is known for its beautiful **Malibu Beach.**

Was **Leonardo Da Vinci** the artist who painted *The Last Supper?*

Singular Nouns

1–44 A singular noun refers to one person, place, or object.

The **telephone** can be connected to a facsimile **machine** or a **computer** to aid communications.

Have you given the **report** to the **statistician?**

Phyllis Brzozowski became the supervising **manager.**

Plural Nouns

1–45 A plural noun refers to two or more persons, places, or objects.

Telephones can be connected to facsimile **machines** or **computers** to aid in communications.

Have you given the **reports** to the **statisticians?**

Phyllis Brzozowski and **Rita Steffen** became the supervising **managers.**

Collective Nouns

1–46 A common noun that identifies a specific group is called a collective noun.

That **organization** has raised a great deal of money for various charities.

The **jury** of five men and seven women has reached a verdict.

The **partnership** is composed of Vargas, Armstrong & Lynn.

Singular Collective Nouns

1–47 The following collective nouns are considered singular, even though each represents a group of more than one person or object.

audience	council	herd
board	crowd	jury
class	department	management
club	faculty	society
committee	family	staff
community	firm	team
company	flock	union
corporation	group	

Singular collective nouns used as subjects of sentences require singular verbs.

The **board** of directors **has decided** to poll the stockholders.

Which **department leads** in total sales this quarter?

Plural Collective Nouns

1–48 The following collective nouns are considered plural.

goods	remains	scissors
pants	riches	shears
pliers	savings	thanks
proceeds		

Plural collective nouns used as subjects of sentences require plural verbs.

> Our **savings are** not quite enough for a trip to Europe.
>
> The **proceeds** of the estate auction **have** been distributed among the heirs.
>
> **Thanks go** to all those who donated their time to the fund-raising event.

1–49 When a collective noun is used to refer to individuals within the group acting separately, the noun is considered a plural subject and requires a plural
verb. Rewrite the sentence to avoid awkwardness.

> Incorrect: The **committee** are not satisfied with the outcome of the vote.
>
> Better: The **committee members** are not satisfied with the outcome
>   of the vote.

Singular or Plural Collective Nouns

1–50 The following collective nouns may be either singular or plural, depending on whether the sentence refers to one person or object or to several
persons or objects.

corps	majority	series
counsel	minority	sheep
deer	moose	species
fish	number	swine

> Her legal **counsel,** Hutchinson & Woods, **is** presenting its closing argu-
> ments today.
>
> My **counsel** of Stan Hutchinson and his associates **have** represented me
> well during the trial.
>
> Which ticket **series is** the least expensive?
>
> The **series** of children's programs **have been** successful.

Compound Nouns

1–51 A compound noun consists of two or more nouns combined as a single
unit. Compound nouns may be written as one word, as separate words, or
hyphenated; they may be singular or plural.

> Please enter these names and addresses in the **database.   [one-word
> singular compound noun]**
>
> Doesn't your **father-in-law** live in the Houston area?   **[hyphenated
> singular compound noun]**
>
> My two **sisters-in-law** work in the same office complex.   **[hyphenated
> plural compound noun]**
>
> Consumers should use their **credit cards** wisely.   **[two-word plural compound
> noun]**

Possessive Nouns

1–52 A possessive noun is a singular or plural noun written with an apostrophe and
used to indicate ownership or possession. (See also Possessives, 4–67 • 4–90.)

The **industry's** profits were down last year. [singular possessive]

Several **industries'** profits were down last year. [plural possessive]

That **child's** toys were hidden by his playmates. [singular possessive]

The **Children's** Museum is located along the waterfront. [plural possessive]

Noun Functions in Sentences

Subject

1–53 A noun as the subject of a sentence is the word about which the sentence is written. Subjects may be singular or plural. A plural subject may consist of a plural noun or a compound subject. (See also 1–4.)

Eugene Pinchuk is a certified public accountant. [singular subject]

How many **children** were enrolled in the computer camp this summer? [plural subject]

Eugene Pinchuk and **Thomas Joyce** are certified public accountants. [compound subject]

Object

1–54 A noun used as an object receives the action of the verb or verb form. (See also 1–6 • 1–8.)

The witnesses for the defense presented corroborating **testimony**. [direct object—presented what?]

She greeted the **media** politely. [direct object—greeted whom?]

Sassan Barkeshli sent the **bank** [indirect object—sent to whom?] his February mortgage payment. [direct object—sent what?]

Complement

1–55 A complement is a word or phrase that completes the meaning of the verb and explains or describes the subject. The complement is connected to the subject by a linking verb. (See also 1–9.)

Mark Leicester became the **director of business valuations and litigation**.

The criminal law instructor is **Professor Martha Bellinger**.

PRONOUNS

1–56 A pronoun takes the place of a noun and refers to the person, place, or object named, asked for, or understood in the sentence. Pronouns are classified as personal, reflexive, relative, indefinite, interrogative, demonstrative, and reciprocal.

Personal Pronouns

1–57 A personal pronoun refers to the person speaking, spoken to, or spoken about. Personal pronouns are divided into three cases: nominative,

TABLE 1.1 **Personal Pronouns**

Person	Nominative Case		Objective Case		Possessive Case	
	Singular	Plural	Singular	Plural	Singular	Plural
First	I	we	me	us	my, mine	our, ours
Second	you	you	you	you	your, yours	your, yours
Third	he, she, it	they	him, her, it	them	his, hers, its	their, theirs

objective, and possessive. Case describes the form of pronoun used to show its relationship to other words in a sentence. (See Table 1.1.)

Nominative Case Personal Pronouns

1–58 Personal pronouns in the nominative case are *I, you, he, she, it, we, you,* and *they.*

1–59 Use a nominative case personal pronoun when the pronoun renames or is substituted for the subject of the sentence.

> Teleconferencing is becoming more popular for economic reasons, but **it [teleconferencing]** has not eliminated the need for face-to-face conferences.
>
> **He [Tedros Yohannes]** is the one who developed the program.

Use the nominative case when the personal pronoun is a complement. A complement follows a form of the verb *to be: am, are, is, was, were, be, been,* and *being.*

> If I were **he [complement],** I would have submitted another estimate for the construction job.

Objective Case Personal Pronouns

1–60 Personal pronouns in the objective case are *me, you, him, her, it, us, you,* and *them.*

1–61 Use an objective case personal pronoun when the pronoun is the direct or indirect object of a verb.

> The claims adjuster for the insurance company called **us.**   **[direct object]**
>
> Did the judge give **them [indirect object]** the court calendar?
>
> Raymond presented Duc Loi and **her [indirect object]** with plaques.

Use an objective case personal pronoun when the pronoun is the object of a preposition.

> Send a fax to **her** in the Singapore office.
>
> **Who** sent the check?
>
> The remainder of the estate was earmarked for **them.**
>
> Between you and **me,** I think the proposal is fair.

Use an objective case personal pronoun when the pronoun is the subject or the object of an infinitive phrase (a phrase that consists of *to* plus a verb). (See Infinitives, 1–143 • 1–145.)

> The office administrator asked **her** *to prepare* the graphics presentations for the report.
>
> Will the vice president ask *to transfer* **him** to the Cincinnati office?

Exception: When the infinitive *to be* has no subject and is followed by a pronoun, use a nominative case personal pronoun *(he, she, we, they, you)*.

> It is likely to *be* **they** attending the seminar.

Possessive Case Personal Pronouns

1–62 Possessive case personal pronouns are *my, mine, your, yours, her, hers, his, its, our, ours, their,* and *theirs.*

1–63 Use a possessive case personal pronoun to indicate ownership or another relationship between a pronoun and its antecedent, the noun to which the pronoun refers.

> Our company offers **its [our company's]** employees a generous profit-sharing plan.
>
> Television actors and actresses recognize **their [actors' and actresses']** outstanding colleagues by awarding Emmys.

Use a possessive case personal pronoun when the noun being modified or described follows the pronoun.

> The latest financial statement reflects **our** best year of operations.
>
> Did **his** qualifications match our job specifications?

Use a possessive case personal pronoun when the pronoun is followed by a gerund (a verb form ending in *-ing*). (See also 1–142.)

> Incorrect: We would appreciate *you* shipping the order by Wednesday, March 8.
>
> Correct: We would appreciate **your** shipping the order by Wednesday, March 8.
>
> Incorrect: *Him* enrolling in the geography course inspired an interest in other cultures.
>
> Correct: **His** enrolling in the geography course inspired an interest in other cultures.

Use the possessive pronouns *mine, yours, hers, his, its, ours,* and *theirs* when the pronoun does not immediately precede the noun being described or modified.

> Those criteria were **theirs** to determine, not ours.

Use the possessive case noun when the noun precedes a gerund (a verb form ending in *-ing*). (See also 1–142.)

15

Adrian Broca's **[possessive noun]** running **[gerund]** the L.A. Marathon is an incredible feat considering he is legally blind.

The human relations manager approved **her [possessive pronoun] taking [gerund]** the auditing course under the tuition reimbursement program.

Reflexive Pronouns

1–64 Reflexive pronouns are formed by adding *-self* or *-selves* to a possessive personal pronoun.

Singular Reflexive Pronouns

1–65 Use *myself, yourself, itself, himself,* and *herself* for emphasis following the singular subject of the sentence.

> She researched and compiled the statistics **herself.**
>
> I wrote the appellate brief **myself.**

Reflexive pronouns should never be used as the subject of a sentence.

> Incorrect: Christopher and *myself* prepared the reports.
>
> Correct: Christopher and I prepared the reports.

Plural Reflexive Pronouns

1–66 Use *yourselves, themselves,* and *ourselves* for emphasis following the plural subject of the sentence.

> Wall Street traders **themselves** were amazed at the volume of trading on the exchanges.
>
> Did we **ourselves** overestimate the credibility of our witness?

Reflexive Pronouns as Objects

1–67 Use a reflexive pronoun as the object of a verb to reflect the action of the verb back to the subject.

> I blamed **myself** for the oversight.
>
> Did the directors vote **themselves** a year-end bonus?

Relative Pronouns

1–68 A relative pronoun refers to a person, place, or object previously named in the sentence. Relative pronouns introduce dependent clauses and should be placed near the word or idea referred to. (See Dependent Clauses, 1–34 • 1–38.) The relative pronouns are listed in Table 1.2.

1–69 *That* refers to people, places, and objects and is used to introduce restrictive (essential) clauses. (See also 1–35 and 1–37.)

> The circumstances **that** were revealed during the investigation surprised us.

TABLE 1.2 Relative Pronouns

Nominative Case	Objective Case	Possessive Case
that	that	that
who	whom	whose
whoever	whomever	
which	which	which, whose
what	what	

1–70 *What* refers to places and objects.

His exceptional college record was **what** made him an outstanding job prospect.

1–71 *Which* refers to objects and is always used to introduce nonrestrictive (nonessential) clauses. (See also 1–36 and 1–38.)

Our new system, **which** was installed last month, has yet to be debugged.

1–72 *Who* and *whom* and *whoever* and *whomever* refer to people and are used to introduce either restrictive (essential) or nonrestrictive (nonessential) clauses. (See 1–35 and 1–36.)

Donalee was the person **who** designed and produced the operations manual.   **[restrictive clause]**

Donalee, **who** designed and produced the operations manual, is a free-lance desktop publisher.   **[nonrestrictive clause]**

Kenneth is the person **whom** we selected to be our delegate.
[restrictive clause]

The bookkeeper, or **whoever** altered the records, was extremely clever.
[nonrestrictive clause]

Nominative Case Relative Pronouns

1–73 The nominative case relative pronouns are *that, who, whoever, which,* and *what*.

1–74 Use a nominative case relative pronoun when the pronoun refers to the subject of the sentence.

The issues **that** were discussed during the hearings surprised us.

Their auditors, **who** certified the statements last year, will return this year.

Use the nominative case relative pronoun *what* when it is used to mean *that which* or *those which.*

What [that which] appeared so obvious eluded the detectives!

The forest life, the watersheds, and the valuable timberlands were **what [those which]** suffered most from the fire.

17

Objective Case Relative Pronouns

1–75 The objective case relative pronouns are *that*, *whom*, *whomever*, *which*, and *what*.

1–76 Use an objective case relative pronoun when the pronoun is the object of a verb.

> The flight attendant disregarded **that** turbulence.
>
> You are free to select **whomever** you want.

Use an objective case relative pronoun when the pronoun is used as the object of a preposition.

> Is it this ledger in **which** the posting error was made?

Possessive Case Relative Pronouns

1–77 Possessive case relative pronouns consist of *that*, *whose*, and *which*. Use a possessive case relative pronoun to show ownership or possession.

> Of all the editors contributing to that story, **whose** reporting was the most objective?

Indefinite Pronouns

1–78 Indefinite pronouns do not refer specifically to any one person or thing. Most indefinite pronouns are singular, some are plural, and a few are either singular or plural. The words that relate to these indefinite pronouns must agree with them in number, tense, and gender.

Singular Indefinite Pronouns

1–79 The following indefinite pronouns are singular:

anything	either	much	one
anybody	every	neither	somebody
anyone	everybody	no one	someone
anything	everyone	nobody	something
each	everything	nothing	

When these pronouns are the subjects of sentences, they require singular verbs.

> **Everyone** *is* expected to participate in some committee work.
>
> **Somebody** *has* to assume the responsibility for the error.
>
> *Does* **anyone** have any idea of the ultimate capacity of computers?

1–80 Pronouns ending in *-one* are written as two words when followed by the preposition *of*.

> **Any one** *of* those runners has a chance to break the record.
>
> **Every one** *of* the panelists possesses very impressive credentials.

When a pronoun ending in -one refers to one of a number of things, it is written as two words.

> Any **one** of the members might be chosen.

Plural Indefinite Pronouns

1–81 The following indefinite pronouns are plural.

both	many	others
few	most	several

When these pronouns are the subjects of sentences, they require plural verbs.

> **Both** Web designers created our award-winning Web site.
>
> **Many** college students *are* realizing the importance of personal financial management.

Singular or Plural Indefinite Pronouns

1–82 The following indefinite pronouns may be either singular or plural.

all	more	other	such
any	none	some	

Depending on their use in the sentence, they take either singular or plural verbs.

> We should **all** take advantage of recycling whenever possible.   **[refers to many people]**
>
> **All** we need *is* an accurate proofreader.   **[refers to the one thing needed]**
>
> **Such** is the nature of the profession when paralegals and attorneys alike must be flexible, creative, able to work under pressure, and able to multitask!   **[refers to the overall environment of law office work]**
>
> Courts can impose confinement or fines, or both, in certain instances; **such** consequences can be expected if violations persist.   **[refers to more than one result]**

1–83 Use the possessive personal pronoun *her* or *his* with an indefinite pronoun when the gender is known or understood.

> *Nobody* reported that it was **her** goal to break the world record during the women's 10K run.

Use *he or she* or *her or his* when the pronouns are used to refer to either gender. To avoid awkwardness, reword the sentence to eliminate the pronoun or use the plural pronoun *they* or *their*.

> Awkward: When someone enters into a contract, **he or she** should read the terms to be aware of **his or her** obligations and potential liabilities.
>
> Better: When individuals enter into contracts, *they* should read the terms to be aware of **their** obligations and potential liabilities.

19

Better: Individuals who enter into contracts should read the terms to be aware of **their** obligations and potential liabilities.

Awkward: **Each** of the applicants must score 70 percent or better to pass **her or his** certification examination.

Better: Each of the applicants must score 70 percent or better to pass the certification examination.

Better: Applicants must score 70 percent or better to pass **their** certification examinations.

Interrogative Pronouns

1–84   Interrogative pronouns are used to ask questions and include *what*, *who*, *whom*, *whomever*, *which*, and *whose*.

What is on your itinerary for your Northwest Territory sales calls?

From **what** source did you find that statute?

Are they the ones **who** are testifying on our behalf?

For **whom** is the request for proposal being prepared?

Which of the two copiers offers the greater reduction and enlargement ratios?

Whose sales quota has not yet been met this quarter?

Demonstrative Pronouns

1–85   Demonstrative pronouns are *this*, *that*, *these*, and *those*. These pronouns limit the numbers or kinds of items or people discussed. *This* and *that* are singular pronouns requiring singular verbs; *these* and *those* are plural pronouns requiring plural verbs.

1–86   *This* and *these* are used to point out items or people nearest in distance or time.

Does **this** videotape capture the details of the accident scene?

These are two key court decisions that support our cause.

1–87   *That* and *those* are used to point out items or people farther away.

That is the more expensive of the two telephone systems.

That other videotape shows distorted images of the accident.

Who researched **those** precedent-setting cases?

Reciprocal Pronouns

1–88   Reciprocal pronouns relate specifically to another person discussed. Reciprocal pronouns are *each other* and *one another*.

1–89   *Each other* relates to two persons.

Stephanie and Christopher appear to work well with **each other.**

1–90   *One another* relates to more than two persons.

Our three administrative analysts are competing against **one another** for the opening at the Lancaster branch.

TABLE 1.3   Possessive Pronouns and Sound-Alike Contractions

Possessive Pronouns	Sound-Alike Contractions
its	it's (it is, it has)
their	they're (they are)
theirs	there's (there is, there has)
whose	who's (who is)
your	you're (you are)

Special Pronoun Usage

Possessives and Contractions

1–91 Possessive pronouns are often confused with contractions. (See Table 1.3.) Possessive pronouns are used to indicate ownership or another relationship between a pronoun and a noun or pronoun referred to earlier in the sentence. Contractions are two words—usually a pronoun subject and a verb—combined into a shortened form: the apostrophe indicates the omission of a letter or letters in the resulting contraction. Apostrophes are never used in possessive pronouns. (See 2–2 and 2–9.)

1–92 Test the correct use of contractions by substituting the complete words represented by the contraction. For example, the contraction *it's* can be read as *it is* or *it has*. If the substitution does not make sense, use the possessive pronoun instead.

> Possessive: The university's alumni association offers its alumni special travel and entertainment benefits.
>
> Contraction: **It's [It is]** the policy of the organization to charge minimum fees for services.
>
> Possessive: **Their** reward for exceeding our sales goals will be an all-expense-paid vacation to Ixtapa, Mexico.
>
> Contraction: Who said, **"They're [They are]** abandoning a sinking ship"?
>
> Possessive: **Whose** architectural rendering for the medical complex was submitted earlier?
>
> Contraction: **Who's [Who is]** responsible for preparing the minutes of meetings?

Comparisons

1–93 The correct pronoun to use with the comparison words *than* or *as* depends on the sentence construction and meaning. Complete the sentence with the same verb or verb form used earlier in the sentence to determine which form of pronoun is correct.

> Loreen Endoso was as enthusiastic about Kenny *as* **I [was]**.
>
> Loreen Endoso was as enthusiastic about Kenny *as* **[she was enthusiastic about]** me.

21

The managers would rather hire Elena as the director *than* [hire] **him**.
Scott is taller *than* **he** [is].

Identification

1–94
When a pronoun identifies the noun that immediately follows it, read the sentence without the noun to determine whether to use a nominative case pronoun (see 1–58) or an objective case pronoun (see 1–60).

> **We** auditors complain about having to be in the field too much.
> [*We* . . . **complain about**]
> The new work schedules have not yet been approved by **us** nurses.
> [**approved by** *us* . . .]

Pronoun–Noun Compounds

1–95
When a noun and a pronoun form a compound subject or object, read the sentence without the noun to determine the correct case for the pronoun.

> Tina and I met to discuss the final construction plans.   [**I met to discuss**—*not* **Me met to discuss**]
> Danny invited Louisa and **me** to attend the moot court competition.
> [**Danny invited me**—*not* **Danny invited I**]

VERBS

1–96
A verb is a word used to express an action, a state of being, or a condition of the subject in a sentence. Every sentence must contain a verb or a verb phrase to express a complete thought. Verbs are classified by the following means: regular or irregular, linking, helping (auxiliary), predicates, mood, transitive or intransitive, voice, and verbals. Verbs are also classified according to tenses to indicate differences in time or relationships.

Regular Verbs

1–97
A regular verb is a verb whose past tense and past participle are formed by adding -*d* or -*ed* to the present tense. In other words, the basic form of the verb is spelled the same in all tenses. (See Table 1.4, Principal Parts of Regular Verbs.)

> Present tense: We generally **discuss** all personnel matters during executive session.
> Past tense: We **discussed** several personnel matters during executive session.
> Past participle: We **had discussed** several personnel matters during executive session.

Irregular Verbs

1–98
The past tense and past participle of an irregular verb are *not* formed by adding -*d* or -*ed* to the present tense. The principal parts of irregular verbs are spelled differently and, in some cases, are entirely different words. The principal parts of common irregular verbs appear in Table 1.5.

TABLE 1.4   Principal Parts of Regular Verbs

Present	Past	Past Participle
add	added	added
agree	agreed	agreed
ask	asked	asked
call	called	called
complete	completed	completed
drop	dropped	dropped
drown	drowned	drowned
hang (put to death)	hanged	hanged
happen	happened	happened
jump	jumped	jumped
lie (tell an untruth)	lied	lied
raise	raised	raised
repeat	repeated	repeated
save	saved	saved
shine (polish)	shined	shined
study	studied	studied
try	tried	tried
walk	walked	walked
work	worked	worked
worry	worried	worried

Present tense: We **choose** new vendors at the annual operations meetings.

Past tense: We **chose** Hahn Supplies Co. as our new vendor.

Past participle: We **have chosen** Hahn Supplies Co. as our new vendor.

Linking Verbs

1–99

Linking verbs are used to connect the subject to an adjective that follows the linking verb. Words commonly used as linking verbs include the forms of the verb to be *(am, are, is, was, were, be, been,* and *being)*; the verbs *appear, become, grow,* and *seem*; and verbs of the senses such as *feel, look, smell, sound,* and *taste*. To test the correct use of a linking verb, substitute the verb *is* or *are* for the linking verb.

Their pharmacy **appears** prosperous.   [pharmacy *is* prosperous]

Do the new employees **seem** pleased with the training?   [employees *are* pleased]

TABLE 1.5 Principal Parts of Common Irregular Verbs

Present	Past	Past Participle
am, are, is (forms of *to be*)	was, were	been
arise	arose	arisen
become	became	become
begin	began	begun
bid (offer)	bid	bid
bid (tell)	bade	bidden
bite	bit	bitten
blow	blew	blown
break	broke	broken
bring	brought	brought
build	built	built
burst	burst	burst
buy	bought	bought
catch	caught	caught
choose	chose	chosen
come	came	come
cost	cost	cost
cut	cut	cut
do	did	done
draw	drew	drawn
drink	drank	drunk
drive	drove	driven
eat	ate	eaten
fall	fell	fallen
feel	felt	felt
fight	fought	fought
find	found	found
flee	fled	fled
fly	flew	flown
forget	forgot	forgotten
forgive	forgave	forgiven
freeze	froze	frozen
get	got	got
give	gave	given
go	went	gone
grow	grew	grown
hang (curtains)	hung	hung

TABLE 1.5 (continued)

Present	Past	Past Participle
have	had	had
hide	hid	hidden
hold	held	held
keep	kept	kept
know	knew	known
lay (to place)	laid	laid
lead	led	led
leave	left	left
lend	lent	lent
lie (to recline)	lay	lain
lose	lost	lost
meet	met	met
pay	paid	paid
ride	rode	ridden
ring	rang	rung
rise	rose	risen
run	ran	run
say	said	said
see	saw	seen
set	set	set
shake	shook	shaken
shine (to give light)	shone	shone
shrink	shrank	shrunk
sing	sang	sung
sink	sank, sunk	sunk
sit	sat	sat
speak	spoke	spoken
spring	sprang	sprung
steal	stole	stolen
strike	struck	struck
swear	swore	sworn
swim	swam	swum
take	took	taken
teach	taught	taught
tear	tore	torn
tell	told	told
throw	threw	thrown
wear	wore	worn
write	wrote	written

Helping (Auxiliary) Verbs

1–100 A helping verb is used with the main verb in the sentence to help convey the action, state of being, or condition of the subject. The helping verb plus the main verb are referred to as the "verb phrase." The following are some common helping verbs.

be	have	shall
can	may	should
could	might	will
do	must	would
had	ought	

> If Darlene and Dennis had the time, they **could spend** a week in Brussels after the exhibition.

> Rhonda **should have known** her specifications were not consistent with the project needs.

1–101 Helping verbs can stand alone as a main verb in a sentence.

> They certainly **will**.

> **Can** we?

> We **ought** to plan for our future now.

Several helping verbs are often combined to form the main verb.

> We **will have** an opportunity to rebut their argument.

> The fire **could have been** a major disaster.

> Only a few people **should have had** access to the password.

1–102 When a statement appears in question form, the verb phrase is usually split. The subject appears between the helping verb and the main verb. (See also 1–12.)

> Statement: She **has completed** three chapters of her book.

> Question: **Has** she **completed** three chapters of her book?

Special Helping (Auxiliary) Verb Usage

Some helping verbs are used to convey a specific thought and are often confused with similar verbs.

1–103 The helping verbs *can* and *could* indicate ability or capacity to do something. Use *can* to refer to the present or the future; use *could* to refer to the past or the future.

> **Can** our flex schedules be changed periodically?

> We **could** have had this equipment delivered earlier if someone had been here to accept delivery.

> The trial **could** be scheduled as early as next month.

1–104 *May* and *might* indicate requests for permission. Use *may* in the present tense; use *might* in the future or the past tense.

May I have a week's personal leave of absence?

Our spot commercial **might** have been responsible for increased sales.

It **might** be more practical to hire a temporary law clerk.

1–105 *Must* and *ought* indicate acts that are commanded, requested, or determined to be done. Use *must* to indicate a stronger obligation than *ought*.

We **must** adjourn by 3:30 p.m. so we can catch our plane.

Surely they **must** have realized the extent of their error!

They **ought** to have confirmed our reservations by now.

College graduates **ought** to know how to spell and to punctuate!

1–106 *Shall* and *will* indicate future action. Use *will* for informal speech and writing, with the personal pronouns <u>he</u>, <u>she</u>, <u>they</u>, <u>you</u>, and <u>it</u>. Use *shall* in formal communications with the first person pronouns <u>I</u> and <u>we</u>.

I **shall** refer this matter to our affirmative action officer.

She **will** notify you of a hearing date.

To express agreement or consent, use *will*.

I **will** follow the contract terms.

1–107 *Should* indicates a duty or obligation in the future. *Would* indicates some condition or state of being in the past or the future.

At some point during an employment interview, an applicant **should** discuss salary terms and benefits.

Who **would** be interested in volunteering for the hospitality booth?

Predicates

1–108 A predicate is a verb or group of words that includes the verb and other words used to describe the action, state of being, or condition of the subject of the sentence.

Simple Predicates

1–109 A simple predicate consists of the verb itself.

Maxine Wilson **retired** in January.

Compound Predicates

1–110 A compound predicate consists of two or more verbs used with the same subject.

The district attorney **will determine** probable cause and **will meet** the burden of proof.

Marcia Hanford and DeAnne Hayes **have organized** many successful fund-raising campaigns.

Complete Predicates

1–111 A complete predicate consists of the verb plus other words—a direct object, an indirect object, or a complement—that describe the subject.

Cindy Chavez **is the law office administrator.**

Is the Constitution **all-inclusive?**

Verb Tenses

1–112 Verbs are written in different tenses to indicate time relationships with their subjects. The three principal verb tenses are present, past, and future, often called the *simple tenses*. Other commonly used tenses are the perfect tenses and the progressive tenses.

Present Tense

1–113 Use the present tense of a verb when an action is currently taking place, when a permanent condition is stated, or when a state of being is expressed.

The delegates **meet** today.

Doris McElwee **is** an excellent family therapist.

Charlyn Brown **teaches** Introduction to Paralegalism.

Past Tense

1–114 Use the past tense of a verb to indicate an action that has already taken place or a condition that no longer exists. The past tense of regular verbs is formed by adding -*d* or -*ed* to the present form. To form the past tense of irregular verbs, see Table 1.5.

The delegates **met** yesterday.

The *New York Times* **featured** the emerging global economy in Sunday's edition.

Baker & Sons **submitted** its bid two weeks before the closing date.

Who **flew** solo around the world nonstop in 2005 without refueling?

Future Tense

1–115 Use the future tense of a verb to indicate an action that will take place or a condition that will exist in the future. To form the future tense, write the word *will* before the present form of the verb. Use *shall* in formal writing. (See 1–106.)

The delegates **will meet** tomorrow at noon.

Orman Sartwell Construction **shall submit** its estimates by Tuesday.

Will Gregg Lee **prepare** the new maps and charts for us?

Perfect Tenses

1–116 Three additional past participle verb tenses are used to indicate differences in time: present perfect, past perfect, and future perfect.

Present Perfect Tense

1–117 Use the present perfect tense to indicate action that began in the past and has been completed in the present. The word *has* or *have* precedes the past participle.

> Sonia Wurst **has assumed** an important role on the arbitration board.
>
> **Have** the artists **drawn** up a package design for the new product?

Past Perfect Tense

1–118 Use the past perfect tense to indicate action that began and was completed in the past. The word *had* precedes the past participle.

> Those two witnesses **had testified** for the prosecution.
>
> Who **had chosen** the location for the archaeological excavation?

Future Perfect Tense

1–119 Use the future perfect tense to indicate action that will be completed by some future date. The phrase *will have* or *shall have* precedes the past participle.

> By next July, the stockholders **will have voted** to select a new auditing firm.
>
> We **shall have demonstrated** our good faith bargaining when the new contract is ratified.

Progressive Tenses

1–120 The progressive tenses are used to indicate some immediate action or existing condition or action that is in progress or taking place over a period of time. The progressive tenses are the present progressive, past progressive, and future progressive. To form the progressive tense, use *am*, *is*, *are*, *was*, *were*, or *be* with the present participle.

Present Progressive Tense

1–121 Use the present progressive tense to indicate an uncompleted action or condition. Use *am*, *is*, or *are* with the present participle.

> I **am** currently **reviewing** our insurance policies.
>
> Louisa **is drafting** a new lease agreement.
>
> Our clients **are rewriting** their personnel policies.

Past Progressive Tense

1–122 Use the past progressive tense to indicate an action or condition that was in progress some time in the past. Use *was* and *were* with the present participle.

> Thomas Armijo **was editing** the film when the producer called.
>
> **Were** you **copying** four pages from this book?

Future Progressive Tense

1–123 Use the future progressive tense to indicate an action or a condition that will be taking place in the future. Use *will be* with the present participle.

> **Will** Doctors Henneberg and Thrun **be relocating** their offices to the new medical complex?
>
> Hard hats **will be worn** by everyone on the construction site.

Emphatic Tenses

1–124 The emphatic tenses are used to emphasize the action, condition, or state of being of the verb. Emphatic tenses are also written in the present, past, and future.

Present Emphatic Tense

1–125 To form the present emphatic tense, use the word *do* or *does* with the present form of the verb.

> She **does** not **sort** her employer's mail before delivering it.
>
> **Do** they **understand** the circumstances fully?

Past Emphatic Tense

1–126 To form the past emphatic tense, use the word *did* with the present form of the verb.

> We **did develop** the new advertising campaign.

Future Emphatic Tense

1–127 To form the future emphatic tense, use *will* for informal speech and writing; *will* is used with the pronouns he, she, you, and they. Use *shall* in formal communications with the first person pronouns I and we.

> You **will report** for work at 8 a.m.
>
> Those lessees **will abide** by the regulations of the Merchants' Association.
>
> I **shall continue** lobbying our representatives to vote in favor of the proposed legislation.

Subjunctive (Mood) Verbs

1–128 The mood of a verb indicates how the speaker feels about the likelihood of the action or situation. The subjunctive mood is used to describe an impossible or uncertain condition or situation; to express a wish or doubt; and to indicate a request, command, or resolution. The subjunctive mood is preceded by words such as *if, as if, that, though, as though, unless,* or *whether.*

Impossibility or Uncertainty

1–129 Use the verbs *be* and *were* (rather than *is* and *was*) to indicate an impossible or uncertain condition or situation.

If I **were** he, I would be preparing earlier for the exam.   [impossibility—one cannot be another person]

If this **be** the case, I will be the first to concede the election. [uncertainty]

It's *as if* the whole world **were** against me.   [uncertainty]

If a condition or situation may be possible or can be a certainty, use *is* and *was*.

If he **was** here, I did not see him.   [possibility he could have been here, but he was not seen]

If this **is** the decision, we will have to accept it.   [certainty]

Wish or Doubt

1–130   Use *were* (rather than *was*) to express a wish or doubt.

I wish I **were** vacationing in Segovia, Spain, right now.   [wish]

If we **were** sure of our situation, we would be less worried.   [doubt]

Request or Command

1–131   Do not use the verbs *shall* or *should* to complete the predicate when indicating a request, command, or resolution. *Shall* and *should* are verbs used to make general statements but are incorrect when used with requests or commands.

Incorrect: Westin's asks that all shoppers *should* exit by the north gate.

Correct: Westin's asks that all shoppers **exit** by the north gate.

Incorrect: Our instructions were that he *should* be required to submit to a handwriting analysis.

Correct: Our instructions were that he **be required** to submit to a handwriting analysis.

Transitive and Intransitive Verbs

Transitive Verbs

1–132   A transitive verb requires a direct object—a noun or a pronoun—after it to complete the meaning of the sentence. A direct object tells who or what receives the action of the verb. (See 1–6.)

Please **set** the table for 12 guests.

When will the contractor **lay** the building foundation?

The pharmacy technician **acknowledged** the billing error.

Intransitive Verbs

1–133   An intransitive verb does not take a direct object. The words following an intransitive verb tell where, how, or to what extent.

The sun **rises** in the east and **sets** in the west.

The assembly line **stopped** abruptly.

Janice **performed** well.

31

Voice

1–134 The voice of a verb indicates whether the subject performs or receives the action. The two voice forms are active and passive.

Active Voice

1–135 A verb in the active voice shows that the subject performs the action of the verb. Use the active voice to emphasize the subject and the action and to convey a positive, direct, and concise message.

> Choy & Choy Architects **drew up** the design for the new clinic.
>
> Wills & Wills Accountancy Corp. **will present** the seminars.
>
> You **did not endorse** the check properly.

Passive Voice

1–136 A passive voice verb shows that the subject of the sentence receives the action of the verb. Use the passive voice to emphasize the object or receiver of the action and to deemphasize the action. The passive voice tactfully conveys bad news or a "no" response.

> The *design* for the new clinic **was prepared** by Choy & Choy Architects.
>
> The *seminars* **will be presented** by Wills & Wills Accountancy Corp.
>
> Your *check* **was not endorsed** properly.

Verbals

1–137 A verbal is a verb form that is used as a noun, an adjective, or an adverb. It is not used as a verb. Verbals include participles, gerunds, and infinitives.

Participles

1–138 A participle is a verbal that serves as an adjective.

Present Participles

1–139 The present participle of a verb ends in *-ing*.

> The **surviving** records are maintained in a separate underground vault.

Past Participles

1–140 The past participle of a regular verb ends in *-d* or *-ed*. See Table 1.5 or a dictionary for the past participles of irregular verbs.

> The **strengthened** house should be able to withstand an earthquake.
>
> Please install those **hidden** cameras facing the vault.

Perfect Participles

1–141 A perfect participle consists of the word *having* plus the past participle form of the verb.

Having renewed the lease agreement, the landlord and the tenant celebrated another five-year relationship.

The race, **having** just **begun**, was called off because of rain.

Gerunds

1–142 A gerund is a verb form that ends in *-ing* but is used like a noun as the subject or object of a sentence.

Studying the various chemical reactions will be a lengthy process. **[subject of sentence]**

Have they discovered any clues in **linking** the contaminated water with other pollutants? **[object of preposition]**

Infinitives

1–143 An infinitive is a verb in its present tense preceded by the word *to*.

Please ask Norm Rittgers **to analyze** the data, **to compile** the report, and **to distribute** it to all managers.

Split Infinitives

1–144 A split infinitive occurs when a modifier is awkwardly placed between the word *to* and the verb. Although split infinitives are no longer considered incorrect, they should be avoided to prevent awkwardness. Place the modifier (adverb) after the object or before or after the infinitive so the meaning of the sentence is clear.

Awkward:	Their idea was **to apparently propose** a one-time retirement incentive.
Better:	Their idea was *apparently* **to propose** a one-time retirement incentive.
Awkward:	Our choice at this time is **to immediately make** an offer.
Better:	Our choice at this time is **to make** an offer *immediately*.

When the infinitive must be split to form a clearer sentence, be sure the modifier is placed so that it clearly refers to the word it modifies.

Awkward:	*Arbitrarily* **to** *award* them a large settlement seems to be a dangerous precedent.
Awkward:	*To award* them a large settlement *arbitrarily* seems to be a dangerous precedent.
Clear:	**To arbitrarily award** them a large settlement seems to be a dangerous precedent.

ADVERBS

1–145 An adverb is a word, phrase, or clause that modifies, describes, limits, or qualifies a verb, an adjective, or another adverb.

Donna Frias programmed the computer **quickly** and **precisely.** **[modify the verb** *programmed***]**

High interest rates dealt a **very** sharp blow to business expansion plans.
[modifies the adjective sharp]

Did the union negotiators fulfill their obligations **quite** diligently?
[modifies the adverb *diligently*]

Adverbs usually answer the questions "how," "when," "where," "why," and "to what extent."

The proposed merger was reported **accurately.** **[how?]**

Several rumors were heard **yesterday.** **[when?]**

Outside the campaign headquarters, the candidate's supporters waited for the election outcome. **[where?]**

Was the factory closed **because of fire damage?** **[why?]**

Details of the bankruptcy were reported **nationwide.** **[to what extent?]**

Many adjectives are converted to adverbs by adding - *ly*.

diligent	diligently
nice	nicely
judicious	judiciously
lawful	lawfully
reasonable	reasonably
vicarious	vicariously

Their investment was a **judicious** choice. **[adjective—what kind?]**

They acted **judiciously** in selecting their investment. **[how?]**

He made a **reasonable** decision based on the facts.

The decision he made based on the facts was **reasonable.**

His decision based on the facts was **reasonably** well thought out.

Her parents were deemed **vicariously** responsible for the daughter's act of vandalism. **[how?]**

Were details of the incident being reported **worldwide** on a **daily** basis? **[to what extent? When or how often?]**

Conjunctive Adverbs

1–146 A conjunctive adverb is used to join two independent clauses. It provides a transition between the two clauses. The following list contains common conjunctive adverbs:

accordingly	however	next
additionally	in addition	nonetheless
also	in fact	otherwise
anyway	incidentally	so
besides	indeed	still
consequently	instead	that is
finally	likewise	then

for example	meanwhile	therefore
for instance	moreover	thus
furthermore	nevertheless	yet
hence		

Few people can plan for all eventualities in life; **nevertheless**, we can plan ahead for our major objectives.

Interest rates seem to be stabilizing; **however**, no one can predict the future trend.

Adverbs Used with Prepositions

1–147 When an adverb is followed by a preposition, the *-ly* form of the adverb is usually preferred. (See also 1–191.)

consistently with	independently of
differently from	separately from
exclusively of	

Our internal auditors should review our financial status **independently of** the federal auditors.

In some instances, the regular adverb form is used with prepositions.

agreeable to	irrespective of
agreeable with	previous to
consistent with	regardless of

Irrespective *of* the motive, we should try to solidify our position.

Our research findings are **consistent** *with* those of other laboratories' findings.

Negative Adverbs

1–148 The adverbs *but* (meaning "only"), *hardly*, *never*, *not only*, and *scarcely* are used to convey a negative thought. Use only one negative adverb in a negative expression. A double negative (two negative adverbs) creates a *positive* meaning.

Incorrect: **No one** could **hardly** pass the civil service exam.

Correct: **No one** could pass the civil service exam.
Hardly anyone could pass the civil service exam.

A double negative may sometimes be used to express a positive thought more emphatically.

This is certainly **not** an **unpleasant** task!   **[Meaning: This is a pleasant task.]**

1–149 *Not* and *never* have different meanings. *Not* expresses a negative; *never* is an absolute term that means "in no way" or "at no time."

Judy and Loren Meredith have **not** considered relocating from Oregon to California.   **[but they may consider it later]**

Judy and Loren Meredith have **never** considered relocating from Oregon to California.   **[at no time had it been considered]**

Adverbs with Two Forms

1–150   Some adverbs are written in two forms, each with a slightly different meaning and function. In many instances, both words may sound correct; however, in most cases, only one form is correct. (The first word of these pairs may also function as an adjective. When in doubt, consult a dictionary.)

clear, clearly	late, lately
close, closely	light, lightly
deep, deeply	loud, loudly
direct, directly	quick, quickly
fair, fairly	quiet, quietly
free, freely	sharp, sharply
hard, hardly	slow, slowly
heavy, heavily	wide, widely
high, highly	

Did Invoice JS736 indicate shipment **direct** to Brick Town, New Jersey?

Was the shipment to be sent **directly** to Brick Town, New Jersey?

The prospectus will be sent **free** to those requesting it.

The prospectus will be distributed **freely** during the open house.

ADJECTIVES

1–151   An adjective is a word, clause, or phrase that modifies, describes, limits, or qualifies a noun or pronoun. Adjectives answer such questions as "what kind," "how many," and "which one."

Our questionnaire surveyed a **limited** population of consumers. **[what kind?]**

Approximately **15** meeting rooms were required for the conference attendees.   **[how many?]**

The **January 20** revision was distributed through the network this morning.   **[which one?]**

1–152   An adjective acts as a complement when it describes the subject of a sentence. (See also 1–9.) Adjectives used as complements follow linking verbs (*am, are, is, was, were, be, been, being; appear, become, grow, seem; feel, look, smell, sound, taste*). To test whether an adjective is the correct modifier, substitute the verb *are, is, was,* or *were.*

Jaime Lee *appears* **innovative**.   **[Jaime Lee *is* innovative.)**

In some cases, linking verbs are used to indicate action rather than to describe the subject. In these cases, use an adverb to modify the verb.

The security guard *looked* **suspiciously** at the visitor.

Adjective Forms

Adjective Clauses

1–153   An adjective clause is a clause modifying a noun or a pronoun. The relative pronouns *that*, *which*, *who*, *whom*, and *whose* are used to introduce the adjective clause. (See 2–46 • 2–50, Essential and Nonessential Phrases.)

> The new product design **that was being tested nationwide** had not been well received.
>
> The new product design, **which was tested nationwide,** was not well received.
>
> Erik Palladino, **whom you recommended highly for the position,** has an impressive background in the industry.
>
> Erik Palladino, **who has an impressive background in the industry,** was recommended highly for the position.

Adjective Phrases

1–154   An adjective phrase is an infinitive phrase, a participial phrase, or a prepositional phrase that functions as an adjective to modify a noun or a pronoun.

> Employees today are required **to possess** up-to-date technological skills and knowledge.   **[infinitive phrase]**
>
> **Having flown from Los Angeles to Hawaii,** I was glad to reach my destination nearly five hours later.   **[participial phrase]**
>
> When was the videotape removed **from the archives?** **[prepositional phrase]**

Proper Adjectives

1–155   An adjective derived from a proper noun can be used to modify or describe another noun.

> **NASA** scientists have made great strides in space exploration since *Apollo 13*.

Compound Adjectives

1–156   A compound adjective consists of two or more words combined to convey a single thought. Compound adjectives are formed by combining adjectives, adverbs, and participles. Some forms of compound adjectives are hyphenated; some are not; others require a hyphen regardless of where they appear in the sentence. Generally, hyphenate the compound adjective when it precedes a noun; if the compound adjective follows the noun, do not hyphenate it.

> The Wild Rose Boutique offers **fine-quality** merchandise.
>
> The Wild Rose Boutique offers merchandise of **fine quality.**

Harriet Beecher Stowe is Connecticut's **best-known** author.

Harriet Beecher Stowe is the Connecticut author who is **best known.**

1–157 An adverb-adjective compound is not hyphenated because the adverb is used to modify the adjective, which in turn modifies the noun.

most challenging research

quite picturesque surroundings

Adverbs ending in *-ly* followed by a participle or an adjective should never be hyphenated.

highly regarded executive

newly renovated facility

barely living organism

wholly invented alibi

1–158 Certain adverb-participle compounds are always hyphenated regardless of whether they appear before or after the noun being modified. (A dictionary listing will show whether a compound adjective is always hyphenated.)

clear-cut responsibilities; responsibilities that are **clear-cut**

far-reaching implications; implications are **far-reaching**

old-fashioned ideas; ideas that are **old-fashioned**

Suspended Hyphens

1–159 A series of hyphenated adjectives with a common ending may modify one noun. Instead of repeating the entire hyphenated adjective phrase, omit the common ending from all but the last adjective. Leave one space after each "suspended" hyphen.

a five- or **a ten-year** loan [a *five-year* or a *ten-year* **loan**]

short- or **long-term** objectives [*short-term* or *long-term* **objectives**]

$100-, $200-, and **$300-a-day** expenses [*$100-a-day, $200-a-day*, and *$300-a-day* **expenses**]

Compound Nouns

1–160 A compound noun may be used as an adjective. Do not use a hyphen with these compound nouns.

child custody issues   real estate market

credit card transaction   voice mail message

income tax regulations

Compound Adjective Phrases

1–161 A phrase used as a compound adjective is hyphenated when it precedes the noun.

on-the-scene reporting   [but **reporting** *on the scene*]

out-of-town clients   [but **clients who are from** *out of town*]

Foreign Words

1–162 Do not hyphenate foreign words and phrases used as adjectives.

> **ad hoc** committee
>
> **bona fide** complaint
>
> **de facto** segregation
>
> **ex officio** member

Number and Noun

1–163 Hyphenate a compound adjective composed of a number and a noun when it precedes the noun. If the compound adjective appears elsewhere in the sentence, do not hyphenate it. The noun following the number is written in its *singular* form when hyphenated.

> a **three-week** holiday   [holiday of *three weeks* or *three weeks'* holiday]
>
> **10-knot** winds   [winds of *10 knots*]
>
> **55-mile-an-hour** speed limit   [a speed limit of *55 miles an hour*]
>
> **258-page** report [a report of *258 pages*]

Ordinal Number and Noun

1–164 Hyphenate compound adjectives that combine ordinal numbers (those ending with -*st*, -*rd*, -*nd* or -*d*, and -*th*, whether written in figures or spelled out) with nouns or participles.

> **first-class** postage
>
> **third-party** beneficiary
>
> **11th-rated** institution
>
> **21st-ranked** position

Proper Names

1–165 Do not hyphenate a proper name used to modify another noun.

> **Trial Lawyers' Association** Conference
>
> **Pacific Rim** marketplace
>
> **Superior Court** docket of cases

When two or more proper names are combined to form a single modifying unit, use a hyphen to connect the entire descriptive phrase.

> The **San Francisco-to-Spokane** mileage is 882.
>
> The **San Francisco-Spokane** mileage is 882.
>
> Our sales during the **June-September** period rose slightly.

Demonstrative Adjectives

1–166 Demonstrative adjectives point or refer to specific nouns or pronouns.

This *and* These

1–167   The singular form *this* and the plural form *these* are used to point out people, places, or objects nearest in distance or time.

> Please update **this** microfiche file.
>
> **These** deeds must be recorded at the recorder's office today.

That *and* Those

1–168   The singular form *that* and the plural form *those* are used to point out people, places, or objects farther removed in distance or time.

> Could **that** property have been on the other side of town?
>
> Some of **those** records dating back to 1950 are stored on microfiche.
>
> Who were **those** people touring our plant yesterday?

Articles

1–169   An article is a word that limits the quantity of a noun or pronoun and specifies which one. There are two types of articles (also called limiting adjectives): indefinite and definite.

Indefinite Articles

1–170   The indefinite articles *a* and *an* are used to refer to an indefinite person, place, or thing.

Use the indefinite article *a* before a noun that begins with a consonant, with the letter *h* when it is pronounced, and with the long *u* (pronounced "yoo").

> **a** reporter   **a** hanger
>
> **a** historic occasion   **a** uniform

Use the indefinite article *an* before a noun that begins with a vowel, with the letter *h* when it is not pronounced, and with the letter *u* except for the long *u*.

> **an** opinion   **an** unusual policy
>
> **an** hour's wait

1–171   When two or more separate persons, places, or objects are referred to, precede each one with *a* or *an*. When the sentence refers to one individual person, place, or object, use *a* or *an* before the entire phrase.

> Our department needs **a** file clerk and **a** receptionist.   **[two individuals]**
>
> Our department needs **a** file clerk and receptionist.   **[one person]**

Definite Article

1–172   The definite article *the* is used to designate a specific person, place, or object or a specific group or class of persons, places, or objects.

> **The** Federal Deposit Insurance Corporation (FDIC) insures savings accounts.

Was this **the** advertising campaign that helped make our product a household word?

1–173 When two or more specific persons, places, or objects are referred to, precede each one with *the*. When the sentence refers to one individual person, place, or object, use *the* before the entire phrase.

> **The** vice president and **the** general counsel spoke at the annual stockholders' meeting   **[two separate individuals]**
>
> **The** vice president and cashier was assisting the bank auditors. **[one person]**
>
> Our investigator is checking **the** damaged seat and **the** seat belt. **[two separate things]**
>
> Our investigator is checking **the** seat and seat belt.   **[one object]**

SIMILAR ADJECTIVES AND ADVERBS

1–174 Many words classified as adjectives and adverbs are similar or identical, although their functions in sentences and their meanings are different. These similarities and differences may be distinguishable by their use as absolute terms, in comparisons, and by the *-ly* word ending. (See Table 1.6, Similar Adjectives and Adverbs.)

TABLE 1.6   Similar Adjectives and Adverbs

Adverbs	Adjectives	Both
absolutely	complete	dead
always	conclusive	full
completely	correct	round
correctly	eternal	square
forever	exact	wrong
never	final	
perfectly	ideal	
	immaculate	
	impossible	
	perfect	
	perpendicular	
	real	
	supreme	
	unanimous	
	unique	
	universal	

Comparison

1–175 Adjectives and adverbs change their forms to indicate degrees of comparison between and among persons, places, and objects. The three degrees of comparison are simple, comparative, and superlative. (See Table 1.7, Comparison of Adverbs and Adjectives.)

Simple Degree

1–176 A simple adjective or adverb is used by itself or with another adjective or adverb to make a simple statement; no comparison is being made in the statement.

TABLE 1.7 Comparison of Adverbs and Adjectives

Simple	Comparative	Superlative
One-Syllable Words		
big	bigger	biggest
close	closer	closest
deep	deeper	deepest
fast	faster	fastest
fine	finer	finest
hard	harder	hardest
large	larger	largest
loud	louder	loudest
mild	milder	mildest
nice	nicer	nicest
poor	poorer	poorest
Two- or More Syllable Words		
active	more/less active	most/least active
careful	more/less careful	most/least careful
clever	more/less clever	most/least clever
costly	more/less costly	most/least costly
lonely	lonelier	loneliest
lovely	lovelier	loveliest
often	more/less often	most/least often
acceptable	more/less acceptable	most/least acceptable
beautiful	more/less beautiful	most/least beautiful
capable	more/less capable	most/least capable
enthusiastic	more/less enthusiastic	most/least enthusiastic

Eugenia Amodei is a **prompt** person.

Our information processing center is a **large** facility.

The research and development staff recommended a **costly** proposal to the board.

The union felt the salary and fringe benefits package to be **acceptable** to the members.

That department is **busy.**

Comparative Degree

1–177 A comparative adjective or adverb is used to compare two persons, places, or objects. The comparative form is usually written by adding either *-er* to the simple form or *more* or *less* before the simple form. The spelling of some words is changed when *-er* is added.

Eugenia Amodei is **more prompt** than most people I know.

Our information processing center is moving to a **larger** facility than its present building.

The research and development staff recommended a **more costly** proposal than was expected.

The union felt the salary and fringe benefits package to be **less acceptable** to the older members than it was to the newer members.

The payroll department is **busier** at month's end than other departments.

Superlative Degree

1–178 A superlative adjective or adverb is used to make comparisons among three or more persons, places, or objects. The superlative form is usually written by adding either *-est* to the simple form or *most* or *least* before the simple form. The spelling of some words changes when *-est* is added.

Eugenia Amodei is the **most prompt** person I know.

We have the **largest** information processing center in the area.

The research and development staff recommended the **most costly** proposal in the company's history.

The union felt the salary and fringe benefits package to be the **least acceptable** of the three plans submitted.

Certain departments tend to be **busiest** on the first and the fifteenth of each month.

Irregular Comparisons

1–179 Some adjectives and adverbs change their forms in the comparative and superlative degrees. Although there are few words in this category, these irregular adjectives and adverbs are commonly used.

Simple	Comparative	Superlative
bad	worse	worst
far	farther, further	farthest, furthest

good	better	best
ill	worse	worst
late	later, latter	latest, last
little	littler, less, lesser	littlest, least
many	more	most
much	more	most
well	better	best

Her professional affiliations were **many**.

Her firm had **more** professional affiliations than the *other* medical groups.

Her firm had the **most** professional affiliations *of all* the groups in the clinic.

The damage to the warehouse was **bad**.

The damage to the warehouse was **worse** than initially thought.

The damage to the warehouse was the **worst** in the city's history.

Comparisons between Two Group Members

1–180 When a comparison is made between two persons, places, or objects within a group, use the comparative form and the word *other* or *else* before the words describing the group.

Their warehouse is **better equipped** for emergencies than any *other* warehouse in the city.

Ms. Cotero defended our department **more enthusiastically** than anyone *else* on the management team.

Comparisons between a Group Member and All Others

1–181 When a comparison is made between one person, place, or object and all others within a group, use the superlative form and the term *of all* before the description of the group.

Marion Graff is the **oldest** of *all* the volunteers.

Of all the diseases known to medical science, cancer is the **most puzzling.**

Words Ending in *-ly*

1–182 Words that end in *-ly* are usually adverbs; however, some adjectives do end in *-ly*. There are also some words ending in *-ly* that can function as both adjectives and adverbs.

Adverb	Adjective	Both
badly	costly	daily
carefully	neighborly	early
clearly		fatherly
completely		friendly

immediately   likely

monthly

only

Russo & Martinez reduced the prices **only** yesterday.   **[adverb]**

Were prices the **only** indicator of an upswing in the economy?
[adjective]

Absolute Terms

1–183 An absolute adjective or adverb is a limiting or descriptive word that represents the highest degree or quality. It cannot be compared with anything else.

complete   round

full   unique

perfect

Does she have **complete** legal title to the land?

The Walt Disney Concert Hall has a **unique** architectural design.

When it is necessary to indicate the degree to which a person or object reaches the absolute quality, use the words *hardly, less, more, nearly, more nearly,* or *most nearly* before the absolute adjective or adverb.

Sherwood's black-and-white image was **more nearly perfect** than Jason's.

Choosing between Adjectives and Adverbs

Fewer *and* Less

1–184 *Fewer* refers to number and is used with plural nouns. *Less* refers to degree or amount and is used with singular nouns.

There were **fewer** than five students at the tryouts.

Less interest on our savings is paid at the savings bank than at a credit union.

Good *and* Well

1–185 *Good* is an adjective used to modify a noun. *Well* is usually used as an adverb. As an adjective, *well* usually refers to health.

Many of the clerks feel that Ms. Qi Shen is a **good** manager.

Norman Rittgers is a **well-known** statistician.

We know that firm **well** enough to depend on its products.

His health is fine; his doctor says he is **well** enough to return to work.

Most *and* Almost

1–186 *Most* is the superlative form of *much* and *many. Almost* is an adverb meaning nearly.

She is the **most** dedicated person I know.

Almost all the employees received bonuses.   **[*not* all of the . . .]**

Real *and* Really

1–187   *Real* is an adjective used to modify a noun. *Really* is an adverb describing the action of a verb. Substitute the word *very* to test the correctness of *really* in a sentence.

> According to the medical examiner, it wasn't a hairpiece; it was **real** hair.
>
> He has been **really** enthusiastic about the new payroll program.
> **[very enthusiastic]**

Some *and* Somewhat

1–188   *Some* is used to modify a noun. *Somewhat* answers the question *what*. Substitute the words *a little bit* to test the correctness of *somewhat*.

> There is **some** authority to dispute that fact.
>
> She was only **somewhat** positive in her description of the runaway car.
> **[*a little bit* positive]**

Sure *and* Surely

1–189   *Sure* is an adjective used to modify a noun. Substitute the word *certain* to test the correctness of *sure*. *Surely* is an adverb used to describe the action of a verb. Substitute the word *certainly* to test the correctness of *surely*.

> She will be a **sure** winner in the moot court competition.
> **[*certain* winner]**
>
> Their visiting the Louvre Museum at the same time was **surely** an unusual coincidence.   **[*certainly* an unusual coincidence]**

PREPOSITIONS

1–190   A preposition is a word that shows the relationship between a noun or pronoun and another word in the sentence. The following are common prepositions.

about	by	opposite
above	down	over
after	except	through
around	for	to
against	from	under
among	in	until
at	into	up
before	like	upon
below	near	with
beside	of	within
between	off	without
but	on	

Using the Correct Preposition

1–191 Certain words require that certain prepositions be used to convey a more precise meaning. Correct preposition usage depends on whether *something* or *someone* follows the preposition. The words in brackets in the following list are examples of completed phrases.

abide **by** something   [regulations]

abide **with** someone   [a supervisor]

accompanied **by** someone   [a parent]

accompanied **with** something   [remorse]

account **for** something   [this mistake]

account **to** someone   [the auditor]

agree **on** or **upon** something   [the terms of a contract]

agree **to** something   [move to Dallas]

agree **with** a person or an idea   [a newscaster or a liberal philosophy]

angry **about** something   [today's news]

angry **at** something   [the computer]

angry **with** someone   [the boss]

argue **about** something   [a difference of opinion]

argue **with** someone   [a colleague]

compare **to** something for similarities [Macintosh apples to Delicious apples]

compare **with** something for differences   [Agatha Christie with P. D. James]

comply (verb) **with** someone or something   [her request or the order]

compliance (noun) **with** someone or something   [the officer's demand or the speed laws]

conform (verb) **to** something   [the letter of the law]

conformity (noun) **with** or **to** something   [strict policies or rules]

convenient **to** something nearby   [the library]

convenient (something being suitable) **for** someone   [a group of homeowners]

correspond **to** something   [your point of view]

correspond **with** someone   [a pen pal in Germany]

differ **from** something else   [what we projected]

differ **with** someone   [a teacher]

different **from** something else   [last year's edition]

discrepancy **in** one thing   [the total]

discrepancy **between** two things   [this year's figures and last year's figures] discrepancy **among** three or more things   [**the annual figures for the last five years**]

enter **into** something   [**a lease**]

identical **to** someone   [**his twin brother**]

identical **with** something   [**the copier bought last week**]

inferior **to** something or someone   [**the brand of paper or that clerk**]

part **from** someone   [**a professor, until the next class**]

part **with** something   [**a favorite watch**]

retroactive **to** a date   [**August 4**]

similar **to** something   [**the copier bought today and the one bought last week**]

speak **to** someone to tell   [**the conference on telecommunications**]

speak **with** someone to discuss   [**the parent of a child**]

superior **to** something or someone   [**this brand of paper or that clerk**]

wait **for** someone or an event   [**the repair technician or Ground Hog's Day**]

wait **on** someone   [**the customers**]

Prepositional Phrases

1–192 A prepositional phrase consists of a preposition and the noun or pronoun that is the object of the proposition. The prepositional phrase may be used either as an adjective or as an adverb, depending on its placement within the sentence.

Used as Adjectives

1–193 When used as an adjective, the prepositional phrase is placed after the noun it modifies.

Computers are business tools **with great time-saving features.**

Used as Adverbs

1–194 When used as an adverb, the prepositional phrase may follow either the verb or its object.

Mr. DeSilva transferred **into the database** all the client records.

Mr. DeSilva transferred all the client records **into the database.**

A prepositional phrase used as an adverb may also be placed at the beginning of the sentence as an introductory dependent element.

During the company's third quarter, sales increased by 18 percent.

Special Preposition Usage

1–195 Difficulties may arise when prepositions are used improperly at the ends of sentences, within a series, included when they should be omitted, and confused with similar prepositions.

Propositions at End of Sentences

1–196 A sentence may end with a preposition to emphasize an idea or a word and to avoid an awkward sentence structure if the preposition were placed elsewhere. Although it was once considered incorrect to end a sentence with a preposition, this is no longer the case. In fact, avoiding prepositions at the end of sentences can lead to awkwardness.

> "That is the kind of nonsense up **with** which I will not put."
>
> —Winston Churchill

Placement of the preposition may depend on whether a formal or an informal tone is desired.

Informal: Whom did he give his report **to?**

Formal: **To** whom did he give his report?

Short questions often end with a preposition.

How many persons can we count **on?**

Prepositional Phrases in a Series

1–197 When a sentence includes a series of prepositional phrases, be sure each item in the series begins or ends with the appropriate preposition.

The ancient silk merchants traveled **over** mountain ranges, **across** plains, and **through** dangerous territory to reach their market.

When a sentence includes a series of prepositions in parallel clauses, be sure each item in the series begins or ends with the appropriate preposition.

He has a deep **devotion to,** and a sincere **interest in,** the philosophy and writings of Thich Nhat Hanh.

Unnecessary Prepositions

1–198 In colloquial speech patterns, do not insert unnecessary prepositions.

Where did you buy that **[at]?**

Where are you going **[to]** on your vacation?

Three percent will be taken off **[of]** the marked price.

Confusing Subjects and Objects of Prepositions

1–199 The noun or pronoun that is the object of the preposition is often incorrectly used to determine the verb of the sentence. Be sure to select an appropriate singular or plural verb based on the subject of the sentence and not on the object of the preposition. (See 1–78 • 1–83, Indefinite Pronouns.)

> Incorrect: *One of the printers were* hooked up incorrectly to the computer.
>
> Correct: **One [*of the printers*] was** hooked up incorrectly to the computer.
>
> Incorrect: *Everyone* except the real estate section's three associates *have* pledged *their* time for the drive.
>
> Correct: **Everyone** except the real estate section's three associates **has** pledged **his or her** time for the drive.

Choosing the Correct Preposition

Beside and Besides

1–200 *Beside* is a preposition meaning "next to." *Besides* as a preposition means "except"; as an adverb, *besides* means "in addition to."

> She sat **beside [next to]** me at the luncheon.
>
> No one is going **besides [except]** Cynthia.
>
> **Besides [in addition to]** the fact that we are overloaded, we are already two weeks behind schedule.

Between and Among

1–201 *Between* is used to refer to two persons, places, or objects. *Among* is used to refer to three or more persons, places, or objects.

> The choice for second chair was **between** Josef and me.
>
> **Among** the three of us, I feel that I have the largest caseload.

Help and Help from

1–202 *Help* as a verb means "to give assistance" or "to aid." *Help* as a noun means "assistance" or "aid." *Help from* requires an object of the preposition to complete the thought.

> The Red Cross offered **to help** those families affected by the disaster. **[verb]**
>
> Which program will offer the most **help** in case of an emergency? **[noun]**
>
> She couldn't **help** offering all her ideas.   **[verb]**
>
> The credit bureau requests **help from** our credit clerks. **[noun and preposition]**

In and Into

1–203 *In* refers to something or someone located within or inside. *Into* implies some motion from the outside to the inside.

> At the courthouse, we ran **in** to see the clerk.
>
> The suspects were transferred **into** the holding cell adjoining the courtroom.

Go **in** the south entrance of the building and then **into** the reception area.

Of and *Have*

1–204   *Of* is a preposition used to indicate a relationship. *Have* is a verb. These two words are misused because of poor pronunciation and incorrect grammar.

Of the two presentations, which one captures the audience's attention?

The notary public verified that he is a resident **of** Inyo County, California.

Incorrect: She should **of** realized her mistake earlier.

Correct: She should **have** realized her mistake earlier.

On to and *Onto*

1–205   *On to* implies physical movement or the action of placing a person or an object. *Onto* refers to the direction of movement.

He went **on to** become the chief financial officer.

Did they go **on to** the stage before they were cued?

She maneuvered the disabled truck **onto** the shoulder of the highway.

CONJUNCTIONS

1–206   A conjunction is a word used to connect two words, phrases, or clauses. The three types of conjunctions are coordinating, correlative, and subordinating.

Coordinating Conjunctions

1–207   A coordinating conjunction is a single word that connects similar words, phrases, or clauses. The most common coordinating conjunctions are *and*, *but*, *or*, and *nor*.

Sara **and** Claire are notaries public.

Tran Ngo made presentations at the seminar **but** not in the individual workshop sessions.

Neither Patty LaMarr **nor** Lois Russell has served as chair of the committee.

1–208   When a coordinating conjunction joins two independent clauses, the conjunction is preceded by a comma.

Tran Ngo made presentations at the seminar, **but** he did not speak in the individual workshop sessions.

Will Margaret Lee head the tax department, **or** will she stay in accounting?

Conjunctions in a Series

1–209   In a series of words, phrases, or clauses separated by commas, the conjunction precedes the last item in the series.

52050

Please verify receipt of the pleadings, copies of pretrial motions, **and** witnesses' depositions.

The reorganization included updating bookkeeping programs, automating inventory controls, **and** shifting billing cycles.

She stated she is a professional journalist, she will not reveal her sources, **and** she will defend her rights to a free press.

If the items in the series are separated by coordinating conjunctions, omit the commas.

Will the Outstanding Hispanic-American Student plaque be awarded to Jorge Mena **or** Julie Camacho **or** Carlos Tejeda?

The comma preceding the last item in a series may also be omitted if no confusion results in the idea to be conveyed and if done consistently.

The breakfast session menu consists of juices, muffins, fresh fruits, and ham and eggs.　**[ham and eggs considered one menu item]**

Today's shopping list includes juices, muffins, fresh fruits, ham, and eggs.　**[ham and eggs are two separate grocery items]**

Conjunctive Adverbs

1–210

Some words act as both adverbs and conjunctions. These conjunctive adverbs are used only to join independent clauses in a compound sentence. (See the list of conjunctive adverbs in section 1–146.) Such adverbs are preceded by a semicolon, not a comma.

The weather pattern in the Northwest has shown some change; **yet** it continues to receive as much rain as in past seasons.

Sealed bids must be received by June 10; **furthermore,** they must be received by 4 p.m. EST.

Correlative Conjunctions

1–211

A correlative conjunction is a pair of words that connects two elements of equal grammatical value—words, phrases, or clauses. A list of correlative conjunctions follows:

both . . . and
either . . . or
neither . . . nor
not . . . but
not only . . . but also
whether . . . or

Both Daryl Taylor **and** Dan Raddon mediated the employment dispute successfully.

Neither our travel itinerary **nor** our scheduled appointments have been confirmed.

The publishers **not only** promoted the book aggressively **but also** sent out advertising pieces across the country.

1–212 Use the correct verb form with the correlative conjunctions. In general, use a singular verb form with singular nouns; use the plural verb form with plural nouns. However, when one of the elements joined by a correlative conjunction is singular and the other is plural, use the verb form that agrees with the element closer to the verb.

> **Neither** the two chemists **nor** the pharmaceutical *firm* **has received** any recognition by the Food and Drug Administration.
>
> **Neither** the pharmaceutical firm **nor** the two *chemists* **have received** any recognition by the Food and Drug Administration.

Subordinate Conjunctions

1–213 A subordinate conjunction is a word used to connect a dependent clause to the main or independent clause. The dependent clause may be placed at the beginning of the sentence or elsewhere within the sentence. The following are common subordinate conjunctions:

after	if	that	whereas
although	in case that	then	wherever
as	in order that	though	whether
as if	inasmuch as	unless	which
as though	otherwise	until	while
because	provided	when	who
before	since	whenever	whom
for	so that	where	

> **As** we must move by the tenth, our rent should be prorated for that month.
>
> Our rent should be prorated for that month, **as** we must move by the tenth.
>
> **Whether** she is promoted, she will surely receive a raise.
>
> **Although** our plant will be closed for two weeks, we will continue to accept orders.

Choosing the Correct Conjunction

Difficulties may arise with conjunctions when making comparisons and when expressing a question or doubt.

And *and* But

1–214 *And* means "in addition." *But* indicates a contrasting view.

> June **and** Lilly are both going.
>
> She is going, **but** I am staying.

As . . . as *and* Not so . . . as

1–215 *As . . . as* is used to make a positive statement. *Not so . . . as* is used to make a negative statement.

He is **as** witty **as** he is clever.

Our fiscal policies are **not so** clear-cut **as** they ought to be.

Like *and* As, As if, As though

1–216 *Like* is a preposition and should not be used as a conjunction. Use the words *as*, *as if*, or *as though* to mean "similar to."

The youngster on the witness stand looks **like** a little doll.

Mamie is acting **as if** she didn't care.

Doesn't he look **as though** he were on top of the world?

Whether *and* If

1–217 *Whether* is used to express a question or to convey a doubt. *If* is used to state a condition. Since "whether" by itself conveys doubt, it is not necessary to use "whether or not."

We have wondered **whether** he would be the suitable person for the promotion.

If the company receives another government contract, everyone will be assured of a job for the next three years.

INTERJECTIONS

1–218 An interjection is a word that expresses strong emotion, such as surprise, elation, or pain. The interjection may be used by itself, or it may be used within a sentence. An exclamation mark is usually written at the end of the word or sentence. The following are common interjections.

Boy!	Hooray!	Ouch!
Bravo!	Never!	Terrific!
Great!	No!	Well!
Ha!	Oh!	Wonderful!

Oh, what a beautiful parade!

Ouch, that bee stung me!

Unit 2

Punctuation

2–1 Punctuation marks are written signals that separate units of writing and clarify the meaning of sentences. Punctuation marks, which can be as effective as a speaker's pauses and voice inflections, help the reader understand the message. Incorrect use of punctuation marks can change the meaning or emphasis of a sentence.

The spacing used with punctuation marks depends on the type of mark, the sentence structure, and any adjacent punctuation used (such as a parenthesis or quotation mark). Leave either one or two spaces after punctuation marks that end sentences, questions, and exclamations. Leaving two spaces at the ends of statements, questions, and exclamations is preferred because it provides a definite separation of ideas and enables easier reading. Leave only one space after internal punctuation marks—commas and semicolons. Be consistent in the spacing used.

APOSTROPHE '

An apostrophe is used to show ownership, indicate the omission of words and letters, set off a quotation within a quotation, and abbreviate.

Possession

2–2 Use an apostrophe to indicate possession or ownership. Before forming a possessive, determine whether a singular noun or a plural noun is required; then insert the apostrophe to form the possessive. To test the ownership, reword the possessive expression by inserting the word *of* or the phrase *belonging to*. (To form possessives, see 4–70 • 4–93.)

> **driver's** registration **[singular noun]**
> **drivers'** registrations **[plural noun]**
> **eyewitness's** testimony **[singular noun]**
> **eyewitnesses'** testimonies **[plural noun]**
> **attorney's** client **[singular noun]**
> **attorneys'** clients **[plural noun]**
> **Stephanie's** and **Christopher's** clothes **[individual ownership]**
> **Brian Lee** and **Jaime Lee's** house **[joint ownership]**

Nouns Not Ending in s

2–3 Add an apostrophe and an *s* (*'s*) to singular or plural nouns that do not end in *s*.

> What will the new administrative **assistant's** duties consist of?
> **[duties of the administrative assistant]**
> My **secretary's** efficiency is a great help to the firm.   **[efficiency of my secretary]**

> The **children's** playtime activities include music and creative arts. **[activities of the children]**
>
> **Women's** rights is an important issue. **[rights belonging to or of women]**

Plural Nouns Ending in s

2–4 Add only an apostrophe (') after plural nouns that end in *s*.

> The new software was installed on the **secretaries'** computers. **[computers belonging to the secretaries]**
>
> The four **diners'** bill came to over $200. **[bill belonging to the diners]**
>
> Those **businesses'** profits have been rising steadily. **[profits of those businesses]**

Proper Nouns

2–5 Add either an apostrophe and an *s* ('*s*) or only an apostrophe (') after a proper noun, depending on whether the proper noun ends in *s*.

> **Jennifer's** new job **[job belonging to Jennifer]**
>
> **Gary's** law practice **[law practice belonging to Gary]**
>
> Mr. **Cox's** accounting class **[accounting class of Mr. Cox]**
>
> **Hawaii's** active volcano **[active volcano of Hawaii]**
>
> Mr. **Jennings'** news report **[news report of Mr. Jennings]**
>
> United **States'** foreign policy **[foreign policy of the United States]**
>
> West **Indies'** tropical climate **[climate of the West Indies]**

Individual Ownership

2–6 Add an apostrophe and an *s* ('*s*) to each proper noun to show individual ownership.

> **Mary's** and **Karla's** cars were damaged in the parking lot. **[individual cars belonging to Mary and to Karla]**
>
> Samples of **John's** and **Steven's** hair had been requested for lab analysis. **[hair of John and of Steven]**

Joint Ownership

2–7 Add an apostrophe and an *s* ('*s*) to the final noun only to show joint possession.

> Bob and **Janice's** racehorse finished second today. **[racehorse belonging to Bob and Janice jointly]**

2–8 When a verb form ending in *-ing* (called a gerund) follows a noun, that noun should be written in its possessive form. Use an apostrophe and *s* ('*s*) or just an apostrophe ('), depending on the noun. (See 1–142, Gerunds.)

> **Jason's** leaving St. Paul for Tucson came as a surprise to his colleagues. **[singular noun Jason with gerund "leaving"]**

Contractions

2–9

Use an apostrophe to indicate the omission of letters in contractions. A contraction is a word formed by combining two words and omitting some letters. Contractions may be used in informal letters and memos and in personal letters, but they should not be used in formal business correspondence and reports.

> **It's** time to close the books for this fiscal year.   **[it is]**
>
> **We've** more orders than we can fill.   **[we have]**
>
> **Doesn't** this style look better?   **[Does not]**
>
> Who indicated that **they're** our competitors?   **[they are or they were]**
>
> **Let's** keep in touch during the year.   **[let us]**
>
> At 7 **o'clock,** the parade will begin.   **[of the clock]**

Omitted Numbers

2–10

Use an apostrophe to indicate the omission of numbers in dates.

> The class of **'96** will be a more technologically aware group.   **[1996]**

Abbreviations for Feet or Minutes

2–11

Use an apostrophe as an abbreviation for *feet* or *minutes* in tables and in technical material. In all other uses, spell out *feet* and *minutes*.

> **40'** carpeting **[40-foot]**
>
> **8'** walk **[8-minute]**
>
> The property measured **150'** × **250'.**   **[150 feet by 250 feet]**
>
> We have ordered 25 **feet** of carpeting for the entryway.
>
> Can anyone keyboard faster than 85 words per **minute?**

Quotation within a Quotation

2–12

Use apostrophes as single quotation marks to set off quoted material that appears within a larger quotation. Space twice after the ending quotation mark when the quoted material is a complete statement or question. (See also 6–175.)

> "Have you completed the chapter titled 'How to Improve Your Memory'?" asked Roxanne.
>
> Mr. Hart concluded, "Successful team members never say, 'That's not my job.'"

Plurals

2–13

Use an apostrophe and an *s* (*'s*) to form the plural of individual letters or small words that could be misread. Omit the apostrophe where no misreading is likely to occur.

> Be sure to cross your **t's** and dot your **i's.**
>
> How many **or's** and **nor's** were included in the contract?

The parent would not accept any **ifs** or **buts** from the child.

The co-valedictorians earned straight **A's** throughout college.

ASTERISK *

An asterisk is used to identify a footnote or other reference source, as well as to indicate an omission of text from quoted material.

Footnotes

2–14 Use an asterisk to indicate one, two, or three footnotes within a document. If there are more than three footnotes or references, use numbers rather than asterisks. (See Reference Notes, 8–65.)

> *Jo Ann Lee and Marilyn L. Satterwhite, *The Law Office Reference Manual,* 2d ed. (Burr Ridge, IL: McGraw-Hill/Irwin, 2008).

Omission of Text

2–15 Use a series of three to five asterisks to indicate the omission of an entire paragraph of text from quoted material. Keyboard the asterisks between paragraphs at the point of omission. (See also 6–181.)

> Four score and seven years ago our fathers brought forth on this continent a new nation, conceived in liberty, and dedicated to the proposition that all men are created equal.
>
> * * * * *
>
> But, in a larger sense, we cannot dedicate—we cannot consecrate—we cannot hallow—this ground. The brave men, living and dead, who struggled here, have consecrated it, far above our poor power to add or detract. The world will little note, nor long remember what we say here, but it can never forget what they did here. . . .
>
> . . . Abraham Lincoln, *Gettysburg Address*

BRACE { }

2–16 Use a brace to connect related information. If your keyboard does not contain the brace, use either the left or the right parenthesis or bracket.

> | | |
> |---|---|
> | THE PEOPLE OF THE STATE | } |
> | OF CALIFORNIA, | } |
> | Plaintiff, | } |
> | | } |
> | v. | } |
> | | } |
> | STEPHEN WALSH, ET AL., | } |
> | Defendants | } |

BRACKETS [ ]

Brackets are used to indicate corrections made within text and to set off explanations.

Corrections or Explanations

2–17 Use brackets to insert a correction or an explanatory statement within quoted material. Use the word *sic* (meaning "thus" or "so") to indicate a spelling, wording, or grammatical error that appears within the original quotation.

> "These **[Civil War]** statistics are crucial to the date."

> As the report stated, "The data was **[sic]** confirmed in the follow-up study."

Parenthetical Expressions or Appositives

2–18 Use brackets to set off a parenthetical expression, an appositive, or other explanatory statement that appears within material already enclosed in parentheses.

> (Refer to Exhibit B **[Deed of Trust and Assignment of Rents]** attached.)

With *Emphasis Added*

2–19 When words are underscored or set in italics in a quotation and that emphasis is not part of the original quotation, use brackets to set off the words *emphasis added* at the end of the quotation.

> "High interest rates, *in my opinion*, are a thing of the past *[emphasis added]*," Mr. Hardy wrote.

COLON :

A colon is used to introduce an idea, an explanation, or a listing and to separate elements of an idea.

Business Letters

2–20 Use a colon after the salutation or greeting of a business letter when mixed or standard punctuation is used. (See Punctuation Styles, 7–14 • 7–16.)

> Dear Mr. Manning:

> Dear Customer Services:

2–21 Use a colon to separate the dictator's or writer's initials from those of the typist's in reference initials.

> KZ:ITI

Time and Ratios

2–22 Use a colon to separate hours and minutes and parts of ratios.

> 10:15 a.m.   ratio of 35:1

Biblical and Publication Citations

2–23 Use a colon to separate biblical and publication citations. Use a colon also to separate a publication title and its subtitle. Leave two spaces after the colon separating a title and subtitle and between the place of publication and the publisher in a bibliographic entry.

Luke 3:16 **[biblical book and verse]**

Vargas (2009: 22–26) **[publication date and page reference]**

The Irwin Law Office Reference Manual, 2d ed. (Burr Ridge, IL: McGraw-Hill/Irwin, 2008) **[place of publication and publisher]**

Managing Workforce 2000: *Gaining the Diversity Advantage*

Enumerations and Listings

2–24 Use a colon, followed by two spaces, before a list that follows an introductory statement written within the sentence. Common words used to introduce lists include *the following*, *as follows*, *namely*, *these*, and *for example*. The list may contain words, phrases, clauses, legal citations, or other references.

When enumerated items are listed on separate lines, leave two spaces after the period before keyboarding each item.

The terms "take" and "harm" within the context of the Endangered Species Act of 1973 are discussed in the following case: *Babbit v. Sweet Home chapter of Communities for a Great Oregon*, 515 U.S. 687, 115 S. Ct. 2407, 132 L. Ed. 2d 597 (1995).

The following receive absolute immunity from discovery because they represent an attorney's subjective thoughts:

1. Legal theories
2. Conclusions
3. Mental impressions
4. Opinions

2–25 Do not use a colon when the introductory expression appears near the beginning of a long sentence. Begin a new sentence with the list.

We must adhere to the *following* principles if we are to succeed in the business world. Be observant of all people and activities around us, listen carefully, and speak intelligently when there is a contribution to be made in the discussion.

When a sentence comes between the introductory expression and the listing, use a period at the end of both sentences rather than a colon.

Courts must consider the following factors in deciding whether to invoke the doctrine of *forum non conveniens*. Such policy issues as convenience to the parties and the interest of the state must be considered.

1. Is the plaintiff a resident of the state?
2. In which forum are the witnesses and sources of proof available?

3. Which forum will be familiar with the laws of the state that will govern the case?

Quotations

2–26 Use a colon to introduce one or more sentences of a quotation when the introductory statement is a complete sentence. Leave two spaces after the colon.

> Their reply was terse: "We are not interested."

> Remember what John F. Kennedy said: "Ask not what your country can do for you. Ask what you can do for your country."

COMMA ,

2–27 Commas provide brief pauses within sentences to separate thoughts and help the reader properly interpret the sentence. In general, commas are used (*a*) to separate independent ideas within a sentence; (*b*) to separate words, clauses, or phrases in a series; (*c*) to set off nonessential explanatory or descriptive words or expressions; (*d*) to clarify words or expressions; and (*e*) to set off direct quotations.

Compound Sentence

2–28 Use a comma to separate the independent clauses in a compound sentence connected by the conjunction *and*, *but*, *or*, or *nor*. The comma may, however, be omitted between two short independent clauses.

> The settlement check has arrived, **but** it cannot be disbursed until June 15.

> She has a 10 o'clock meeting and she's late.

2–29 Do not use a comma in a compound sentence when there is no coordinating conjunction joining the two independent clauses. This incorrect comma usage (called a comma splice) creates a run-on sentence. Use a semicolon or a dash, or begin a new sentence.

> Incorrect: Refer this matter to our affirmative action officer, Ms. Kate Meehan will assist you.

> Correct: Refer this matter to our affirmative action officer; Ms. Kate Meehan will assist you.

> Correct: Refer this matter to our affirmative action officer. Ms. Kate Meehan will assist you.

Do not use a comma to separate independent clauses connected by a transitional expression. (See Parenthetical Expressions 2–40 and 2–41.) Use a semicolon before the transitional expression and a comma following it, or begin a new sentence. Do not, however, use a comma after a one-syllable transitional expression such as *then*, *thus*, or *yet*.

Semicolon:	The conference fee includes access to the network database; **therefore,** each participant will have access to the same data for the business simulation.
Period:	The conference fee includes access to the network database. **Therefore,** each participant will have access to the same data for the business simulation.
No comma:	The conference fee includes access to the network database; **thus** each participant will have access to the same data for the business simulation.

2–30 When a sentence contains one subject with two verbs, do not use a comma before the conjunction. The sentence is a simple sentence—not a compound sentence.

> The settlement check **has arrived** but **cannot be disbursed** until June 15.   **[simple sentence with one subject and two verbs]**

> The settlement check has arrived, **but** it cannot be disbursed until June 15.   **[compound sentence with two subjects and two verbs]**

Complex Sentence

2–31 A complex sentence contains one independent clause and one or more dependent clauses. The dependent clause may appear at the beginning, middle, or end of the sentence. A comma is generally used to separate the two clauses, although it may be omitted in certain instances.

Dependent Clause at Beginning of Sentence

2–32 Use a comma to separate an introductory dependent clause from the independent clause.

> Because of the damage caused by the recent fire, we will close our plant until further notice.

Essential Dependent Clause

2–33 A dependent clause is essential when it cannot be omitted without changing the meaning of the sentence. Do not use commas to set off an essential dependent clause.

> Those council members **who favor the moratorium** are in the minority.

> Your deposit will be returned **when the equipment is returned.**

Nonessential Dependent Clause

2–34   A dependent clause is considered nonessential (nonrestrictive) when it can be omitted without changing the sentence meaning. Use commas to set off a nonessential dependent clause.

> Greg Lee, **who favors the moratorium,** spoke on its behalf.
>
> The grand opening will be postponed, **because the storm delayed the shipment of goods.**

Appositives

2–35   An appositive is a descriptive or explanatory word or words following a noun. Use commas to set off an appositive within a sentence.

> Fran Chandler, **a business professor,** has become a member of our organization.
>
> Obeying his first instinct, **to leave the podium,** would have caused him more embarrassment later.
>
> Tsui & Lopez has introduced its latest merchandise line, **hypoallergenic bedding.**

Use two commas to set off an appositive phrase beginning with *or.*

> Court reporting, **or machine shorthand,** skills now incorporate computer-related skills as well.

2–36   When a noun and its appositive are considered one unit or so closely related that it is essential to the meaning of the sentence, do not set off the appositive with commas.

> Maria Aguilar **herself** knew her future job potential would be increased with her accounting experience.

Contrasting Expressions

2–37   Use commas to separate or set off contrasting expressions that begin with such words as *but, not, yet, rather than,* and *instead of.*

> Escrow is due to close Wednesday, **rather than** Monday.
>
> The recall notices will be sent out soon, **but not** until we get official factory authorization.

Rhetorical Questions

2–38   Use a comma between a statement and a question in the same sentence. A rhetorical question is added for effect or emphasis and no response is expected.

> That team thinks it will exceed its sales quota this quarter, **doesn't it?**

Clarity

2–39   Use a comma to separate words or figures that could be misread or misunderstood.

What the quoted figure **is, is** for you to determine.

Instead of **15, 35** potential witnesses may be called to testify.

Parenthetical Expressions

2–40 A parenthetical expression is a nonessential word or phrase that is used for emphasis or as a transition between related thoughts. A parenthetical expression can be omitted without changing the meaning of a sentence. Table 2.1 lists commonly used parenthetical expressions.

2–41 Set off a parenthetical expression with commas, whether it appears at the beginning of a sentence, in the middle, or at the end.

Beginning:	**Moreover,** the merger was well accepted by stockholders of both companies.
	In the meantime, we will continue to obtain estimates for the highway project.
Middle:	It appears evident, **however,** that the lack of supervision caused the employee's work to deteriorate.
	We are, **as a matter of fact,** planning our 20th reunion for next February.
	Dorothy Estrada, **too,** knows about reprographics management.

TABLE 2.1   Commonly Used Parenthetical Words and Expressions

accordingly	hence	of course
actually	however	on the contrary
after all	in addition	otherwise
again	in fact	perhaps
also	in other words	personally
as a matter of fact	inclusive	respectively
as a result	indeed	so
as you know	meanwhile	still
besides	moreover	that is
certainly	namely	then
consequently	naturally	therefore
finally	needless to say	thus
first	nevertheless	too
for example	next	well
fortunately	no doubt	without a doubt
further	now	yes
furthermore	obviously	yet

End: Bridget Furiga and Patricia Sahagian were voted president and vice president, **respectively.**

2–42   Commas may be omitted with certain parenthetical expressions, depending on the emphasis given and the intended meaning of the sentence.

Melanie Roco is **indeed** capable.

The board has **therefore** reaffirmed its decision.

2–43   When *too* (meaning "also") appears at the end of a sentence or when it is used to mean "excessively," do not use commas to set the word off.

Please send my congratulations to Jim **too [also].**

The neon lights are **too [excessively]** bright.

Additional Thoughts

2–44   Use commas to set off parenthetical expressions beginning with such words as *as well as*, *accompanied by*, *attached to*, *in addition to*, and *besides* when they appear between the subject and the verb. Select a singular or plural verb based on the subject of the sentence rather than on any noun included in the additional thought.

Your written proposal, **in addition to** any supporting documents, **was** to have been submitted to Hector Ramirez before January 13.

Don Busché, **as well as** Alicia Vargas and Marly Bergerud, **is** a well-known author of information processing textbooks.

Interruptions

2–45   Use commas to set off expressions that interrupt the flow of the sentence. These expressions may be afterthoughts or independent comments expressing the writer's attitude.

She was, **it appears,** entitled to worker's compensation benefits.

Compu-Tome, **I will admit,** has done an outstanding job of promoting its software.

If I recall correctly, the attack on Pearl Harbor occurred in December of 1941.

Essential and Nonessential Phrases

2–46   Essential (restrictive) infinitive, participial, or prepositional phrases are important to the meaning of the sentence and cannot be omitted without changing its meaning. A nonessential (nonrestrictive) infinitive, participial, or prepositional phrase provides information that can be omitted without changing the meaning of the sentence.

Nonessential (Nonrestrictive) Phrases

2–47   Use a comma to set off a nonessential (nonrestrictive) infinitive, participial, or prepositional phrase.

To be an efficient legal assistant, the individual must possess excellent research and writing skills.   **[nonessential infinitive phrase]**

The witness, **having invoked her Fifth Amendment rights against self-incrimination,** did not respond to any questions posed to her. **[nonessential participial phrase]**

Turn north on Longden and drive north three miles, **toward the mountains.**   **[nonessential prepositional phrase]**

2–48 If the introductory prepositional phrase is short (five or fewer words) or if the sentence flows smoothly after the phrase, the comma may be omitted.

The minutes disclosed that **in November** several resolutions were adopted.

During the recess the parties decided to settle their dispute.

2–49 If an introductory prepositional phrase contains a verb form—regardless how short the phrase is—use a comma after the phrase.

Upon reading the prospectus, I decided this would be an appropriate investment.

Essential (Restrictive) Phrases

2–50 Do not use commas to set off essential (restrictive) phrases.

A decision **to reject the nonconforming goods** must be accompanied by notice to the seller within a reasonable time after the tender of goods.   **[essential infinitive phrase]**

The package **addressed to June Tatsuno** contained the audit report.   **[essential participial phrase]**

Will we be meeting **in the Wentworth Room on November 10 at 6 p.m.?**   **[essential prepositional phrases]**

Personal Titles

2–51 Commas may be used to set off personal titles written after a person's name if that is the person's preference. Otherwise, the comma may be omitted.

Richard G. Fong **Jr.** has been practicing law for several years.

Address all correspondence to Carol Kellogg-Toogood, **Esq.**

The same applies when roman or arabic numerals (such as *II, III, 2d, 3d*, etc.) are used as personal titles to indicate rank.

Henry **VIII** had six wives.

Theodore T. Roelfsema **2d** opened the new branch bank.

Dates

2–52 Use commas to set off the year from the month and the day when written in a sentence.

Are they aware that May **28, 2010,** is the deadline under the statute of limitations?

67

When only the month and year are used, omit the comma.

> The United States will celebrate its tricentennial in **July 2076.**

Addresses

2–53 Use commas to separate the parts of an address written within a sentence.

> Please renew my subscription at the following address: 1550 West Canoga Avenue, Abilene, TX 79604-8403.

Geographic Locations

2–54 Use commas to separate the names of a city, county, state, and country.

> The company's office is in Annapolis, Maryland.
>
> The fraud case is being tried in Superior Court, Pasadena, Los Angeles County, California.

Abbreviations in Company Names

2–55 Use commas to separate business abbreviations, such as *Co.*, *Inc.*, and *Ltd.*, from the company name if that is how the company name appears on its letterhead. Otherwise, the comma may be omitted.

> Data Tech **Inc.** specializes in network troubleshooting.
>
> Johnson, Napier & Meyers, **Inc.,** has agreed to handle our advertising campaign.

2–56 When an ampersand (&) appears in a company name, it takes the place of the word *and*. Do not use a comma before the ampersand.

> Is your counsel Freeman, Coke **&** Johnson?

Letters

Salutation

2–57 Use a comma after the salutation or greeting in a social business letter when mixed or standard punctuation is used. (See 7–32.)

> Dear Carolyn,

Complimentary Closing

2–58 Use a comma after the complimentary closing of personal and business letters when mixed or standard punctuation is used. (See 7–47.)

> Sincerely yours,

Direct Address

2–59 A direct address is the name, title, or other designation of the person being spoken to or addressed in correspondence. Use commas to set off a direct address.

Your account balance, **Mr. Carpentier,** is as you have stated.

What are your thoughts, **Diane?**

Transposed Names

2-60 When an individual's name is transposed or inverted, use a comma to separate the surname from the rest of the name.

Lauricella, Joan M.

2-61 When a title or degree designation follows an inverted name, use a comma to separate it from the name.

Clark, Sally N., **Mrs.**

Hutchinson, Stanley A., **Attorney-at-Law**

When an inverted name appears within a sentence, use a comma after the complete name (and any title or degree designation) to separate it from the remainder of the sentence. (See also 8–71, Bibliographies.)

The opinion listed Roberts, C. J., writing for the Court.

Omissions

2-62 Use a comma to indicate the omission of a word or words from a sentence. These omitted words are usually verbs whose meanings are understood.

Data entry clerks must take the keyboarding test; administrative assistants, spelling and proofreading tests as well.   [*must take* is understood]

Numbers

2-63 Use commas to separate thousands and millions in numbers of four or more digits.

3,783   128,983,105   109,000

$3,783 $128,983,105 $109,000

Large numbers normally written without such separating marks as colons, hyphens, or diagonals/slashes may be separated by commas to aid in reading and filing numbers more easily.

Invoice No. 416,281

Patent No. 124,331,400

2-64 When millions and billions are written in even amounts within a sentence, the commas and zeroes can be omitted and the word *million* or *billion* written out.

Our projection is to sell **4 million** units overseas.

Estimated losses amounted to nearly **$2 billion.**

Series

2–65 Use commas to set off three or more items in a series. A series may consist of words, phrases, or short clauses. Include a comma after the next-to-the-last item before the conjunction. The comma may be omitted if done so consistently without causing a misreading or misunderstanding.

> Is Whitney Barrick in charge of operations in Hong Kong, Taiwan, **or** Japan? **[series of words]**

> A paralegal uses analytical skills to understand case law and statutes, apply the legal principle to the client's situation, **and** interpret and summarize documents. **[series of phrases]**

> Yee Man To practices defense litigation, Lindsay Ugland practices family law, **and** Alex Razo practices corporate law. **[series of clauses]**

> We will be serving coffee, cakes, fruit, beverages, ham, **and** eggs.

> We will be serving coffee cakes, fruit beverages, **and** ham and eggs.

2–66 When two or more adjectives modify a noun, insert a comma where the conjunction *and* could have been used but was omitted.

> Cindy Chavez is a competent, experienced legal assistant. **[competent *and* experienced]**

> Lynn Aspeth has been a dedicated, conscientious, hard-working deputy assistant. **[dedicated *and* conscientious *and* hard-working]**

Do not use commas when coordinating conjunctions (*and* or *or*) are written between each item in a series.

> There are openings for buyers **and** assistant managers **and** managers in all our franchises.

> Please call on Rosie **or** Sally **or** Jayne.

With *etc.*

2–67 Use commas to set off *etc.* as the last item in a series unless it is at the end of a sentence. *Etc.* means "and so forth"; the conjunction *and* is not needed. If *etc.* ends the sentence, the ending period is not needed; the period following the abbreviation is sufficient.

> The fields of intellectual property, workers' compensation, elder law, environmental law, **etc.,** are particularly challenging for new paralegals.

> Remember to organize such tax records as receipts, business expenses, cancelled checks, W-2 statements, 1099 forms, **etc.**

Incorrect Comma Usage

The following are frequent comma usage problems. Do not use commas in these instances. The diagonals (/) indicate where commas should *not* be inserted.

Between Subject and Verb

2–68 Do not separate a subject of the sentence from its verb.

> Carol Blasczynski / is a pleasant person.

Between Verb and Complement

2–69 Do not separate a verb from its complement.

> Elizabeth Polenzani became / project coordinator.

Between Verb and Object

2–70 Do not separate a verb from its object.

> Carol White manages / the project.

Compound Adjective and Noun

2–71 Do not separate a compound adjective from its noun.

> The flight attendants have to work that short, tedious / route between New York and Washington, D.C.

DASH —

2–72 A dash can be used in place of commas, a semicolon, a colon, or parentheses to emphasize or highlight an idea when strong emphasis is needed. A dash is keyboarded as two hyphens (--) with no space before, between, or after them. However, a dash when keyboarded on word processing software and a dash appearing in printed matter will appear as a long, solid line.

To Set Off Parenthetical Expressions

2–73 Use a dash to set off a parenthetical expression more clearly than commas. (See 2–40 and 2–42.)

> The mechanical aspects of writing--punctuation and capitalization--help clarify and emphasize one's ideas.

2–74 Use a dash to set off a parenthetical expression that contains commas.

> Representatives from the Western Region—especially those from California, Hawaii, and American Samoa—should attend the meeting in San Francisco.

To Set Off Descriptive or Explanatory Expressions

2–75 Use a dash instead of a comma to set off an appositive, a descriptive, or explanatory expression. (See 2–35.)

> Will we hire Amedee LaCroix—the consultant—or should we conduct a nationwide search?

Use a dash in place of parentheses to set off an explanatory statement.

> Please refer to Policy 1040—the one concerning leaves of absence—for appropriate reporting procedures.

In Compound Sentences

2–76 For emphasis, use a dash instead of a comma before the conjunction in a compound sentence. (See 2–28 and 2–30.)

> The country was reacting to the recession—and the attitude was evident in the decline in retail sales.

2–77 For emphasis, use a dash in place of a semicolon before the second independent clause.

> Our client signed the lease—it was submitted well before the deadline.

In Informal Writing

2–78 Use a dash in place of a colon in informal writing.

> When the company started, our duties were simple—I made the product and Sam sold it.

To Introduce a Series

2–79 Use a dash instead of a colon to introduce a series of words, phrases, or clauses within a sentence.

> These sales representatives were our top sellers last month—Maxine Wilson, Lois Russell, and Ha Lam.

> Follow these procedures—complete the application, submit your entry fee, and report to the registration area.

For Special Emphasis

2–80 Use a dash before or after a single word for special emphasis.

> Listen—that is the key to learning.

> Our objectives focus on one thing—survival!

Restatement or Summary

2–81 Use a dash to repeat, emphasize, restate, or summarize information.

> Make an IRA contribution before April 15—and receive a credit on last year's tax return.

> The effective date of the contract is June 30—not July 1 as was previously stated.

> Nola Widin kept the books properly, deposited checks in the account promptly, and performed her job in a businesslike manner—she's the most efficient treasurer we've had!

Hesitation or Afterthoughts

2–82 Use a dash to indicate hesitation or an afterthought.

> Cory, Inc., started expanding—I think—in the early 1990s.

> Cory, Inc., started expanding in the early 1990s—after Jim joined the firm.

Abrupt Change in Thought

2–83   Use a dash to indicate an abrupt change of thought within a sentence.

> The training session has been moved up to February 10—no, make that February 12.

DIAGONAL /

2–84   A diagonal, also called a *slash*, a *solidus*, or a *virgule*, is used to separate or to connect numbers, dates, and words.

Fractions

2–85   Use a diagonal when keyboarding fractions. In mixed numbers (whole number plus a fraction), insert either a space or a hyphen between the whole number and the fraction. (See also 5–29 • 5–30.)

> The sum of 6 1/3 and 2 2/3 is 9.
>
> What is the sum of 3-1/4 plus 4-5/8 minus 1-1/4?
>
> Find the lowest common denominator of 1/3, 1/6, 1/5, and 3/5.

Dates

2–86   Use a diagonal to separate numbers used in shortened forms of dates. Spell out the date in business correspondence and reports.

> Birthdate: 10/5/99
>
> Revised   8/2008
>
> The incident occurred on December 1, 1999.
>
> Our contract, signed April 17, 2007, expires March 16, 2010

When referring to dates of different centuries, write out the year in full to avoid confusion.

> Birthdates: 6/12/1928
>
>   11/23/2008 **[not 11/23/08, confused with 1908]**

With *and/or* and *either/or*

2–87   Use a diagonal in the expressions *and/or* and *either/or* to indicate that either word could be used in the sentence.

> Joan **and/or** Jennifer will attend the estate auction.
>
> We are in an **either/or** situation: either we win the contract or we don't!

Discount Terms

2–88   Use a diagonal to indicate certain discount terms.

> The discount term **2/10, n/30** means that a 2 percent discount may be taken if the invoice is paid within 10 days; otherwise, the net amount is payable within 30 days.

Abbreviations

2–89 Use a diagonal with certain abbreviations.

> B/L **[bill of lading]**
>
> c/o **[in care of]**

ELLIPSIS POINTS . . .

2–90 An ellipsis is a series of three periods with a space before, between, and after each period. Ellipses are used to indicate omissions in quoted material. (See also 6–176.)

Omissions of Part of Sentence

2–91 Use an ellipsis of three periods to indicate an omission in the middle of a sentence.

> "More than 250 representatives will arrive . . . for the summit."

Omissions of Words at End of Sentence

2–92 Use a period followed by ellipsis points (four periods) to indicate an omission of quoted material at the end of a sentence. Do not leave a space between the last word of the sentence and the period.

> "More than 250 representatives will arrive on the morning of November 23. . . ."

Omissions of Several Sentences

2–93 Use a period followed by ellipsis points (four periods) to indicate the omission of several sentences of quoted material. Leave two spaces after the ellipsis points and begin a new sentence with a capital letter.

> "More than 250 representatives will arrive on the morning of November 23. . . . We expect the conference hall to be packed."

Omissions at Beginning of a Sentence

2–94 Use ellipsis points (three periods) to indicate an omission of the beginning of a sentence. When the sentence begins with an omission, do not capitalize the first word unless it is a proper noun.

> ". . . 250 representatives will arrive on the morning of November 23 for the summit."

EXCLAMATION POINT !

An exclamation point is used to show strong emotion.

Strong Feeling or Emotion

2–95 Use an exclamation point to indicate a strong emotion such as excitement, surprise, anger, or fear. Exclamation points should be used sparingly in business and legal writing. Leave two spaces after the exclamation point.

> Wonderful!   These are the results we were hoping to obtain.

Use with Quotation Marks

2–96 Place an exclamation point *inside* the quotation mark only when it is part of the quoted remark. Place the exclamation point *outside* the quotation mark when the complete sentence is exclamatory. Leave two spaces after the final quotation mark and after the exclamation point. (See also 2–138, Direct Quotation.)

> He said at the top of his voice, "I need help!"   **[quoted material is the exclamation]**
>
> I can't believe he actually said, "I'm going to the movies"!   **[entire statement is the exclamation]**

HYPHEN -

The hyphen is used to divide words as well as to separate compound words, word elements, or numbers.

Word Divisions

2–97 Use a hyphen to indicate word division at the end of a line. (For word division rules, see 4–91 • 4–106.)

> If you are not sure about the divi-
> sion of words at the ends of key-
> boarded lines, consult a dictionary.

Numbers

Inclusive Numbers

2–98 Use a hyphen in inclusive numbers as a substitution for the word *to* or *through*.

> 2009-2012   §§ 20(b)-21(f)
>
> 4:30-5:45 p.m.   pp. 128-255

Written Numbers

2–99 Use a hyphen when writing out numbers from 21 to 99 that are used alone or as part of a larger number.

> twenty-six
>
> twenty-first of October
>
> one hundred ninety-nine
>
> ten thousand eighty-five
>
> Sixty-four and 28/100 Dollars

Written Fractions

2–100 Use a hyphen when a fraction used as an adjective is spelled out.

> She was elected by a **two-thirds** vote.

With Numbers in Compound Adjectives

2–101 Use a hyphen with numerals in a compound adjective written before a noun.

> 80-cent increase
>
> 55-mile-an-hour speed limit

ZIP Codes

2–102 Use a hyphen between the parts of the nine-digit ZIP code.

> San Gabriel, CA 91775-**1602**
>
> Boston, MA 02215-**2391**

Prefixes and Suffixes

2–103 *Prefixes* are syllables added to the beginning of a word or phrase to form another word. *Suffixes* are syllables attached to the end of a word or phrase to form a different word. Some prefixes are written with hyphens and others are not. Consult a dictionary when in doubt.

2–104 Use a hyphen with certain prefixes and suffixes.

> high-tech industry
>
> quasi-judicial
>
> self-defense
>
> vice president-elect

Some words may either be hyphenated or not. When a word contains two vowels written together, the hyphen may be omitted if it would not cause a misreading or mispronunciation. Be consistent in the use of the hyphen in such instances.

> **P**re-emptively, the defense attorney called the witness to testify before the prosecution had a chance to do so.
>
> All applicants are required to complete certain pre-employment tests. If a new attorney is not accustomed to the dynamics of the courtroom, he or she will often have **p**re-litigation jitters.

2–105 Use a hyphen to separate a prefix from a proper noun or numeral.

> post-2008 economy
>
> pre-Civil War years
>
> pre-Raphaelite art form

2–106 When the prefix ends in *a* or *i* followed by a word beginning with the same letter, use a hyphen to avoid a misreading.

> extra-ambitious effort
>
> semi-independent

The hyphen may be omitted when the prefix ends in *e* or *o* followed by a word beginning with the same letter.

> reelect   coordination
>
> preeminent   cooperation

2–107 Use a hyphen after the prefix *re-* (meaning "repeat") to avoid confusion in the meaning or pronunciation of a word.

> re-creation of the accident scene *but* recreation vehicles
>
> re-form the committee *but* reform the policies
>
> re-sign the agreement *but* resign from the position

Compound Nouns

2–108 Use a hyphen between words in a compound noun (two or more words used as a single unit).

> When will the new **editor-in-chief** be named?
>
> She recently became a licensed **attorney-at-law**.

Compound Adjectives

2–109 Use a hyphen between the words of a compound adjective that appear before the noun it modifies. (See 1–156 • 1–165 for more discussion of compound adjectives.)

> fourth-class mail
>
> state-of-the-art technology
>
> well-known publicist

2–110 Use a hyphen to indicate that a series of compound adjectives have the same last element and modify the same noun. Leave a space after each "suspended" hyphen.

> Parcels of 10-, 15-, and 20-pound books will be sent by sea.

Single Letters

2–111 Use a hyphen to join one or more letters and a word.

> CD-ROM   U-shaped table arrangement
>
> DVD-R   X-ray technology

PARENTHESES ( )

2–112 Parentheses are used to set off nonessential explanatory information from the main idea of a sentence. Parentheses usually deemphasize the material they enclose. Use dashes to emphasize or highlight an idea; use commas if the explanatory expression helps clarify the sentence meaning.

Dates

2–113 Use parentheses to set off dates following a name, event, or period of time.

> Philologists generally divide the story of the English language into three periods; namely, Old English **(499-1100)**, Middle English **(1100–1500)**, and Modern English **(1500-present day)**.

Explanations

2–114 Use parentheses to set off special references, instructions, or other explanatory statements.

> The Bill of Rights **(the first ten amendments to the Constitution of the United States)** describes the fundamental liberties of the people.

Definitions

2–115 Use parentheses to enclose an expression that defines a word.

> Some acronyms include radar **(radio detecting and ranging)**, sonar **(sound navigation ranging)**, and laser **(light amplification by stimulated emission of radiation).**

Numbers and Amounts

2–116 Use parentheses to set off a number or an amount of money that follows a written-out amount in business or legal documents.

> The balance of one hundred fifty-two dollars **($152.00)** is due in two **(2)** equal monthly installments of seventy-six dollars **($76.00)** each.

Enumerations

2–117 Use parentheses to enclose numbers or letters in a listing written within a sentence.

> General requirements include **(1)** the ability to see relationships, **(2)** mature judgment, **(3)** the ability to analyze problems before solving them, and **(4)** efficient work habits.

Outlines

2–118 Use parentheses to enclose numbers in the fifth division of an outline. (See also 8 – 4 • 8 – 5.)

    I. Major Division
        A. Secondary division
           1. Third division
               a. Fourth division
                  (1) Fifth division

Replacement for Comma

2–119 Use parentheses to set off expressions when commas would be confusing.

> Our international relations representative for the Pacific Rim **(Japan and Hong Kong)** will be headquartered in Tokyo.

Punctuation and Capitalization Usage

2–120 Follow the normal rules for punctuation and capitalization of the material enclosed within parentheses.

2–121 Punctuation marks that apply to the complete sentence rather than to the parenthetical item should be written outside the closing parenthesis. Punctuation that applies solely to the parenthetical expression should be placed inside the closing parenthesis.

> The report will be sent priority mail tomorrow **(Thursday);** you should have it by Friday at 10 a.m.

> He insisted on reporting on every detail of the event **(including who wore whose designer fashions!)** for the next two issues!

2–122 Capitalize the first word of the parenthetical expression enclosed in parentheses only if it is a proper noun, a proper adjective, the pronoun *I*, or the first word of a quotation.

> One of our engineers **(Christopher Steven Lee)** invented the system.

> The videodisk **(I believe that was the medium)** stores both graphic images and sound.

2–123 Insert a period before the closing parenthesis only if the parenthetical expression is an abbreviation. The spacing after the closing parenthesis depends on the punctuation preceding it. If a period, question mark, or exclamation point precedes the right parenthesis, space twice after the parenthesis before beginning the next sentence. If a comma precedes the right parenthesis, space once after it before continuing the sentence.

> Our headquarters office **(Washington, D.C.)** is the site of several magnificent monuments to past presidents.

PERIOD .

2–124 A period marks the end of a complete thought, an independent clause. It signals the reader to pause before reading the next idea.

Ends of Sentences

2–125 Use a period after sentences that are statements, commands, and requests. Leave one or two spaces after the period. Leaving two spaces provides a definite separation of ideas for easier reading. Be consistent in the spacing used. The spacing following the period used in other contexts varies; follow the guidelines presented.

> Punctuation marks are mechanical aids to assist the reader in understanding the meaning of an idea.   **[statement]**
>
> Please report to Community Relations immediately.   **[request]**
>
> Submit your expired passport to the agency at once.   **[command]**

2–126 Use a period rather than a question mark after a request stated as a question. If no response is expected, use a period.

> Will you please confirm the reservation by Tuesday.

Abbreviations

2–127 Use a period after abbreviations (other than for units of measure), titles, and degrees. Leave one space after the period at the end of an abbreviation. Generally, no space follows a period *within* an abbreviation. (See 6–186 for abbreviations used in legal citations.)

> **Ms.** Judy Meredith   **Co.**
>
> Richard G. Fong, **J.D.**   **Inc.**
>
> **Sept.** 14   **Mon.**

When a sentence ends with an abbreviation followed by a period, do not use another period.

> Orders will be shipped to the Bingham Co.

States and Countries

2–128 Use a period after the standard state and country abbreviations. Do not use periods with the two-letter state abbreviations used by the U.S. Postal Service. (See Tables 5.6 and 5.7.)

> U.S.A.   Can.   P.R.C.
>
> Calif.   Minn.   Ont.

Initials

2–129   Use a period, followed by one space, after initials in a person's name. Do not use periods after radio and television broadcasting call letters and well-known abbreviated organization names.

Ronald S. Lee	CNN	MSNBC
L. C. Nanassy	IRS	NPR

Decimal Points

2–130   Use a period as a decimal point in dollar amounts and percentages. Align decimal points when figures and percentages are written in columns. Insert zeroes after the decimal point when mixed amounts or percentages are written.

$200.95	12.65%
36.00	6.00
14.63	6.75
$251.58	

2–131   Do not use a decimal point when all the amounts in a sentence or a column are even dollar amounts.

$ 130
100
1,899
$2,129

Petty cash payments were for $22, $135, and $16.

Outlines

2–132   Use a period after numbers and letters in the first four divisions of an outline and after all complete sentences. (See 8–5.) Two spaces follow the periods in the outline.

   I.   Introduction

       A.   State the problem to be solved.

       B.   Summarize the background and significance.

Enumerations and Listings

2–133   Use a period after the numbers or letters in a listing, each of which is written on a separate line. Leave one or two spaces after the periods.

Please note the following:

1. Inactive records will be transferred to central storage on February 8.
2. Active records will be reorganized on March 15.
3. Nonessential records will be gathered by May 15 for disposal or destruction.

81

QUESTION MARK ?

A question mark is used after direct questions and to express doubt.

Direct Questions

2–134 Use a question mark at the end of a sentence that asks a question. Two spaces follow the question mark.

> On whom should the subpoena be served?   Does the court have proper jurisdiction over the defendant?

2–135 Use a period rather than a question mark after a courteous request or where no response is expected. (See also 2–126.) If a response is expected, use a question mark.

> Will you please respond to our credit inquiry by December 2.

Series of Questions

2–136 When a series of questions appears within one sentence, use a question mark after each question. Leave one space after the internal question mark. Do not capitalize the items within the series of questions unless proper names are included.

> Was he the driver? the passenger? the witness?
>
> Who will be the new treasurer? Ms. Kline? Mr. Ortell? Ms. Konomoto?

Expressions of Doubt

2–137 Use a question mark in parentheses to express doubt.

> The captain of the team is 7(?) feet tall.
>
> His uncle was born in 1921 (?).

QUOTATION MARKS " "

Quotation marks are used to set off direct quotations, definitions, and the titles of published works; to indicate emphasis or irony; and to represent certain abbreviations.

Direct Quotations

2–138 Use quotation marks to enclose a direct quotation, the exact words used by a writer or speaker. Quotations of 50 or fewer words are keyboarded within the paragraph. Quotations of more than 50 words are keyboarded as a separate paragraph, indented from the left and right margins, and single-spaced; no quotation marks are used. (See also 6–174.)

> According to *Sell,* "The defendant's failure to take drugs voluntarily . . . may mean lengthy confinement in an institution for the mentally ill. . . ." *Sell v. U.S.,* 539 U.S. 166, 180.
>
> "I will be the next top-selling agent!" Rose Monde said.

The spacing after the end quotation mark depends on the punctuation preceding it. If a period, question mark, or exclamation point precedes the end quotation mark, space once or twice after the quotation mark before beginning the next sentence. If either a comma or no punctuation precedes the end quotation mark, space once after the quotation mark before continuing the sentence.

2–139   Incorporate a quotation of fewer than 50 words within the paragraph and enclose it within quotation marks.

> Douglas Drill gave an example of the use of "heroine" in a sentence as follows: "Yesterday we left our heroine in an impossible situation."

2–140   Keyboard a quotation of more than 50 words as a separate paragraph, indented from both margins, and single-spaced without quotation marks. (See 6–174 • 6–175.)

Quotations within Quotations

2–141   Use single quotation marks (apostrophes) to enclose a quotation within a larger quotation.

> Her last remark was, "When I say, 'Sell,' that's the time for immediate action!"

Restatements/Indirect Quotations

2–142   Do not use quotation marks when someone's remarks are being restated. An indirect quotation is often preceded by *that* or *whether*.

> Direct Quotation: She said, "I'm the new defense attorney."
>
> Indirect Quotation: She said **that** she is the new defense attorney.

Definitions

2–143   Use quotation marks to enclose a definition. Underscore or italicize the word being defined.

> The word *television* comes from Greek and Latin words meaning "to see far."

Emphasis

2–144   Use quotation marks to set off jargon, slang, coined words, and technical terms in nontechnical material. When indicating that slang or poor grammar is not the writer's normal pattern of speech, enclose the expression in quotation marks.

> The future of robotics is evidenced today with "global positioning systems" (also known as "navigational systems") in our automobiles, trucks, and motorcycles.
>
> According to the design analysts, it "ain't" going to be easy to create the Web site quickly; but they'll just have to "wing" it.

Humor or Irony

2–145 Use quotation marks to enclose a word that is used humorously or ironically.

Does the "new" product design look the same as the old one to you?

Titles of Published Works

2–146 Use quotation marks to indicate the titles of magazine articles, chapters of books, speeches, short poems, short stories, lectures, songs, and radio and television programs. (See also Publication Titles, 2–160.)

"The Artificially Intelligent Office" is the title of Chapter 3.

M*A*S*H was one of the most successful television series ever broadcast.

The concert began with "The Star Spangled Banner."

Inches and Seconds

2–147 Use a quotation mark as an abbreviation for inches or seconds in technical material. In all other uses, spell out *inches* and *seconds*.

16-1/2" [inches] of fabric

5" pipe [5-inch pipe]

30" radio ad [30-second radio ad]

The plumber replaced almost 18 **inches** of copper piping.

A 15-**second** television commercial is costly.

2–148 When an expression includes both feet and inches or minutes and seconds, spell out the words.

The tallest woman in the dance competition is **6 feet 1 inch**.

The car skidded **23 feet 6 inches** before hitting the hydrant.

Quotation Marks with Other Punctuation Marks

Certain punctuation marks are written inside the final quotation mark while others are written outside, depending on appearance and the meaning of an idea within quotation marks.

Commas and Periods

2–149 Place commas and periods *inside* the final quotation mark. Follow the spacing appropriate for the punctuation mark inside the final quotation mark: leave one space after the final quotation mark when preceded by a comma; leave one or two spaces after the final quotation mark when preceded by a period.

"I heard a car backfire at about 10:15 that evening," the witness stated.

Gabriella said, "Now is the time to make a decision."

Semicolons and Colons

2–150 Place semicolons and colons *outside* the final quotation mark because they apply to the entire sentence rather than just the quotation. Follow the spacing appropriate for the punctuation mark outside the final quotation mark: leave one space after the final quotation mark when preceded by a semicolon; leave two spaces after the final quotation mark when preceded by a colon.

> I sent you the article, "The Future of Alternative Dispute Resolution"; therefore, you should be well prepared for your presentation.
>
> Only one character comes to mind from "The Red-Headed League": Sherlock Holmes.

Exclamation Points and Question Marks

2–151 Place an exclamation point or a question mark *inside* the final quotation mark when it applies only to the quoted statement. When it applies to the entire statement, place the exclamation point or question mark *outside* the final quotation mark. Leave one or two spaces after the entire quotation whether the exclamation point or question mark is written inside or outside the quotation mark.

> He shouted, "Stop!"
>
> Stop saying, "Everything happens for the best"!
>
> The child kept asking, "When can we go home?"
>
> Did Jonathan say, "I'm quitting"?

SEMICOLON ;

2–152 The semicolon temporarily holds the reader at a particular point in the sentence before continuing to read. A semicolon can be used in place of a period. A semicolon can also be used instead of a comma in sentences containing internal commas.

Between Independent Clauses

2–153 Use a semicolon between the independent clauses of a compound sentence when a conjunction (*and*, *but*, *or*, or *nor*) is omitted.

> His first payment was due in March; the second payment was not due until June.

2–154 Use a semicolon instead of a comma to separate independent clauses joined by a conjunction when a stronger break is desired.

> Someone must have realized the error; but apparently that person did not think the mistake important enough to question.

Transitional Expressions

2–155 Use a semicolon when the second independent clause begins with a transitional expression (see 1–146); use a comma after the expression.

> Spelling is not always logical or consistent; **nevertheless,** an educated person is expected to know how to spell.

Internal Commas

2–156 Use a semicolon to separate one or more clauses that contain internal commas and that could be misread.

> The publications department is responsible for reports, proposals, and analyses; and the public information office handles brochures, press releases, and publicity.

> Reneé is drafting the possible objections; Kevin is compiling the photos, charts, and other evidence; and Ting Mai is checking the citations.

Series

2–157 Use a semicolon to separate the items in a series already containing commas.

> Branch offices are located in Tulsa, Oklahoma; Tuscaloosa, Alabama; Portland, Maine; Madison, Wisconsin; and Santa Barbara, California.

UNDERSCORE ___

2–158 An underscore is used to highlight or emphasize words. Underscoring used in keyboarded material may be substituted for italics. Most word processing programs have the capability to print italics; if so, use the italics rather than underscores.

If underscoring is used, the underscore may be a solid line below all characters and spaces, or it may appear only under characters. When citing case names in court opinions, use a solid underscore. (See 6–83.)

Emphasis or Highlighting

2–159 Underscore individual letters, words, or expressions being highlighted, emphasized, or identified.

> The h in Lindbergh is silent.

> The word contract never entered our discussion.

> Gracias, merci, and cnacudo all mean "thank you."

Publication Titles

2–160 Underscore the titles of books, magazines, newspapers, plays, movies, and musical compositions. Such titles may also be written in italics.

> Introduction to International Business has been a popular textbook.   **[book title]**

> Consult Consumer Reports for reviews of this year's new automobiles.   **[magazine]**

> Aida is being performed this afternoon at a charity benefit.   **[opera]**

> The Chicago Tribune, San Francisco Examiner, Los Angeles Times, and the New York Times are available at public libraries.   **[newspapers]**

The long-running Broadway play *South Pacific* was adapted from James Michener's book, *Tales of the South Pacific*. **[play and book titles]**

The Orson Wells classic, *Citizen Kane*, continues to be a favorite film. **[movie]**

Legal Citations

2–161 Underscore the names of the parties involved in a dispute when a case is cited in a case reporter, periodical, legal memorandum, legal brief, or other court documents. Separate the parties' names with a lowercase *v.* (for "versus"). Follow the correct format for capitalization, spacing, and abbreviations. (See Unit 6, Legal Citations.)

Unit 3

Capitalization

3–1 Capitalization helps clarify the meaning and importance of words. The most commonly accepted and widely used rules of capitalization are included in this unit. Consult the dictionary for additional capitalization rules.

FIRST WORDS

Sentences

3–2 Capitalize the first word of a sentence.

> Having a dictionary nearby may help an employee develop the "dictionary habit."

Parenthetical Expressions

3–3 Capitalize the first word of a complete sentence written within parentheses if the sentence is a separate idea and not a part of the larger sentence.

> Because of the late hour, the judge decided to recess for the day. (She asked to see counsel in her chambers.)
>
> Because of the late hour (the judge asked to see counsel in her chambers), the judge decided to recess for the day.

Capitalize a word, a series of words, or an abbreviation written in parentheses to represent a shortened form or definition of a spelled-out name. Capitalize the defined word throughout the document.

> . . . leases to Jackson Financial Associates, LLP ("Lessee")

3–4 Capitalize a sentence fragment written within parentheses only if the words would normally be capitalized.

> Our associates (the Bonnes) will be traveling to Australia this fall.
>
> Did the former executive (Liz Polenzani) retire to Maui?

Outlines

3–5 Capitalize the first word in each subdivision of an outline.

> I. Company fringe benefits
> A. Paid vacations
> B. Accumulated sick leave
> C. Medical insurance

Enumerated Listings

3–6 Do not capitalize the first word of an enumerated listing written within a sentence—even if the item is a complete sentence—unless the first word would normally be capitalized.

> The following items must be taken care of: (1) the Ohio office must make hotel reservations; (2) David Helmstadter must organize the conference program; and (3) the Delaware office must submit a preliminary budget.

Quotations

3–7   Capitalize the first word of a statement within quotation marks if the statement is a complete sentence or a one-word exclamation.

> Dr. Laurence J. Peter's financial principle is, "Money is the root of all evil; everyone needs to have roots."
>
> After the company team won the match, everyone shouted, "Hooray!"

Do not capitalize a portion of a quotation that is part of a larger sentence.

> Referring to the "severe problem facing our modern cities," the speaker cited some alarming statistics.

Following a Colon

Complete Sentences

3–8   Capitalize the first word of a sentence following a colon when the sentence is an independent clause expressing a rule or a guideline.

> This is a good rule to follow: Consult the dictionary when in doubt.

3–9   Do not capitalize the first word following a colon when an independent clause explains, illustrates, or expands upon the expression it follows:

> Many law firms require specialized skills of their legal assistants: competency in identifying issues and researching are essential as well as proficiency in producing a variety of legal documents and correspondence.
>
> Our quality circle keeps one motto in mind: quality begets quality.

3–10   When an expression following a colon is not a complete sentence, do not capitalize the first word unless the word is normally capitalized.

> Our group counseling sessions abide by one rule: no personal attacks.
>
> The store is closed two days a year: Thanksgiving and Christmas.

Quotations

3–11   Capitalize the first word following a colon when quoted material follows.

> Ms. Basil gave me these instructions: "Record this deed by January 8."

Listings

3–12   Capitalize the first word of each listed item when the items are written on separate lines, although the items may not be preceded by numbers or letters.

> Clients will have access to a full range of legal services:
>
> Wills, trusts, and probate services
>
> Family law
>
> Tax law
>
> Real property law

PROPER NOUNS

3-13 A proper noun identifies a specific person, place, or thing. Capitalize each significant word of a proper noun. Do not capitalize articles *(the, a, an)*, coordinating conjunctions *(and, or, nor)*, or prepositions (such as *of, at, in, on, for*) unless they are the first word of a sentence or unless specific usage requires it.

> **A**ssociation of **L**egal **A**dministrators
> **F**ederal **R**eserve **B**ank
> **N**obel **M**emorial **P**rize in **E**conomic **S**cience
> **O**pera **T**heatre of **S**aint Louis

Capitalize words in names of acts and codes only when specific acts and codes are cited. When an act or code is referred to subsequently in its shortened form, capitalize the first letter.

> **A**mericans with **D**isabilities **A**ct of 1990; the **A**ct
> **S**arbanes-**O**xley **A**ct of 2002; the **A**ct (or its acronym, **SOX**)
> The **U**niform **C**ommercial **C**ode; the **C**ode

Proper Adjectives

3-14 Capitalize words that are derived from proper names.

> **E**lizabethan language   **S**cottish terrier
> **G**regorian calendar   **V**ictorian architecture

3-15 Do not capitalize certain derivatives that have acquired a common usage. Consult a dictionary when in doubt about capitalization.

> manila envelope   plaster of paris

Nouns with Letters or Numbers

3-16 Capitalize a noun appearing before a letter or number that clarifies and emphasizes a specific person, place, or object.

> **A**ppendix A   Case LAV07–3490
> **B**adge 3920   *In re* **B**aby D, a Minor
> **C**atalog **N**o. 321

3-17 As a rule, do not capitalize words such as *page, paragraph, section*, or *line* unless these words appear at the beginning of the sentence.

> The revised provisions appear on **p**age 341.
> **P**aragraph IX of the plaintiff's complaint sets out details of her fraud allegation.
> Refer to **p**age 8, **l**ine 10, of the trial transcript for her statement.

When citing constitutions, statutes, and pleadings, capitalize such words to refer to specific passages.

> The 2006 Supplement shows that Section 120(b) was amended in 2005.
>
> In Paragraph V of the amended complaint, the plaintiff set out general details of her personal injuries.

3–18 When the noun and the number are separated in the sentence, do not capitalize the noun.

> The number of the case referred to is LAV07–3490.
>
> In the catalog, the course number is listed as 112B.

COMMON NOUNS

3–19 Common nouns refer to people, places, or things in general and should not be capitalized.

agents	lease	minors
bailee	legislation	venue

3–20 The following words may be used as common or proper nouns.

act	committee	department
avenue	company	division
board	corporation	president
board of directors	county	state
city	court	supervisor
college		

Capitalize a common noun when it is written as part of a proper name. In general, do not capitalize a common noun when it is used alone to stand for the entire name or for the general category to which the name belongs. When referring to the U.S. Supreme Court or a state's highest court, capitalize Court.

> The Court in *In re Pulliam*, 262 B.R. 539 (Bankr. D. Kan. 2001), stated . . . **[citing a Bankruptcy Court decision]**
>
> The Arlington Title Company was established in 1899.
>
> Their company was investigating a complicated title search.
>
> Contact the U.S. Department of Agriculture.
>
> That department publishes several booklets on proper health care and diet.
>
> In *Bank One Chicago v. Midwest Bank & Trust*, 516 U.S. 264, 116 S. Ct. 637, 133 L. Ed. 2d 635 (1996), the Court . . .   **[citing a U.S. Supreme Court decision]**
>
> The federal courts are bound by Federal Rules of Procedure.

ACADEMIC SUBJECTS AND DEGREES

3–21 Capitalize specific course titles, but do not capitalize academic subject areas. Names of languages, however, are always capitalized.

> Jorge's spring schedule includes Contracts I, Torts I, and Legal Writing and Research.

> Preparation for law practice requires not only knowledge of contracts and tort laws and remedies but also effective English skills for legal writing.

3–22 Capitalize an academic abbreviation or academic degree when it follows a name. Academic degrees are not capitalized when used in general terms.

> He holds a Ph.D. in psychology.

> Dawn Balog, Doctor of Philosophy, will be our guest speaker.

> She earned her doctorate in psychology.

> Sonia earned her doctorate in public administration.

ACRONYMS

3–23 An acronym is a word form derived from the first letters of a longer name. The acronym is pronounced as written. Capitalize all the letters of an acronym and do not use periods. Some acronyms have become "ordinary" words and are now written in lowercase letters.

CAT	computerized axial tomography
FAQs	frequently asked/answered questions
GUI	graphic user interface (pronounced goo-ey)
OSHA	Occupational Safety and Health Act
RICO	Racketeer Influenced and Corrupt Organizations (Laws)
laser	light amplification by stimulated emission of radiation
radar	radio detecting and ranging
sonar	sound navigation ranging
Wi-Fi	wireless fidelity

ASTRONOMICAL BODIES

3–24 Capitalize the names of specific planets and satellites (except *earth* and *moon*), stars (except *sun*), and constellations.

Capitalize *earth*, *moon*, and *sun* only when they are included within a listing or a series of astronomical bodies.

> the Big Dipper   Jupiter

> the Milky Way   Saturn

> The global objective is achieving peace on earth.

A solar eclipse occurs when the **S**un, **M**oon, and **E**arth line up, and the **M**oon's shadow falls on **E**arth.

COMPASS TERMS

3–25 Capitalize points of the compass (*north*, *south*, *east*, *west*) only when they refer specifically to a particular region or are used as part of a proper name. Do not capitalize them when they are simply used to show direction.

North Dakota	north side of the street
the **S**outhwest	southwest corner
South Third Avenue	just south of Laguna Canyon
the **W**est Side	drive west three miles

3–26 Capitalize the adjectives *northern*, *eastern*, *southern*, and *western* when they are written as part of a place name.

Northern Ireland	northern coastal area
Southern Section Conference	southern Illinois
Western Samoa	midwestern drought
Eastern Hemisphere	eastern mountains

CORRESPONDENCE

Letter Parts

3–27 Capitalize the first and other important words in the salutation, attention line, subject line, and complimentary closing of business and personal letters. Sometimes an entire element, such as the word *ATTENTION* or *SUBJECT* or the keyboarded company name, may appear in all capital letters. (See Unit 7, Law Office Correspondence.)

Dear Joseph:

Attention: **M**s. Esperanza Hernandez

SUBJECT: Policy **N**o. IRE0930

Sincerely yours,

Memorandum Parts

3–28 Capitalize the headings of memorandums when preprinted memorandum stationery is not used. Capitalize important words in the names of the addressee and sender, department or division name, and the subject.

TO:	Elaine C. Fong
FROM:	Jeffrey Winter
DATE:	September 25, 20—
SUBJECT:	Morrison Electronics Contract

DATES AND TIME

Days and Months

3–29   Capitalize the days of the week and the months of the year.

> **Wednesday, February 15**
> the second **Monday** in **October**
> the fifteenth of **April**

Holidays

3–30   Capitalize holidays and holy days, including the word *Day* written with the event.

> Labor **Day**   Christmas **Eve**
> Mother's **Day**   Thanksgiving
> Ramadan   Veterans **Day**
> Yom **Kippur**

Seasons

3–31   Do not capitalize seasons of the year unless they refer to a specific time period or event.

> spring seed catalogs   **Spring Quarter, 2007**
> our winter stock   **Winter Clearance Sale**

Time Periods

3–32   Capitalize important words in periods of time. Do not capitalize decades or centuries.

> the **Great Depression**   the **Middle Ages**
> the **Ice Age**   the **Roaring Twenties**
> the nineties   the twenty-first century

Historic Events

3–33   Capitalize important words in the names of historic events.

> Battle of **Trenton**
> Boston **Tea Party**
> the **Civil War**

GEOGRAPHIC NAMES

3–34   Capitalize the names of continents, nations, states or commonwealths, cities, towns, mountains, and bodies of water.

> Atlantic **Ocean**
> Democratic **Socialist Republic** of **Sri Lanka**
> **Grand Duchy** of **Luxembourg**
> **Nile River**

Pittsburgh, Pennsylvania

Principality of Monaco

the Rockies

Saint Vincent and the Grenadines

3–35 Do not capitalize terms such as *lake*, *river*, *mountain*, *ocean*, or *city* when used alone or when they appear with two or more proper nouns.

Roger and Marie planned a rafting trip down the river.

They have sailed both the Atlantic and the Pacific oceans.

Of the Great Lakes, only Lake Michigan is wholly in the United States.

3–36 Capitalize regions, localities, and nicknames of cities and states.

the Aloha State

Land of Enchantment

the Keystone State

Salem Township

the North and South Poles

Third World countries

3–37 Capitalize sections of countries or other geographic subdivisions.

Central Europe   the Midwest

the Mississippi Basin   the Pacific Rim region

GOVERNMENTAL AGENCIES AND BODIES

Legislative Bodies

3–38 Capitalize the full names of national, state, and city or municipal legislatures. Do not capitalize the shortened form of smaller legislative units.

the United States Congress; Congress

the Wisconsin Legislature; the legislature

the New Jersey Senate; the senate

Boston City Council; city council; the council

Departments and Agencies

3–39 Capitalize the important words in the names of governmental agencies, authorities, boards, commissions, and departments when spelled in full. Generally, do not capitalize the shortened form in subsequent references.

Pennsylvania Higher Education Assistance Agency; the agency

Department of Justice; the department

Federal Trade Commission; the commission

the Federal Bureau of Investigation; the bureau

97

Armed Forces and Military Terms

3–40 Capitalize the names of specific branches of the armed forces. The words *army*, *navy*, and so on are not capitalized when used alone or when they are not part of an official title.

U.S. Air Force Academy	the academy
U.S. Army	army life
U.S. Coast Guard	coastguardsman
U.S. Navy	naval officer
Sixth Fleet	the fleet
First Division	the division
U.S. Marine Corps	the corps

HYPHENATED WORDS

3–41 Capitalize only those parts of hyphenated words that are normally capitalized.

> Merriam-Webster dictionaries
> President-elect Jannings
> high-spirited horses

Prefixes

3–42 Capitalize hyphenated prefixes only when they are the first word in a sentence. Generally, hyphenate a prefix when it precedes a proper noun.

> Post-settlement conferences have been scheduled for March 18, 26, and April 4.
> The parties have agreed on a pretrial conference date of January 10.

LEGAL CITATIONS

3–43 Capitalize important words in legal citations. Citations of case names are underscored, although in printed matter they appear in italics. (Refer to *A Uniform System of Citation* published by The Harvard Law Review Association, Cambridge, Massachusetts, for correct citation format.) (See Unit 6, Legal Citations, for citation forms and elements.)

> Roe v. Wade, 410 U.S. 113, 93 S. Ct. 705 (1973).
> Palsgraf v. Long Island R.R. Co., 248 N.Y. 339, 162 N.E. 99 (1928).
> Accuracy, Efficiency and Accountability in the Litigation Process—The Case for the Fact Verdict, 59 U. Cin. L. Rev. 15 (1990).

THE COURTS

3–44 Capitalize the name of the highest court in the nation (*the United States Supreme Court*) when it is written in full; capitalize *Court* when used in subsequent references. Capitalize the names of special courts and the highest court in any jurisdiction when written in full; but do not capitalize in subsequent references.

> the United States Supreme Court; the Court
>
> New York Supreme Court; the Court
>
> the Bankruptcy Court; the court

LEGAL TERMS

3–45 Capitalize certain introductory terms and other words in legal documents.

> **SECOND:** I hereby give, devise, and bequeath . . .
>
> **IN WITNESS WHEREOF,** the parties . . .
>
> **THEREFORE, BE IT RESOLVED,** that . . .

NAMES

Personal Names

3–46 Personal names consist of a first name (given name) or initial, a middle name or initial, and a last name (surname). Capitalize the first letter of each part of the name.

> Nancy P. Lee
>
> J. Donald Curry
>
> Carolyn Jensen

When double initials precede a surname, keyboard a period and a space after each letter. Some initials may be written without the period and spacing. (See 6–86 for citing party names.)

> E. I. Du Pont de Nemours
>
> C. S. Lewis

First-Name and Surname Prefixes

3–47 Capitalize the first letter of a first-name prefix whether the prefix is separated by a space or written as one word.

> DeAnne Hayes
>
> De Witt Williams
>
> FaLaine Cooper

Surname prefixes of foreign origin frequently follow no specific capitalization rule. Certain surnames with prefixes begin with a capital letter; others are written with a space between the prefix and the name. Follow the individual's preference in spelling such surnames.

De La Cruz	McCray
De La Torre	McElwee
DeMille	O'Brien
MacRae	von Kalinowski
Macmillan	Von Posch

Nicknames

3–48 Capitalize words used as nicknames designating particular people, places, or things.

the First Lady   the Windy City   Old Ironsides

Business Names

3–49 Capitalize important words in business names. Capitalize *the* when it is the first word of a company's name.

American Chemical and Research Corp.
the American Red Cross
The Bank of San Diego
Giovanni's Barber Shop
Leonard's Restaurant by the Sea

Organization Names

3–50 Capitalize important words in organization names. Organizations include associations, clubs, foundations, political parties, and societies.

American Board of Forensic Accountants
American Institute of Certified Public Accountants
Association of Certified Fraud Examiners
Barlow Foundation
Center for Conflict Resolution
National Association of Legal Secretaries

Institution Names

3–51 Capitalize important words in institution names. Institutions include churches, libraries, schools, hospitals, synagogues, and colleges and universities.

Beth El Temple
Chinatown Branch Library
John Marshall High School

Nova Southeastern University
The Old North Church
Verdugo Hills Hospital

3–52 Capitalize important words in school, college, department, or division names within a college or university. When a general reference is made to a school, college, department, or division name, however, do not capitalize it. (See also 3–21.)

School of Law	the law school
Department of English	the English department
Department of History	the history department

NATIONALITIES AND RACES

3–53 Capitalize names of nationalities, tribes, and races.

African American	Polynesian
Caucasian	Samoan
German	Native American
Hispanic	Cherokee

Thurgood Marshall became the first Black associate justice of the U.S. Supreme Court in 1967.

RELIGIOUS TERMS

3–54 Capitalize specific religious terms, including the names of saints and deities, sacred works, religious groups, and holy days. General terms such as *biblical* and *godlike* are not capitalized.

the Bible	Muslim
Buddhism	Roman Catholic Church
Catholicism	Judaism
Easter Sunday	the Koran
God	Talmud
the Holy Ghost	the Ten Commandments
Islamic	

TITLES

3–55 In general, capitalize titles preceding a name. Titles that follow a name are capitalized only with positions that indicate special distinction. (See also Forms of Address, 7–82 • 7–85.)

Assistant Director Dave Pastrana will lead the investigation.

Dave Pastrana, assistant director, will lead the investigation.

John G. Roberts, Jr., the Chief Justice of the Supreme Court, wrote the opinion for the court.

Will Commissioner Mina Dumas Fried take the matter under submission?

Party Names in Pleadings

3–56 Capitalize parties' names in pleadings. Capitalize only the first letter of the parties' designations.

> I'M A PATIENT,
>   Plaintiff,
>
>   v.
>
> D. R. SCRUBBS, M.D.,
> MAINSTREET CLINIC,
> DOES 1–11,
>   Defendants.

Government Titles

3–57 Capitalize titles of high-ranking government officials at the international, national, and state levels when such titles are written before or in place of a specific individual's name. When titles are used to refer to an entire class of officials, however, do not capitalize such titles.

Ambassador	President
Attorney General	Prime Minister
Chief Justice	Representative
Governor	Secretary-General of the United Nations
Premier	Vice President

President Abraham Lincoln issued the Emancipation Proclamation in 1862.

The President issued the Emancipation Proclamation in 1862.

The Constitution requires that all candidates for president be at least 35 years old.

Who was the first woman justice to serve on the United States Supreme Court?

Family Titles

3–58 Capitalize family titles when they precede a person's name and when the title itself is used as a name. Do not capitalize family titles when they appear by themselves or when they do not refer to a specific individual.

Uncle Francis was generous to everyone in his will.

It seems Grandma was eager to continue her volunteer activities.

Her uncle had traveled extensively during his lifetime.

Publication Titles

3–59 Capitalize the first letter of all important words in the titles and subtitles of books, magazines, newspapers, articles, encyclopedias, dictionaries, and artistic works. (Titles of these publications are underscored; in printed material they appear in *italics*. Titles of articles and chapters from these works are written within quotation marks.)

> <u>1,000 Places to See Before You Die</u> or *1,000 Places to See Before You Die*
>
> "Diving in the Red Sea," <u>1,000 Places to See Before You Die</u>
>
> <u>Black's Law Dictionary</u> or *Black's Law Dictionary*
>
> <u>Eats, Shoots & Leaves</u> or *Eats, Shoots & Leaves*
>
> <u>Second Concerto for Orchestra</u> or *Second Concerto for Orchestra*
>
> <u>The Wall Street Journal</u> or *The Wall Street Journal*

3–60 Do not capitalize the word *the* when it precedes a publication title appearing within a sentence. Do not capitalize articles (*a, an*), prepositions (*of, to, for*), and coordinating conjunctions (*and, or, but, nor*).

> Have you read the latest issue of the <u>National Geographic</u>?

Historical Documents

3–61 Capitalize the first letters of all important words in the titles of historical documents.

> Bill of Rights
>
> Declaration of Independence
>
> Magna Carta
>
> United States Constitution

TRADEMARKS AND BRAND NAMES

3–62 Words registered as trademarks and brand names are capitalized. However, certain trademarks that have become accepted as generic words do not require capitalization. Also, some brand names are intentionally written in lowercase letters.

aspirin	nylon
Coca-Cola	Scotch tape
Kleenex	Xerox
Pyrex	zipper

Unit 4

Spelling, Word Division, and Word Usage

SPELLING

4–1 In following these general guidelines for spelling, remember that there are often exceptions to spelling "rules." Also, many English words are not spelled the way they are pronounced. When in doubt, refer to a dictionary.

Words with *ie* or *ei*

4–2 In general, use *i* before *e*.

achieve	believe	piece
belief	field	relieve

Use *e* before *i* after the letter *c*.

ceiling	conceive	receipt	*but:*	ancient
conceit	deceit	receive		efficient

Use *ei* when it is pronounced as *a*.

eight	neighbor	weigh
freight	vein	weight

The following words are exceptions to the general rule.

foreign	leisure	seize
height	neither	weird

Words Ending in *-cede*, *-ceed*, and *-sede*

4–3 There are no rules for these word endings. Memorize the few words in which these word endings appear.

-cede

4–4 Only eight words end in *-cede*. However, note that words derived from these words are often spelled differently from the root word.

accede	but:	accession
antecede		
cede		
concede	but:	concession
intercede		
recede	but:	recession
precede		
secede	but:	secession

-ceed

4–5 Only three words end in *-ceed*. Words derived from these three words are often spelled differently from the root word.

exceed   but: ex**cess**
proc**eed**   but: pro**cedure**, pro**cession**
suc**ceed**   but: suc**cession**, suc**cessive**

-sede

4–6 Only one word ends in *-sede*.

super**sede**

Suffixes

4–7 Suffixes are word endings used to express a specific meaning. Suffixes can change a word to a different part of speech and affect its usage.

-able *and* -ible

4–8 Both suffixes mean "capable of." In general, add *-able* to words.

pay**able**	acces**sible**
reason**able**	convert**ible**
tax**able**	deduct**ible**

With *y* Endings

4–9 Change a *y* ending to an *i* before adding *-able*.

deny + able   =   den**iable**
justify + able   =   justif**iable**
rely + able   =   rel**iable**

With *d* and *de* Endings

4–10 Use *-ible* for words that end in *d* and *de*. Change the *d* to *s* before adding *-ible*. Drop the silent *e* at the end of a word.

defend + ible   =   defen**sible**
divide + ible   =   divi**sible**

Exceptions:

depend	depend**able**
expand	expand**able**

With *s* and *se* Endings

4–11 Use *-ible* for words that end in *s* and *se*. Drop the silent *e*.

dismiss + ible   =   dismiss**ible**
response + ible   =   respon**sible**
reverse + ible   =   rever**sible**
sense + ible   =   sen**sible**

4–12 Other uses of *-ible* do not follow any rule. Such words must be memorized.

admiss**ible**	intellig**ible**
correct**able**	suscept**ible**
elig**ible**	terr**ible**
flex**ible**	

-ant *and* -ance

4–13 Use *-ant* and *-ance* with most words. A word that requires an *-ant* suffix will also require an *-ance* ending where appropriate.

accept**ance**	
assist**ant**	assist**ance**
complain**ant**	
disinfect**ant**	
expect**ant**	expect**ance**
hesit**ant**	hesit**ance**

4–14 If the word ends in *y,* change the *y* ending to an *i* before adding *-ant* or *-ance.*

comply + ant/ance	=	compl**i**ant/compl**i**ance
defy + ant/ance	=	def**i**ant/def**i**ance
rely + ant/ance	=	rel**i**ant/rel**i**ance

-ent *and* -ence

4–15 Use *-ent* or *-ence* with words that end with *d, de,* or *fer.* Drop the silent *e* at the end of a word. A word that requires an *-ent* suffix will also require an *-ence* ending where appropriate.

confide + ent/ence	=	confid**ent**/confid**ence**
differ + ent/ence	=	differ**ent**/differ**ence**
incident + ent/ence	=	incid**ent**/incid**ence**
prefer + ence	=	prefer**ence**
reside + ent/ence	=	resid**ent**/resid**ence**

-ize, -ise, *and* -yze

4–16 There are no rules for these word endings. Memorize the correct spelling of words containing these suffixes.

-ize	**-ise**	**-yze**
apolog**ize**	advert**ise**	anal**yze**
author**ize**	comprom**ise**	paral**yze**
character**ize**	enterpr**ise**	
critic**ize**	exerc**ise**	
liberal**ize**	merchand**ise**	

| realize | supervise |
| summarize | surprise |

Words Ending in ll

4–17 Retain the double letters *ll* when a suffix is added. If the suffix is -*like* or -*less,* add a hyphen before the suffix.

full	fullest
install	installed, installment
skill	skilled, skillful
spell	spelling
shell	shell-like

Drop the final *l* in the root word before adding the suffix -*ly*.

| full | fully |

Words Ending in y

When a suffix is added to a word ending in *y,* the *y* ending may be retained or it may be changed, depending on the letter preceding it.

y Ending Preceded by Consonant

4–18 When the final *y* of a word is preceded by a consonant, change the *y* to *i* before adding a suffix. If a suffix begins with *i,* however, retain the *y* to maintain the sounded syllable.

beauty	beautiful	but:	beautifying
biography	biographical		
carry	carries, carrier	but:	carrying
clumsy	clumsiness		
weary	weariness	but:	wearying

In one-syllable words ending in *y* preceded by a consonant, retain the *y* before the -*ly* and -*ness* suffixes.

| dry | dryly | dryness |
| sly | slyly | slyness |

y Ending Preceded by Vowel

4–19 In most cases, when the final *y* is preceded by a vowel, retain the *y* when adding the suffix.

convey	conveyed	conveyance
employ	employer	employment
relay	relayed	relaying

In other cases, change the *y* to *i*.

day	dai**ly**
lay	la**id**
gay	gai**ety**
pay	pa**id**

Doubling the Final Consonant

4–20 The final consonant of some words may be doubled depending on how many syllables the word has, where the accent is, and whether the suffix begins with a consonant or a vowel.

Final Consonants Preceded by a Single Vowel

4–21 Double the final consonant when a one-syllable word ends in a consonant preceded by a single vowel and the suffix begins with a vowel.

bag	ba**gg**age	ba**gg**y
drop	dro**pp**ed	dro**pp**ing
fit	fi**tt**ed	fi**tt**ing
skim	ski**mm**ed	ski**mm**ing

Exceptions:

fix	fixed
gas	gaseous
saw	sawing
tax	taxing
tow	towed

Multisyllable Words with the Final Syllable Accented

4–22 Double the final consonant if a multisyllable word ends in a consonant preceded by a single vowel, the suffix begins with a vowel, and the final syllable of the root word is accented.

begin	begi**nn**ing		
commit	commi**tt**ing	*but*	commitment
confer	confe**rr**ing	*but*	conference
occur	occu**rr**ing, occu**rr**ed, occu**rr**ence		
recur	recu**rr**ing, recu**rr**ed, recu**rr**ence		

Multisyllable Words with the First Syllable Accented

4–23 Do not double the final consonant in a word ending in a consonant preceded by a single vowel when the first syllable is accented.

catalog	catalog**ing**	catalog**ed**
credit	credit**ing**	credit**ed**

differ	differing	differed	difference
offer	offering	offered	

Some words can be spelled correctly with or without doubling the final consonant. Consult a dictionary to determine preferred spellings. Be consistent in using one form or the other.

cancel	canceling	canceled
	cancelling	cancelled
program	programing	programed
	programming	programmed
travel	traveling	traveled
	travelling	travelled

Suffixes Beginning with Consonants

4–24 Do not double the final consonant in a word ending in a consonant preceded by a single vowel when the suffix begins with a consonant.

develop	development	
glad	gladly	gladness
harm	harmful	harmless

Final Consonants Preceded by Several Vowels

4–25 Do not double the final consonant in a word when the ending consonant is preceded by more than one vowel.

brief	briefly	briefing
cheer	cheerful	cheering
cloud	cloudy	

Exception:

equip	equipped	equipping

Words Ending in Several Consonants

4–26 Do not double the final consonant when a word ends in more than one consonant.

attach	attachment
condemn	condemned

Words Ending in Silent e

4–27 Generally, the *e* at the end of a word is dropped if it is silent (not pronounced) and the suffix begins with a vowel. Retain the silent *e* if the suffix begins with a consonant or if there is a chance for mispronunciation or confusion. Some words can be correctly spelled with the silent *e*. Consult a dictionary for the preferred spelling. (See also 4–28.)

like	likeable	likable
service	serviceable	
size	sizeable	sizable
use	useable	usable

Suffixes Beginning with Vowels

4–28 Drop the silent *e* at the end of a word when it is followed by a suffix that begins with a vowel.

advise	advisable
age	aging
desire	desirable
hope	hoping

Words Ending in *ce* or *ge* with Suffixes Beginning with Vowels

4–29 Do not drop the silent *e* of a word ending in *ce* or *ge* if doing so may change the pronunciation of a preceding syllable or letter.

change + able	=	changeable
courage + ous	=	courageous
manage + able	=	manageable
notice + able	=	noticeable

Exceptions:

change + ing	=	changing
force + ible	=	forcible
practical + able	=	practicable

Words Ending in *ie* with an *-ing* Suffix

4–30 When a word ends in *ie*, change the *ie* to *y* before adding *-ing*.

die	dying	[relating to death]
lie	lying	[telling an untruth]
tie	tying	
vie	vying	

Suffixes Beginning with Consonants

4–31 Retain the final *e* in a word if the suffix begins with a consonant.

enforce	enforcement
hope	hopeful
manage	management

Exceptions:

acknowledge	acknowledgment (or acknowledgement)
argue	argument

idle	id**ly**
judge	judg**ment**
subtle	subt**ly**

4–32 Do not drop the silent *e* at the end of a word if the word could be mispronounced or confused.

dye	dyeing (related to coloring or tinting; confused with **dying**)
eye	eyeing
hoe	hoeing (confused with **ho, ho, hoing**)

Double Letter Combinations

4–33 When a double letter combination is formed by adding a prefix or suffix or by combining words, retain the double letters. If a word must be divided at the end of a line, divide between the double letters.

book + keeper	=	boo**kk**eeper
dis + satisfaction	=	di**ss**atisfaction
dis + similar	=	di**ss**imilar
dis + solve	=	di**ss**olve
ir + respective	=	i**rr**espective
ir + responsible	=	i**rr**esponsible
mean + ness	=	mea**nn**ess
mis + spelled	=	mi**ss**pelled
room + mate	=	roo**mm**ate
ski + ing	=	ski**i**ng
taxi + ing	=	taxi**i**ng
under + rated	=	unde**rr**ated
with + holding	=	wit**hh**olding

Prefixes

4–34 Prefixes are word beginnings used to express a specific meaning. Prefixes can change a word to a different part of speech and affect its usage.

Prefixes Meaning **Not**

4–35 Certain prefixes are used to express the idea of *not.* Common prefixes include "*dis-*," "*il-*," "*im-*," "*in-*," "*ir-*," "*mal-*," "*non-*," and "*un-*." Add the appropriate prefix to the main word; generally, only one form of prefix is used with specific words. (Refer to a dictionary to determine the correct prefix.) To avoid misunderstanding and overly long words, use the word "not" for clarity in writing.

113

The following are examples of commonly used prefixes:

dis-

    dis + pleased

    dis + connected

    dis + engaged

    dis + satisfaction (or un + satisfied)

il-

    il + legal

    il + legible

    il + legitimate

    il + literate

    il + logical

im-

    im + balanced

    im + material

    im + mobile

    im + movable

    im + partial

    im + passive

    im + penetrable

    im + probable

    im + prudent

in-

    in + accessible

    in + advisable

    in + alienable

    in + applicable

    in + appropriate

    in + civility

    in + coherence

    in + comprehensible (or non + comprehensible)

    in + controvertible (or un + controvertible)

    in + curable (or un + curable)

    in + distinguishable

    in + effective

    in + effectual

    in + equitable

    in + tangible

ir-

ir + rational

ir + reconcilable

ir + regular

ir + reverence

ir + revocable

ir + reparable

mal-

mal + adjusted

mal + functioning

non-

non + applicable

non + assessable

non + assignable

non + committal

non + communicative (or un + communicative)

non + essential

non + negotiable

non + participating

non + restrictive

un-

un + acceptable

un + allowable

un + apologetic

un + ascertained

un + assignable

un + authenticated

un + changeable

un + controllable

un + corroborated

un + scrupulous

Double Negatives

4–36   A double negative is formed when the word *not* is used in a sentence with
a word that contains a prefix meaning *not*. The resulting meaning becomes
a positive idea.

> The partners' differences are **not irreconcilable**.   [meaning: the
> **differences are reconcilable**]

Did the judge rule that the evidence was **not inadmissible**?   **[meaning: the evidence was admissible]**

Our customers have **not** been **dissatisfied** with either our merchandise or our prices.   **[meaning: customers have been satisfied]**

PLURAL WORD FORMS

4–37   In general, form plurals by adding an *s* to the singular form; add *es* to singular nouns that end in *s* or an *s* sound.

network	networks
park	parks
student	students
plaintiff	plaintiffs
Donald	Donalds
North and South Dakota	the Dakotas
tort	torts
Liz	Lizes
Thomas	Thomases

Words Ending in *f* and *fe*

4–38   The plurals of some nouns ending in *f* and *fe* are formed by changing the ending to *ves*. In other cases, the plural is formed by adding *s* to the singular form.

brief	briefs
chief	chiefs
dwarf	dwarfs or dwarves
half	halves
knife	knives
leaf	leaves
life	lives
proof	proofs

4–39   Some plural nouns are spelled identically to singular verb forms. Distinguish between the spellings and usage of these nouns and verbs.

Singular Noun	Plural Noun	Singular Verb
belief	beliefs	believes
proof	proofs	proves
safe	safes	saves

Exceptions:

leaf	leaves
life	lives

Words Ending in *s, x, ch, sh,* and *z*

4–40 Add *es* to form the plurals of words ending in *s, x, ch, sh,* and *z*. (See also 4–57 and 4–61 • 4–62.)

boss	boss**es**
business	business**es**
church	church**es**
mix	mix**es**
quartz	quartz**es**
rush	rush**es**
tax	tax**es**
waltz	waltz**es**
wish	wish**es**

Exception:

bus	bus**es,** buss**es**

Words Ending in *o* Preceded by Consonant

4–41 Add *s* to form the plurals of most words ending in *o* preceded by a consonant. Some plurals are formed by adding *es*, and others may be formed with either ending.

domino	domino**s,** domino**es**
hero	hero**es**
memo	memo**s**
tomato	tomato**es**
veto	veto**es**
zero	zero**s,** zero**es**

Words Ending in *o* Preceded by Vowel

4–42 Add *s* to form the plurals of words ending in *o* preceded by a vowel.

duo	duo**s**
radio	radio**s**

Musical Terms Ending in *o*

4–43 To form the plurals of musical terms ending in *o*, add *s*.

alto	alto**s**
arpeggio	arpeggio**s**
piano	piano**s**
solo	solo**s**
soprano	soprano**s**
tango	tango**s**
trio	trio**s**

Words Ending in *y* Preceded by Consonant

4–44 To form the plurals of words ending in *y* preceded by a consonant, change the *y* to *ies*.

authority	authori**ties**
country	countr**ies**
facility	facili**ties**

Words Ending in *y* Preceded by Vowel

4–45 Add *s* to form the plurals of most words ending in *y* preceded by a vowel.

attorney	attorney**s**
bay	bay**s**
donkey	donkey**s**
journey	journey**s**
money	money**s** (or mon**ies**)

Irregular Nouns

4–46 The plurals of certain nouns are formed by changing letters within the words.

child	child**ren**
foot	f**ee**t
goose	g**ee**se
louse	l**ice**
man	m**e**n
mouse	m**ice**
tooth	t**ee**th
woman	wom**e**n

4–47 When irregular nouns are used in compound words, retain the irregular plural form.

dormouse	dor**mice**
eyetooth	eye**teeth**
stepchild	step**children**

Words

4–48 To form the plurals of individual words, add either *s* or *es*, depending on the last letter. Do not use an apostrophe unless the word could be misread.

the aye**s** have it	the noe**s** [or nos] have it
do**s** and don't**s**	pro**s** and con**s**
in**s** and out**s**	dot your i'**s**; cross your t'**s**
if**s**, and**s**, and but**s**	

Compound Words

4–49 A compound word consists of two or more words used as a single unit. (See also 1–51.) Some compound words are hyphenated; others are not. Follow the general rules for forming plurals of words, as well as these specific guidelines.

4–50 Make the most significant word in the compound word plural. In most cases, the significant word refers to a person.

attorney general	attorneys general
court-martial	courts-martial, court-martials
deputy chief of protocol	deputy chiefs of protocol
father-in-law	fathers-in-law
lieutenant colonel	lieutenant colonels
notary public	notaries public, notary publics
passerby	passersby

If both words in the compound word are of equal significance, make both words plural.

coat of arms	coats of arms
secretary-general	secretaries-generals

If there is no one significant word in the compound and neither word is a noun, pluralize the last word.

go-between	go-betweens
higher-up	higher-ups
trade-in	trade-ins
follow-up	follow-ups

Foreign Words

4–51 The plural forms of foreign words do not follow the same guidelines used for English words. Table 4.1 lists common foreign words in their singular and plural forms. Memorize the singular and plural word endings, noting the general pattern of spelling certain word endings. A few foreign words may be pluralized by adding an *-s* or *-es* although it is not the preferred spelling. Note the change in pronunciation from the singular *-is* to the pluralized *-es* ending.

> Please add this contract as **Addendum** 1 to the report.
>
> The contract, financial statement, and letter are to be included as **addenda** to the report.
>
> The only **criterion** for the receptionist position is a pleasant personality.

119

TABLE 4.1 Singular and Plural Forms of Common Foreign Words

Singular	Plural
addendum	addenda
alumna (feminine)	alumnae
alumnus (masculine)	alumni (masculine and feminine)
analysis	analyses
appendix	appendices, appendixes*
basis	bases
crisis	crises
criterion	criteria
curriculum	curriculums, curricula
datum	data
executrix	executrices, executrixes
formula	formulas, formulae
index	indexes, indices
medium	media
memorandum	memoranda, memorandums
parenthesis	parentheses
stimulus	stimuli
thesis	theses

* This form is the only correct usage in medical references.

Applicants for word processing operator must meet these **criteria:** keyboard 65 words per minute and proofread accurately.

This **datum** should be incorporated in the analysis.

What were the sources of these **data** shown on page 32?

Abbreviations

4–52 Add *s* to form the plurals of most abbreviations.

mo.	mos. (months)
no.	nos. (numbers)
yr.	yrs. (years)

Capitalized Abbreviations

4–53 To form the plurals of abbreviations written in all capital letters, add an *s* only. If the word could be misread, add an apostrophe and *s* (*'s*).

ABCs	M.D.s
CDs	three Rs
CPAs	TVs
GIs	PLSs

Abbreviations for Weights and Measures

4–54 Abbreviations for both the standard and metric weights and measures are written the same way in both the singular and plural forms. The trend is toward eliminating the period after abbreviations for both standard and metric units of weights and measures. (See 5–100, Weights and Measures.)

cm (centimeter or centimeters)	lb (pound or pounds)
ft (foot or feet)	m (meter or meters)
g (gram or grams)	mi (mile or miles)
hr (hour or hours)	oz (ounce or ounces)
in (inch or inches)	qt (quart or quarts)
kg (kilogram or kilograms)	yd (yard or yards)
km (kilometer or kilometers)	

Doubling Consonants

4–55 The plurals of some abbreviations are formed by doubling the consonants in the singular form.

p. 482	pp. 482–96 (pages)
v. 24	vv. 24–38 (verses)

Numbers and Fractions

Numbers Written in Figures

4–56 Add only an *s* to form the plurals of numbers written in figures.

during the 1990s

in the high 300s

mid-20s

Spelled-Out Numbers

4–57 Depending on the word ending, add either *s* or *es* to form the plurals of numbers that are spelled out. (See 4–40.)

fifty-two	fifty-twos
sixth	sixths
forty	forties
six	sixes
sixteenth	sixteenths

Spelled-Out Fractions

4–58 Add *s* to form the plurals of spelled-out fractions.

three-fourths of an ounce

forty one-hundredths

Personal Titles

4–59 The plurals of personal titles are as follows:

Singular	Plural
Dr. (or Doctor)	Drs. (Doctors)
Miss	Misses
Mr.	Messrs.
Mrs.	Mmes. (Mesdames)
Ms.	Mses.
Prof. (or Professor)	Professors
Rev. (or Reverend)	Reverends

My internist is **Dr**. Carol J. Thrun.

Doctors Thrun and Henneberg are dedicated physicians.

Mrs. Gloria Winscott and **Mrs**. Marge Hutchinson are coordinating the fund-raising event.

Mesdames Winscott and Hutchinson are coordinating the fund-raising event.

Personal Titles with Two or More Surnames

4–60 When the same personal title applies to two or more surnames, precede the first surname with the plural personal title. You may also precede each surname with the singular personal title.

Mr. Klein and Mr. McDonough	Messrs. Klein and McDonough
Mrs. Irving and Mrs. Laskota	Mesdames Irving and Laskota
	Mmes. Irving and Laskota
Miss Limón and Miss Sanders	Misses Limón and Sanders
Ms. Meehan and Ms. Orsini	Mses. Meehan and Orsini

Proper Names

First Names

4–61 Depending on the last letter in the name, add either *s* or *es* to form the plurals of first (or given) names. (See also 4–40.)

Alejandro**s**	David**s**	Margo**s**
Alex**es**	Debi**s**	Mitch**es**
Charles**es**	Jessie**s**	Rosa**s**
Chuck**s**	Jorge**s**	Scott**s**
Christopher**s**	Kenneth**s**	Tracy**s**

Can you imagine one teacher having three Michael**s** in the class?

Surnames

4–62 Add either *s* or *es* to form the plurals of family names (surnames), depending on the last letter in the name. Do not change the spelling of the name in any other way. (See 4–40.) When referring to the family name in its singular or plural form, precede the name with *the*.

Serene and Dick Clayton	the Clayton**s**
Sally and Don Clark	the Clark**s**
Mr. and Mrs. Gonzalez	the Gonzalez**es**
Louise and Byron Peebles	the Peebles**es**
the Cox family	the Cox**es**
the Shimasaki family	the Shimasaki**s**
the Thomas family	the Thomas**es**
the Wolf family	the Wolf**s**

Add only an *s* to form the plurals of surnames that end in a silent letter. Follow the pronunciation of a surname when the name ends in a letter (or combination of letters) or a sound that is pronounced differently from its spelling.

Virginia Gignoux and family ("noux" pronounced "noo")	the Gignoux**s**
Mr. and Mrs. Koch ("ch" pronounced "k")	the Koch**s**

Exception:

Mr. and Mrs. Koch (pronounced with the "ch" sound)	the Koch**es**

Geographic Names

4–63 Add *s* to form the plurals of geographic names.

Waterloo (in Iowa, Ontario, and Belgium)	the Waterloo**s**
North Carolina and South Carolina	the Carolina**s**
the Cascade Mountains	the Cascade**s**

Exception:

the Rocky Mountains	the Rock**ies**

4–64 The following geographic names are already in their plural forms.

Grand Rapids, Michigan

Niagara Falls, New York

United States

West Indies

Singular and Plural Noun Forms

4–65 The singular and plural forms of the following words are spelled the same way. Use an appropriate verb with these words, depending on their use as singular or plural subjects in sentences.

123

counsel	moose	sheep
deer	number of	species
majority of	series	swine

Our legal **counsel is** Darlene Willis.

Stan Hutchinson and Richard Fong, my legal **counsel, have advised** me not to speak to the press.

Have the **majority** of voters cast their ballots yet?

Has the **majority** of the staff approved the new benefits package?

Plural Nouns

4–66 The following words are always plural. Use a plural verb when these words are used as plural subjects in sentences.

cattle	pliers
credentials	proceeds
goods	remains
grounds	savings
headquarters	scissors
pants	thanks

The **goods are** being shipped f.o.b. Seattle.

When **are** the **proceeds** to be distributed?

Thanks go to all our dedicated peer counselors.

Words Ending in Silent s

4–67 When a word ends in a silent *s* in its singular form, retain the same spelling for the plural form.

corps   chassis   faux pas

The Army **Corps** of Engineers **is** in charge of various civil engineering projects.

Thirty drum and bugle **corps are** competing for the trophy this weekend.

Who noted how many **faux pas** the speaker made?

She made a **faux pas** by not extending a handshake to the president.

Single Letters

Lowercase Letters

4–68 Add an apostrophe and *s* (*'s*) to form the plurals of individual lowercase letters.

dotting i**'s** and crossing t**'s**

solving for the x**'s**, y**'s**, and z**'s** in the equation

watching your p**'s** and q**'s**

Capital Letters

4–69 To avoid confusion, add an apostrophe and *s* (*'s*) to form the plurals of individual capital letters, particularly the letters *A*, *I*, *M*, and *U*.

> straight A**'s** on his grade report   [**could be confused with the word** *As*]
>
> no U**'s** for "unsatisfactory"   [**could be confused with the word** *Us*]
>
> using fewer I**'s**   [**could be confused with the word** *Is*]

In some instances, plurals may be formed by adding either an *s* or an apostrophe and *s* (*'s*).

> Bs   B**'s**

POSSESSIVES

4–70 A possessive form of a word indicates ownership of an object or concept. Possessives also indicate a relationship of time, distance, or value.

4–71 Possessive nouns and descriptive adjectives are often confused. Possessive nouns answer the question *Whose?* and require either an apostrophe (*'*) or an apostrophe and *s* (*'s*). Descriptive adjectives answer the questions *Which one(s)?* and *What kind(s)?* and do not require any apostrophes.

Descriptive adjective:	The **Tom Joyce** accounting principle [**which principle?**]
Possessive noun:	**Tom Joyce's** accounting principle [**whose principle?**]
Descriptive adjective:	Greetings from the **Lee** family [**which family?**]
Possessive noun:	Greetings from the **Lees'** home [**whose home?**]
Descriptive adjective:	legal **secretaries** conference [**which conference?**]
Possessive noun:	Legal **Secretaries'** Conference [**whose conference?**]
Descriptive adjective:	**IRS** tax rulings [**which rulings?**]
Possessive noun:	**IRS's** tax rulings [**whose rulings?**]

4–72 In general, an apostrophe and *s* (*'s*) or only an apostrophe (*'*) is added to a word to form a possessive. Determine whether the possessive noun is singular or plural. To test the correct possessive form, reword the phrase by adding *of*, *of the*, or *belonging to the* after the object or concept being owned.

firm**'s** attorney	an attorney **of the** *one firm*; an attorney **belonging to the** *one firm*
firms**'** attorneys	attorneys **of the** *several firms*; attorneys **belonging to the** *several firms*

125

employee's time card	time card **of the** *one employee;* time card **belonging to the** *one employee*
employees' time cards	time cards **of the** *several employees;* time cards **belonging to the** *several employees*

Singular Nouns

Singular Nouns Not Ending in s

4–73 Add an apostrophe and *s* ('*s*) to form the possessive of singular nouns that do not end in *s*.

partner's staff   [**staff of the sole partner**]

clerk's computer   [**computer belonging to the one clerk**]

Singular Nouns Ending in s

4–74 Add only an apostrophe (') to form the possessive of singular nouns that end in *s*, even if the final *s* or *ps* is not pronounced.

planet **Mars'** surface   [**surface of the planet Mars**]

drum and bugle **corps'** performance   [**performance of the drum and bugle corps**]

Add an apostrophe and *s* ('*s*) to form the possessive of singular nouns that end in *s* when the additional *s* sound is pronounced.

my boss's appointments   [**appointments of my boss**]

our business's earnings   [**earnings of our business**]

witness's testimony   [**testimony of the witness**]

Plural Nouns

Regular Plural Nouns

4–75 Regular plural nouns end in either *s* or *es*. Add only an apostrophe (') to form the possessive of regular plural nouns.

those boss**es'** appointments   [**appointments of those bosses**]

several business**es'** earnings   [**earnings of several businesses**]

doctor**s'** offices   [**offices of several doctors**]

judge**s'** chambers   [**chambers of several judges**]

witness**es'** testimonies   [**testimonies of several witnesses**]

Irregular Plural Nouns

4–76 Irregular plural nouns are formed by changing the spelling of the word. (See 4–46.) Add an apostrophe and *s* ('*s*) to form the possessive of irregular plural nouns.

chidren's privileges   [**privileges belonging to more than one child**] women**'s** rights   **[rights of more than one woman]**

men**'s** discussion group   **[discussion group for more than one man]**

Compound Nouns

4–77   A compound noun combines two or more words into a single idea to describe a person, place, or object. To show possession, add an apostrophe and *s* (*'s*) to the final word only. (See 4–49 • 4–50 for rules on forming the plurals of compound words.)

attorney general**'s** opinion   **[opinion of one attorney general]**

president-elect**'s** acceptance speech   **[speech by one president-elect]**

sister-in-law**'s** escrow company   **[company belonging to one sister-in-law]**

editors-in-chief**'s** remarks   **[remarks made by two or more editors-in-chief]**

administrative secretaries**'** classification   **[classification of all administrative secretaries]**

brothers-in-law**'s** businesses   **[businesses belonging to two or more brothers-in-law]**

lieutenant colonels**'** commands   **[commands made by two or more lieutenant colonels]**

Proper Nouns

Singular Proper Nouns

4–78   Generally, add an apostrophe and *s* (*'s*) to form the possessive of a singular proper noun not ending in *s*.

Mrs. Hurley**'s** mobile home   **[home belonging to Mrs. Hurley]**

Fox**'s** studio   **[studio belonging to the Fox Corporation]**

Edgar Allen Poe**'s** "The Raven"   **[poem written by Edgar Allen Poe]**

Add an apostrophe and *s* (*'s*) to form the possessive of singular proper nouns that end in *s* when the additional *s* sound is pronounced.

John Keats**'s** poems   **[poems of John Keats]**

Sara Hawkins**'s** promotion   **[promotion of Sara Hawkins]**

Thomas**'s** English Muffins   **[English muffins made by Thomas]**

Plural Proper Nouns

4–79   Add only an apostrophe (*'*) to form the possessive of a plural proper noun that ends in *s*.

the Hurleys**'** hacienda   **[hacienda belonging to the Hurleys]**

Tri-Cities**'** rapid transit system   **[transit system of the Tri-Cities]**

the Simmonses**'** Pharmacy   **[pharmacy of the Simmonses]**

the Martinezes**'** children   **[children belonging to the Martinezes]**

Understood Possessive Form

4–80 When the item owned is understood from the sentence meaning, the noun in its possessive form stands alone.

> David's grades are better than Jane's [grades].
>
> Nancy's closing argument was more persuasive than Jan's [closing statement].
>
> Please fax this contract to the McFarlands' [business].
>
> Remember to send these to the architect's [office] by 4:30.

Separate and Joint Ownership

4–81 Ownership may be either separate or joint. In separate ownership, one person owns or possesses her or his own particular item or idea. With joint ownership, several people own or possess a single object or idea. The placement of the apostrophe (') or apostrophe and *s* ('*s*) determines whether separate or joint ownership is stated.

Separate Ownership

4–82 To indicate separate and individual ownership of an item by two or more individuals, add either an apostrophe (') or an apostrophe and *s* ('*s*) to each individual's name, depending on whether the name ends in *s*. The item owned is in the plural form to indicate two separate items.

> Gene Pinchuk's and Harvey Pine's mountain cabins   [separate mountain cabins owned by each person]
>
> the Davises' and the Taylors' vacation itineraries   [separate itineraries belonging to each family]

Joint Ownership

4–83 To indicate joint ownership of one item by two or more individuals, add either an apostrophe and *s* ('*s*) or an apostrophe (') (depending on whether the name ends in *s*) to the final name only.

> Bullock & Yamaguchi's landscaping service   [landscaping service owned jointly]
>
> Rita Steffen and Diane Young's nephew   [the nephew of both women]
>
> Nancy and Ron's automobiles   [several automobiles owned jointly by Nancy and Ron]

Business and Organization Names

4–84 The names of many businesses, organizations, institutions, and societies contain possessives. Some organizations omit the apostrophe in the possessive. Other organizations retain the apostrophe (') or apostrophe and *s* ('*s*). Follow the spelling preferred by the organization as shown on its stationery or in the telephone directory listing.

The Farmers and Merchants Bank

Hawkins Realty

Hawkinses' Frozen Yogurt Shoppe

Lindell's Pharmacy

Lindells Pharmacy

4–85 To form the possessive, add either an apostrophe and *s* (*'s*) or an apostrophe (') to the last word in the name of a business, organization, institution, or society.

American Red Cross's disaster preparedness kits

Parkwood Townhomes Association's CC&Rs

California State University's campuses

Mars, Snacks & Hershey's statement

Technico Bondsmen's bailiwick

Possessive Pronouns

Personal and Relative Pronouns

4–86 The possessive of personal and relative pronouns is not formed by adding an apostrophe. These pronouns have their own possessive forms. (See 1–62 • 1–63 and 1–77.)

Possessive personal pronouns and contractions are often confused because they sound alike. Do not use an apostrophe in a possessive personal pronoun. See Sections 1–91 • 1–92 and Table 1.3 for a list of possessive pronouns and sound-alike contractions.

Indefinite Pronouns

4–87 Indefinite pronouns do not refer specifically to any one person, place, or object. Add an apostrophe and *s* (*'s*) to form the possessive of an indefinite pronoun.

another's responsibility

anybody's guess

no one's fault

someone else's job

Possessives before Gerunds

4–88 A gerund is an *-ing* verb used as a noun. The noun or pronoun preceding the gerund must be in the possessive form. Add either an apostrophe and *s* (*'s*) or an apostrophe ('), depending on the ending of the ownership word.

Do not confuse the possessive noun or pronoun with a contraction. (See Section 1–91 and Table 1.3.) Test for the correct form by reading the proper noun with the verb *is* or *was* to see if the sentence makes sense; if it does not, use the possessive noun or pronoun in the sentence.

129

Your assisting in this surgery is appreciated.

Joan**'s** receiving the award is a special honor.   [not Joan *is* receiving the award is a special honor]

Was it **their** persevering that enabled us to win the award?   [not them persevering]

Was it because of Dr. Yu**'s** and Dr. Williams**'s** performing the biopsy that the tumor was ultimately discovered?

Abbreviations

4–89 Add an apostrophe (') or an apostrophe and *s* (*'s*) to form the possessive form of abbreviations, depending on whether the abbreviation is singular or plural.

NASA**'s** new launch site

FTC**'s** investigation

one M.D.**'s** diagnosis

several M.D.s**'** diagnoses

IRS**'s** tax rulings

Inanimate Objects

4–90 Do not use the possessive form for inanimate objects since such objects cannot own or possess another thing. To show the relationship, rewrite the expression using an "of the" phrase or a descriptive adjective.

Incorrect:	the law**'s** enactment
Correct:	enactment **of the** law
Incorrect:	mortgage**'s** current rate
Correct:	current rate **of the** mortgage
Descriptive:	current mortgage rate

Figures

4–91 Add an apostrophe (') to the plural form of a year or other time period to indicate an event or a trend belonging to that time period.

the 2000s**'** Digital Age

the 1990s**'** recession

Personification

4–92 Add either an apostrophe and *s* (*'s*) or an apostrophe (') with expressions that personify an organization, business, or other entity.

my club**'s** charity banquet   [charity banquet of my club]

our competitors**'** new product lines   [new product lines of our competitors]

Time, Distance, and Measurement

4–93 Add either an apostrophe and *s* (*'s*) or an apostrophe (') with expressions of time, distance, and measurement that are spelled out.

> last quarter's financial standing   **[financial standing of last quarter]**
>
> a mile's drive   **[drive of a mile]**
>
> one year's profits   **[profits of one year]**
>
> dealing at arm's length   **[length of an arm]**
>
> three weeks' leave of absence   **[leave of absence of or for three weeks]**
>
> several years' profits   **[profits of several years]**

Time, distance, or measurement may also be expressed as a hyphenated compound adjective.

> a one-mile drive   **[drive of one mile]**
>
> a three-week leave of absence   **[leave of absence of three weeks]**
>
> our second-quarter earnings   **[earnings for our second quarter]**

WORD DIVISION

4–94 Word division refers to dividing a word at the end of a line when the entire word cannot fit on the line. Dividing a word may confuse the reader, so divide the word where appropriate and *only when necessary*. Words should always be divided between syllables. Consult a dictionary or other reference when in doubt about syllabication. Word division in this manual conforms to *Webster's New College Dictionary*, 4th ed., 2005.

Word processing programs contain a hyphenation feature. The keyboarder may select "automatic hyphenation," which automatically divides the word at the end of the line if the entire word does not fit within the set line length. Such programs also enable the keyboarder to select when to divide certain words and where they should be divided. Although most programs follow general guidelines for word division, they do not always produce the "best" division point.

The following word division guidelines apply to keyboarded material; typesetters' guidelines may vary. The following guidelines also include certain word divisions that should be avoided to prevent a misreading or mispronunciation of a partial word at the end of a line.

Keyboard a hyphen at the end of a line to indicate the word division.

Short Words and One-Syllable Words

4–95 Do not divide a word that has six or fewer letters or that has only one syllable.

allot	could	fuel	penal
change	echo	length	through

One-Letter Syllables

4–96 Divide a word so as to leave two or more letters with the first part of the word and three or more letters with the last part of the word. The diagonal in the following examples indicates where *not* to divide words.

a/chieve	e/clipse	live/ly
a/gain	hang/er	o/blige
bacteri/a	heav/en	waiv/er

Divide a word after a one-letter syllable in the middle of a word.

conju-gal	particu-lar	testi-mony
judi-ciary	recidi-vist	
mani-fest	sepa-rate	

Compound Words

4–97 Divide a hyphenated compound word at the hyphen.

　　heir-apparent　　　　self-confidence

A compound word written as one word without a hyphen should be divided between the parts of the compound.

business-person	sales-person
peace-keeper	tax-payer
policy-holder	under-writer

Double Vowels

4–98 In words containing two separately accented (pronounced) vowels written together, divide between the vowels.

abbrevi-ate	continu-ance
medi-ocre	recre-ation

Contractions and Abbreviations

4–99 Do not divide contractions or abbreviations.

can't	doesn't	should've
Calif.	et al.	S. Rep.
CBS	D.C.	S & L

Amounts and Numbers

4–100 Do not divide amounts and numbers. (The diagonals indicate where *not* to divide.)

$15,750./36	4,673,/550
25/ cents	$25/ million

Avoid dividing numeric information that is read as one unit.

Article/ IV	page/ 113	June/ 2009
Chapter/ 6	Section/ 1A	18/ inches
November/ 10	15/ U.S.C.	90 Stat./ 2985 (2007)

Proper Names

4–101 In general, avoid dividing proper names. When necessary, however, divide before the surname (last name) of a person, between the parts of a compound name, or after the hyphen in a hyphenated name.

. . . Annie F.	. . . Billy
Kennedy	Joe Yang
. . . Winston-	. . . C. J.
Salem	Klein

Prefixes and Suffixes

4–102 Divide a word after a prefix and before a suffix (see 4–7.)

Prefixes	**Suffixes**
ambi-dextrous	glad-**ness**
circum-stances	litiga-**tion**
dis-associate	prece-**dent**
re-arranged	promis-**ing**
tran-script	tax-**able**

Avoid divisions that might cause confusion or a mispronunciation of the first part of a divided word. (Diagonals indicate where *not* to divide; hyphens indicate where *to* divide.)

dem-on/strate	re-ap/por-tion-ment	super/flu-ous

Doubled Consonants

4–103 When a final consonant of a root word is doubled before adding a suffix, divide between the doubled consonants.

ba**g-g**age	ge**t-t**ing
begi**n-n**ing	si**t-t**ing
shi**p-p**er	swi**m-m**ing

Two Suffixes

4–104 When two suffixes are added to a word, divide them to form a logical grouping.

Confusing:	fear/lessness
Better:	fearless-ness

Suffix and Prefix

4–105 When a word has both a prefix and a suffix, divide the word so that syllables are grouped intelligibly.

    Confusing: indiffer/ence
    Better: in-difference

Successive Lines

4–106 Do not divide words in more than two lines in succession. Also, do not divide the last word on the page since it interrupts the train of thought for the reader.

WORD USAGE

Troublesome Words

4–107 Words are not necessarily pronounced as they are spelled. Some words with the same or almost the same pronunciation are spelled and/or used differently. (Words that are spelled differently but that are pronounced alike are *homonyms*.) The most commonly confused groups of words are listed and defined in this section. (Abbreviations for parts of speech are as follows: "adj" for adjective; "adv" for adverb; "conj" for conjunction; "n" for noun; "prep" for preposition; "pron" for pronoun; "v" for verb.)

accede *and* exceed

4–108 accede (v): to express approval or give consent
accede (v): to extend outside or go or be beyond; to surpass

  Whether our department will **accede** to their wishes is not known.
  Employees who **exceed** their goals will receive a bonus.

accept *and* except

4–109 accept (v): to receive
except (v): to leave out
 (prep): with the exclusion of

  Was the seller willing to **accept** a 20 percent down payment?
  Jane **excepted**, no one in the office really enjoys filing.
  Everyone took the CPR training **except** Johan.

access *and* excess

4–110 access (n): admittance or approach
excess (n): more than necessary

  In her position as personnel manager, she had **access** to the files.
  There was an **excess** of inventory in the warehouse.

ad *and* add

4–111
ad (n): advertisement
add (v): to total

The legal notice took the form of an **ad** in the newspapers.
How many people can **add** a long column of figures easily?

adapt *and* adept

4–112
adapt (v): to make suitable
adept (adj): skilled or proficient

Ramos Industries will **adapt** the prosthesis to suit the customer's needs.
Janice Luciero is an **adept** data entry operator.

addition *and* edition

4–113
addition (n): increase
edition (n): copy or version

We expect an **addition** of three assistants to our paralegal team.
This Personnel Policy and Procedures Manual is in its third **edition.**

adverse *and* averse

4–114
adverse (adj): unfavorable; opposition
averse (adj): disinclined; distasteful

Did the patient suffer an **adverse** reaction to the medication?
We were not **averse** to the proposal; we merely wanted to negotiate further.

advice *and* advise

4–115
advice (n): recommendation
advise (v): to counsel or tell

His **advice** about local area networking was excellent.
Will you please **advise** us about the advantages of telecommunications?

affect *and* effect

4–116
affect (v): to influence
effect (v): to bring about
(n): result

The quality of the lighting on the stage might **affect** the actor's makeup.
The new manager could not **effect** as many changes as she wanted.
One **effect** of inflation is higher prices for most goods and services.

aid *and* aide

4–117
aid (n): help or assistance
(v): to help or give assistance
aide (n): a person who acts as an assistant

Doctors Without Borders/Médecins Sans Frontières provides humanitarian **aid** in developing countries.

We should **aid** the poor and homeless in whatever ways we can.

Did the colonel's **aide** issue the commands as ordered?

all ready *and* already

4–118

all ready (adj):　prepared
already (adv):　　previously

The attorney was **all ready** to leave for the hearing when she received the fax message.

Had the train **already** left when Anna reached the station?

all together *and* altogether

4–119

all together (pron and adj):　in a group
altogether (adv):　　　　　　　wholly; in all; all told

This special occasion has brought us **all together** for a joyous family reunion.

Including the four managers, there are nine employees at this office **altogether.**

After the trial, the jurors will appear **altogether** to meet the press.

allude *and* elude

4–120

allude (v):　to make indirect reference
elude (v):　to evade; to avoid skillfully

You should not **allude** to an event that others might misunderstand.

The burglars **eluded** the police for only a few minutes.

allusion *and* illusion

4–121

allusion (n):　indirect reference
illusion (n):　misleading image or idea

The mayor's **allusion** to the cost of mass transit was not ignored by the reporters.

The heavy fog contributed to the **illusion** that the house was miles from its nearest neighbor.

all ways *and* always

4–122

all ways (adj and n):　every respect
always (adv):　　　　　at all times, without exception

He is in **all ways** a competent and fair attorney.

Isn't Ingrid **always** traveling somewhere?

allowed *and* aloud

4–123

allowed (v):   past tense of *allow;* permitted
aloud (adv):   manner of speaking out loud

> The company **allowed** them to take a two-week paid leave.
>
> Since Bill enjoys public speaking, he presented the report **aloud.**

altar *and* alter

4–124

altar (n):   raised structure as a center of religious worship
alter (v):   to change

> The couple took their vows before the **altar.**
>
> It is against the law to **alter** the reading on an automobile odometer.

any one *and* anyone

4–125

any one (pron):   any single thing or person
anyone (pron):   any person at all; anybody

> **Any one** of the four mannequins would be appropriate for our window display.
>
> Did **anyone** witness the accident?

any way *and* anyway

4–126

any way (n):   any manner or fashion
anyway (adv):   nevertheless; in any case

> If we can help in **any way,** please call.
>
> **Anyway,** she made every effort to succeed.

appellate *and* appellant

4–127

appellant (n):   a party who seeks an appeal of a decision from one court or jurisdiction to a higher-level court
appellate (n):   authority to review and decide appeals
          (adj):   referring to a court's authority to review a prior opinion or decision made by a lower-level court or agency

> Josephine was dissatisfied with the trial court's decision; on appeal, she is the **appellant.**
>
> The U.S. Supreme Court is the highest **appellate** court in the nation.

appraise *and* apprise

4–128

appraise (v):   to estimate the value of
apprise (v):   to inform

> The lender needs to **appraise** the property to determine its current value.
>
> Be sure to **apprise** the buyers of the exact escrow and closing fees.

are, hour, *and* our

4–129

are (v):   plural present tense of the verb *to be*
hour (n):   time of day
our (pron):   first person plural possessive pronoun

> **Are** the Greens testifying as hostile witnesses?
>
> The crew went home at a late **hour.**
>
> **Our** division exceeded its sales quota.

assistance *and* assistants

4–130

assistance (n):   help or support
assistants (n):   helpers

> Please call us whenever you need **assistance** with your new system.
>
> My **assistants,** Joan de la Cruz and George Retana, are thorough legal researchers.

attendance *and* attendants

4–131

attendance (n):   the number present
attendants (n):   persons who wait on others

> The seminar had 350 jurists in **attendance.**
>
> A large group of **attendants** usually travels with ambassadors.

biannual *and* biennial

4–132

biannual (adj):   twice a year
biennial (adj):   every other year

> The **biannual** report is published on March 15 and September 15.
>
> Since the statistical material is not published annually, the **biennial** report is important.

canvas *and* canvass

4–133

canvas (n):   a firm, closely woven cloth used for tents, sails, and clothing
canvass (v):   to examine or solicit

> Covering the boat with **canvas** will protect it from the elements.
>
> Volunteers will **canvass** the neighborhood for charitable contributions.

capital, capitol, *and* Capitol

4–134

capital (adj):   important; excellent; punishable by death
        (n):   wealth; seat of government (city)
capitol (n):   building in which a state legislature meets
Capitol (n):   building in which the U.S. Congress meets

> The **capital** point of his paper was the need for energy conservation.
>
> James Michener's *Texas* is a **capital** novel.
>
> In some states, premeditated murder is a **capital** crime.

Zhirong Liang had $50,000 in **capital** to expand her business.

Trenton is the **capital** of New Jersey.

The General Assembly meets on the second floor of the **capitol.**

Our U.S. senators and representatives spend each congressional session at the **Capitol.**

casual *and* causal

4–135

casual (adj):	uncertain or unexpected
(adv):	occurring irregularly, on an occasional basis
causal (adj):	that which precedes and brings about an effect or result; reason for an action or condition to occur

The plaintiff and the defendant had been only **casual** acquaintances.

Our community group meets on a **casual** basis.

There was a **causal** relationship between the collision of the two cars and the spilled gasoline that resulted in the explosion.

cease *and* seize

4–136

cease (v):	to discontinue or stop
seize (v):	to confiscate or capture

Because of increasing costs, we must **cease** publishing a newsletter.

The police must **seize** and tag all evidence.

censor *and* censure

4–137

censor (n):	official who removes objectionable material
(v):	to remove objectionable material
censure (n):	judgment involving condemnation
(v):	to criticize adversely; to blame or reprimand

The job of the **censor** is difficult when individuals and groups have differing ideas about what is acceptable.

The Russian poet's books were **censored.**

Several academy members used their power of **censure** during the demonstration.

How often does Congress **censure** a member?

cite, sight, *and* site

4–138

cite (v):	to quote
sight (n):	vision
site (n):	location

You may **cite** *The Irwin Law Office Reference Manual* as your source.

Although he was over 90 years old, his **sight** was excellent.

The **site** chosen for the warehouse was adjacent to the railroad yards.

139

collision *and* collusion

4–139

collision (n):   A sudden contact of one or more moving objects into or against another

collusion (n):   an agreement between two or more persons to conduct themselves illegally or fraudulently; a conspiracy to engage in an act for unlawful purposes

The **collision** of the train and the car occurred at a marked railroad crossing zone.

The medical clinic and the defendants were suspected of **collusion** in submitting false medical insurance claims.

complement *and* compliment

4–140

complement (n):   that which completes

      (v):   to add to; to correspond to

compliment (n):   approval, praise

      (v):   to give praise

Now that a new vice president has been named, the executive board has a full **complement** of officers.

The designer planned the elegant reception room to **complement** the company's prestige.

John's supervisor gave him a well-deserved **compliment** on his presentation.

Robin was **complimented** several times after the press conference.

complementary (adj):   completing in a favorable way

The mauve draperies are **complementary** to the dark walnut paneling in the conference room.

complimentary (adj):   free; description of a closing for a letter

David received a **complimentary** CD when he purchased his new CD player.

The **complimentary** closing Steve prefers on his letters is "Sincerely."

conscience, conscious, *and* conscientious

4–141

conscience (n):   one's awareness of moral implications

conscious (adj):   aware; deliberate

conscientious (adj):   careful or meticulous

Because she had a guilty **conscience,** she admitted that she had not been polite to the visitor.

McGee's supervisors made a **conscious** decision to overlook his absenteeism.

The teenagers were not **conscious** of the seriousness of their prank.

Her personnel appraisals indicated she had been a **conscientious** worker.

consul, council, *and* counsel

4–142

consul (n): representative for a nation's commercial interests abroad
council (n): group of elected or appointed advisers
counsel (n): advice
    (v): to advise; to give advice

The French **consul** provided input about European Union problems.

The city **council,** which meets monthly, turned down the city manager's recommendation.

After receiving the letter, he went to his attorney for **counsel.**

Does human resources need someone to **counsel** new employees?

correspondence *and* correspondents

4–143

correspondence (n): letters or other written communications
correspondents (n): letter writers; news reporters

Please enclose these documents with the **correspondence** to Adelaide & Co.

Our foreign **correspondents** are scattered throughout the world.

decent, descent, *and* dissent

4–144

decent (adj): adequate; satisfactory; proper
descent (n): downward step; one's relation to an ancestor
dissent (n): difference of opinion
    (v): to differ in opinion

Without a high school education, few can expect to earn a **decent** living.

The astronauts' **descent** to earth was slow but steady.

Pierre Gant is an Englishman of French **descent.**

Was there much **dissent** among the three candidates?

Justice Ginsburg wrote the **dissenting** opinion.

depositary *and* depository

4–145

depositary (n): person entrusted with something
depository (n): place of safekeeping

The executor of the estate was named **depositary** of the funds.

Use the bank's night **depository** for your cash and checks.

desert *and* dessert

4–146

desert (n): dry area
    (v): to abandon
dessert (n): final course in a meal

A number of camels were seen in the **desert.**

Was she the type of person who would **desert** her friends?

We are serving pie, cake, and fruit for **dessert.**

device *and* devise

4–147   device (n):   instrument or invention; plan
devise (v):   to plan or invent
devise (n):   a testamentary disposition of land or other real property

> The automated teller machine is an ingenious banking **device.**
>
> The car is so old that the mechanic had to **devise** a new part to repair it.
>
> The testator included a **devise** of his 100-acre farmhouse to his favorite nephew.

devisable *and* divisible

4–148   devisable (adv):   relating to real or personal property included in a testamentary disposition by will
divisible (adv):   capable of being divided or apportioned

> Real or personal property is **devisable** by testamentary disposition.
>
> Is the estate parcel **divisible** so it can be partitioned among the parties?

devisee *and* devisor

4–149   devisee (n):   one who receives land or other real property through a will
devisor (n):   one who gives land or other real property through a will; testator of a will

> Mr. Sloan's daughter Jennifer was named as sole **devisee** to receive all the Sloan estate land.
>
> The **devisor** is Jonathan Sloan, the testator.

disapprove *and* disprove

4–150   disapprove (v):   to pass unfavorable judgment upon
disprove (v):   to prove something false

> The city council was quick to **disapprove** the mayor's proposal.
>
> This evidence will **disprove** his written statement.

disburse *and* disperse

4–151   disburse (v):   to pay out
disperse (v):   to spread or scatter

> Please **disburse** $3,500 for the consultant's services.
>
> The advertising department will **disperse** fliers to the test market area.

discreet *and* discrete

4–152   discreet (adj):   careful; prudent in action or speech
discrete (adj):   separate and distinct; unrelated

> The witness has been **discreet** in revealing what she saw.
>
> Had the pair acted more **discreetly**, their affair would not have been discovered.

What are some **discrete** strategies for expanding into the Pacific Rim and western Europe?

Some voice recognition software programs require a user to input information using **discrete** speech.

disinterested *and* uninterested

4–153 disinterested (adj):   impartial, having no interest or stake in the outcome; being indifferent
uninterested (adj):   having a lack of interest

The arbitrator's role is to act as a neutral **disinterested** party.

A large number of **uninterested** voters did not go to the polls.

drawee *and* drawer

4–154 drawee (n):   a person or institution that is requested to pay an amount of money stated
drawer (n):   a person or institution that signs an instrument as an order to pay another the specified amount

The First National Bank is the **drawee** of that check.

The **drawer** is the banking customer who writes a check against his or her account.

dual *and* duel

4–155 dual (adj):   double
duel (n):   conflict or combat
    (v):   to fight a duel

Julie Settimo assumed **dual** responsibilities as legal secretary and law librarian.

Aaron Burr and Alexander Hamilton used pistols in their 1804 **duel.**

Who reported that Burr and Hamilton would **duel** at dawn?

elicit *and* illicit

4–156 elicit (v):   to draw forth
illicit (adj):   unlawful

Let the mediators try to **elicit** the facts from the union officials.

Some people thought that the merger was **illicit.**

emigrate *and* immigrate

4–157 emigrate (v):   to leave a country to live elsewhere
immigrate (v):   to enter a country to settle there

Unless the country's economy improves, more citizens will **emigrate.**

Scores of people have been allowed to **immigrate** to the United States.

143

eminent *and* imminent

4–158 eminent (adj):   conspicuous; famous
imminent (adj):   threatening or impending

> Stone walls are an **eminent** feature of the New England landscape.
>
> Anthony Eden was an **eminent** British statesman.
>
> Are gasoline and oil price increases **imminent?**

ensure *and* insure

4–159 ensure (v): to make certain, sure, or safe; to guarantee; to assure
insure (v): to underwrite; to provide or receive insurance on or for some-
            thing or someone

> Can you **ensure** that the sample products will be available for shipment by March 5?
>
> Our insurance company will **insure** the shipment of goods for $50,000 in case of loss or damage.

envelop *and* envelope

4–160 envelop (v):   to enclose
envelope (n):   container for correspondence

> The fire had begun to **envelop** the firefighters.
>
> The quality of the **envelope** should match that of the letterhead.

estop *and* stop

4–161 estop (v):   to bar, prevent, preclude, or stop
stop (v):   to restrain or cease
    (n):   restraint of one's freedom by physical force or show of authority

> The agent was **estopped** from claiming he was not acting on behalf of the corporation when he was an officer of the firm.
>
> How can we **stop** the flow of illegal arms?
>
> The officers ordered a **stop** on that vehicle.

expand *and* expend

4–162 expand (v):   to spread out or open wide; to unfold; to increase
expend (v):   to spend, pay out, or distribute; to consume by use

> We should **expand** the width of the freeway to allow more lanes of traffic.
>
> Efficient office workers should not have to **expend** much physical energy to perform their work.

explicit *and* implicit

4–163 explicit (adj):   clearly expressed
implicit (adj):   not clearly expressed but is understood

Didn't I give you **explicit** instructions to send the letter by registered mail?

His silence during the negotiations indicated **implicit** acceptance of the terms of the agreement.

farther *and* further

4–164 farther (adj): at a greater distance (measurable)

further (adv): in addition, a greater extent

(adj): additional, extending beyond

(v): to promote or advance

The planet Neptune is **farther** from the sun than Jupiter is.

It is **further** understood that a $1,000 deposit will be paid by the tenth.

What will result if our competitors expand their market **further** west?

Successful employees are those who continue their education to **further** their careers.

flaunt *and* flout

4–165 flaunt (v): to show off or to parade oneself

flout (v): to show contempt for or scorn; to show disregard

keep (n): an insult or a contemptuous remark or action

After her recent surgery, she **flaunted** her new figure.

His sarcastic remarks **flouted** his dislike for his supervisor.

foreword *and* forward

4–166 foreword (n): preface

forward (adj): situated in advance

(adv): toward what is before or in front of

(v): to advance or transmit

The **foreword** to the book is well written.

Mr. Phan, would you prefer a **forward** seat on the plane?

The troops moved **forward** at the general's command.

Will you please **forward** three copies of the book to me.

formally *and* formerly

4–167 formally (adv): in a formal manner

formerly (adv): before; once

The new training officer **formally** assumes office on January 20.

She was **formerly** a deputy district attorney.

forth *and* fourth

4–168 forth (adv): forward

fourth (adj): number

The delegates showed their skill when they went **forth** into negotiations.

Margaret Lee was the **fourth** member to become senior partner.

guarantee, guaranty, *and* warranty

4–169

guarantee (n): a promise or pledge; an assurance that something is as represented

guaranty (n): an agreement or promise whereby one person agrees to satisfy the debt of another (debtor) in case of failure to repay or to perform a specific act

(v): to assume responsibility for the repayment of another person's debts or to perform another person's duties or obligations

warranty (n): a written guarantee of a product's integrity and the maker's responsibility for repair or replacement

Accompanying your new coffee maker is our **guarantee** of the finest product we make.

We **guarantee** that your coffee maker brews the tastiest coffee you have ever had.

Mr. Reichert signed the **guaranty** on behalf of his son.

Mr. Reichert will **guaranty** the repayment of his son's loan.

Your coffee maker comes with a written one-year **warranty** for all parts and labor.

in re *and* in rem

4–170

in re (prep): in the matter of, regarding, concerning

in rem (prep): designation of proceedings or action instituted against the thing or to enforce a right in the thing

Refer to **In re** *Alexander V. Stein v. Mitchell* (2001).

Has the court instituted **in rem** proceedings against the stock certificates held in another jurisdiction?

incidence *and* incidents

4–171

incidence (n): rate of occurrence

incidents (n): events

The **incidence** of heart attacks among women is alarming.

Several unfortunate **incidents** involving misappropriations of funds led to his dismissal from the job.

ingenious *and* ingenuous

4–172

ingenious (adj): clever

ingenuous (adj): natural; naive

The microchip is an **ingenious** invention.

Is she so **ingenuous** as to assume that most people are always truthful?

interstate *and* intrastate

4–173   interstate (adj):   between states
intrastate (adj):   within a state

> Regulation of **interstate** commerce is one of Congress's major functions.

> The governor's main responsibility is to concentrate on **intrastate** affairs.

irony *and* coincidence

4–174   irony (n):   words used to express a different or opposite meaning
coincidence (n):   an accidental or remarkable occurrence of events

> The **irony** is that as a youngster, she was clumsy at the piano; but now she is a gifted pianist.

> What a **coincidence** that the two women wore identical dresses to the dinner.

irrespective, regardless, *and* irregardless

4–175   irrespective (adj):   independent of; without regard for persons or consequences

regardless (adj):   unmindful; careless; without regard for objections or difficulties

irregardless: nonstandard, incorrect usage (a blending of *irrespective* and *regardless*)

> **Irrespective** of the heavy fine, he rode his motorcycle beyond the speed limit.

> **Regardless** of the outcome of the negotiations, the parties will continue their business relationship.

Its *and* it's

4–176   its (pron):   third person possessive pronoun
it's: contraction for *it is*

> The cable connection to the printer is **its** main problem.

> **It's [it is]** easy to learn this rule!

judicial *and* judicious

4–177   judicial (adj):   relating to a judge; judgment in courts of justice or the administration of justice; characteristics of a judge

judicious (adj):   having or exercising sound or discriminating judgment; prudent, wise

> The **judicial** robe is a symbol of authority on the bench.

> Did the attorney make a **judicious** choice of expert witness?

later *and* latter

4–178   later (adv):   after a particular time; at another time
latter (adj):   relating to the second of two

Donalee Fong was **later** seen in the information systems center.

The Cincinnati and Dayton representatives will plan the conference; the **latter** group **[referring to the Dayton representatives]** will host the dinner meeting.

lay *and* lie

4–179   lay (v):   to set or put down; past tense of *to lie* (to recline)
lie (v):   to recline or to be situated; to tell an untruth
    (n):   an untruth

Please **lay** the report on my desk.

I **lay** in the sun for hours yesterday.

Lie with your feet above your head for improved circulation.

Did he **lie** about his age on his application form?

The age he wrote on his application form was a **lie.**

lead *and* led

4–180   lead (v):   to guide on a way by going ahead; to direct operations, activity, or performance
    (n):   the position at the front; initiative
    (n):   heavy, soft metal; graphite
led (v):   the past tense of *to lead*

Which Sherpa will **lead** this year's expedition to Mt. Everest?

Musical Director Esa-Pekka Salonen will **lead** the Los Angeles Philharmonic in a Mozart tribute.

The drum and bugle corps will take the **lead** in the parade.

Use only a No. 2 **lead** pencil on the test.

The suspect had **led** the officers on a high-speed chase.

leased *and* least

4–181   leased (v):   granted or held for a term, as in a rental
least (adj):   lowest; smallest

Leicester & Associates **leased** the office suite for a two-year term.

We were **least** impressed with the second candidate.

Which department reported the **least** employee turnover last year?

lessen *and* lesson

4–182   lessen (v):   to decrease or make smaller
lesson (n):   unit of instruction

Our receiving the new contract would **lessen** the chances of worker layoffs next year.

Today's **lesson** will include ways to prevent identity theft.

liable *and* libel

4–183

liable (adj): responsible or susceptible

libel (n): written defamatory statement; harm to the reputation of someone or something

(v): to hurt one's reputation and/or good name; give misleading or false reports that are negative or evil in nature

The company was **liable** for the accident because of its negligence in providing safety precautions.

Did the untrue article constitute **libel** on the part of the newspaper?

The report **libeled** my reputation.

loan *and* lend

4–184

loan (n): the act of lending or borrowing; an amount or item borrowed or lent

lend (v): to let someone use or have something temporatily; to make a loan

I applied for a $10,000 **loan** from the credit union.

She asked her supervisor for a **loan** of two clerks from another department.

Can you please **lend** me your laptop computer?

She asked her supervisor to **lend** her two clerks from another department.

Because of my poor credit, the bank could not **lend** me the money.

local *and* locale

4–185

local (adj): nearby, confined

(n): public form of transportation; regional branch; neighborhood resident

locale (n): location, site, situation

Brogan's Pharmacy has been in the **local** area for many years.

She belongs to the downtown union **local**.

The **locale** for next year's conference is San Francisco.

loose, lose, *and* loss

4–186

loose (adj): not tightly bound

(v): to release or detach

lose (v): to be unable to keep

loss (n): act of losing, casualty

The front porch has a **loose** board that John tripped over.

Be sure to **loosen** your bow before engaging the arrow.

Although Sara always tries her best, she managed to **lose** her temper.

Several airlines suffered a financial **loss** last year.

malfeasance, misfeasance, *and* nonfeasance

4–187 malfeasance (n): wrongdoing; wrongful, evil, or ill conduct that affects or interferes with the performance of one's official duties

misfeasance (n): wrongful or injurious exercise of lawful authority; improper performance of a lawful act

nonfeasance (n): omission or failure to perform an act that one is obligated to do

> The bystander was cited for **malfeasance** for obstructing the scene of a police investigation.

> An officer who misappropriates funds under his or her control will be charged with **malfeasance**.

> The failure of the lifeguard to attempt to rescue the drowning swimmer is **nonfeasance**.

maybe *and* may be

4–188 maybe (adv): perhaps

may be (v): indicating possible action

> **Maybe** we'll vacation in Scandinavia next summer.

> Loretta **may be** able to substitute for Danny at the board meeting.

overdo *and* overdue

4–189 overdo (v): to do something to excess

overdue (adj): past due

> Some actors have a tendency to **overdo** their gestures.

> The credit report showed several **overdue** payments.

passed *and* past

4–190 passed (v): moved or transferred

past (adj): former; recently elapsed

(prep): beyond

(n): time gone by

(adv): reaching and going beyond a point

> She passed the bar examination on her first attempt.

> Is Dorothy a past president of our association?

> Carl could not see past the problem to the possible solution.

> Each nation celebrates great events from its past.

> Do not drive past the detour sign ahead.

personal *and* personnel

4–191 personal (adj): private

personnel (n): employees

(adj): related to employees and employment

Please restrict **personal** calls to emergencies.

The bank **personnel** were delighted with the increase in customers.

All **personnel** matters should be directed to human resources.

precede *and* proceed

4–192 precede (v): to be, to go, or to come ahead or in front of; to be earlier than someone or something else

proceed (v): to continue after a pause or interruption; to begin or carry on an action, process, or movement; to advance

Graduates from the School of Business will **precede** those from the Center for Public Administration in the procession.

Ken's presentation will **precede** mine.

We will **proceed** with our discussion after our lunch break.

The project will **proceed** when the final plans have been approved.

Even though the microphone did not work, the speaker **proceeded** with the presentation.

precedence *and* precedents

4–193 precedence (n): an act or occurrence taking place before; priority in importance

precedents (n): cases or legal decisions by a court used as authority or example for similar or identical future cases or decisions; course of conduct to be followed in the future based on past conduct

Preparing the report due next week should take **precedence** over next month's meeting agenda.

Cases decided by the highest court in a state serve as **precedents** for other decisions in that jurisdiction only.

That Court's 1998 decision stands as **precedent** for future cases involving the same fact pattern.

prescribe *and* proscribe

4–194 prescribe (v): to impose, direct, or point in an authoritative way; to assert a right or title

proscribe (v): to apply a sentence or punitive action

What dosage of medication did the physician **prescribe** to her patient?

Should the courts **proscribe** restitution or incarceration?

principal *and* principle

4–195 principal (adj): most important, main

(n): administrator; amount

principle (n): rule

The double indemnity clause was the **principal** article they quoted.

Maureen Smith, formerly an English teacher, became the high school **principal.**

Monthly mortgage payments include both **principal** and interest.

In making a decision of this type, be sure to consider the **principle** of probability.

raise, raze, and rise

4–196

raise (v):   to lift something or someone; to increase
raze (v):   to destroy or tear down
rise (v):   to get up or to go upward

Hospitals have had to **raise** their patient costs drastically.

Have you ever watched a bulldozer **raze** a building?

The sun **rises** in the east and sets in the west.

raise (n):   an increase in amount; an act of elevating
rise (n):   an ascent or a slope; an increase in height, volume, or pitch; an elicited response

The new clerk received a $25 per month salary **raise** upon completing his probationary period.

There was a dramatic **rise** in the stock's value by the end of the trading day.

The composition required a **rise** in pitch in the alto section of the choir.

His passing the bar exam on the first try gave **rise** [noun] to his ability to **rise** [verb] to the occasion when necessary.

residence and residents

4–197

residence (n):   structure that serves as a home
residents (n):   individuals living in a particular place

One's domicile is where one maintains his or her primary **residence.**

There must be several hundred **residents** in that condominium complex.

respectfully and respectively

4–198

respectfully (adv):   with reverence or respect
respectively (adv):   successively with each in the order given

I **respectfully** request a one-month leave of absence.

In some states, the *plaintiff* and the *defendant* are referred to as the *petitioner* and the *respondent*, **respectively.**

role and roll

4–199

role (n):   part in a play or situation
roll (n):   list or roster

(v):   to move forward; to pass by

The investigator played a key **role** in the case.

Our alumni **roll** includes several legal assistants who went on to law school.

The maintenance crew will **roll** the desk to a better location.

Keeping busy helps the hours **roll** by quickly during a workday.

set *and* sit

4–200

set (v):   to place or put

   (n):   a unit or grouping

sit (v):   to rest in a seated position; to be located or situated; to occupy a judicial, legislative, or other important position.

Please **set** the closed case files on the cabinet.

Please try to find a matching piece for this **set** of luggage.

Because he had no furniture to **sit** on, he ate and slept on the floor of his new apartment.

Their new home **sits** atop the hill overlooking the ocean and the mountains.

Commissioner Bellinger **sits** as the presiding bench officer in Division D.

stationary *and* stationery

4–201

stationary (adj):   still, not moving

stationery (n):   writing materials

The trucker ran into the **stationary** pole on the highway shoulder.

Company policy requires the use of white letterhead **stationery** only.

suit *and* suite

4–202

suit (n):   type of clothing; court action (lawsuit)

   (v):   to adapt or to agree

suite (n):   a group of rooms; instrumental musical form

She should have worn a more conservative **suit** for her interview.

Has the lawyer filed a **suit** on behalf of his client yet?

Our present plant facilities should **suit** our future needs as well.

A special **suite** of rooms is reserved for distinguished government officials.

The *Peer Gynt Suite* is a unique musical composition.

than *and* then

4–203

than (conj):   used with a comparison

then (adv):   at that time; next

   (n):   a particular time

Kazuko has more law office experience **than** Donna.

Please check these requisitions; **then** you can issue the vouchers.

If the authors submit the manuscript on May 1, the publication would be scheduled a year from **then.**

their, there, *and* they're

4–204   their (pron):   third person plural possessive pronoun
there (adv):   in or at that place
     (n):   that particular point
they're: contraction for *they are*

Do **their** plans include expanding the staff?

That forklift over **there** needs to be repaired.

"You take it from **there,** Dan," stated the director.

They're [they are] going to face some stiff competition from our firm.

threw *and* through

4–205   threw (v):   past tense of *throw*; to project or propel through the air
through (prep):   movement from one area to another
     (adv):   concluded or finished
     (adj):   extension from one surface to another

The center fielder **threw** the ball to second base, and the runner was called out.

Patti runs **through** the park during her morning jog.

The clerk was **through** sorting the mail by 11.

Is Laurel Avenue a **through** street?

to, too, *and* two

4–206   to (prep):   indicates direction toward
too (adv):   also, excessively
two (adj):   a number

Student groups are welcome **to** the courthouse for tours.

I **too** believe that the audit should be done immediately.

Our operating expenses have been **too** high.

"I was one of **two** eyewitnesses," said the bystander.

tortious *and* tortuous

4–207   tortious (adj):   wrongful conduct; involving wrongful conduct against a person, property, or reputation; a tort
tortuous (adj):   not direct or straightforward; deceitfully indirect or morally crooked; devious

The defendant was accused of the **tortious** act of breaching a contract.

The unfounded gossip about the actor was **tortious** behavior that ruined his professional career.

The group's **tortious** activities—vandalism and theft—caused $5,000 in damages.

Why did the witness have to concoct such a **tortuous** alibi for her whereabouts?

void *and* voidable

4–208

void (adj): having no legal force or effect; not legally binding or enforceable; null, inoperative

(n): an empty space; emptiness

(v): to vacate, nullify, to annul; to have no effect; to empty the contents of something

voidable (adj): ineffective, inoperative, nonenforceable; ability to be voided or declared void; a document, transaction, or defect that can be cured or corrected so it can have legal force and effect

How often do judges **void** the decisions of juries?

Void a check when the payee name or the amount is incorrectly written.

The sale of the home was **void** because there was no written agreement as required by the Code.

When the law firm moved to new quarters, there was a large **void** in the office complex.

The minor's contract for nonnecessities is **voidable;** upon reaching 18, one can have the contract rescinded.

weak *and* week

4–209

weak (adj): lacking skill, strength, or effectiveness

week (n): a period of seven days

Did the attorney concede that her case was based on **weak** evidence?

In spite of her excellent research skills, she was **weak** in human relations skills.

It should take approximately a **week** to complete the report.

weather *and* whether

4–210

weather (n): atmosphere or state of the climate during a short period of time

(v): to undergo change; to endure or resist exposure to weather conditions; to go or come safely through bad weather, difficulty, or troubled times

whether (conj): if

155

The **weather** in San Diego varies little the year round.

Will the company **weather** these unstable economic times?

Because of illness, Nancy couldn't decide **whether** to make the trip.

whose *and* who's

4–211 whose (pron):　possessive pronoun
who's:　　　　contraction of *who* is

Whose cash register terminal will you be using today?

Who's [who is] going to the bank to make the deposit?

your *and* you're

4–212 your (pron):　second person possessive pronoun
you're:　　　contraction of *you are*

Why is it that **your** desk always looks so neat?

Your being promoted to manager is exciting news!

You're [you are] going to the conference, aren't you?

Words with Similar Meanings

The following groups of words are commonly misused because of similarities in meaning.

amount *and* number

4–213 Use *amount* to refer to quantities. Use *number* to refer to individual persons or items. *The number* is singular and requires a singular verb; *a number* is plural and requires a plural verb.

The chef miscalculated the **amount** of wine to add to the casserole.

Will the **number** of college graduates increase in the next decade?

Our researcher found that **a number** of cases support our theory.

anxious *and* eager

4–214 Use *anxious* to refer to worry or anxiety. Use *eager* to refer to an enthusiastic or impatient desire or interest.

Richard was **anxious** about his daughter's surgery.

Brian Lee was **eager** to start his vacation in Hawaii.

between *and* among

4–215 Use *between* to refer to two persons, places, or objects. Use *among* to refer to three or more persons, places, or objects.

Between Jackie and me, I am better qualified for the position.

Must our selection be made from **among** just these five books?

continual *and* continuous

4–216 Use *continual* to mean successive or one after another. Use *continuous* to mean without interruption.

> A receptionist must be able to handle **continual** telephone calls while performing his other work.
>
> Isn't the **continuous** beeping noise from the car alarm annoying?

different *and* differently

4–217 Use *different* (an adjective) to mean dissimilar. Use *differently* (an adverb) to mean in a different manner.

> One component is **different** from the others that were tested.
>
> The results appeared **differently** than the researchers anticipated.

every one *and* everyone

4–218 every one (adj, n):   each person, item, or idea within a group
every one (pron):   all persons within a group

> **Every one** of these graphs must be replotted.
>
> Our policy is that **everyone** must sign a confidentiality agreement.

ex-, former, *and* past

4–219 Sometimes the prefix *ex-* is used to refer to a person who has immediately preceded someone else in a current position. *Former* and *past* are also used to refer in general to people who have held a particular position.

> Carol Blaczynscki is the **ex-director** of our industry council.
>
> Many of our country's **former** presidents have written memoirs of their years in office.
>
> The **past** presidents of the Daughters of the American Revolution were honored for their service.

farther *and* further

4–220 Use *farther* to refer to distance. Use *further* to mean additional or to a greater extent. Only *further* is a verb, meaning to advance or to help the progress of.

> The planet Jupiter is **farther** away from Earth than Mars is.
>
> Please refer to Appendix C for **further** details of the proposal.
>
> To **further** her job skills, she is taking additional computer classes.

fewer *and* less

4–221 Use *fewer* when referring to numbers that can be counted. Use *less* when referring to a collective or an abstract amount.

> Fewer than 30 brands of office equipment were displayed at this year's office Expo.
>
> We should strive to accomplish more work with **less** stress!

flammable, inflammable, *and* nonflammable

4–222

flammable (adj):	easily capable of being ignited and burning rapidly; combustible
inflammable (adj):	easily capable of being ignited and burning rapidly; combustible
nonflammable (adj):	inability to catch on fire

> Hydrogen sulphide is a **flammable** gas, subject to catching fire readily!
>
> Hydrogen sulphide is an **inflammable** gas, subject to catching fire readily!
>
> Children's clothing and bedding are made of **nonflammable** fabrics that have been specially treated.

former *and* latter

4–223

Both words are used to refer to one of two persons, places, or objects previously mentioned in a sentence. Use *former* to refer to the first-named individual or item. Use *latter* to refer to the second-named individual or item.

> Dallas and Washington are both good teams, but I think the **latter** [referring to Washington] will win the championship.
>
> If I had to choose between Sunny and Bridget, I would reelect the **former**   [referring to Sunny].

good *and* well

4–224

Good is used as an adjective, not an adverb. As an adjective, it can modify a noun or follow a linking verb. *Well* is an adverb used to modify verbs.

> You took a **good** picture for your yearbook.
>
> Hard-working students generally do **well** in their chosen careers.
>
> The elderly patient has not been feeling **well** lately.

healthy *and* healthful

4–225

Healthy refers to a state of well-being. *Healthful* refers to a climate, food, or environment that is beneficial to one's well-being.

> Daily jogging and swimming have helped Mark remain a **healthy** individual.
>
> Cutting down one's consumption of fats, calories, and cholesterol contributes to more **healthful** eating habits.

imply *and* infer

4–226

Use *imply* to mean suggest. Use *infer* to mean to conclude or to come to the conclusion. (Speakers and writers imply; listeners and readers infer.)

> Did the authorities **imply** the robbery was planned by someone inside the company?
>
> From these budget figures, we can **infer** that the company has serious financial problems.

last *and* latest

4–227 Use *last* to refer to the final one, where there are no others to follow. Use *latest* to mean the most recent.

What was the date of the **last** issue of *Look* magazine?

Did you read the **latest** issue of the *National Geographic?*

some time, sometime, *and* sometimes

4–228 some time (adj with):   a future period of time
sometime (adv):   nonspecific time; at a time in the future
sometimes (adv):   occasionally or on various occasions

Our committee will meet again **some time** soon.

You can expect your reimbursement **sometime** in the next 10 days.

Our staff **sometimes** holds breakfast meetings at a nearby restaurant.

waiver *and* waver

4–229 waiver (n):   the voluntary relinquishment of a right, claim, or privilege
waver (v):   to be indecisive; to fluctuate back and forth

She signed a **waiver** giving up her right to sue in court in case of a dispute.

Some people tend to **waver** on important issues rather than make a decision.

who *and* whom

4–230 Use *who* as the subject of a sentence and when the pronoun *he, she, we,* or *they* can be substituted. Use *whom* as the object of a preposition and when the pronoun *him, her, them,* or *us* can be substituted.

Who [He or she] will be the next president?

Our firm's scholarships will be given to **whom [him or her]** this year?

whoever *and* whomever

4–231 Use *whoever* as the subject of a sentence and when the pronoun *he, she, we,* or *they* can be substituted. Use *whomever* as the object of a preposition and when the pronoun *him, her, them,* or *us* can be substituted.

Whoever [He or she] can benefit the most will receive the funds.

You may invite **whomever [him, her, or them]** you wish.

More Effective Words

4–232 How words are used within a letter, memo, legal document, or report determines the effectiveness of the message. Facts and ideas should be communicated in a logical order and in direct, simple language. Avoid awkward, trite, and wordy expressions such as those in Table 4.2.

4–233 Avoid using several words that mean essentially the same thing. In the following list, one word or another would be adequate.

agreeable and satisfactory	give, devise, and bequeath
and therefore	hope and trust
cease and desist	null and void
courteous and polite	remise, release, and discharge
false and untrue	rest, residue, and remainder
full and complete	

4–234 Eliminate trite expressions; they are worn-out expressions that are wordy and meaningless.

along these lines	I am writing this letter
as a matter of fact	I have your letter
beg to acknowledge	permit me to say
beg to inform	replying to yours
contents duly noted	respectfully urge
enclosed herewith please find	this letter is for the purpose of

TABLE 4.2 **Word Usage for Effective Writing**

Avoid	Use
above listed	those
above mentioned	those
absolutely complete	complete
actual experience	experience
along these lines	similar to; like this
arrived at the conclusion	concluded
articulate	explain
as per	as; according
assemble together	assemble
at a cost of	at
at a later date	later
at all times	always
at the present time	now
attached please find	attached is/are
basic fundamentals	fundamentals
by means of	by
circumstances surrounding	circumstances

TABLE 4.2 *(continued)*

Avoid	Use
close proximity	close; near
consensus of opinion	consensus
continue on	continue
disseminate	distribute
due to the fact that	because; since
during the course of the day	during the day
during the time that	while
each and every one of us	each of us; all of us; everyone
enclosed please find	enclosed is/are
entirely completed	completed
for the purpose of	for; to
for the reason that	because; since
held a meeting	met
if it is possible	if possible
in accordance with your request	as you requested
in connection with	about
in order that	so
in regard to	regarding; about
in the event that	if
in the neighborhood of	about
in the normal course of our procedures	normally
in the very near future	soon
in this day and age	today
in view of the fact that	because; since
inasmuch as	since
inside of the	inside the
later on	later
might possibly	might
my personal opinion	my opinion
necessary requisite	requisite
party	person
past experience	experience
previous to	before

TABLE 4.2   *(concluded)*

Avoid	Use
prior to	before
reason is because	reason is
remembering the fact that	remembering that
repeat again	repeat
revert back	revert to
same identical	same; identical
significant	important
small in size	small
square in shape	square
still persists	persists
subsequent to	after; later
the reason is because	the reason is that
the reason is due to	because
thrust	direction; emphasis
under date of	on
under separate cover	separately
uniformly consistent	consistent
unique	somewhat different
until such time	until
up until	until
utilize	use
whether or not	whether
will you be kind enough	please
with a view to	to
with regard to	about; regarding
with respect to	about
with the result that	so that
without further delay	now; immediately

Unit 5

Numbers and Abbreviations

NUMBERS

5–1 Numbers may be expressed in figures or words. Figures (called "arabic numbers") stand out from the text and are more quickly read than words. Use figures exclusively in tables, statistical matter, and financial reports. In business correspondence, use either figures or words depending on the situation. Follow the general guidelines and specific rules in this unit to determine which form to use.

General Guidelines

5–2 In routine business correspondence, spell out numbers one through ten, and use figures for numbers above ten. If a short block of type or copy contains both numbers under ten and over ten, use figures for all numbers. Be consistent in expressing numbers throughout a document.

> Our company added **three** divisions this year alone.
>
> Our company began the year with only **11** divisions.
>
> Our company added **3** divisions this year alone. By next year, we expect to have a total of **17** divisions.

In the most informal written communications such as interoffice memos, figures may be used exclusively to save time.

5–3 In legal text and documents, spell out numbers one through ninety-nine; use figures for larger numbers.

> The court clerk had to process **sixty-eight** exhibits.
>
> Before the jury was selected, the judge and the attorneys had to interview **120** potential jurors.

5–4 Certain numbers are preassigned to individuals (such as Social Security numbers or drivers' license numbers) and to documents (such as purchase orders, invoices, or vouchers). Some numbers are written with spaces, hyphens, or diagonals; some contain letters. For example, Social Security numbers consist of a nine-digit number, separated by hyphens: 560-30-5591. Write the numbers as they appear on the document or record.

Beginning a Sentence

5–5 Always spell out a number that begins a sentence—regardless of the number of words it takes. If necessary, rewrite the sentence to avoid beginning it with a number.

> **Two hundred fifty** people were registered for the conference.
>
> There were **250** people registered for the conference.

Inclusive Numbers

5–6 The second number of inclusive numbers may be abbreviated if it contains a repeated figure. When consecutive page numbers, sections, or subsections are cited, keyboard the inclusive numbers; do not use *et seq.*

Follow this guideline for abbreviating the second number when the numbers appear frequently in a document. In general, do not abbreviate.

> 1994–9 *instead* of 1994–1999
>
> pages 205–6 *instead* of pages 205–206

Do not abbreviate the second number of the sequence if the first number is a multiple of 100, if the second number begins with a new series of digits, or if the numbers are under 100.

> pages 315–408   pp. 315–408
>
> 1999–2010
>
> pages 54–98   pp. 54–98

When inclusive numbers are code sections from statutes, regulations, and other sources—especially when the number includes a combination of arabic and/or roman numerals and/or upper- and lowercase letters, repeat the inclusive numbers in the range. If hyphens appear within a number, use the word *to* to indicate the range of numbers.

> Sections 426.35(A)(1)-426.35(A)(1)(c)(i)
>
> §§ 3-502-3 **to** 3-502-3(II)(a)

Ordinal Numbers

5–7 Ordinal numbers indicate a ranking or place within a series and are formed by adding *st*, *nd*, *rd*, or *d*, or *th* after the arabic number.

> Use *st* after numbers ending in 1: 31st or 221st
>
> Use *nd* or *d* after numbers ending in 2: 52nd or 342d
>
> Use *rd* or *d* after numbers ending in 3: 23rd or 153d
>
> Use *th* after numbers ending in 4–9 and 0: 66th or 70th

5–8 Ordinal numbers that can be written as one or two words should be spelled out (a hyphenated number counts as one word). Use figures and the ordinal endings for larger numbers.

> first, second, and third place
>
> their one hundredth customer
>
> twenty-fifth in line
>
> three-thousandths of an inch
>
> the film's 125th anniversary

In advertising copy, use figures even when the ordinal number could be written as one word.

> Our **30th** Anniversary Celebration!

Reference to Numbers

5–9 When referring to particular numbers within a sentence, always use figures.

> Add **50** to each column of figures.
>
> Choose a number from **1** to **10**.

Round Numbers

5–10 Use words rather than figures to indicate round or approximate numbers.

> Never in **a million** years will this happen again.
>
> **Several hundred** people work in this plant.

5–11 Very large round numbers may be written in a combination of figures and words. Use the decimal equivalent for rounded fractions.

> Our earnings last year exceeded **$2 billion.**
>
> Approximately **1.5 million** people gathered to witness the launch of the space shuttle.

Successive Numbers

5–12 When two related numbers are used successively in a sentence, spell out the smaller number and use figures for the larger number.

> John bought **50** thirty-nine-cent stamps.

Insert a comma between two unrelated numbers written in figures.

> In **2007, 403** experienced lab technicians attended the seminars.

Punctuation with Numbers

Compound Numbers

5–13 Compound numbers from 21 to 99 are hyphenated when written out, as is any number that is part of a compound adjective.

> twenty-one   forty-two thousand
>
> one hundred eighty-two   a ten-cent stamp

With Commas

5–14 Use a comma in whole numbers of four or more digits. Counting from right to left, place a comma after every third digit.

> 1,942   10,926,367
>
> 682,745 $2,345.74

Inclusive Numbers

5–15 Use hyphens to connect figures representing a continuous sequence such as calendar dates and page numbers. Do not space before or after the hyphen. The hyphen takes the place of the word *to* or *through* in the sequence.

> the years 1998-2018   pages 11-18

Specific Rules

Addresses

5–16 Use figures for house and building numbers in addresses, except for the number One. Use figures for numbered streets beginning with 11. To avoid a misreading, place a hyphen between a house or building number and a numbered street.

> One East Tenth Street
>
> 2 East 13th Street
>
> 2 West Tenth Street
>
> 751-34th Street

5–17 The five-digit ZIP (Zone Improvement Plan) code number is written in figures, beginning one space after the state name or the U.S. Postal Service two-letter state abbreviation.

> Dallas, TX 75204
>
> Wilkes-Barre, PA 18702

5–18 ZIP + 4 adds a four-digit number to the five-digit ZIP code. The four digits enable electronic sorting of mail to a particular area of a postal carrier's route: one side of an individual city block, one building in a large apartment complex, one office in a large office building, and so forth.

Use a hyphen to separate the ZIP code and the four digits. Keyboard the ZIP + 4 one space after the two-letter state abbreviation on both the inside address of the letter and on the envelope. (Refer to the *National ZIP + 4 Code Directory* to determine the mailing codes.)

> Washington, DC 20260-3100

Ages

5–19 In statistical or technical writing, use figures for ages.

> Employees are entitled to receive retirement benefits at age **62**.

In general writing, spell out ages.

> Darren will be **two** years old in September; his brother is **twelve** years old.

167

For anniversaries, spell out number of years.

> As of July 10, Reynard celebrated **twenty** years with the firm.

5–20   Ordinal numbers in birthdays and anniversaries written as one or two words should be spelled out. (Hyphenated numbers count as one word.) (See 5–6 • 5–7, Ordinal Numbers.)

> Darren will celebrate his **second** birthday in September.
>
> This June, Judy and Loren will celebrate their **twenty-fifth** anniversary in New Zealand.

Dates

5–21   A complete date consists of the month (spelled out), day, and year. Do not use ordinal endings (*st*, *th*, *nd*, *d*, or *rd*) with a complete date. Separate the day and year with a comma.

> January 28, 2006

Include the complete date on all correspondence and in other documents where space permits. If the complete date appears within a sentence, place a comma after the year.

> **July 16, 2005,** was a memorable date for the couple.

5–22   In informal correspondence, on forms, or where space is limited, the complete date may be written in figures. Separate the month, day, and year with either diagonals (/) or hyphens (-). Be consistent in the form used.

> 6/14/09   6-14-09

In business correspondence, do not write dates in figures because the numbers may be keyboarded incorrectly or misinterpreted as military dates. (See 5–26, Military Dates.)

5–23   When the day precedes the month, use ordinal numbers. Common endings are *st*, *nd*, *rd*, *d*, and *th.* (See Ordinal Numbers, 5–7.)

> 23rd of March

5–24   When dates are included in legal documents or on formal announcements and invitations, spell out the day and the year. The year may be written in its shortened form or spelled out.

> the fifteenth of October
>
> the thirty-first day of January
>
> nineteen hundred ninety-nine   **[shortened form]**
>
> one thousand nine hundred ninety-nine   **[full date]**
>
> twenty fifteen   **[shortened form]**
>
> two thousand ten   **[full date]**

5–25 When a date consists of only the month and year, do not use a comma between the two. When the day is included, use a comma after the day and the year.

> July **1976** was the country's bicentennial.
>
> Independence Day, **July 4, 2076,** will be very special.

Military Dates

5–26 Dates written in the military are expressed in day, month, and year order with no punctuation. If the sentence requires it, set off the entire date with commas. (See also Military Time, 5–54.)

> 17 April 2010
>
> Recruits will report for orientation on Thursday, **10 February 2008.**

Decimals

5–27 Write decimal amounts in figures, using the period for the decimal point. Write decimal equivalents of less than 1 percent in figures, preceded by a zero.

> 3.75 inches   0.075 inch

5–28 Do not add zeros to the right of any decimal figures except when the numbers are aligned in columns. Decimals in tables and columns should have the same number of decimal places.

> 15.051
>
> 1.000
>
> .875
>
> 3.050

Fractions

5–29 When keyboarding mixed numbers, use a space or a hyphen to separate the whole number from the fraction so that the number is read correctly. Using the hyphen ensures that the fraction is correctly written.

> 8 4/5 [or 8-4/5]

Fractions used without whole numbers are spelled out except when used in a series.

> three-fourths of a mile
>
> tolerances of 1/32, 1/16, and 1/8 inch

5–30 Some word processing programs include the character set of symbols for the fractions ½ and ¼. When only these two fractions are used in a document, use these characters. If other fractions are also included, for consistency make all fractions using figures and the diagonal. For mixed fractions, insert a space or a hyphen between the whole number and the fraction.

169

Incorrect: $7/8 + 2/3 + 5\frac{1}{2}$

Correct: 7/8 + 2/3 + 5 1/2 [or 5-1/2]

In Legal Documents

5–31 Numbers and amounts included in legal documents and contracts are spelled out as well as written in figures within parentheses. Spell out amounts fully rather than use the shortened form. The spelled out number or amount may appear in all capital letters or with only the first letter of important words capitalized.

Incorrect: The principal amount of Thirty-Five Hundred Fifty Dollars ($3,550.00) is due within thirty (30) days.

Correct: The principal amount of Three Thousand Five Hundred Fifty Dollars ($3,550.00) is due within thirty (30) days.

Measurements

5–32 Use figures to indicate capacities, dimensions, distances, measures, temperature, and weights in technical or scientific contexts. (See Symbols, Section 5–55, and Table 5.1.)

1 pt [1 pint]	120 hp [120 horsepower]
3 miles	4′ × 6′ area [4-foot by 6-foot area]
20° [20 degrees]	8-1/2″ paper [8-1/2-inch paper]
45 lb [45 pounds]	10 feet 6 inches

Money

5–33 Use figures, preceded by a dollar sign, for amounts over one dollar. Do not use a decimal point or zeros with even dollar amounts in a sentence.

Your **$1.10** refund check is in the mail.

Maureen has a balance of exactly **$2,836** in her credit union account.

For amounts under one dollar, use figures and the word *cents*. If the cents amount appears in a series with amounts greater than one dollar, use a dollar sign followed by a decimal point.

A simple device, costing **75 cents,** repaired the million-dollar machine in minutes.

John's collections were **$.95, $1.50, $.75, $2.25, and $1.85.**

5–34 Whenever amounts are spelled out, write the word *dollars* or *cents* after the amount.

thirty-five dollars

sixteen and 50/100 dollars

seventy-one cents

5–35 When a series of dollar amounts appears in a sentence, repeat the dollar sign before each amount.

The quarterly dividends for the past year have been **$1.05, $1.15, $1.04, and $1.02.**

5–36   In tables or columns, use the decimal point and zeros after even dollar amounts if the column contains mixed amounts (dollars-and-cents amounts). Insert the dollar sign only before the first amount in the column, any subtotals, and the total.

$ 18.95
7.00
95.30
$121.25

5–37   On business forms such as purchase orders and invoices, use the cents symbol (if available) and figures for amounts under one dollar. If the list includes both cents and amounts above one dollar, use a dollar sign followed by a decimal point before the cents amount.

3 doz at 39¢

2 pr at 19¢

4 dozen at $1.24 and 3 dozen at $.29

Percentages

5–38   Unless they begin a sentence, write percentages in figures followed by the word *percent*. Use the percent symbol (%) only in tables, in statistical matter, and on business forms.

The credit manager approved a **5 percent** discount for us.

Ten percent of the students had never taken keyboarding in high school.

5–39   Percentages of less than 1 percent should be written in fractions and spelled out or converted into their decimal equivalents.

three-fourths of a percent *or* .75 percent

one-half of 1 percent *or* .5 percent

5–40   Express fractional percentages of more than 1 percent in figures, using either mixed numbers or a decimal equivalent.

9 1/2 percent *or* 9.5 percent

10 3/4 percent *or* 10.75 percent

5–41   When presenting inclusive percentages or a series of percentages, write the word *percent* after the last percentage only. If, however, the percent symbol is used with these percentages, it must be used with each percentage figure.

15–20 percent

returns of up to 15, 20, and 25 percent

15% to 20%

returns of up to 15%, 20%, and 25%

Ratios and Proportions

5–42 Numbers indicating ratios and proportions are written in figures. Keyboard the word *to* or a colon (:) between the numbers; do not space before or after the colon.

> 5 **to** 1 ratio or 5:1 ratio
>
> odds of 1,000 **to** 1
>
> 3 parts paint **to** 1 part thinner

Roman Numerals

5–43 Roman numerals are often used to indicate chapter numbers, volumes of books, preliminary pages in books, years in formal reports, and family titles.

> Chapter III   Volume VI
>
> pp. ii–ix   Sections IV–XII
>
> p. ii   MMVII (2007)
>
> Charles L. Steel III   MCMXCIX (1999)

5–44 Use roman numerals to form numbers by adding the appropriate sequence of symbols as required. Roman numerals are keyboarded by using the capital letters **I, V, X, L, C, D**, and **M**. When a small roman numeral (such as *C*) precedes a larger roman numeral (such as *M*), subtract the smaller number from the larger. The major roman numerals are shown below.

1	I	11	XI	30	XXX
2	II	12	XII	40	XL
3	III	13	XIII	50	L
4	IV	14	XIV	90	XC
5	V	15	XV	100	C
6	VI	16	XVI	400	CD
7	VII	17	XVII	500	D
8	VIII	18	XVIII	900	CM
9	IX	19	XIX	1000	M
10	X	20	XX		

Lowercase roman numerals are used to number preliminary pages (table of contents, introduction, etc.) of books and formal reports. Use the lowercase letters **i, v, x, l, c, d**, and **m**.

5–45 When roman numerals are used to indicate major divisions in outlines, keyboard a period followed by two spaces after the numeral. Align the roman numerals at the right. (See also Outlines, 8–3.)

    I.   Issue

    II.   Rule

    III. Analysis

    IV. Conclusion

Telephone Numbers

5–46 A complete telephone number for North America consists of the three-digit area code followed by a seven-digit telephone number. Enclose the area code within parentheses, preceded and followed by a space. If the complete telephone number is written within parentheses within a sentence, separate the area code with a hyphen (-).

> Please fax us at **(631) 555-1222.**
>
> Please send a fax to **631-555-1222.**
>
> Please call my office **(818-555-7341)** to schedule an appointment.

International Telephone Numbers

5–47 A complete telephone number for international calls consists of a three-digit International Access Code (011), a country code, a city code (if required), and the local telephone number. (Refer to a telephone directory.) Enclose the International Access Code within parentheses; separate other codes by hyphens. For example, the telephone number for New Zealand (country code 64), city of Auckland (city code 9) would be written as follows:

> (011) 64-9-[local telephone number]

Time Periods

5–48 General references to periods of time are expressed in words, unless the number requires more than two words.

> ten seconds
>
> three hundred years
>
> thirty minutes
>
> 350 years
>
> Steve Fossett's solo flight around the world in 2005 took **67** hours, **2** minutes, and **38** seconds.

When specific business expressions incorporate numbers, use figures.

> 30-day overdue obligation
>
> payable in 12 months

In legal documents, spell out the time period and include the numbers in parentheses.

> . . . payable in twenty-two (22) monthly payments

173

Times of Day

5–49   Use figures with the abbreviation *a.m.* or *p.m.* to express the exact time of day.

> 7:55 a.m.
>
> 10:45 p.m.

Avoid redundant expressions such as *10 a.m. in the morning.* Choose one or the other.

> 10 a.m. *or* 10 in the morning

5–50   Use the word *noon* or *midnight* to indicate the 12 o'clock hour when another time is referred to in the sentence; otherwise just refer to noon or midnight.

> 12 noon to 6 p.m.
>
> 12 midnight until 4 a.m.
>
> The deadline for submitting bids is **12 noon**.
>
> At **12 midnight,** eager fans waited for *Harry Potter* to make his debut.

5–51   When *o'clock* is used in formal writing, the time should be expressed in words.

> eight o'clock
>
> quarter past seven o'clock

5–52   When time on the hour is expressed with either *p.m.*, *a.m.*, or *o'clock*, do not add zeros for minutes even for a series of times written within a sentence.

> 6 a.m.   6 o'clock   six o'clock (for formal writing)
>
> The departure times are **6:15 a.m., 10 a.m.,** and **1:10 p.m.**

5–53   When times are written in a table, include zeros for minutes. Align all times at the right.

Arrival	Departure
6:00	6:15
6:45	7:00
11:00	11:50

Military Time

5–54   Military time is stated using the 24-hour clock. Hours are written in four figures, without colons, and are read as *hundred hours*. A listing of the 24-hour military time follows.

> For 3:30 a.m.: 0330 hours   **[pronounced oh-three hundred thirty hours]**

For 3:30 p.m.: 1530 hours   **[pronounced fifteen hundred thirty hours]**

1 a.m.	0100 hours (oh one hundred hours)	1 p.m.	1300 hours
2 a.m.	0200 hours	2 p.m.	1400 hours
3 a.m.	0300 hours	3 p.m.	1500 hours
4 a.m.	0400 hours	4 p.m.	1600 hours
5 a.m.	0500 hours	5 p.m.	1700 hours
6 a.m.	0600 hours	6 p.m.	1800 hours
7 a.m.	0700 hours	7 p.m.	1900 hours
8 a.m.	0800 hours	8 p.m.	2000 hours (twenty hun- dred hours)
9 a.m.	0900 hours	9 p.m.	2100 hours
10 a.m.	1000 hours (ten hundred hours)	10 p.m.	2200 hours
11 a.m.	1100 hours	11 p.m.	2300 hours
12 noon	1200 hours	12 midnight	2400 hours

SYMBOLS

5–55 Symbols reduce the time and effort needed to write or keyboard a given word. Avoid using symbols in formal correspondence.

Use the combination of keyboard keys or the character sets of symbols in your word processing software to make the symbols. If a symbol cannot be found, leave extra spaces so that the symbols can be handwritten after the keyboarding has been completed.

The American Standard Code for Information Interchange (ASCII) is a standard coding system that allows information to be transferred from computer to computer. In conjunction with word processing (and other) programs, ASCII codes enable you to create and print various diacritical marks and other special symbols and characters not contained on the computer keyboard. (Refer to your computer or printer operating manual for a listing of such codes.)

5–56 Use figures with abbreviations or symbols.

      4 doz $20

      @ 96¢   #19436

Business Symbols

5–57 Certain symbols are used commonly and are therefore readily understood by readers. Table 5.1 contains some of these commonly used business symbols. Generally, space once before and after the symbol. Do not

175

TABLE 5.1   **Commonly Used Business Symbols**

Symbol	Definition	Example
´	acute accent	résumé
&	ampersand (*and*)	Merrick & Poore, Inc.
*	asterisk (for footnotes)	$128,344*
@	at, each	@ 12 cents
¢	cents	75¢
©	copyright	© 2008 McGraw-Hill/Irwin
°	degree(s)	78°
/	diagonal	and/or, 15/16, c/o
$	dollar(s)	$12.75
′	foot/feet	6′ tall
ƒ	florin/guilder	ƒ
″	inch(es)	3″ × 5″ card
	ditto	4″ × 6″ ″
#	number	#402
	pound	20#
¶	paragraph	¶ 45b
¶ ¶	paragraphs	¶ ¶ 45b–48
%	percent	100% turnover
€	Euro	€26
£	pound/sterling	£5
§	section	refer to § 1104
§§	sections	refer to §§ 1104–1108
¥	Japanese yen	¥

space between the numbers and the following symbols: cents, degree(s), dollar(s), foot/feet, inch(es), number, and pound(s).

10¢ (10 cents)	$145.95
180° (180 degrees)	7′ (7 feet)
#10 (No. 10)	10# (10 pounds)

Mathematical Symbols

5–58   Table 5.2 contains some commonly used mathematical symbols. Generally, space once before and after the symbol. Do not space between the numbers and the following symbols: ratio, degrees, minutes, and seconds.

TABLE 5.2 Commonly Used Mathematical Symbols

Symbol	Definition	Example
+	plus	5 + 5
−	minus	10 − 7
±	plus or minus	±6
∓	minus or plus	∓8
×	multiplied by	10 × 10
*	multiplied by	10 * 10
÷	divided by	12 ÷ 2
/	divided by	12/4
	fraction	1/8
=	equal to	$x = 8$
>	greater than	15 > 12
≥	greater than or equal to	$x \geq 8$
≠	not equal to	$x \neq y$
<	less than	10 < 11
≤	less than or equal to	$x \leq 10$
∥	parallel to	Line *AB* ∥ line *CD*
⊥	perpendicular to	Line *BD* ⊥ line *MN*
∟	right angle	∟ = 90°
√	radical, root, square root	$\sqrt{4} = 2$
:	ratio, is to	5:1
°	degrees	142°
′	minutes	35′
″	seconds	10″

Many commonly used symbols do not appear on the computer keyboard. However, these symbols are provided in the extended character sets in word processing programs. Keyboard mathematical symbols and equations in italics if available.

　　5:1 ratio　　$a \geq 2$

Section(s) Symbol

5–59　Use the section symbol § when citing a specific section number of a code, rule, or regulation within a legal citation. Space once after the section symbol. If the § is not available, spell out the word section in lowercase

177

letters. Spell out the word section or sections when used in textual material.

UCC § 3-413 or UCC **section** 3-413

Evid. Code § 952 or Evid. Code **section** 952

5–60 To cite several section numbers—whether the numbers are inclusive or noninclusive—keyboard two section symbols §§; space once after the symbols. If the section symbol is not available, spell out the word **sections** in lowercase letters.

UCC §§ 3-502 and 3-503(2)(a) or UCC **sections** 3-502 and 3-503(2)(a)

Evid. Code §§ 952-954 or Evid. Code **sections** 952-954

Paragraph Symbol

5–61 Use the paragraph symbol ¶ when citing a specific paragraph number of a code, rule, or regulation. Keyboard two paragraph symbols (¶¶) to indicate more than one paragraph number, whether inclusive or noninclusive. Space once after the paragraph symbol(s). If the ¶ is not available, use the abbreviation **para.** in lowercase letters. Space once after the paragraph symbol. Spell out the word paragraph when used in textual material.

¶ 19.88 or **para.** 19.88

Refer to ¶¶ 23.95(a) et seq.   ¶¶ 14.3(c) and 15.20

GENERAL ABBREVIATIONS

5–62 An abbreviation is a shortened form of a word, title, name, or expression. Abbreviations may be used to refer to commonly recognized terms or names, when space is limited, or in tables and graphs. Abbreviations are used to simplify word usage within certain technical documents, business forms, and tables and charts.

In general, do not use abbreviations in business correspondence except for titles (such as *Mr.* or *Ms.*), degrees (such as *M.D.*), in company names (such as *Co.* or *Inc.*), in expressions of time (such as *a.m.* or *p.m.*), or in some commonly abbreviated expressions (such as *A.D.* or *R.S.V.P.*).

When in doubt about when and how to write abbreviations, use the generally accepted form, including punctuation and capitalization, shown in a dictionary or other reference source. If a choice of usage is offered, use the form that will be recognized easily by anyone reading the document. Be consistent in using abbreviations, since some may be correctly written in either lower- or uppercase letters, and some may be punctuated or not.

Punctuation and Spacing

Single-Word Abbreviations

5–63 Use a period after a single-word abbreviation.

cont.   amend.   Fig.   Inc.   Wed.

Two or More Words

5–64 As a rule, use a period and one space after each element in an abbreviation that stands for two or more words and consists of more than single letters. However, do not leave a space in abbreviations of academic degrees (see 5–67).

N. Dak.   Lt. Cmdr.   op. cit.

Ph.D.   Litt.D.

Lowercase Letters

5–65 Generally, in an abbreviation of lowercase letters, use a period after each letter and no internal spacing.

f.o.b.   e.g.   i.e.   c.o.d.

Exceptions:

rpm   mph   psi

Capital Letters

5–66 Use all capital letters and no internal periods or spaces in abbreviations written in all capital letters.

APR   KPCC

COD   NAACP

EEOC   VA

Academic Degrees

5–67 Abbreviations of academic degrees may be used after an individual's name, in addresses, within the body of business correspondence, or in listings of information. A list of the most common academic degrees appears in Table 5.3.

Daryl J. Taylor, **Ph.D.**

You don't need an **M.B.A.** to understand this.

5–68 Spell out a degree in full, without capitals, when a general reference to the degree is made in text.

The **doctor of jurisprudence** degree requirements are extensive.

5–69 Do not use both a personal title (such as *Mr.*, *Mrs.*, *Miss*, *Ms.*, or *Dr.*) before the name and a degree after the name unless each conveys a different meaning.

179

TABLE 5.3 Abbreviations of Common Academic Degrees

A.A.	Associate in Arts
A.A.S.	Associate in Applied Science
A.S.	Associate in Science
B.A. or A.B.	Bachelor of Arts
B.B.A.	Bachelor of Business Administration
B.S.	Bachelor of Science
D.B.A.	Doctor of Business Administration
D.C.	Doctor of Chiropractic
D.D.	Doctor of Divinity
D.D.S.	Doctor of Dental Surgery
D.V.M.	Doctor of Veterinary Medicine
Ed.D.	Doctor of Education
Ed.M.	Master of Education
J.D.	Doctor of Jurisprudence; Doctor of Laws
Litt.D.	Doctor of Letters
LL.B.	Bachelor of Laws
LL.M.	Master of Laws
M.A. or A.M.	Master of Arts
M.B.A.	Master of Business Administration
M.D.	Doctor of Medicine
M.Div.	Master of Divinity
M.P.A.	Master of Public Administration
M.P.H.	Master of Public Health
M.S.	Master of Science
Ph.D.	Doctor of Philosophy
Th.D.	Doctor of Theology

Incorrect: Dr. Roberta Shimasaki, DDS
Correct: Roberta Shimasaki, DDS
Incorrect: Mr. Donald L. Southworth, Esq.
Correct: Donald L. Southworth, Esq.

Acronyms

5–70   An *acronym* is an abbreviation formed by combining the first letter(s) or sounds of several words into a pronounced word. Acronyms are generally written in capital letters, although some commonly used acronyms are written in lowercase letters. In general, do not use punctuation within an acronym. In correspondence and other writing, use an acronym only when the reader is likely to understand its meaning. Many acronyms are included in Table 5.4.[1]

AIDS	acquired immune deficiency syndrome
ERISA	Employee Retirement Income Security Act
ESOP	Employee Stock Option Plan
hazmat	hazardous material(s)
IRA	Individual Retirement Account
laser	light amplification by stimulated emission of radiation
PIN	personal identification number
RICO	Racketeer Influenced and Corrupt Organization

TABLE 5.4   **Commonly Used Abbreviations and Acronyms**

acct.	account
addl.	additional
adm. or admin.	administration, administrative
a.k.a. or AKA	also known as
agcy.	agency
agt.	agent
amt.	amount
anon.	anonymous
ann.	annotated, annotation, annual, annuity
A/P or AP	accounts payable
APR	annual percentage rate
A/R or AR	accounts receivable
ARM	adjustable rate mortgage
ASAP	as soon as possible
assoc. or Assoc.	associate(s)
assn., Assn.	association(s)
Attn.	attention
atty.	attorney
a.v. or A.V.	audiovisual
avg.	average

[1] Although abbreviations are usually followed by a period, it is becoming standard practice to eliminate the period in legal writing.

TABLE 5.4 *(continued)*

bal.	balance
bbl	barrel(s)
bc	blind copy
B/L or BL	bill of lading
bldg.	building
B/S or BS	bill of sale
c	copy
cc	carbon copy, courtesy copy
CD	certificate of deposit, compact disc
CEO	chief executive officer
CFO	chief financial officer
COO	chief operating officer
chg.	charge, change
c/o	care of
COD or c.o.d.	cash or collect on delivery
COLA	cost-of-living adjustment
cont.	continued
cr.	credit
ctn.	carton
cu in	cubic inch
cwt	hundredweight
dba	doing business as
dept.	department
dis.	discount
div.	division
doz.	dozen
dr.	debit, debtor, dram(s)
dstn.	destination
dtd.	dated
ea.	each
ed.	editor, edition
EOM or e.o.m.	end of month
ETA	estimated time of arrival
FAQ(s)	frequently asked/answered question(s)

TABLE 5.4 *(continued)*

fax	facsimile
F.B.O. or fbo	for benefit of
FIFO	first in, first out (inventory)
fl oz	fluid ounce(s)
f.o.b. or FOB	free on board
ft	foot, feet
fwd.	forward
FY	fiscal year
FYI	for your information
g	gram(s)
gal	gallon(s)
GB	gigabyte(s)
GDP	gross domestic product
gr.	gram(s), gross
gr. wt.	gross weight
hdlg.	handling
HMO	health maintenance organization
HQ	headquarters
hr	hour(s)
in	inch(es)
ins.	insurance
inv.	inventory, invoice
IRA	Individual Retirement Account
K	thousand
K or KB	kilobyte(s)
kg	kilogram(s)
L	liter(s)
l., ll.	line, lines
lb	pound(s)
LIFO	last in, first out (inventory)
m	meter(s)
M	Roman numeral for 1,000
max.	maximum
min.	minimum
mdse.	merchandise

TABLE 5.4 *(continued)*

mfg.	manufacturing
mfr.	manufacturer
mg	milligram(s)
mgmt.	management
mgr.	manager
MHz	megahertz
mi	mile(s)
min	minute(s); minimum
misc.	miscellaneous
mm	millimeter(s)
mo., mos.	month(s)
MO	mail order, money order
mph	miles per hour
n/30	net in 30 days
NA	not applicable or not available
n/a	no account
n.d.	no date
No., Nos.	number, numbers
n.p.	no page or pagination; no place of publication; no publisher
NSF	not sufficient funds
nt. wt.	net weight
opt.	optional
o/s, OS	out of stock
OTC	over the counter
oz	ounce(s)
p., pp.	page, pages
pd.	paid
pk.	peck
pkg.	package(s)
PO	purchase order
P.O.	post office
p.o.e. or POE	port of entry
ppd.	prepaid, postpaid
PR	public relations

TABLE 5.4 *(concluded)*

pr.	pair(s)
psi	pressure per square inch
pstg.	postage
pt	pint(s); part; points(s); port
qt	quart(s)
qtr.	quarter(ly)
R&D	research and development
recd.	received
reg.	registered; regular
req.	requisition; required
rev.	revised; revision
rm	ream(s)
rpm	revolutions per minute
/s/	signed (before a copied signature)
sq. in	square inch(es)
std.	standard
stmt.	statement
supp.	supplement
UPC	Universal Product Code
URL	Universal Resource Locator
VAT	value-added tax(es)
VIP	very important person
VP	vice president
wt.	weight
WWW	World Wide Web
yd	yard(s)
yr	year(s)
YTD	year to date

Broadcasting Stations

5–71 Radio and television broadcasting stations are known by their call letters. Write these call letters in capital letters with no periods or spaces between them.

BBC   KNBC   PBS   WCCO

If a frequency or mode of transmission is included with the call letters, insert a hyphen between them. If a radio station or television channel is written, do not use a hyphen.

> KPCC-FM   KHJ-TV   98.7 FM

Business Names

5–72
A business name may include an abbreviation that identifies its legal status, the type of organization, or the nature of its business. Common abbreviations used within business names are as follows. Forms of business names in citations appear in Unit 6, Legal Citations.

Assn.	Association
Bros.	Brothers
Cie	Compagnie
Co.	Company
Corp.	Corporation
GmbH	Geschellschaft mit beschraukte Haftung
Inc.	Incorporated
LLC	Limited Liability Corporation
LLP	Limited Liability Partnership
Ltd.	Limited
Mfg.	Manufacturing
PLC	Public Limited Co.
SA	Société Anonyme

Depending on where the abbreviation appears within the business name or the sentence, a comma may precede and/or follow the abbreviation.

> Sarkisian Bros., **Ltd.,** offers fine imported antiques.

5–73
Follow the company's style for writing its name, including abbreviations, punctuation, capitalization, and spacing as indicated on its stationery.

> JCPenney   Johnson & Johnson   Kmart

5–74
Many corporations are better known by their abbreviated names. Capitalize all letters in the abbreviation. As a rule, do not use periods or spacing within such abbreviations.

> AT&T   GMC   IBM   RCA

Business Terms

5–75
Common abbreviations used in informal business correspondence and on business forms are listed in Table 5.4. Note the differences in the use of lowercase and capital letters, spacing, and punctuation.

The **APR** on an 8.6 percent loan is 8.793 percent.

Thank you for your recent order, which will be shipped **COD** to your Ferris Street address.

Will you please send the parcel **c/o** Mr. Jan Nannings de Vries.

Payment terms are **2/10, n/30.**

Compass Points

5–76 Within sentences, compass points that indicate general direction or a region should be spelled out. (See also 3–25.)

Our new site will be at the **southeast** corner of Oak and Ogden.

The aircraft made a landing somewhere in the **Northwest.**

In Addresses

5–77 Spell out compass points preceding a street name in an address.

10570 **West** Camden Boulevard

5–78 When a compass point follows the street name in an address, use the abbreviated form. Insert a comma after the street name to separate it from the compass point. Capitalize each letter. If a city name follows, insert a comma after the compass point to separate the parts of the entire address.

Street name: 1401 Sixteenth Street, **NW**

Complete address: Please send the subscription to me at 1401 Sixteenth Street, **NW,** Washington, DC 20036.

If the complete street name appears within a sentence, insert a comma after the compass point to set it off from the other words.

Please deliver the parcel to 1263 Queensberry Street, **SE,** before 4 p.m.

In Technical Material

5–79 In technical material, omit the periods in compass point abbreviations.

E NE NNE

Foreign Expressions

5–80 Foreign expressions commonly used in formal business report writing and in legal documents appear in Table 5.5. These expressions need not be underscored or otherwise highlighted because they are commonly understood. Refer to *Black's Law Dictionary* to determine current use of italicizing or underlining such foreign expressions. Note the differences in the use of capital and lowercase letters, spacing, and punctuation.

TABLE 5.5   Commonly Used Foreign Expressions

ad hoc	for a particular purpose
a.m.	*ante meridiem:* before noon
A/V or ad val.	*ad valorem:* according to value
ca.	*circa:* approximately
cf.	*confer:* compare
e.g.	*exempli gratia:* for example
et al.	*et alii:* and others
et seq.	*et sequens:* and the following *et sequentes:* and those that follow
etc.	*et cetera:* and so forth
ibid.	*ibidem:* in the same place
id. or idem	the same
i.e.	*id est:* that is
L.S.	*locus sigilli:* in place of the seal
loc. cit.	*loco citato:* in the place cited
N.B.	*nota bene:* note well
op. cit.	*opere citato:* in the work cited
p.m.	*post meridiem:* after noon
pro tem.	*pro tempore:* for the time being
PS	*postscriptum:* postscript
q.v.	*quod vide:* which see
re (in re)	regarding, in the matter of
R.S.V.P.	*répondez s'il vous plaît:* please reply
ss	*scilicet:* namely
ult.	*ultimo:* in the last month
viz.	*videlicet:* namely
v.	*versus:* opposed to, against

Did the chairperson create an **ad hoc** committee to study the proposal?

The job description will be more detailed; **e.g.,** it will state minimum education, work experience, and other requirements.

A classic legal action that focused on the theory of unforeseeable consequences is that of Palsgraf **v.** Long Island R. R. Co., a 1928 case.

Geographic Names

5–81   Names of countries, republics, nations, and other geographic areas are generally abbreviated by capitalizing the first letter of each word in the name. Each letter may be followed by a period (without spaces), or the periods may be omitted. Follow one practice or the other consistently.

U.S.A. (or USA)   United States of America

U.K. (or UK)   United Kingdom

5–82 Spell out geographic names within the body of correspondence and reports. Abbreviate city, state, and country names on correspondence and envelopes following local or international postal service guidelines.

State, District, and Territory Names

5–83 Names of states, districts, and territories of the United States are abbreviated as shown in Table 5.6. Use the two-letter abbreviations adopted by the U.S. Postal Service on all envelope addresses. Forms of state abbreviations in citations also appear in Unit 6.

TABLE 5.6   U.S. State, District, and Territory Abbreviations

States, District, and Territories	Abbreviations	
	Standard	Two-Letter
Alabama	Ala.	AL
Alaska	Alaska	AK
Arizona	Ariz.	AZ
Arkansas	Ark.	AR
California	Calif.	CA
Colorado	Colo.	CO
Connecticut	Conn.	CT
Delaware	Del.	DE
District of Columbia	D.C.	DC
Florida	Fla.	FL
Georgia	Ga.	GA
Guam	Guam	GU
Hawaii	Hawaii	HI
Idaho	Idaho	ID
Illinois	Ill.	IL
Indiana	Ind.	IN
Iowa	Iowa	IA
Kansas	Kans.	KS
Kentucky	Ky.	KY
Louisiana	La.	LA
Maine	Maine	ME

TABLE 5.6 *(concluded)*

States, District, and Territories	Abbreviations	
	Standard	Two-Letter
Maryland	Md.	MD
Massachusetts	Mass.	MA
Michigan	Mich.	MI
Minnesota	Minn.	MN
Mississippi	Miss.	MS
Missouri	Mo.	MO
Montana	Mont.	MT
Nebraska	Nebr.	NE
Nevada	Nev.	NV
New Hampshire	N.H.	NH
New Jersey	N.J.	NJ
New Mexico	N. Mex.	NM
New York	N.Y.	NY
North Carolina	N.C.	NC
North Dakota	N. Dak.	ND
Ohio	Ohio	OH
Oklahoma	Okla.	OK
Oregon	Oreg.	OR
Pennsylvania	Pa.	PA
Puerto Rico	P.R.	PR
Rhode Island	R.I.	RI
South Carolina	S.C.	SC
South Dakota	S. Dak.	SD
Tennessee	Tenn.	TN
Texas	Tex.	TX
Utah	Utah	UT
Vermont	Vt.	VT
Virgin Islands	V.I.	VI
Virginia	Va.	VA
Washington	Wash.	WA
West Virginia	W. Va.	WV
Wisconsin	Wis.	WI
Wyoming	Wyo.	WY

TABLE 5.7 Canadian Province Abbreviations

| | Abbreviations | |
Province	Standard	Two-Letter
Alberta	Alta.	AB
British Columbia	B.C.	BC
Labrador	Lab.	LB
Manitoba	Man.	MB
New Brunswick	N.B.	NB
Newfoundland	Nfld.	NF
Northwest Territories	N.W.T.	NT
Nova Scotia	N.S.	NS
Ontario	Ont.	ON
Prince Edward Island	P.E.I.	PE
Quebec	P.Q. or Que.	PQ
Saskatchewan	Sask.	SK
Yukon Territory	Yuk.	YT

Canadian Province Names

5–84

Names of Canadian provinces are abbreviated as shown in Table 5.7. Use the two-letter abbreviations on all envelope addresses.

Addresses

5–85

Words used in street addresses should be written out in business correspondence and envelope addresses. The following words may be abbreviated where space is limited. If the abbreviation appears as part of a complete address within a sentence, follow it with a comma.

Ave.	Avenue
Bldg.	Building
Blvd.	Boulevard
Ct.	Court
Dr.	Drive
La.	Lane
Pkwy.	Parkway
Pl.	Place
Rd.	Road
Sq.	Square
St.	Street
Terr.	Terrace

191

Mailing address: 1570 East Colorado **Blvd.**, Pasadena, CA 91106.

Certain other words appearing in names of streets, cities, or countries are generally abbreviated. If these words appear by themselves, spell them out.

Ft.	Fort
Mt.	Mount
St., Ste.	Saint or Sainte

Please report to **Ft. Ord** on 3 September; the **Fort** will greet recruits from 0900 to 1500 hours.

Government Agencies

5–86

Abbreviations for the more common American and international government agencies are usually written in capital letters with neither periods nor spaces between the letters. Table 5.8 contains a listing of the more common government agencies. Refer to Section 6–6 on abbreviating government agency names in citing statutes, codes, administrative materials, and other sources.

TABLE 5.8   **Abbreviations of Government Agencies**

AEC	Atomic Energy Commission
BIA	Bureau of Indian Affairs
CAB	Civil Aeronautics Board
CIA	Central Intelligence Agency
CSC	Civil Service Commission
EEOC	Equal Employment Opportunity Commission
EU	European Union
FAO	Food and Agriculture Organization
FBI	Federal Bureau of Investigation
FCC	Federal Communications Commission
FDA	Food and Drug Administration
FDIC	Federal Deposit Insurance Corporation
FHA	Federal Housing Administration; Farmers Home Administration
FRB	Federal Reserve Bank; Federal Reserve Board
FTC	Federal Trade Commission
GAO	Government Accountability Office
HHS	Department of Health and Human Services
HUD	Department of Housing and Urban Development
ICC	Interstate Commerce Commission; Indian Claims Commission
IMF	International Monetary Fund
IRS	Internal Revenue Service

TABLE 5.8 *(concluded)*

NASA	National Aeronautics and Space Administration
NBS	National Bureau of Standards
NLRB	National Labor Relations Board
NRC	Nuclear Regulatory Commission
NTSB	National Transportation Safety Board
OMB	Office of Management and Budget
OSHA	Occupational Safety and Health Administration
PHA	Public Housing Administration
PRC	Postal Rate Commission
SBA	Small Business Administration
SEC	Securities and Exchange Commission
SSA	Social Security Administration
TVA	Tennessee Valley Authority
UNESCO	United Nations Educational, Scientific, and Cultural Organization
UNICEF	United Nations International Children's Fund
USIA	United States Information Agency
VA	Veterans Administration
WHO	World Health Organization

After all air disasters, **NTSB** investigative teams are sent to the site of the accident.

President Franklin D. Roosevelt is remembered for his role in creating the **TVA.**

Organization Names

5–87 Many unions, professional and trade organizations, charitable societies, and other groups are known by their abbreviated names. These abbreviations are generally written in all capital letters with no periods or spaces. A list of abbreviations for well-known organizations appears in Table 5.9. Refer to a dictionary for a complete listing of abbreviations for organized groups.

TABLE 5.9 **Abbreviations of Organizations**

AAA	American Automobile Association
AARP	American Association of Retired Persons
ABA	American Bankers Association; American Bar Association
ABFA	American Board of Forensic Accountants
ACFE	Association of Certified Fraud Examiners

TABLE 5.9 *(concluded)*

ACLU	American Civil Liberties Union
AFL-CIO	American Federation of Labor and Congress of Industrial Organizations
AICPA	American Institute of Certified Public Accountants
ALA	Association of Legal Administrators
AMA	American Medical Association
AMS	Administrative Management Society
API	American Petroleum Institute
ARC	American Red Cross
ARMA	Association of Records Managers and Administrators
ASA	American Standards Association; American Statistical Association
ASCAP	American Society of Composers, Authors, and Publishers
ASCE	American Society of Civil Engineers
ASME	American Society of Mechanical Engineers
ASTA	American Society of Travel Agents, Inc.
BBB	Better Business Bureau
NAACP	National Association for the Advancement of Colored People
NALA	National Association of Legal Assistants
NALS	National Association of Legal Secretaries (International)
NAM	National Association of Manufacturers
NANA	North American Newspaper Alliance, Inc.
NAS	National Academy of Sciences
NASDAQ	National Association of Securities Dealers Automated Quotations
NEA	National Education Association; National Endowment for the Arts
NFPA	National Federation of Paralegal Associations
NOW	National Organization for Women
PSI	Professional Secretaries International
PTA	Parent-Teacher Association
SPCA	Society for the Prevention of Cruelty to Animals
UAW	United Auto Workers
WCC	World Council of Churches
WIPO	World Intellectual Property Organization

Refer to Section 8–94 on abbreviating organization names in citing court decisions.

> The three enterprising young women applied for an **SBA** loan.

> Funds deposited in federal savings institutions are guaranteed by the **FDIC**.

> Internal Revenue Service **(IRS)** rulings are published in the United States Codes; however, cite to the Revenue Code as *I.R.C.*

> **ASCAP** becomes prominent in the media when Grammy nominees are announced each year.

Personal Names

Abbreviations of personal names vary in how they are written and punctuated and in the spacing.

First (Given) Names

5–88

Some people prefer using the abbreviated forms of their given names in correspondence and in their signatures. Space once after the period before keyboarding the middle name or surname.

Chas.	(Charles)	Jos.	(Joseph)
Edw.	(Edward or Edwin)	Robt.	(Robert)
Geo.	(George)	Thos.	(Thomas)
Jas.	(James)	Wm.	(William)

First or Middle Initials

5–89

Some people use initials in place of their first and/or middle names. Space once after each period following an initial.

> Patricia R. Lynn

> L. Edmund Kellogg

> Christine E. M. Allen

> G. P. Sutherland

5–90

Some well-known people are referred to by their initials. Use the initials if the reader is likely to know the individuals referred to. These initials should not be used in formal correspondence.

JFK	(John F. Kennedy)
LBJ	(Lyndon B. Johnson)
FDR	(Franklin D. Roosevelt)

Titles

5–91

A title written before a complete name is commonly written in abbreviated form. One space follows the period after the abbreviation.

> **Dr.** Frederick Ho

> **Prof.** Ralph S. Spanswick

Ms. Doris Daou

Mrs. Olga González

5–92 With the exception of the titles *Mr.*, *Mrs.*, *Ms.*, and *Dr.*, spell out the title when it precedes only a last name. Always spell out the formal titles *The Reverend* and *The Honorable*.

Professor Vargas   **The Reverend** Roland Shorter

Captain Pearce   **The Honorable** Martha Bellinger

5–93 Abbreviate title and academic degrees that follow an individual name.

June Barrett Tatsuno, **ALS**

John S. Wong **Jr.**

Gary L. Woods, **Esq.**

Time Periods

5–94 In letters, memos, and other correspondence, spell out days of the week and months of the year. Days and months may be abbreviated in tables, charts, graphs, and financial reports and in other situations where space is limited.

Days of the Week

5–95 Abbreviate days of the week when they appear in tables. The period following the abbreviation may be omitted.

Sun.	or	S
Mon.	or	M
Tues.	or	Tu or Tue
Wed.	or	W
Thurs.	or	Th
Fri.	or	F
Sat.	or	Sa

Months

5–96 Use the following abbreviations for months. With the exception of May, June, and July, the months may be abbreviated without periods. *June* and *July* may be abbreviated where space is limited.

Jan.	May	Sept. or Sep.
Feb.	June or Jun.	Oct.
Mar.	July or Jul.	Nov.
Apr.	Aug.	Dec.

Time of the Day

5–97 Use *a.m.* and *p.m.* with expressions of time. In very formal writing, use o'clock. When stating time on the hour, do not add zeros. (See also 5–49 • 5–53.)

7:30 a.m.   8:15 p.m.   9 p.m.

Informal: The meeting will begin at **9 a.m.**

Formal: The reception will begin at **seven o'clock.**

5–98 Use the word *noon* or *midnight* rather than *a.m.* or *p.m.* Do not add zeros after the time.

12 noon   12 midnight

Time Zones

5–99 The North American continent is divided into eight time zones. The time zones are abbreviated as shown in Table 5.10. Write the abbreviation one space after the time.

Tune in at 6 a.m. **PST** or 9 a.m. **EST.**

TABLE 5.10   North American Time Zone Abbreviations

Zones	Standard Time	Daylight Saving Time
Atlantic	AST	ADT
Eastern	EST	EDT
Central	CST	CDT
Mountain	MST	MDT
Pacific	PST	PDT
Yukon	YST	YDT
Alaska	AKST	AKDT
Hawaii	HAST	HADT
Newfoundland	NST	NDT

Weights and Measures

5–100 Units of measure, such as length, weight, volume, and temperature, are generally abbreviated when they appear in technical and scientific contexts. Spell out units of measure when they appear in other contexts. No punctuation appears after the abbreviation unless the sentence ends with the abbreviation. (See Table 5.4 and related text.)

720°K   3 ft by 6 ft

145 lbs   14 sq yd

3-1/2 qts

Unit 6

Legal Citations

6–1 Writing in the law office consists mainly of preparing various legal documents and briefs to be presented to the court and other attorneys. Although each court jurisdiction may have its own rules and procedures, the method for reporting, or citing, various primary and secondary authorities is standardized. Legal citations should be written according to the rules set out in *The Bluebook: A Uniform System of Citation* published by the Harvard Law Review Association. (This unit is not intended to be a comprehensive source of citations; refer to the *Bluebook* for a complete reference source.)

LEGAL CITATIONS

6–2 Legal citations refer to cases, statutes and codes, constitutions, treatises, legislative materials, administrative and executive materials, books, pamphlets, periodicals, unpublished works, electronic media, and nonprint materials. When information from these works is quoted verbatim or paraphrased, the source of such information must be cited. The citation (or "cite") must be properly referenced (1) to satisfy the requirements of the document, the court, or other recipient and (2) to provide adequate information so that the reader can locate the published source.

Primary and Secondary Authorities

6–3 Legal references are divided into two types: primary authority and secondary authority. *Primary authority* are sources that serve as "the law" for the U.S. government and legislative bodies at the federal, state, and local levels. Primary authority consists of the following materials:

1. Constitutions   **[see 6–7 • 6–21]**
2. Statutes   **[see 6–22 • 6–50]**
3. Legislative materials   **[see 6–51 • 6–59]**
4. Administrative and executive materials   **[see 6–60 • 6–73]**
5. Rules governing practice and procedures   **[see 6–39 • 6–73]**
6. Case reporters   **[see 6–74 • 6–152]**

6–4 *Secondary authority* are sources that do not carry the force or effect of primary authority but are used as persuasive authority. Secondary authority consists of the following:

1. Annotations   **[see 6–154 • 6–155]**
2. Dictionaries and thesauruses   **[see 6–156 • 6–157]**
3. Encyclopedias   **[see 6–158 • 6–159]**
4. Legal periodicals   **[see 6–160]**

5. Restatements   **[see 6–161]**

6. Textbooks and treatises   **[see 6–162 • 6–165]**

Abbreviations and Spacing

6–5 Standard forms of abbreviation are used for parties in case names, case reporters, legal periodicals, statutes, constitutions, and administrative and legislative materials.

6–6 The spacing used with abbreviations is also specified in the *Harvard Bluebook*. In general, do not space within an abbreviation when it consists of a series of capital letters or when a series number follows a single-word reporter name. Space once between abbreviations consisting of multiple letters.

U.S.	[No spacing between capital letters]
C.F.R.	[No spacing between capital letters]
P.2d	[No spacing between capital letter and volume number; series number considered a single-letter]
So. 2d	[Spacing after multiletter abbreviation with series number]
F. Supp.	[Spacing within multiletter abbreviation]
Cal. App. 3d	[Spacing within multiletter abbreviation]

CITING PRIMARY AUTHORITY

Constitutions

6–7 The Constitution of the United States and the constitutions of the 50 United States describe the powers and authority granted the federal government and the states, respectively. Local governments, such as cities and other municipalities, also have similar powers granted them in their municipal charters.

The United States Constitution

6–8 The United States Constitution is abbreviated as *U.S. Const.* and is followed by specific reference to the preamble or to an article, section, clause, or paragraph.

Elements of the United States Constitution

6–9 Name of the document

Article number

Section number

Clause number

Paragraph number

Date of any amendment or adoption (in parentheses)

Citing the United States Constitution

6–10 When citing the United States Constitution, identify the document as *U.S. Const.* Then cite the article (abbreviated *art.*) with a capital roman numeral. If a current United States Constitution provision is being cited, it is not necessary to include a date.

> U.S. Const. **art. V.**

Article, Section, Clause, and Paragraph Numbers

6–11 Numbers of articles, sections, clauses, paragraphs, and other portions of the Constitution are written in arabic numerals, uppercase roman numerals, and lowercase roman numerals.

Section Numbers

6–12 When citing a section number of the Constitution, use the symbol § (or §§ for several sections). If the section symbol is not available, spell out the word in lowercase letters. Cite the section in arabic numerals. Space once after either the symbol or the word.

> U.S. Const. art. I, **§** 9.
>
> U.S. Const. art. I, **section** 9.

Inclusive Section Numbers

6–13 When citing several sections of the Constitution, cite the specific section numbers following the proper number format used in that published work.

> U.S. Const. art. IV, **§§ 1-2.**

Clause

6–14 When referring to a clause, cite the clause (abbreviated *cl.*) in arabic numbers.

> U.S. Const. art. I, § 9, **cl.** 2.
>
> U.S. Const. art. I, section 9, **cl.** 2.

Amendment

6–15 When citing an amendment to the Constitution, identify the amendment (abbreviated *amend.*) in roman numerals, followed by the section number.

> U.S. Const. **amend. XV,** §§ 1, 2.

6–16 If an amendment or article has been amended or repealed, include at the end of the citation the word *amended* or *repealed*; cite the date in parentheses. A complete explanation of the action and its subsequent provision may be written after the citation.

```
U.S. Const. art. 3, § 2, cl. 1 (amended 1793).
U.S. Const. art. 3, § 2, cl. 1, amended by U.S. Const.
amend. XI (1798).
```

6–17 When the parts of the Constitution are referred to in text by their popular names, capitalize the first letters of the key words.

```
the Fourteenth Amendment
the Equal Protection Clause
```

Preamble

6–18 When citing the preamble to the Constitution, use the abbreviation *pmbl.*

```
U.S. Const. pmbl.
```

State Constitutions

6–19 The elements of state constitutions are similar to those of the United States Constitution. The format for section, article, clause, and paragraph numbers varies: some are written in parentheses and some with periods. Some numbers are separated by hyphens and some are written using a combination of numbers, letters, parentheses, and punctuation marks. Follow the particular format in the document cited.

Citing State Constitutions

6–20 State constitutions are cited by the state name in its abbreviated form, followed by the article number and section number. If a current constitutional provision is being cited, it is not necessary to include a date. Use the symbol ¶ for paragraph (or ¶¶ for several paragraphs); or abbreviate as *para.*

```
Cal. Const. art. 13, § 1.
Tenn. Const. art. II, § 6.
N.J. Const. art. 4, § 3, ¶ 1.
```

6–21 If a state constitution has been amended or if a particular provision was adopted on a date other than the original date, cite the year in parentheses.

```
Cal. Const., art. 1, § 1 (amended 1972).
```

Statutes

6–22 Statutes are laws enacted by the federal government and the 50 states. Statutes are published in both official and unofficial publications and are arranged alphabetically by subject matter.

Federal Statutes

6–23 Proposed laws are introduced in Congress by either the United States Senate or the House of Representatives. Once enacted, the federal statutes are published in various forms: Statutes at Large, codes, and rules of procedure.

Statutes at Large

6–24 Statutes at Large consist of federal session laws—both public and private laws—passed by Congress during each legislative period. *Public laws* are statutes that apply to the general public; *private laws* apply to a particular person or group of persons. The laws are numbered according to the congressional session and the sequential number of the law passed. Thus laws are arranged chronologically; amendments or repeals to those laws are not reflected in these volumes of Statutes.

6–25 When citing a statute, include the name of the law or act, the identification as a Public Law *(Pub. L.)* or Private Law *(Priv. L.)*, and its number and sequence in the series. Include the citation to the *Statutes at Large (Stat.)* and the year of enactment unless it is included in the name of the act or law.

> Act: The Uniting and Strengthening America by Providing Appropriate Tools Required to Intercept and Obstruct Terrorism Act.
>
> Popular Name: USA PATRIOT Act of 2001, **Pub. L.** No. 107-56, 115 **Stat.** 272.
>
> 21st Century Nanotechnology Research and Development Act, **Pub. L.** No. 108-153, 117 **Stat.** 1392 (2003).
>
> The Sarbanes-Oxley Act of 2002, **Pub. L.** No. 107-2047, 116 **Stat.** 745.

United States Code

6–26 The *United States Code* contains the official codified Statutes at Large. The codes are compiled into 50 subject classifications called "titles"; each numbered title contains all the general and permanent laws of the federal government. Abbreviate the *United States Code* as *U.S.C.*

Elements of a United States Code Citation

6–27   Title number
Federal code abbreviation *(U.S.C.)*
Section number(s)
Date of publication
Popular name, if appropriate
Date of supplement (in parentheses)
Publisher of an unofficial code (in parentheses)

United States Code Title

6–28 The title of each federal code identifies the subject matter by its numeric code. Keyboard the title number of the code in arabic numerals followed by a space. Cite the code section number using the section symbol (§). If the symbol is not available, spell out the word *section* in lowercase letters. Leave one space after the section symbol or word.

> **42** U.S.C. **§** 1983.
>
> **42** U.S.C. **section** 1983.

6–29 If several inclusive or nonconsecutive section numbers are cited, use two section symbols (§§) or the word *sections*.

> 17 U.S.C. §§ 501–502, 504
>
> 17 U.S.C. sections 501–502, 504

Date of Publication

6–30 The date refers to the date the code was published. Keyboard the date of the code in parentheses to indicate the version being cited.

> 23 U.S.C. § 109 **(2000)**
>
> 42 U.S.C. § 246 **(2003)**
>
> 25 U.S.C. § 1911 **(2004)**

Code Supplement

6–31 If the cited statute appears in a supplement to the code volume, include the year of the supplement in parentheses.

> 40 U.S.C. §§ 7703–7704 **(Supp. III 2003)**

Popular Name

6–32 When citing the *United States Code (U.S.C.)*, include the popular name of the code (optional), title/volume number, section number, and date (in parentheses).

> **Federal Food, Drug, and Cosmetic Act,** 21 U.S.C. § 355(j) (2002)
>
> **U.S. Holocaust Memorial Museum,** 36 U.S.C. §§ 2301–2310
>
> **The Sarbanes-Oxley Act of 2002,** 18 U.S.C. §§ 1341, 1343

United States Code Annotated (U.S.C.A.) and United States Code Service (U.S.C.S.)

6–33 The unofficial publications of the codes are the *United States Code Annotated (U.S.C.A.)*, published by Thomson/West, and the *United States Code Service (U.S.C.S)*, published by Lawyers Cooperative. Cite to an unofficial code when a statute does not appear in the *United States Code*. The titles and the section numbers contained in these unofficial code publications are identical to those contained in the official code.

> **Citations to *United States Code Annotated***
>
> 41 **U.S.C.A.** § 5 (1994)
>
> 42 **U.S.C.A.** § 246 (West 2003)

Citations to *United States Code Service*

41 **U.S.C.S.** § 5 (1994)

15 **U.S.C.S.** § 19 (Law. Co-op 1991)

Code Supplement

6–34   If the statute appears in a supplement to the code volume, include the publisher of the supplement and the year in parentheses.

41 U.S.C.A. § 403 **(West Supp. 2005)**

31 U.S.C.S. § 1710 **(West Supp. 2004)**

Popular Name

6–35   When citing either of the two unofficial codes, include the popular name of the code (optional), title/volume number, section number, and the publisher name and copyright date (in parentheses).

Federal Subject-Matter Codes

6–36   Two special sets of federal codes are published in their own volumes although they also appear in the *United States Code*: the Internal Revenue Code and various federal subject matter codes of procedure.

Internal Revenue Code

6–37   When citing the *Internal Revenue Code*, refer to that code rather than its corresponding title in the *United States Code*. Cite the *Internal Revenue Code* as *I.R.C.*, followed by the section symbol (§) or the word *section*, followed by the appropriate section number(s). Cite subsections as they appear in the codes, with upper- or lowercase letters, parentheses, or arabic numerals. Include the copyright date in parentheses.

I.R.C. § 220(b)(3)(A)(B) (2005)

I.R.C. § 61 (2000)

6–38   When citing an unofficial publication of the *Internal Revenue Code*, include the publisher's name and copyright date in parentheses after the code citation.

I.R.C. § 334(b)(2) (CCH)

I.R.C. § 1247 (West 1988)

Federal Rules of Procedure

6–39   A set of federal rules governs civil procedure, criminal procedure, evidence, and appellate procedure in the federal courts. When citing the *Federal Rules of Procedure*, cite to these special subject matter codes directly, even though they are also contained in the *United States Code*.

6–40   Use the following abbreviations to cite to the various Federal Rules of Procedure:

Fed. R. Civ. P.	Federal Rules of Civil Procedure
Fed. R. Crim. P.	Federal Rules of Criminal Procedure
Fed. R. App. P.	Federal Rules of Appellate Procedure
Fed. R. Evid.	Federal Rules of Evidence

6–41   When referring to a federal rule of procedure, cite the rule in its abbreviated form, followed by the rule number.

Fed. R. Civ. P. 26.

Fed. R. Crim. P. 21(a).

Fed. R. App. P. 45.

Fed. R. Evid. 410.

6–42   A cited procedural rule may include section and subsection numbers. Cite sections and subsections as they appear in the codes, with upper- or lowercase letters, arabic numerals, or upper- or lowercase roman numerals. Use parentheses, brackets, and punctuation as they are written in the rule. Do not space between the rule number or any section or subsection.

Fed. R. Civ. P. 26**(b)(3).**

Fed. R. Civ. P. 26**(b)(4)(A)(i).**

Fed. R. Crim. P. 16**(a)(2)(b).**

Federal Rules of Appellate Procedure

6–43   The 13 federal appellate courts have rules governing procedures to be followed in those courts at the circuit level. Each circuit has its own operating rules. A rule is cited in its abbreviated form, followed by the rule number.

Fed. R. App. P. 39.

State Statutes

6–44   Statutes enacted by the 50 states are published chronologically as session laws called acts, public laws, resolutions, or other names. State laws are further classified into codes or statutes.

Elements of State Statutes

6–45   The elements of state statutes consist of the following:

Name of the state (abbreviated) **[see Table 6.2]**

Name of the statute or code

Number, where appropriate

Section or chapter number

Year (in parentheses)

Publisher, editor, or compiler, where appropriate

6–46 State statutes may be referred to as Codes, Code Annotated, Revised Statute, Statute Annotated, or other names; they may be identified by title number, section number, or chapter number.

6–47 The numbers of the codes or statutes may be written within parentheses, with periods, with hyphens, or with a combination of punctuation. Follow the format of the particular document cited. When citing section numbers, use the symbol § (or §§ for inclusive or nonconsecutive section numbers).

Citing State Statutes

6–48 When citing a state statute or code, indicate the name of the state in its abbreviated form (see Table 6.2), followed by appropriate words identifying the statute or code. Then indicate the section number(s). Many state codes and statutes are published by private companies. When appropriate, cite the name of the publisher, editor, or compiler in parentheses, followed by the year of publication.

> Cal. **Stat. Ann.** § 2311 (West 2003)
>
> Fla. **Stat. Ann.** § 1401 (West 1990)
>
> Haw. **Rev. Stat.** § 710.12
>
> Ind. **Code Ann.** § 22-9-1-1
>
> Minn. **Stat.** § 257.022 (1990)
>
> R.I. **Gen. Laws** § 18-13-1 (1988)

6–49 If a statute appears only in a supplement or a pocket part, cite the publication and the copyright date.

> Alaska Stat. § 1401 **(Supp. V 1986).**
>
> Haw. Rev. Stat. § 707-702.5 **(Supp. 1992).**

If a statute has been published in a hardbound volume and an amendment appears in a supplement or a pocket part, cite the original date of the statute; identify the supplement or pocket part and its publication date in parentheses.

> Vt. Stat. Ann. tit. 16 § 822(a)(1) **(1989 & Supp. 1999)**

State Subject Matter Codes

6–50 Some states publish their codes in separate subject matter volumes. In such cases, cite the name of the subject matter code in its abbreviated form. Indicate the publisher and the copyright date in parentheses. If a code amendment appears in a supplement or a pocket part, identify it along with the publication date (see 6–49).

```
Cal. Veh. Code § 11506 (West 2000)
Tex. Fam. Code § 162.005 (2003)
West's Ann. Cal. Bus. & Prof. Code § 17200
```

Legislative Materials

6–51 Legislative materials include bills, resolutions, reports of hearings, and committee reports produced by the United States Senate or House of Representatives or by a state legislature. Such materials trace a piece of legislation from its introduction through committee discussions and debates to final enactment.

Federal Legislation

6–52 The United States Congress meets for a two-year period that consists of two sessions. The first year of the congressional period is called the First Session *(1st Sess.)*; the second period, the Second Session *(2d Sess.)*. The First Congress met in 1789–91; thus members of the Senate and the House of Representatives meeting in 2005–2006 comprise the 109th Congress. Abbreviate Congress as *Cong.*

```
George W. Bush, State of the Union Message, 109th
Cong., 2d Sess. (January 31, 2006).
```

Congressional Record

6–53 The *Congressional Record* (abbreviated *Cong. Rec.*) contains bills that have been introduced and/or passed by either house of Congress.

Committee Reports

6–54 As bills are discussed in committees and members agree on their content, a committee report of that committee is published. The House and the Senate each publishes such reports, which courts refer (and defer) to as Congress's *legislative intent* for enacting a law.

United States Code Congressional and Administrative News

6–55 House and Senate Committee Reports are also published in an unofficial source, the *United States Code Congressional and Administrative News* (abbreviated *U.S.C.C.A.N.*), published by West Publishing.

Elements of Legislative Materials

6–56 The elements of legislative materials are as follows:

> Name of the legislative body
>
> Number of the document
>
> Number of the term of Congress
>
> Volume number, where appropriate
>
> Name of the publication
>
> Year of publication

House and Senate Bills

6–57 When citing a bill introduced by the House of Representatives, identify that legislative body as *H.R.* When citing a bill introduced by the Senate, indicate that body as *S.* Space once after the abbreviation, and keyboard the bill number in arabic figures.

> **H.R.** 2887
>
> **S.** 1789

6–58 When a bill is published in the *Congressional Record*, cite the complete House or Senate bill. Include the volume number of the *Congressional Record* and the page number. Include the year in parentheses.

> S. 338, 101st Cong., 1st Sess., 135 **Cong. Rec.** 4 (1989).
>
> H.R. 3445, 103d Cong., 1st Sess., 139 **Cong. Rec.** 8 (1993).

Committee Reports

6–59 When citing a House or Senate committee report on a bill, indicate the legislative body, the report number, the Congress and the session of Congress, the page number(s) of the bill, and the year (in parentheses).

> H.R. **Rep. No.** 23, 97th Cong., 1st Sess. 20 (1981).
>
> S. **Rep. No.** 84, 101st Cong., 1st Sess. 951 (1989).
>
> H.R. **Rep. No.** 358, 103d Cong., 1st Sess. 8 (1993).

Administrative and Executive Materials

6–60 Administrative and executive materials include federal rules and regulations, agency reorganizations, opinions, presidential papers, presidential messages or addresses to Congress, executive orders, and administrative law court orders. These materials are published in the *Federal Register* as they are issued. When codified, they are published in Title 3 of the *Code of Federal Regulations* (abbreviated *C.F.R.*).

6–61 If material does not appear in the *C.F.R.* because it was issued recently, cite the executive order or proclamation to the *Federal Register* (abbreviated *Fed. Reg.*). The *Federal Register* is cited by volume and page number with the year written in parentheses. A comma separates every three digits to the left in the number of the orders and in the page numbers.

> Exec. Order No. 13,318, 68 **Fed. Reg.** 66,317 (2003)

6–62 Administrative laws include those enacted by specialized government agencies at the federal, state, or local levels. These agencies function independent of the executive, judicial, and legislative branches of the government. Within each agency are departments, authorities, divisions, boards, or offices that make rules, enforce administrative orders, render administrative decisions and opinions, and interpret regulations.

Federal Administrative Materials

6-63 Federal administrative materials consist of codifications of regulations and any amendments contained in the *Code of Federal Regulations* (abbreviated *C.F.R.*). These materials are arranged by 50 topics similar to those contained in the *United States Code*. Updates to *C.F.R.* entries are contained in the *Federal Register.*

Elements of Administrative Citations

6-64 Elements of an administrative or executive order consist of the following:

> Number of the title
>
> *Code of Federal Regulations (C.F.R.)*
>
> Section or page (where appropriate)
>
> Year of publication

Citing Administrative Materials

6-65 When citing administrative and executive materials, cite to the official *Code of Federal Regulations (C.F.R.)* even though the same materials are also published in the *Federal Register*, the *United States Code*, *United States Code Service*, *United States Code Service Annotated*, and *United States Code Congressional and Administrative News*. Cite the number of the title, followed by *C.F.R.*, and the section or page number. Include the publication year in parentheses.

> 29 **C.F.R.** § 1926.64 (2005)
>
> 42 **C.F.R.** § 413.1 at 602 (2005)
>
> 26 **C.F.R.** § 1.31-2 (rev. April 2005)

6-66 A commonly known federal rule or regulation may also be cited by its popular name, followed by the citation to the *C.F.R.*

> **School Breakfast Program,** 7 C.F.R. § 220 (1991)

6-67 If a federal regulation has not yet been codified in *C.F.R.*, cite the *Federal Register*. Include in parentheses the citation to the proposed *C.F.R.* codification if such information is indicated in the *Federal Register*.

> 71 Fed. Reg. 36,979 (2006) [to be codified at 7 **C.F.R. § 457]**

Presidential Proclamations and Executive Orders

6-68 Identify the name of the executive order, citing to the *Code of Federal Regulations (C.F.R.)*. Include a citation to the *United States Code* to indicate where the order or proclamation is reprinted. If the *U.S.C.* is not available, cite next to *United States Code Service* or *United States Code Annotated*.

> `Exec. Order No.` 12,866, 7 `C.F.R.` § 457 (2006), `reprinted`
> `in` [volume no.] U.S.C. § [number] [year]

Presidential Addresses and Messages

6–69   Identify the title of the president's address or message, a description of the nature of the address, and the date of the address. Include a reference to indicate where the address is reprinted.

> `Bill Clinton, "Our Common Humanity Is What's Most Im-`
> `portant," Commencement Address to Cornell University`
> `(May 29, 2004), reprinted in` *The Los Angeles Times,*
> `June 13, 2004, at M1.`

6–70   If material has not yet been codified in *C.F.R.*, cite the executive or presidential order to the *Federal Register (Fed. Reg.)*. Indicate the volume number and page number; include the year in parentheses.

> `Exec. Order No.` 12,926, 59 ***Fed. Reg.*** `472,271 (1994)`
>
> `Exec. Order No.` 13,402, 71 ***Fed. Reg.*** `27,945 (2006)`
>
> `Proclamation No.` 7973, 71 ***Fed. Reg.*** `3,199 (2006)`

Advisory Opinions

6–71   Formal advisory opinions include those rendered by the attorney general's office. When citing such advisory opinions, include the volume number, the name of the advisory agency and type of opinion, and the page number. Keyboard the year of the opinion in parentheses.

> Opinion: `Attorney General's Opinion, No. 47 issued in`
> `1985, dealing with Treasury Regulations, at`
> `page 16`
>
> Citation: `47` **`Op. Att'y Gen.`** `16 (1985).`
>
> Opinion: `Louisiana Attorney General's Opinion No. 82-630,`
> `paragraph 25,658, issued July 27, 1982, dealing`
> `with the 1984 Copyright Law Decision`
>
> Citation: `82-630 La.` **`Op. Att'y Gen.`** `¶ 25,658 (1982).`
>
> Opinion: `Nebraska Attorney General's Opinion No. 06007`
> `issued May 25, 2006, regarding whether an origi-`
> `nal bill of sale is required by the Nebraska`
> `Brand Act in sales transactions of cattle.`
>
> Citation: `No. 06007 Neb.` **`Op. Att'y Gen.`** `¶ 2 (2006).`

6–72   The popular name of the advisory opinion may also be included in the citation. Keyboard the name, followed by a comma and a space, before the citation.

> **Treasury Regulation,** 47 Op. Att'y Gen. 16 (1985).
>
> **1984 Copyright Law Dec.,** 82-630 La. Op. Att'y Gen. ¶ 25,658 (1982).

Administrative Decisions

6–73   Administrative decisions are made by administrators of the various government agencies. When citing an administrative decision, include the complete name of the party or the title of the subject matter. Cite the volume, name of the administrative agency (abbreviated), the published source, the page or section number, and the year in parentheses. If a specific paragraph number is cited, include it with either the paragraph symbol (¶) or the abbreviation *para*.

> Decision: The Great Atlantic and Pacific Tea Co., Inc., decision, published January 17, 1982, by Commerce Clearing House
>
> Citation: <u>Great Atlantic & Pacific Tea Co.</u>, 1982 **N.L.R.B. Dec.** (CCH), ¶ 17,289 (1982).

Case Law

6–74   Cases refer to opinions that have been decided by appellate courts at the federal and state levels. These opinions are reported, or published, in volumes of federal reporters, state reporters, regional reporters, and other publications. Cases are cited or referred to in legal memorandums, court documents, briefs, and other legal writings.

6–75   The information that must be included in a case citation (or "cite") depends on the purpose and the intended recipient of a particular document; whether the document will be presented to a court in one's own jurisdiction, to a court in another jurisdiction, or to the U.S. Supreme Court; or whether a legal memorandum, court brief, or scholarly work (such as a treatise or journal article) is being prepared.

6–76   Cases cited in any legal document or published work should follow the standardized citation format as outlined in *The Bluebook: A Uniform System of Citation* (known as the *Harvard Bluebook*). However, some state court jurisdictions may require a different format when cases are cited in documents prepared for courts within those jurisdictions. Follow the appropriate statutory requirements and court rules.

Elements of Case Citations

6–77   Case citations contain the following elements:

> Name of the case   **[see 6–82 • 6–104]**
>
> Name(s) of the reporter(s) in which the case is published **[see 6–105 • 6–120 and 6–123 • 6–135]**

Court and jurisdiction, if appropriate, in parentheses
[see 6–121 • 6–122]
Date on which the case was decided   **[see 6–119]**

A citation may also include the following additional information:
Parallel citation   **[see 6–141 • 6–148]**
Prior history of the case   **[see 6–120]**

Format of Case Citations

6–78 There are two ways to cite case names in legal documents: (1) case name cited as a source note and (2) case name cited in textual sentences.

Citation as a Source Note

6–79 As a *source note*, the case name is placed outside the sentence or discussion as a reference or credit to the quoted or paraphrased information. The elements of a source note are generally heavily abbreviated. (See 6–81 • 6–148.) A source note may appear with various citation signals, identifying relevance, priority, and/or significance of the source note to the citation. (See 6–206 • 6–209.)

Citation in Textual Sentences

6–80 A case name appearing in *textual sentences* becomes an integral part of the sentence structure and meaning and relates to the concept or discussion of the sentence. The elements of the case name are generally spelled out rather than heavily abbreviated so the reader can see the complete case citation and its relevance to the sentence context. The case name must be preceded or followed by appropriate wording to form a complete sentence. (See 6–149 • 6–152.)

> In *Sell v. U.S.,* **539 U.S. 166 (2003),** the Court had to decide, among other issues, whether a defendant's choice not to "to take drugs voluntarily . . . may mean lengthy confinement in an institution for the mentally ill . . . ."

> The Court in *Sell v. U.S.,* **539 U.S. 166, 181 (2003),** had to decide, among other issues, whether a defendant's choice not to "to take drugs voluntarily . . . may mean lengthy confinement in an institution for the mentally ill. . . ."

Citation as a Source Note

6–81 A citation as a source note stands alone to provide a reference for the reader. A period follows the entire case citation.

> "Hearsay is a statement, other than one made by the declarant while testifying, that is 'offered in evidence to prove the truth of the matter asserted.' Fed. R. Evid. 801(c)." *U.S. v. Serrano,* **434 F.3d 1003, 1004 (7th Cir. 2006).**

Name of Case

6–82 The case name contains the names of the parties in the dispute. The parties may consist of one or more plaintiffs or defendants. Parties may be individuals, companies, organizations, cities, states, the federal government, or government agencies. The parties may be designated in the court opinions as plaintiff and defendant, appellant and appellee, or appellant and respondent. Abbreviations, where appropriate, are used to identify the parties to save space. (See Table 6.5.)

Parties: Tennessee Student Assistance Corporation, as petitioner; and Pamela L. Hood, as respondent.

Citation: *Tennessee Student A. C. v. Hood,* 541 U.S. 440, 158 L. Ed. 2d 764, 124 S. Ct. 1905 (2004).

6–83 Capitalize the first letter of each party's name and other important words. Separate the parties' names with a lowercase *v.* (meaning "versus"). Use a continuous underscore to underline the words and spaces in the case name; or keyboard all words in the name in italics. Keyboard a comma and a space after the case name.

Case name underscored: **Miranda v. Arizona,** 384 U.S. 436, 16 L. Ed. 2d 694, 86 S. Ct. 1602 (1966).

Case name italicized: *Miranda v. Arizona,* 384 U.S. 436, 16 L. Ed. 2d 694, 86 S. Ct. 1602 (1966).

Individual as a Party

6–84 When the dispute involves one individual as plaintiff (or appellant) or one individual as defendant (or respondent), cite the party's name by surname (last name) only. Always adhere to the surname-only rule.

Parties: Shirley Ree Smith, petitioner-appellant, and Gwendolyn Mitchell, Warden, respondent-appellee.

Citation: *Smith v. Mitchell,* 437 F.3d 884 (9th Cir., 2006).

Parties: Henry G. Baxter and Jody Amanda Baxter

Citation: *Baxter v. Baxter,* 423 F.3d 363 (3d Cir. 2005).

Foreign Names

6–85 When a party's complete name is a foreign name or when the surname and given name (first name) cannot be distinguished, cite the complete name.

Parties: The United States government and Ahmed Omar Abu Ali

Citation: *United States v. **Ahmed Omar Abu Ali,*** 395 F. Supp. 2d 338 (E.D. Va 2005).

Parties: Fong Yue Ting and the United States government
Citation: ***Fong Yue Ting*** v. *United States*, 149 U.S. 698,
           133 S. Ct. 1016, 37 L. Ed. 905 (1893).

Party's Legal Status, Designation, or Description

6–86 The complete case name as shown in the opinion itself will include the
legal status, designation, or other description of a party, such as *administrator*, *guardian*, *trustee*, *executor*, or *plaintiff-appellant*. Disregard such
descriptive words when citing cases.

Parties: The Wilderness Society, appellant, and Gale A.
           Norton, Secretary of the United States
           Department of the Interior, and Fran Mainella,
           Director, National Park Service, appellees
Citation: ***The Wilderness Soc.*** v. ***Norton,*** 434 F.3d 584
           (D.C. Cir. 2006).

Parties: Kenton E. Moore, as Trustee, etc., plaintiff
           and appellant, and Nancy A. Shaw, et al.,
           defendants and appellants
Citation: ***Moore*** v. ***Shaw,*** 10 Cal. Rptr. 3d 154 (Cal. App.
           2d Dist. 2004).

Name and/or Initial(s) Only

6–87 When a party's name is written with only a surname, given name and surname initial, or only initial(s) to preserve confidentiality or to shorten the
citation, include the initials in the citation. The abbreviation *In re*, meaning
"in the matter of" or "petition of," precedes the surname and/or initial(s).

Case: Dissolution proceedings regarding the Olsens
Citation: *In re Marriage of* ***Olsen***, 24 Cal. App. 4th 1702
           (1994).

Case: Bankruptcy proceedings in the matter of an
           individual, Flaherty
Citation: *In re* ***Flaherty,*** 335 B.R. 481 (Bkrtcy. D.
           Mass. 2005).

6–88 When only initials are used in the case name, keyboard the initials with a
period in between; but do not space between the initials.

Case: Proceedings involving an unidentified child
           whose initials are W.A.
Citation: *In re* ***Baby Boy W.A.***, 773 N.Y.S.2d 255 (Surr.
           Ct., Broome Cty. 2004).

Case: Adoption proceedings by an unidentified person
           whose initials are GPB, Jr.
Citation: *In the Matter of the Adoption of Children by*
           GPB, Jr., 161 N.J. 396, 736 A.2d 1277 (1999).

Business as Party

6–89 Names of businesses include such designations as *Company* or *Co.*, *Incorporated* or *Inc.*, *Corporation* or *Corp.*, and *Limited* or *Ltd.* Names may also identify the nature or type of business such as *Manufacturing*, *Railway*, *Railroad*, *Bank*, *Insurance*, or *Investment.* Cite the business name, using common abbreviations for designating business entities as listed in Table 6.5.

Parties: Massachusetts Mutual Life Insurance Company, et al., and Doris Russell

Citation: *Massachusetts* **Mut. Life Ins. Co.** *v. Russell*, 473 U.S. 134, 105 S. Ct. 3085, 87 L. Ed. 2d 96 (1985).

Case: Neutrino Development Corporation and Sonosite, Inc.

Citation: Neutrino Development **Corp.** *v. Sonosite,* **Inc.**, 410 F. Supp 2d 529 (S.D. Tex. 2006).

6–90 If the business name includes words descriptive of the company (such as *R.R.* or *Corp.*), disregard any additional abbreviations as *Inc.* and *Ltd.* The name of the company is sufficient to identify the party as a business. When two or more initials appear together, follow each with a period but do not space between them.

Parties: The Atchison, Topeka & Santa Fe Railway Co. and John C. Hadley

Citation: *Atchison,* **T. & S.F. Ry. Co.** *v. Hadley*, 168 Okla. 588, 35 P.2d 463 (1934).

Parties: The Wisconsin Central Railroad Company and Price County

Citation: *Wisconsin* **Cent. R.R. Co.** *v. Price County*, 133 U.S. 496, 10 S. Ct. 341, 33 L. Ed. 687 (1889).

Parties: Grable & Sons Metal Products, Inc., and Darue Engineering & Manufacturing

Citation: *Grable & Sons Metal Prod. v. Darue Engineering & Mfg.*, 377 F.3d 592 (2004).

"The" in Business Name

6–91 Generally, when the word *The* appears as the first word in a business name, disregard it. However, include the word *The* when the "party" is an object or property involved in an *in rem* action.

Case: Dean Long, Jr., et al., and **The** Walt Disney Company, et al.

Citation: ***Long v. Walt Disney Co.,*** 10 Cal. Rptr. 3d 836 (Cal. App. 2 Dist. 2004).

Case: The action involved *The Fred Smartley,
            Jr.*, a barge.

Citation: ***The*** *Fred Smartley, Jr.*, 108 F.2d 603 (C.A.
            Va. 1940).

Individual's Initial or Name in Business Name

6–92

When an individual's given name and/or initial is part of the business name, include the given name, initial, and surname followed by other words in the business name. When two or more initials appear together, follow each with a period but do not space between them.

Parties: Norman I. Krug Real Estate Investment, Inc., as
            plaintiff and appellant, and Roman Praszker,
            et al., as defendants and respondents

Citation: ***Norman I.*** *Krug Real Estate v. Praszker*, 24
            Cal. Rptr. 2d 632 (Cal. App. 2 Dist. 1993).

Parties: J. C. Penney Co. and H. D. Lee Mercantile Co.

Citation: ***J.C.*** *Penney Co. v.* ***H.D.*** *Lee Mercantile Co.*,
            120 F.2d 949 (C.C.A. 1941).

Parties: U.S. Equal Employment Opportunity Commission
            and E. I. Du Pont De Nemours & Co.

Citation: *U.S. E.E.O.C. v.* ***E.I. Du Pont De Nemours*** &
            Co., 406 F. Supp. 2d 645 (E.D. La. 2005).

Geographical Words in Names

6–93

When a case name includes words relating to a geographic location, abbreviate geographical words where appropriate.

Parties: South Florida Water Management District and
            Miccosukee Tribe of Indians, et al.

Citation: ***S. Fla.*** *Water Mgmt. Dist. v. Miccosukee Tribe
            of Indians*, 541 U.S. 95, 124 S. Ct. 1537, 158
            L. Ed. 2d 264 (2004).

Parties: Town of Stratford, Connecticut, petitioner;
            and Federal Aviation Administration and Jane
            F. Garvey, Administrator, respondents

Citation: *Town of Stratford,* ***Conn.*** *v. F.A.A.*, 292 F.3d
            251 (D.C. Cir. 2002).

Organization or Association as a Party

6–94

Names of organizations and associations include such designations as *Association* or *Assn.* as well as other business designations. Cite the organization or association name, using common abbreviations for such entities as listed in Table 6.5.

Parties: Catholic Charities of Sacramento, Inc., and The
            Superior Court of Sacramento County; Department

of Managed Health Care, et al., Real Parties
in Interest

Citation: ***Catholic Charities*** *of Sacramento v. Sup. Ct.,*
10 Cal. Rptr. 3d 283, 32 Cal. 4th 527, 95 P.3d
67 (2004).

Parties: Engine Manufacturers Association, et al., and
South Coast Air Quality Management District,
et al.

Citation: *Engine* ***Mfrs. Ass'n*** *v. South Coast Air Quality*
Management ***Dist.****, 541 U.S. 246 (2004).*

Labor Unions as Parties

6–95 Names of labor unions are generally lengthy; however, any abbreviated
form of such names must be descriptive of the party involved. Generally,
cite the party name using the smallest identifying unit of the name, dis-
regarding other descriptive words. Omit information related to the union's
location (local, national, regional, etc.) or status.

Parties: Robert Murray, plaintiff; and Local 2620,
District Council 57, American Federation of
State, County, and Municipal Employees

Citation: *Murray v.* ***Local 2620****, District Council 57, 192*
F.R.D. 629 (N.D. Cal. 2000). [a Federal Rules
Decision opinion]

Union Craft/Industry Designation

6–96 When a union name includes the craft or industry designation, cite only
the first craft or industry given.

Parties: Lawrence Moore and International Brotherhood
of Electrical Workers, Local 6, et al.

Citation: *Moore v. Int'l Brotherhood of* ***Elec. Workers****,*
Local 6, 541 U.S. 1006, 124 S. Ct. 2035, 158
L. Ed. 2d 522 (2004).

Abbreviated Name/Acronym

6–97 When a union is commonly referred to by an abbreviated name or an acronym, cite the organization name using the standard abbreviation or acronym.

Parties: United Automobile, Aerospace and Agricultural
Implement Workers of America, Local 33, and
Kirk Golden, et al., and R. E. Dietz Company

Citation: ***UAW****, Local 33 v. R.E. Dietz Co., 996 F.2d 592*
(2d Cir. 1993).

Multiple Parties

6–98 When a dispute involves several parties as plaintiffs or defendants, cite
only the first-named plaintiff or defendant. Do not include the abbreviation

et al., any initials, any personal or professional titles, or other descriptive
words or legal status.

Parties: Iseut G. Velez-Rivera; Fernando Pena-Castro,
             plaintiffs-appellants; and Hon. Juan Agosto-
             Alicea, in his personal capacity and in his
             official capacity as President of the Govern-
             ment Development Bank; Government Development
             Bank of Puerto Rico; Alba Caballero-Fuentes;
             Lilliam Jimenez-Montijo, defendants-appellees.

Citation: *Velez-Rivera v. Agosto-Alicea,* 437 F.3d 145
             (1st Cir. 2006).

Parties: Tritent International Corp.; Dwi, LLC; and
             Cibahia Tabacos Especias Ltda.; and Common-
             wealth of Kentucky

Citation: *Tritent Int'l Corp. v. Kentucky,* 395 F. Supp.
             2d 521 (E.D. Ky. 2005).

Governments as Parties

6–99 Governments and governmental agencies—the United States, states, cities,
counties, or other municipalities—are involved in both civil and criminal
legal disputes. In criminal actions, governments and their various agencies
are the prosecuting parties; in civil actions, the government may be either
the plaintiff or the defendant.

United States of America as Party

6–100 When the federal government is a party to an action, cite it as *United
States.* Do not abbreviate.

Parties: The federal government and Merrill D. Olvey, Jr.
Citation: *United States* v. *Olvey,* 437 F.3d 804
             (8th Cir. 2006).

Parties: The federal government and Roberto Serrano
Citation: *United States* v. *Serrano,* 434 F.3d 1003
             (7th Cir. 2006).

Federal Government Agency

6–101 When a specific agency of the federal government is a party in an action,
cite the agency name in its standard abbreviated form or acronym.

Parties: The Food and Drug Administration and Brown &
             Williamson Tobacco Corp.

Citation: *FDA* v. *Brown & Williamson,* 529 U.S. 120, 120
             S. Ct. 1291, 146 L. Ed. 2d 121 (2000).

Parties: Hoffman Plastic Compounds, Inc., and National
             Labor Relations Board

Citation: *Hoffman Plastic Compounds v. NLRB,* 835 U.S.
             137, 122 S. Ct. 1275, 152 L. Ed. 2d 271 (2002).

Parties:	The Equal Employment Opportunity Commission and The A. E. Staley Manufacturing Co.
Citation:	**EEOC** *v. A.E. Staley Mfg. Co.*, 711 F.2d 780 (7th Cir. 1983).

Government Agency/Representative as Party

6–102   When a governmental agency—commission, department, agency, bureau, etc.—is represented by an individual agent or representative in an action, cite the individual's name and his or her title. Such case names may be lengthy; follow accepted forms of abbreviation.

Parties:	John D. Ashcroft, Attorney General, et al, and The Free Speech Coalition, et al.
Citation:	**Ashcroft** *v. Free Speech Coalition*, 535 U.S. 234, 122 S. Ct. 1389, 152 L. Ed. 2d 403 (2002).
Parties:	Donald H. Rumsfeld, Secretary of Defense; and Jose Padilla and Donna R. Newman, as next friend of Jose Padilla.
Citation:	**Rumsfeld** *v. Padilla*, 542 U.S. 426, 124 S. Ct. 2711, 159 L. Ed. 2d 513 (2004).

State as Party

6–103   When a state is a party in an action, cite the state name as *State*, *People, or Commw.* (for "Commonwealth"), as appropriate for the jurisdiction. The citation to the specific state reporter will identify the party as one of the 50 states and which state is involved in the action.

Parties:	Randall L. Frank and the State of Michigan, acting through the Michigan Unemployment Agency of Consumer & Industry Services
Citation:	*Frank v.* **State** *of Michigan*, 261 B.R. 909 (E.D. Mich. 1999). [Barkruptcy Reporter case]
Parties:	State of Kansas and Roy D. Woodling
Citation:	**State** *of Kansas v. Woodling*, 957 P.2d 398 (Kan. 1998).
Parties:	People of the State of New York and Ronald T. Esposito
Citation:	**People** *v. Esposito*, 640 N.Y.S.2d 274 (A.D. 3 Dept. 1996).
Parties:	The People of the State of California and One 1941 Cadillac Club Coupe
Citation:	**People** *v. One 1941 Cadillac Club Coupe*, 63 Cal. 2d 418, 147 P.2d 49 (1944).

State Agent or Representative as Party

6–104   When a state governmental agency—commission, department, or board or a city or municipality—is a party in an action, identify the name of the agency and/or its representative as well as the geographic entity as a city, township, etc. Such case names may be lengthy; follow accepted forms of abbreviation.

Parties:	Robert James Tennard and Doug Dretke, Director, Texas Department of Criminal Justice, Correctional Institutions Division
Citation:	*Tennard v.* **Tex. Dep't of Crim. Just.**, 542 U.S. 274, 124 S. Ct. 2562, 159 L. Ed. 2d 384 (2004).
Parties:	Timothy Sullivan, et al., and City of Augusta
Citation:	*Sullivan v. City of* **Augusta**, 406 F. Supp. 2d 92 (D. Me. 2005).
Parties:	Cleveland Holloway and Wyoming Game and Fish Commission
Citation:	*Holloway v.* **Wyo. Game and Fish Comm.**, 2005 Wy. 144, 122 P.3d 959 (2005).
Parties:	Town of St. John, Indiana, and the State Board of Tax Commissioners
Citation:	*Town of St. John v.* **State Bd.**, 665 N.E.2d 965 (Ind. Tax 1996).

Reporter Name

6–105 The key element in a case citation is the name of the reporter in which the complete court opinion is published. This information refers the reader to one or more sources where the court's opinion appears. The reporter name may also identify the jurisdiction and the court that decided a particular case.

6–106 The United States Supreme Court, some federal courts, and most of the state courts publish their opinions in *official reporters*. The West Publishing Company publishes *unofficial reporters* for all court cases that are also reported in the official reporters. The Lawyers Co-operative Publishing Company also publishes unofficial reporters for United States Supreme Court and federal court opinions. The Bureau of National Affairs (BNA) publishes Supreme Court opinions weekly in *United States Law Week* (abbreviated *U.S.L.W.*). A particular case may appear in at least four different reporters:

The 2000 *FDA v. Brown & Williamson* decision is reported in 529 **U.S.** 120 (official reporter), 120 **S. Ct.** 129 (unofficial West reporter), 146 **L. Ed. 2d** 121 (unofficial Lawyers Co-operative reporter).

The 2005 *Bowling v. Kerry* decision of the United States District Court, Eastern District, in Missouri is reported in 406 **F. Supp. 2d** 1057 (West Federal Supplement, 2d Series, reporter for U.S. District Court cases).

The 1990 *U.S. v. Haggerty* decision is reported in 496 **U.S.** 310 (official reporter), 110 **S. Ct.** 2404 (unofficial West reporter), 110 **L. Ed. 2d** 287 (unofficial Lawyers Co-operative reporter), 58 **U.S.L.W.** 4744 (unofficial BNA reporter).

6–107   Reporters are published in series of bound volumes, with each volume numbered consecutively as issued. As a series grows and the number of volumes increases, the publisher begins a new series of numbered volumes. The subsequent series number is identified after the reporter name.

Vermule v. Shaw, 4 **Cal.** 214 (1854). **[citation in first series of *California Reports*]**

Leonard v. Superior Court, 4 **Cal. 2d** 215 (1935). **[citation in second series of *California Reports*]**

People v. Montalvo, 4 *Cal. 3d* 328 (1971). **[citation in third series of *California Reports*]**

Catholic Charities of Sacramento v. Sup. Ct., **32 Cal. 4th 527** (2004). **[citation in fourth series of *California Reports*]**

Elements of a Reporter Citation

6–108   A citation to a reporter consists of the following elements:

Name of case **[see 6–82 • 6–104]**
Volume number in the series **[see 6–109]**
Reporter name and series, if appropriate **[see 6–110 • 6–114]**
Beginning page number of the opinion **[see 6–115 • 6–118]**
Year of the decision (in parentheses) **[see 6–119]**

Volume Number

6–109   The number of the volume in which a case is published appears on the spine of the reporter. Keyboard the volume number in arabic numerals. Space once after the number.

Sell v. U.S., **539** U.S. 166. **[Case reported in volume 539 of the reporter]**

Orion IP, LLC, v. Staples, Inc., **406** F. Supp. 2d 717 (E.D. Tex. 2005). **[Case reported in volume 406 of the reporter]**

Citing Reporter Name

6–110   Keyboard the name of the reporter, using the appropriate form of abbreviation for the federal, state, and regional reporters (see Table 6.2).

Sell v. U.S., 539 **U.S.** 166 **[official reporter]**, 123 **S. Ct.** 2174 **[unofficial West reporter]**, 156 L. Ed. 2d 197 (2003). **[unofficial Lawyers Co-operative reporter]**

> *Orion IP, LLC, v. Staples, Inc.*, 406 **F. Supp. 2d** 717
> (E.D. Tex. 2005). **[Case reported in unofficial West Federal
> Supplement 2d Series]**

Abbreviations and Spacing

6–111 When citing abbreviations used in reporter names, follow the spacing
rules as outlined in *The Bluebook: A Uniform System of Citation (the
Bluebook).*

Capital Letters

6–112 When a name consists of a series of capital letters, do not space between
the letters.

U.S.	**[for *United States Reports*]**
R.I.	**[for Rhode Island Supreme Court]**
N.E.	**[for *North Eastern Reporter*]**
U.S.L.W.	**[for *United States Law Week*]**

Reporter and Series Number

6–113 When a series number (2d, 3d, 4th, etc.) follows a reporter name written
as a series of single letters, do not space between the reporter name and
the number. The series number is considered a single-letter abbreviation.

F.3d	**[for *Federal Reporter 3d Series*]**
S.W.2d	**[for *South Western Reporter 2d Series*]**
N.Y.S.2d	**[for *New York Supreme Court Reports 2d Series*]**

Multiple-Letter Abbreviations

6–114 When an abbreviation in a reporter name consists of two or more letters, space once between the abbreviations. If a series number follows the
reporter name, space once before the number.

F. Supp. 2d	**[for *Federal Supplement 2d Series*]**
S. Ct.	**[for *Supreme Court Reporter*]**
So. 2d	**[for *Southern Reporter 2d Series*]**
Cal. App. 4th	**[for *California Appellate Reporter 4th Series*]**
L. Ed. 2d	**[for *Lawyer's Edition 2d Series*]**

Page Number

6–115 The page number always refers to the number of the *first page* on which
an opinion appears in the reporter. Keyboard the page number in arabic
numerals; space once after the number.

> *Sell v. U.S.*, 539 U.S. **166**, 123 S. Ct. **2174**, 156 L. Ed.
> 2d **197** (2003). **[Beginning page numbers of opinions in official
> and unofficial reporters]**

Orion IP, LLC, v. Staples, Inc., 406 F. Supp. 2d **717** (E.D. Tex. 2005). **[Opinion begins on page 717]**

Specific Page Number(s) Cited

6–116 If cited information appears on the first page of the opinion, repeat the first page number. This tells the reader that the cited information appears on that specific page rather than the entire opinion itself. Keyboard a comma after the opinion's first page, followed by a space; then repeat the page number followed by a space.

Intel Corp. v. Advanced Micro. Dev., 542 U.S. **241, 242** (2004). **[The case begins on page 241; quoted or paraphrased information appears on page 242.]**

Inclusive Page Numbers

6–117 If inclusive pages of an opinion are to be cited, keyboard the *first page* on which an opinion appears in the reporter, followed by a comma and a space. Then keyboard the first page number of the range, a hyphen, and the last page number of the range of inclusive page numbers. Keyboard the page numbers in arabic numerals; space once after the number.

Sell v. U.S., 539 U.S. **166, 167–170** (2003). **[The case begins on page 166; quoted or paraphrased information appears on consecutive pages 167–170.]**

Nonconsecutive Page Numbers

6–118 If a citation refers to information that appears on one or more nonconsecutive pages of the opinion, keyboard the *first page* on which the opinion begins. Keyboard each page number followed by a comma and a space.

New York Times Co. v. Sullivan, 376 U.S. **254, 270, 277** (1964). **[The cited case begins on page 254; quoted or paraphrased information appears on pages 270 and 277.]**

People v. Calbo, 122 P.3d **1101, 1102, 1104** (Colo. O.P.D.J. 2005). **[The cited case begins on page 1101; quoted or paraphrased information appears on nonconsecutive pages 1102 and 1104.]**

Year of the Decision

6–119 The year refers to the year in which the case was decided and the opinion written. Keyboard the year in parentheses beginning one space after the page number(s). If several reporter citations are given, cite the date after the last reporter.

Stephen v. Ford Motor Co., 37 Cal. Rptr. 3d 9 (Cal. App. 2 Dist. **2005**).

Mosley v. Industrial Claim Appeals Office, 119 P.3d 576 (Colo. App. **2005**).

Case History

6–120 If a case was further appealed, the case citation must include an explanation of the history of the case: the subsequent action taken, which court
received the appeal, and the date of any subsequent action to regional
reporters. Keyboard the citation for the original decision, including any
parallel citations to regional reporters (see 6–123 • 6–129), followed by a
comma and a space. Identify the subsequent action—either underscored
or in italics—in lowercase letters followed by a comma and a space. Then
give the case citation(s) for the subsequent court decision(s).

> *United States v. Marshall*, 908 F.2d 1312 (7th Cir.
> 1990), **aff'd subnom** *Chapman v. U.S.*, 500 U.S. 453, 111
> S. Ct. 1919, 114 L. Ed. 2d 524 (1991) **[In subsequent action
> in 1991, the court affirmed under new case name.]**

> *Shiavo ex rel. Schindler v. Shiavo*, 357 F. Supp. 2d
> 1378 (M.D. Fla.), **aff'd**, 403 F.3d 1223 (11th Cir. 2005),
> **reh'g en banc den.**, 403 F.3d 1261 (11th Cir. en banc),
> **stay den.**, 125 S. Ct. 1692 (2005) **[In subsequent action, the
> decision was affirmed; on a rehearing, the case was denied; ultimately,
> the stay was denied.]**

Court and Jurisdiction

6–121 Each case citation must identify the jurisdiction—whether federal or
state—and which court within that jurisdiction decided the case. Cases
decided by the United States Supreme Court identify that court and the
jurisdiction in which cases were decided; for example, a case cited in *U.S.*
refers to a U.S. Supreme Court case.

  The courts and jurisdictions of state cases that are or have been reported
in an official state reporter are also identified by the name of the state reporter
cited; for example, *Ala.* for an Alabama Supreme Court case; *Tex. App.* for a
Texas Court of Appeals case; and *La.* for a Louisiana Supreme Court case.

> *Wilsonville Heights Ass'n, Ltd. v. Dep't of Revenue*,
> 339 **Or.** 462 (2005) **[Oregon Supreme Court case]**

> *People v. Elliot*, 37 **Cal.** 4th 453 (2005) **[California
> Supreme Court case]**

Identifying Court and/or Jurisdiction

6–122 A citation to a reporter may not identify the federal court or the name of
the state or the court that decided the case. The state's court opinions may
have been published in an official reporter that has since been discontinued; all cases decided in the various state courts were or are currently
published in one official state reporter; or the opinions are published only
in a regional reporter. In these situations, the case citation must include

additional information to identify either or both the jurisdiction and the court. (See 6–123 • 6–129.)

Citing Regional Reporters

6–123 West Publishing Company arranges case opinions according to seven regions of the country and publishes a separate set of *regional reporters* for each of the regions. (See Table 6.6.) A regional reporter may be used as a *parallel citation* along with an official and/or unofficial citation; or it may be used by itself. Since the citation to a regional reporter identifies only the region in which the case was decided, the specific court must be identified in parentheses.

6–124 A regional reporter is cited when a state's court decisions are published only in a regional reporter. For those states that have no official state reporter or whose official reporter has been discontinued, the regional reporters covering those states would contain decisions for those states' courts.

> *People v. Esposito*, 640 N.Y.S.2d 274 (A.D. 3 Dep't 1996)   **[Citation to a New York Supreme Court, Appellate Division, case cited in the regional West *New York Supplement*]**

> *In Re Estate of Johnson*, 119 P.3d 425 (Alaska 2005) **[Citation to an Alaska Supreme Court case cited in the regional *Pacific Reporter*]**

Elements of a Regional Reporter Citation

6–125 Citations to a regional reporter contain the following elements:

Name of the case   **[see 6–82 • 6–104]**

Volume number   **[see 6–107]**

Name of the regional reporter and series, if appropriate **[see 6–110 • 6–114]**

Beginning page number of the opinion   **[see 6–115 • 6–118]**

State and state court, if appropriate   **[see 6–121 • 6–122; 6–126 • 6–129]**

Year of the opinion   **[see 6–119]**

State Court Cases in Regional Reporters

6–126 When citing a state court case published in a regional reporter, cite the complete case name in the usual manner. (See 6–82 • 6–104.) Keyboard the volume number, the name of the regional reporter in its abbreviated form, and the page number. (See 6–109 • 6–124.) Keyboard the name of the state that decided the case (in its abbreviated form), followed by the year in which the case was decided, in parentheses. Space once between the state name and the year. When only the state abbreviation is given, it is assumed that the case was decided by the state's highest court.

> *Alvin v. St. Paul Saints Baseball Club, Inc.*, 672 N.W. 2d 570 **(Minn. Ct. App. 2003)**. [Citation to a Minnesota Appellate Court case cited in the *North Western Reporter*]

> *People v. Brown*, 119 P.3d 486 **(Colo. App. 2004)**. [Citation to a Colorado Appellate Court case cited in the *Pacific Reporter*]

> *Helbush v. Helbush*, 122 P.3d 288 **(Haw. 2005)**. [Citation to a Hawaii Supreme Court case cited in the *Pacific Reporter*]

All State's Court Opinions Cited in One Official Reporter

6–127 When all cases of a state's courts are reported in *only* a regional reporter, the region in which the state is located is known but the particular state and court that decided the case are not identified. Cite the case name, volume number and name of the regional reporter, and the page number in the usual manner. Then keyboard the name of the state and the court in their abbreviated forms, followed by the year in which the case was decided, in parentheses.

> *McHose v. Physician & Clinic Serv, Inc.*, 548 N.W. 2d 158 **(Iowa App. 1996)** [Case decided by the Iowa Appellate Court in 1996 and reported in the *North Western Reporter*]

States with Discontinued Reporter or No Official Reporter

6–128 When a state does not have an official reporter or its reporter has been discontinued, the case will be reported in a regional reporter. Because the regional reporter citation does not identify either the state or which court in that state decided the case, such information must be included in parentheses after the complete case citation. When only the state name is given, it is assumed that the case was decided by that state's highest court. If another state court decided the case, its name must be included after the state name.

> *State v. Kimsel*, 122 P.3d 1148 **(Haw. App. 2005)**. [Case decided by the Hawaii Appellate Court in 2005. No official reporter for Hawaii court cases after 1994; cases thereafter reported in the regional *Pacific Reporter*]

> *People v. Brown*, 119 P.3d 486 **(Colo. App. 2004)**. [Case decided by the Colorado Appellate Court in 2004. No official reporter for Colorado court cases; cases reported in the regional *Pacific Reporter*]

Citing to Regional Reporters Only

6–129 When a state case is being cited and submitted to a court *outside* its own jurisdiction, cite only to the regional reporter. The court receiving the document will likely have access to regional reporters and not reporters for the individual states. Keyboard the state name and the date in parentheses after the citation.

Helbush v. Helbush, 122 P.3d 288 (**Haw. 2005**) [Case decided by the Hawaii Supreme Court in 2005; reported in the *Pacific Reporter*]

People v. Calbo, 122 P.3d 1101 (**Colo. O.P.D.J. 2005**) [Case decided by the Colorado Office of the Presiding Disciplinary Judge of the Supreme Court in 2005; cited to the regional *Pacific Reporter*]

Alvin v. St. Paul Saints Baseball Club, Inc., 672 N.W. 2d 570 (**Minn. Ct. App. 2003**) [Case decided by the Minnesota Court of Appeal in 2003; cited to the regional *North West Reporter*]

Federal Courts

6–130 Citations to decisions of the circuit courts of appeals and those of the district courts do not indicate which federal court decided those cases. The respective court and its jurisdiction must be included in parentheses at the end of each citation. (See Table 6.3 and Figure 6.1 at the end of this unit.)

United States Courts of Appeals

6–131 Cases decided in the 13 U.S. Courts of Appeals are reported in the unofficial *Federal Reporter (F.)* or *Federal Reporter, 2d Series (F.2d)*. Use the following abbreviations for citing the number of the circuit courts:

First Circuit	1st Cir.
Second Circuit	2d Cir.
Third Circuit	3d Cir.
Fourth Circuit	4th Cir.
Fifth Circuit	5th Cir.
Sixth Circuit	6th Cir.
Seventh Circuit	7th Cir.
Eighth Circuit	8th Cir.
Ninth Circuit	9th Cir.
Tenth Circuit	10th Cir.
Eleventh Circuit	11th Cir.
District of Columbia District	D.C. Cir.
Federal Circuit	Fed. Cir.

Keyboard the name of the court and the year of the decision in parentheses; space once between the court name and the year.

U.S. v. Olvey, 437 F.3d 804 (**8th Cir. 2006**).

American Disability Ass'n, Inc. v. Chmielarz, 289 F.3d 1315 (**11th Cir. 2002**)

United States District Courts

6–132 Cases decided in the seven U.S. district courts are reported in the unofficial *Federal Supplement (F. Supp.)*. (See Table 6.3. and Figure 6.1.) Use abbreviations for citing district court cases. The abbreviations are written in capital letters and periods with no internal spacing.

Northern District	N.D.
Southern District	S.D.
Eastern District	E.D.
Western District	W.D.
Central District	C.D.
Middle District	M.D.
States with one District	D.

6–133 After the case citation, keyboard in parentheses the district court abbreviation in capital letters. Space once before keyboarding the abbreviated state name, followed by the date of the decision.

> *Neutrino Development Corp. v. Sonosite, Inc.,* 410 F. Supp. 2d 529 **(S.D. Tex. 2006)** **[Case decided in the Southern District Court in Texas in 2006]**

> *Bristol West Ins. Co. v. Whitt,* 406 F. Supp. 2d 771 **(W.D. Mich. 2005)** **[Case decided in the Western District Court in Michigan in 2005]**

Specialized Court Reporters

6–134 Case decisions for the special federal lower courts are published in the *Federal Reporter (F.)* and *Federal Reporter 2d (F.2d)* and in the *Federal Supplement (F. Supp.)*. Specialized reporters include those for the United States Claims Court and the Bankruptcy Court. Case decisions of the United States Tax Court are cited as *court decisions* although they are administrative agency decisions.

> *Estate of Huntington v. IRS,* 100 **T.C.** 313 (1993). **[Tax proceeding reported in the *United States Tax Court Reports*]**

> *In re Robert S. Miller,* 335 **B.R.** 335 (Bkrtcy. E.D. Pa. 2005) **[Bankruptcy proceeding reported in the *Bankruptcy Court Reporter*, Eastern Division of Pennsylvania)**

> *Town of St. John v. State Board,* 665 N.E.2d 965 (**Ind. Tax** 1996) **[Tax case decided in Indiana in 1996. No official reporter for Indiana; cases reported in the regional *North East Reporter*]**

Case History

6–135 If cases from the lower federal courts proceed to the apellate court level, those decisions will be published in one of the unofficial federal court reporters. Include the appropriate citations to any subsequent proceedings.

> *Bridgeport Music, Inc. v. Still N The Water Publ'g,* 327 F.3d 472 (6th Cir.), *cert. den.,* 540 U.S. 948, **124 S. Ct. 399, 157 L. Ed. 2d 279** (2003) **[Circuit Court case**

appealed to the Supreme Court; subsequent action reported in the unofficial *Supreme Court Reports* and the *Lawyers' Edition*]

Citing State Court Opinions

6–136 Twenty-eight of the 50 states publish official state reporters. Some publish a separate reporter for each level of their court system, and others publish only one reporter for all of its courts' decisions. (See Table 6.2.) Depending on the court and the jurisdiction, citations to state court case decisions may include not only the official reporter but also one or more unofficial reporters.

Elements of State Court Citations

6–137 Case citations for state court opinions include the following elements:

Name of the case   **[see 6–82 • 6–104]**

Volume number   **[see 6–109]**

Name of the state's official reporter, if available (abbreviated)

Beginning page number   **[see 6–115 • 6–118]**

Date on which the case was decided   **[see 6–119]**

A citation may also include the following information:

Name of the court (in parentheses)   **[see 6–121 • 6–123, 6–126]**

Jurisdiction of the court (in parentheses)   **[see 6–127 • 6–133]**

Prior history of the case   **[see 6–120]**

Citing Official State Reporters

6–138 For states that publish an official reporter for its opinions, cite the case name, volume number, beginning page number in the reporter, and year of the decision (in parentheses) in the usual manner. (See 6–126.)

State Reporter Name

6–139 The name of the state reporter is cited in its abbreviated form (see Table 6.2). When only the state name is cited, it is assumed that the decision was rendered by that state's highest court.

Wilsonville Heights Ass'n, Ltd. v. Dep't of Revenue, 339 **Or.** 462 (2005).   **[Case decided by the Oregon Supreme Court and reported in the state's official reporter]**

People v. Elliot, 37 **Cal. 4th** 453 (2005).   **[Case decided by the California Supreme Court and reported in the state's official reporter]**

Town of Hilton Head Island v. Morris, 324 **S.C.** 30 (1997).   **[Case decided by the South Carolina Supreme Court and reported in the state's official reporter]**

Unofficial State Reporter Name

6–140 If an unofficial state reporter for a state court opinion is available, include a parallel citation for the case.

Wilsonville Heights Ass'n, Ltd. v. Dep't of Revenue, 339 **Or.** 462, **122 P.3d 499** (2005). **[Case decided by the Oregon Supreme Court and reported in both the official state reporter and the unofficial regional *Pacific Reporter*]**

People v. Elliot, 37 **Cal. 4th** 453, **35 Cal. Rptr. 3d 759, 122 P.3d 968** (2005). **[Case decided by the California Supreme Court and reported in both the official and unofficial state reporters as well as the regional *Pacific Reporter*]**

Town of Hilton Head Island v. Morris, 324 **S.C.** 30, **484 S.E.2d 104** (1997). **[Case decided by the South Carolina Supreme Court and reported in both the official state reporter and the unofficial regional reporter]**

Regional Reporters

6–141 West Publishing Company's seven regional reporters provide alternative sources of published court decisions. Citations to a regional reporter are required when a state's official reporter is not available. If an official state reporter is available, it should be cited when appropriate. (See also 6–125.)

6–142 Regional reporters may be cited alone—without a citation to an official state reporter. Whether to include a regional reporter as a parallel citation or to include it as the main case citation depends on the jurisdiction to which a document will be submitted.

Document Submitted to Court of State Reported

6–143 If a state case is being submitted to a court of that state, cite the official reporter, if available. (See Table 6.2.) Also include a parallel citation to the appropriate West's regional reporter. (See 6–125.)

Avery v. Steele, 414 Mass. 450, **608 N.E.2d 1014** (1993). **[Case decided by the Massachusetts Supreme Court, citation presented to a Massachusetts court; reported in the regional *North Eastern Reporter*]**

Holloway v. Wyoming Game & Fish Comm., 205 Wyo. 144, **122 P.3d 959** (2005). **[Case decided by the Wyoming Supreme Court, citation presented to a Wyoming court; reported in the regional *Pacific Reporter*]**

People v. Elliot, 37 Cal. 4th 453, 35 Cal. Rptr. 3d 759, **122 P.3d 968** (2005). **[Case decided by the California Supreme Court, citation presented to a California court; reported in the regional *Pacific Reporter*]**

Credit Alliance Corp. v. Arthur Andersen & Co., 65 N.Y.2d 536, **493 N.Y.S.2d 435, 483 N.E.2d 110**

(1985). **[Citation to a New York case reported in the official and un-official New York reporters and the regional *North Eastern Reporter*]**

Document Submitted Outside of State Reported

6–144

If a state case is being submitted to a court outside that state, cite only to the regional reporter in which the case appears. The state's official reporter citation—even if one is available—is not included. Keyboard the state name and the date in parentheses. When only the state name is cited, it is assumed that the decision was rendered by the highest court in that state.

Alvin v. St. Paul Saints Baseball Club, Inc., 672 **N.W.2d 570 (Minn. Ct. App.** 2003). **[Case decided by a Minnesota court and submitted to an out-of-state court; citation to the North *Western Reporter*]**

People v. Brown, 119 **P.3d 486 (Colo. App.** 2004). **[Case decided by a Colorado court and submitted to an out-of-state court; citation to the *Pacific Reporter*]**

Wichman v. Naylor, 487 **N.W.2d 291 (Neb.** 1992). **[Case decided by the Nebraska Supreme Court and submitted to an out-of-state court; reported in the regional *North Western Reporter*]**

Henningsen v. Bloomfield Motors, Inc., 161 **A.2d 69 (N.J.** 1960). **[Citation to a New Jersey Supreme Court case reported in the regional *Atlantic Reporter*]**

Fairmount Glass Works v. Crunden-Martin Woodenware Co., **51 S.W. 196 (Ct. App. Ky.** 1899). **[Citation to a Kentucky Court of Appeal case reported in the regional *South Western Reporter*]**

State with No Official Reporter

6–145

When a state does not have an official reporter or it no longer publishes one, cite only to the appropriate regional reporter. Include the state name and the date in parentheses.

Alvin v. St. Paul Saints Baseball Club, Inc., 672 **N.W.2d** 570 (Minn. Ct. App. 2003). **[Minnesota Court cases have not been reported in an official state reporter since 1977; case reported in the regional *North West Reporter*]**

In re Estate of Johnson, 119 **P.3d** 425 (Alaska 2005). **[Alaska Supreme Court cases are not reported in an official state reporter; case reported in the regional *Pacific Reporter*]**

San Juan-Torregosa v. Garcia, 80 **S.W.3d** 539 (Tenn. Ct. App. 2002). **[Tennessee cases are not reported in an official state reporter; case reported in the regional *South West Reporter*]**

One Reporter for All Court Decisions

6–146

When a state reporter contains published cases of all its courts' opinions, the particular court that decided a case must be identified. Cite the state reporter and include a parallel citation to the regional reporter. Keyboard the name of the specific court that decided the case followed by the year, in parentheses.

> *McKaskle v. Industrial Comm'n of Ariz.*, 135 Ariz. 168, 659 P.2d 1313 **(Ariz. App. 1982).**

Court and Jurisdiction

6–147 When any citation, including one with a parallel citation, identifies the name of the state but not the particular court that decided the case, include the name of the court followed by the year in parentheses.

> *In re Baby Boy W.A.*, 773 N.Y.S.2d 255 **(Surr. Ct., Broome Cty.** 2004). **[Case decided in the Surrogate Court of Broome County, New York, in 2004]**

Prior History

6–148 When a case proceeds through the appellate process, either within the state or to a higher jurisdiction, its subsequent history must also be cited. Keyboard the original case citation, including any parallel citations; then either italicize or underscore the abbreviation(s) for any subsequent action.

> *Duarte v. Chino Community Hosp.*, 85 Cal. Rptr. 2d 521 (Ct. App. 1999) (***rev. den.*** 1999).
>
> *Shiavo ex rel. Schindler v. Shiavo,* 357 F. Supp. 2d 1378 (M.D. Fla.), ***aff'd,*** 403 F.3d 1223 (11th Cir.), ***reh'g en banc den.,*** 403 F.3d 1261 (11th Cir. en banc), ***stay den.,*** 125 S. Ct. 1692 (2005).

Case Citations in Textual Sentences

6–149 Case citations in *textual sentences* are those that appear within sentences in journal articles, treatises, and other legal publications. The citation is incorporated into the grammatical structure of the sentence so it must be preceded and/or followed by appropriate wording to form a complete sentence.

6–150 Case names appearing in textual sentences are not as heavily abbreviated, so more complete information about the parties is provided the reader. Any abbreviations used should follow the form set out in the *Bluebook.*

All other elements of case citations for state and federal opinions follow the standard format as discussed in 6–82 • 6–122, 6–130 • 6–135.

Citation at Beginning of Sentence

6–151 A cited case can begin the sentence or otherwise become the subject of the sentence. Keyboard a comma after the entire citation before continuing the sentence.

> ***Doe v. Attorney General,*** 487 N.W.2d 484 (Mich. App.
> 1992), dealt with the respective constitutional rights
> of infertile couples and prospective surrogate mothers
> under the state's Surrogate Parenting Act.
>
> ***Doe v. Attorney General,*** 487 N.W.2d 484, 485 (Mich.
> App. 1992), addressed the issue of whether plaintiffs–
> infertile couples and prospective surrogate mothers—
> were entitled to protection under the Due Process
> Clauses of both the state and the federal Constitutions
> regarding matters of child-bearing and specifically
> surrogate parenting.
>
> Referring to the Surrogate Parenting Act, ***Doe v.
> Attorney General,*** 487 N.W.2d 484, 485 (Mich. App. 1992),
> addressed whether the act had the effect of denying
> infertile couples and prospective surrogate mothers
> privacy rights guaranteed by the Fourteenth Amendment.

Citation in Middle of Sentence

6–152 A cited case appearing within the sentence can function grammatically in different ways; for example, as a direct object, an indirect object, an object of the preposition, and so on. Keyboard a comma after the entire citation.

> The issue in ***Doe v. Attorney General,*** 487 N.W.2d 484
> (Mich. App. 1992), was whether there was a compelling
> government interest intended by the Legislature to jus-
> tify its intrusion into a woman's surrogacy choice.
>
> As plaintiffs claimed in ***Doe v. Attorney General,*** 487
> N.W.2d 484, 485 (Mich. App. 1992), the Surrogate Par-
> enting Act had the effect of denying infertile couples
> and prospective surrogate mothers privacy rights guar-
> anteed by the Fourteenth Amendment.
>
> The Court found that ***Doe v. Attorney General,*** 487 N.W.2d
> 484, 485 (Mich. App. 1992), represented a situation in
> which the trial court had erroneously granted summary
> judgment in favor of the Defendant-Appellee.
>
> The Court summarized ***Doe v. Attorney General,*** 487
> N.W.2d 484, 489 (Mich. App. 1992), by setting forth
> two specific conditions under which surrogate parentage
> contracts would be void and unenforceable.

CITING SECONDARY AUTHORITY

6–153 Secondary authority consists of annotations, encyclopedias and dictionaries, restatements of the law, uniform laws, treatises and textbooks, and various legal periodicals and services.

Annotations

6–154 Annotations contain comprehensive analyses of significant cases and the laws and issues related to those cases. The *American Law Reports* (A.L.R.), published by the West Group Publishing Co., is published in five series plus a special series, *Federal Law Reports* (F.L.R.), covering federal legal issues.

6–155 When citing an annotation, cite the author's name (if available), the word *Annotation*, the title of the work, the *A.L.R.* or *F.L.R.* and its series number, the section number, and the page on which the cited material appears. Include in parentheses the date of the publication.

> Edward A. Nolfi, **Annotation,** Standing to Sue for Copyright Infringement Under 17 U.S.C.S. § 501(b), -F.L.R. 509 (1987).
>
> Admissibility of Sound Recordings in Evidence, **Annotation**, 58 A.L.R. 2d § 1034 (1991).
>
> Limitation of Actions: Invasion of Right of Privacy, **Annotation**, 33 A.L.R. 4th 479 (2004).

Dictionaries and Thesauruses

6–156 Dictionaries provide not only definitions of legal words and phrases but also spelling, pronunciation, and usage. Some dictionaries also provide citations to cases in which a particular word or term was defined. Specialized medical and technical dictionaries are also available. (See 12–5.) A thesaurus contains words and their synonyms and other words having similar meanings. Legal *word books* may contain a combination of definitions and synonyms.

6–157 When citing a dictionary, keyboard its name followed by the page number on which the word appears. Include in parentheses the edition and the year of publication.

> In foro conscientiae (meaning "in the forum of conscience") is the term used by courts to say that a "moral problem cannot be dealt with by . . . [a] court, but only in foro conscientiae"; i.e., that such matters must be dealt with "[p]rivately or morally rather than legally." **Black's Law Dictionary** 795 (8th ed. 2004).

Encyclopedias

6–158 Legal encyclopedias present in-depth discussions of various topics within a particular field of law but are not intended to be comprehensive works. Encyclopedias provide references to other sources of information, as well as to cases. Two legal encyclopedias are *American Jurisprudence 2d (Am. Jur. 2d)* published by West Group Publishing, and *Corpus Juris Secundum*

(*C.J.S.*) published by West Publishing Company. Encyclopedias are also available in state editions that cover fields of law relevant to those states.

> 23 **Am. Jur. 3d** Proof of Facts § 9B at 341–344 (1993).
>
> 24 **C.J.S.** Criminal Law § 1493 (1989) (Supp. 2004).

6–159 When citing an encyclopedia, keyboard the volume number, the name of the encyclopedia (in its abbreviated form), the topic, and the section number of the referenced text; keyboard the year of publication in parentheses. Include in parentheses the edition and the year of publication.

> 64 **Cal. Jur. 3d (Rev.)** Wills § 182 (1994).

Legal Periodicals

6–160 Periodicals include journals, law review articles, magazines, and other works that are published on a regular basis. When citing a legal periodical, keyboard the author's name (if available), title of the article (underscored or italicized), name of the periodical, date of the periodical, and beginning page number of the article (preceded by *at*).

> Kristin Henning, Loyalty, Paternalism, and Rights: Client Counseling Theory and the Role of Child's Consent in Delinquency Cases, 81 **Notre Dame L. Rev.** 245–324 (2005). **[law review article]**
>
> Michael Warburton, Toward Greater Certainty in Water Rights: Public Interests Require Inherent 'Uncertainty' to Support Constitutional Governance of Our States' Waters, 36 **McGeorge L. Rev.** 139–163 (2005). **[law review article]**
>
> John Gibeaut, A Matter Over Mind, **A.B.A. J.** (April 2006) at 33. **[professional journal article]**
>
> Charles Collier, Affirmative Action and the Decline of Intellectual Culture, **J. of Legal Education** (March/June 2005), at 3. **[professional publication article]**
>
> Ira S. Kuperstein, Determination of Cause of Damage to an Automobile, 29 **J. Forensic Sci.** (1984) at 923. **[professional scientific journal article]**

Restatements

6–161 The American Law Institute (A.L.I.) has produced simplified series of restatements of common law. Restatements of the law are available for agency, conflict of laws, contracts, foreign relations law of the United States, judgments, property, restitution, security, suretyship, torts, and trusts. When citing a restatement, include the volume number (if appropriate), name of the restatement (spelled in full), the series number if appropriate, the section number(s), and the date of publication in parentheses.

> Restatement of Foreign Relations Law § 101 (rev. 1986).
>
> Restatement (Second) of Conflicts of Laws § 305 (1971).
>
> Restatement (Second) of Trusts § 348 (1965).

Textbooks and Treatises

6–162 Legal textbooks—referred to as *hornbooks*—are treatises written about various subjects: criminal law, torts, contracts, wills, trusts, community property, and so on. Some hornbooks are comprehensive works that cover several volumes. Some treatises may contain the author's name as part of the publication title.

6–163 When citing a treatise, keyboard the author's name, followed by the name of the treatise (underscored or italicized). Include in parentheses the edition and the year of publication. When reference is made to a specific section and/or page number, include the section number and the page number of the cited information. No punctuation is used between the treatise title and the section number; a comma precedes the *at* and the page number.

> Roy J. Lewicki and Joseph A. Litterer, <u>Negotiation</u> (Homewood, IL: Richard D. Irwin, Inc., 1985).
>
> John E. Cribbet, et al., <u>Property: Cases and Materials</u>, 6th ed. (Westbury, NY: The Foundation Press, 1990).

6–164 When a treatise has multiple authors, list only the first author's name followed by a comma and the abbreviation *et al.* (for "and others").

> Jack H. Friedenthal, **et al.,** <u>Civil Procedure</u> § 551 (1999).
>
> W. Page Keeton, et al., <u>Prosser and Keeton on the Law of Torts</u> § 30 (5th ed. 1984).
>
> William B. Lockhart, **et al.,** <u>The American Constitution</u> (8th ed. 1996).

6–165 When citing a multivolume treatise, begin the citation with the volume number.

> **1** <u>Witkin Summary of Cal. Law</u> § 6 (2005).
>
> **2** David Bender, <u>Computer Law Software Protection</u> § 4.04(1) (1994).
>
> **21** Charles Alan Wright & Arthur R. Miller, <u>Federal Practice and Procedure</u> § 1005 (2d ed. 1987).

When citing information from a pocket part or supplement, identify the updated information and publication date in parentheses.

> **3** <u>Lane's Goldstein Tr Tech</u> § 19.42 (**Supp. Nov. 1994**).

Uniform Laws and Model Codes

6–166 The National Conference of Commissioners on Uniform State Laws proposes uniform laws that each state and the District of Columbia may adopt. Uniform codes, such as those for sales, negotiable instruments, and secured transactions, provide a uniform set of standards by which the states can function.

Uniform Laws

6–167 When citing a uniform law, cite the name of the code, the section number, and the year of publication.

> Model Tribal Secured Transactions Act, § 9-102 (August 2005).
>
> U.C.C. art. 9 (rev. 2001).
>
> Uniform Statute of Limitations for Maritime Torts, 46 U.S.C. § 183 (1980).

Model Rules and Model Codes

6–168 Model rules and model codes serve as guidelines of professionalism and conduct. When citing the *Model Code of Professional Responsibility* or the *Model Rules of Professional Conduct,* do not identify the American Bar Association as the "author" of these ethical rules.

> California Rules of Prof'l Conduct Rule 1-110 (2006). **[State rule]**
>
> Model Code of Prof'l Responsibility EC 7-9 (1993). **[ABA Code]**
>
> National Association of Legal Assistants Model Standards and Guidelines for Utilization of Legal Assistants-Paralegals (1984, rev. 2005).

QUOTED MATERIAL

6–169 When information is taken from another source or when a direct quotation is cited in a document, credit must be given to the source of the material. Reworded or paraphrased information taken from any published source must also be credited.

6–170 When a citation credits a quotation or paraphrased information, the source note is keyboarded after the quoted or paraphrased information. (See 6–81, Citations as Source Notes.) Citations that appear within the text are incorporated as part of the grammatical structure of sentences. (See 6–149, Citations in Textual Sentences.)

6–171 When footnotes are used with quoted or paraphrased information within the body of a legal document, they are identified by superscripts (numbers printed slightly above the text line). Complete reference or source information appears as a footnote at the bottom of the page on which the superscript appears. (See 6–218 • 6–273 for information on footnotes.)

Short Quotations

6–172 Short quotations consisting of fewer than 50 words are keyboarded within the paragraph and enclosed in quotation marks. The source note is keyboarded immediately following the quoted material; a period follows the entire citation, which is considered a complete sentence.

> The court stated that "[t]he primary duty is owed to the testator-client, and the attorney's paramount obligation is to serve and carry out the intention of the testator." *Featherson v. Farwell*, 20 Cal. Rptr. 3d 412, 417 (Cal. App. 2 Dist. 2004).

Quotation within a Short Quotation

6–173 If the quotation contains a quoted passage or individual words or phrases to be highlighted, enclose such information in single quotation marks using the apostrophe (').

> Citing *Starkman v. Mann Theatres Corp.*, 227 Cal. App. 3d 1491, 1497, 378 Cal. Rptr. 543, the court stated that "Age-based distinctions often appear in statutory programs . . . 'Social Security and Medicare are but two examples of congressional enactments designed to assist senior citizens once they retire.'" *Pizarro v. Lamb's Players Theatre*, 37 Cal. Rptr. 3d 859, 862 (Cal. App. 4 Dist. 2006).

Long Quotations

6–174 A long quotation consisting of more than 50 words is keyboarded as a separate paragraph, single-spaced, and indented one-half to one inch from the right and the left margins. No quotation marks are used before or after the text. The source note is keyboarded a double space below the quotation, at the left margin.

> In deciding whether an attorney representing a testator-client who dies before the deed is executed owes a duty to a third-party beneficiary, the court stated:
>
> > . . . liability to a third party will not be imposed where there is a question about whether the third party was in fact the *intended* beneficiary of the decedent, or where it appears that a rule imposing liability might interfere with

the attorney's ethical duties to his client or
impose an undue burden on the profession.

Featherson v. Farwell, 20 Cal. Rptr. 3d 412, 416 (Cal.
App. 2 Dist. 2004).

Quotation within a Longer Quotation

6–175 If the quotation contains a quoted passage or if words or phrases are to be
highlighted, enclose such information in quotation marks.

The Pizarro Court, relying on *Koire v. Metro Car
Wash*, 40 Cal. 3d 24, 219 Cal. Rptr. 133, 707 P. 195
(Wash. 1985), affirmed the practice of California courts
allowing "private parties to extend or withhold benefits
based on age." *Id.* The Pizzaro Court stated that

"'[c]harging different prices to children and
senior citizens is sometimes permissible and
socially desirable. (*Id*. at 36, 219 Cal. Rptr.
133, 707 P.2d 195)' . . . that rental car
companies were permitted to refuse to rent to
drivers under the age of 25 (*Lazar v. Hertz
Corp.*, 69 Cal. App. 4th 1494, 82 Cal. Rptr. 2d
368 [1999], [and] a condominium association's
age restriction favoring those age 40 and older
was held valid (*Huntington Landmark Adult
Community Assn. v. Ross*, 213 Cal. App. 3d 1012,
261 Cal. Rptr. 875 [1989]."

Pizarro v. Lamb's Players Theatre, 37 Cal. Rptr. 3d
859, 862 (Cal. App. 4 Dist. 2006).

Ellipsis Points

Omission at Beginning of a Sentence

6–176 Use ellipsis points to indicate an omission of the beginning of a sentence.
When a sentence begins with an omission, do not capitalize the first word
unless it is a proper noun or otherwise requires capitalization.

". . . offering discount admission prices to 'baby
boomers' to attend a musical about that generation does
not involve an arbitrary class-based generalization
protected by the [Unruh Civil Rights] Act." *Pizarro v.
Lamb's Players Theatre*, 37 Cal. Rptr. 3d 859, 861 (Cal.
App. 4 Dist. 2006).

6–177 If the omitted words are part of the first sentence of a paragraph, indent
one-half inch before keyboarding the ellipsis points.

. . . we emphasize the basic principle that,
while out of an agreement to provide legal services to the testator, a duty also arises to act
with due care with regard to the interests of

> the intended beneficiary, *the scope of duty owed*
> *to the beneficiary is determined by reference to*
> *the attorney-client relationship.*
>
> *Featherson v. Farwell*, 20 Cal. Rptr. 3d 412, 417 (Cal.
> App. 2 Dist. 2004).

Omission of Part of Sentence

6–178   Use an ellipsis of three periods to indicate an omission in the middle of a sentence. Space once after each ellipsis point before continuing the sentence.

> "Disbarment is generally appropriate when a lawyer
> knowingly converts client property and causes injury or
> potential injury to the client. . . . Therefore,
> disbarment is the presumptive sanction for Respondent's
> misconduct in this case." *People v. Calbo*, 122 P.3d
> 1101, 1102 (Colo. O.P.D.J. 2005).

Omission of One or More Sentences

6–179   Use a period followed by ellipsis points (four periods) to indicate the omission of one or more sentences of quoted material. A new sentence beginning with a capital letter indicates that at least one full sentence has been omitted.

> In such cases, the documents are not in-
> troduced for the truth of the matters they
> assert—for example, that the defendant rented a
> car, bought a television, or used 500 kilowatt
> hours of electricity. . . . Rather, the docu-
> ments are "introduced for the inferences that
> may be drawn circumstantially from [their] exis-
> tence or from where [they are] found, regardless
> of whether the assertions contained therein are
> true or not. [citation omitted]"
>
> *U.S. v. Serrano,* 434 F.3d 1003, 1005 (7th Cir. 2006).

Omission of Words at End of Sentences

6–180   Use a period followed by ellipsis points (four periods) to indicate an omission of quoted material at the end of a sentence. Do not leave a space between the last word of the sentence and the period.

> "Age discrimination may violate the Act if used as an
> arbitrary class-based generalization. . . ." *Pizarro v.*
> *Lamb's Players Theatre*, 37 Cal. Rptr. 3d 859, 862 (Cal.
> App. 4 Dist. 2006).

Omission of Paragraphs

6–181   Use ellipsis points to indicate that one or more paragraphs of a quotation have been omitted. Double-space below the previous paragraph of quoted material. Keyboard a period followed by ellipsis points (four periods) at the point of the omission. Double-space after the ellipsis to continue the next quoted paragraph if appropriate.

> The Court in *Sell v. U.S.*, 539 U.S. 166, 156 L. Ed. 2d 197 (2003), stated that "[t]he defendant's failure to take drugs voluntarily, for example, may mean lengthy confinement in an institution for the mentally ill . . . and that would diminish the risks that ordinarily attach to freeing without punishment one who has committed a serious crime." *Id.* at 180
>
> . . . .
>
> Third, the court must conclude that involuntary medication is necessary to further those interests. . . . *Id.* at 180, 181.

New Paragraph after Quotation

6–182 If a new paragraph of text (not a direct quotation) follows the citation, double-space below the citation. Keyboard the new paragraph in the usual way.

> Plaintiff cites her civil rights under 42 U.S.C. § 1983 as follows:
>
> > Every person who, under color of any statute, ordinance, regulation, custom, or usage, of any State. . . , subjects, or causes to be subjected, any citizen of the United States or other person within the jurisdiction thereof to the deprivation of any rights, privileges, or immunities secured by the Constitution and laws, shall be liable to the party injured in an action at law, suit in equity, or other proper proceeding for redress. . . .
>
> 42 U.S.C. § 1983. In such a situation where Plaintiff has been deprived of her civil rights, the statute reinforces the rights to remedies that have been established elsewhere.

6–183 If another long quotation follows the citation, double-space below the citation. Keyboard the long quotation as a separate paragraph, single-spaced, and indented from both the left and the right margins. (See 6–174.)

Subsequent References/Shortened Forms of Citations

6–184 After a case, book, article, statute, or other work has been cited in full the first time in a document, subsequent references to that work may be shortened. A shortened form of citation should be clearly written so the reader can easily refer to the complete citation provided earlier in the document. There are different guidelines for citing subsequent references to court opinions, constitutions, statutes, and other legal publications.

Page Numbers

6–185 Page numbers in legal citations and references are not identified by the word *page* or *pages*. The number following the abbreviation for a case reporter, periodical, statute, code, constitution, or other published work is understood to represent the page number(s) of the cited information.

Case Citations

6–186 Subsequent references to case opinions previously cited in full may be shortened in the following ways:

> Citing one party's name with the reporter name and page number
>
> Citing only the reporter name and page number
>
> Citing *Id.* (or *Id. at*), where appropriate
>
> Citing one party's name only

In shortened forms of subsequent references, omit the first page of the case decision and any parenthetical information such as the court, jurisdiction, or year of the decision.

Case citation:	*Pizarro v. Lamb's Players Theatre,* *37 Cal. Rptr. 3d 859 (Cal. App.* *4 Dist. 2006)*
Subsequent references:	*Pizarro, 37 Cal. Rptr. 3d at 861* **[cited material appears on page 861 of the opinion]**
	37 Cal. Rptr. 3d at 861 **[first page of opinion omitted; page number refers to source of cited material]**
	Id. **[cited material appears in exact work and at the same page as immediately cited]**
	Id. at 862 **[cited material appears in exact work but on different page from the preceding reference]**
	In Pizarro, the court. . . . **[general reference to case previously cited in full]**

Id.

6–187 The abbreviation *id.* means "in the same place." It is used to cite subsequent references to any published work—case, statute, constitution, book, treatise, periodical—previously cited in full. *Id.* is used only to refer to the *immediately preceding* citation to cite consecutive references to that work and only when the subsequent reference is *identical to* the source just cited.

6–188 Capitalize *id.* if the abbreviation stands alone as a source note at the end of a quotation or paraphrased text. Do not capitalize *id.* if the abbreviation is included within a textual sentence or is part of a larger quotation being cited.

Original citation:	*American Disability Ass'n v. Chmielarz*, 289 F.3d 1315 (11th Cir. 2002).
Subsequent reference:	*Id.* **[cited material came from the exact source immediately cited and on the identical page]**

6–189 If a party in the case is the United States or a government agency, do not use such words as *United States*, *State*, or *People* in shortened forms of citation. Refer to the other party's name in subsequent references.

Original citation:	*People v. Brown*, 119 P.3d 486 (Colo. App. 2004).
Shortened forms:	***Brown***, 119 P.3d at 487 119 P.3d at 487 *Id.* at 486 In *Brown*, the court . . .

Id. *with Page Number*

6–190 When a subsequent reference is made to an immediately preceding source just cited, but the page number is different from that originally cited, include the new page number(s) in the subsequent reference. Cite as *Id. at*, followed by the page number(s).

Original citation:	*U.S. v. Thornton*, 197 F.3d 241 (7th Cir. 1999).
Subsequent reference:	*Id.* **at 251.**
Original citation:	*Nichols v. Tri-State Brick & Tile Co.* 608 So., 2d 324 (Miss. 1992).
Subsequent reference:	*Id.* **at 329.**

6–191 When a reference previously cited in full is referred to later in a document, although not consecutively, keyboard a shortened form of the reference, followed by *Id.* or *id. at.* Then include the page number(s).

Original citation:	*Helbush v. Helbush*, 122 P.3d 288 (Hawai'i App. 2005).
Subsequent nonconsecutive reference:	***Helbush, id.* at 289.**
Original citation:	*Featherson v. Farwell*, 20 Cal. Rptr. 3d 412 (Cal. App. 2 Dist. 2004).
Subsequent nonconsecutive reference:	***Featherson, id.* at 416.**

Id. *with Page Number in Parallel Citations*

6–192 When a parallel citation to an unofficial reporter and/or regional reporter is provided for a court decision, any subsequent reference to the case citation must include a corresponding reference to the page number(s) within the parallel case(s) where the quoted material appears. Include the parallel citation reference in its shortened form. Precede the page number of the parallel citation with *at*, followed by a space.

Original citation:	*Baker v. Carr*, 369 U.S. 186, 208–210 **[official reporter]**, 82 S. Ct. 691, 705–706, 7 L. Ed. 2d 663, 680–682 (1962). **[unofficial reporters]**.
Shortened forms with parallel citations:	*Baker*, 369 U.S. **at 208**, 82 S. Ct. **at 705**, 7 L. Ed. 2d **at 680**. 369 U.S. **at 208**, 82 S. Ct. **at 705**, 7 L. Ed. 2d **at 680**. *Id.*, 369 U.S. **at 208**, 82 S. Ct. **at 705**, 7 L. Ed. 2d **at 680**.
Original citation:	*Ott v. Boston Edison Co.*, 413 Mass. 680 **[official state reporter]**, 602 N.E.2d 566 (1992). **[regional reporter]**.
Shortened forms with parallel citation:	*Ott*, 413 Mass. **at 685**, 602 N.E.2d **at 569**. 413 Mass. **at 685**, 602 N.E.2d **at 569**. *Id.*, 413 Mass. **at 685**, 602 N.E.2d **at 569**.

Constitutions

6–193   Subsequent references to the Constitution must be repeated in their proper citation forms. The subsequent references to articles, titles, sections, or paragraphs may be shortened using only *Id.* or *Id. at*, followed by the appropriate citation.

Original citation:	U.S. Const. art. I, sec. 3, cl. 2.
Subsequent reference:	U.S. Const., ***Id.***

Statutes and Codes

6–194   Citations to statutes and code provisions may be shortened in subsequent references in any form that clearly identifies the statute or code. Subsequent references to articles, titles, sections, or paragraphs may be shortened using only *id.* or *id. at*, followed by the appropriate citation.

Original citation:	The Sarbanes-Oxley Act of 2002, **Pub. L.** No. 107-2047, 116 **Stat.** 745.
Subsequent citation:	Sarbanes-Oxley Act, ***Id.***

Section and Paragraph Numbers in Subsequent References

6–195   When a section or a paragraph number is referred to in a subsequent reference, cite the section or paragraph number *without* the word *at*.

Original citation:	42 U.S.C. § 1983.
Subsequent citation:	42 U.S.C. § 1983.

Secondary Authority

6–196   Citations to secondary authorities—legal periodicals, annotations, restatements, encyclopedias, and treatises—may be shortened in subsequent references by using *id.*, *id. at*, *supra*, *supra at*, or *infra*.

Id. *and* Id. at

6–197   *Id.* and *id. at* may also be used to refer to subsequent references to any secondary authority. Cite the source in its shortened form (see 6–184 • 6–185). Use *id.* if the source and the reference are identical to that previously cited. (See 6–187 • 6–188.) Use *id. at* if the reference is different from that previously cited. (See 6–190 • 6–191.)

Original citation to book:	Martin A. Frey, <u>Alternative Methods of Dispute Resolution</u> (New York: Delmar Learning, 2003) at 206.
Subsequent consecutive citation:	Frey, ***id.***
Subsequent nonconsecutive citation:	Frey, ***id.* at** 207.

Supra

6–198   The term *supra* means "above" and is used to refer to the same book, article, or other secondary source of authority cited in full earlier ("above") in the document. (Do not use *supra* to refer to cases, statutes, or constitutions.) The previous reference may appear anywhere in the document and need not immediately precede the point at which *supra* is used. Keyboard the surname of the author of the article or book, followed by *supra* either underscored or italicized.

Original citation:	W. Page Keeton, et al., <u>Prosser and Keeton on the Law of Torts</u>, § 38 at 239 (5th ed. 1984).
Subsequent nonconsecutive reference:	Prosser and Keeton, ***supra.***

6–199   Use *id.* instead of *supra* to refer to an immediately preceding authority.

Original citation:	W. Page Keeton, et al., <u>Prosser and Keeton on the Law of Torts</u>, § 38 at 239 (5th ed. 1984).
Subsequent consecutive reference:	***Id.***
Subsequent nonconsecutive reference:	***Id.* at 240.**

Supra with Page Number

6–200 To refer to a specific volume or page number of a previously cited work, keyboard the word *supra* after the source name, followed by a comma; then keyboard the word *at* and the page number(s).

> Subsequent
> nonconsecutive reference: `Keeton, ` **`supra`**`, ` **`at 241.`**

Cross-Referencing Previous Citations with *Supra*

6–201 When a lengthy document contains multiple citations and subsequent references to any of them, *supra* alone may not be adequate to direct the reader to the precise place within the current document where the complete citation first appeared. When referring to an earlier cited source, state the source name, the word *supra*, and the page number location *within the current document* where the source was first cited in full.

> Subsequent reference: `Frey, ` **`supra, 4.`** **[refers to page 4 of the current document where the complete citation first appears]**

6–202 If the subsequent reference came from a different page number than the one originally cited, include the page number of the source. Include the source name, *supra*, and the page number location *within the current document* where the source was first cited. Then keyboard a comma, the word *at*, followed by the page number on which the cited source of information appears.

> Subsequent reference: `Frey, ` *`supra`*`, 4 ` **`at 207.`** **[complete citation appears on page 4 of the current document; the cited information appears on page 207 of the book]**

Infra

6–203 The term *infra* means "below" and is used to refer the reader to a book, article, or other *secondary source of authority* cited later in the document. Do not use *infra* to refer to primary authority—cases, statutes, or constitutions—which should be cited in standard or shortened forms. The use of *infra* is awkward since it directs the reader to the complete source after discussing or mentioning its relevance earlier in the document. *Infra* is most commonly used to refer the reader to a specific section, chapter, or unit of the current document. Keyboard the reference source, followed by *infra*, either underscored or italicized.

> `See Unit 9, ` **`infra.`**

Hereinafter

6–204 An authority may contain a lengthy name or a title too cumbersome for its complete citation to be repeated in subsequent references. After citing the complete authority the first time, identify in brackets how that source will be referred to subsequently in the document. Keyboard the complete citation in the usual manner; then keyboard within brackets the word *hereinafter*, followed by the word(s) to be used to refer to that source.

> *U.S. Postal Service* **[hereinafter** USPS**]** *v. Flamingo Indus.* **[hereinafter** Flamingo**],** 540 U.S. 736, 124 S. Ct. 1321, 158 L. Ed. 2d 19 (2004).

> USA PATRIOT Act of 2001, Pub. L. No. 101-56, 115 Stat. 272 **[hereinafter** PATRIOT Act**].**

> *Fidelity Mort. Trustee Service* **[hereinafter Fidelity]** *v. Ridgegate East Homeowners Ass'n* **[hereinafter Ridgegate],** 94 Daily J. D.A.R. 10969 (Cal. C.A.2, 1994).

"Hereinafter" with *Id.* and *Id. at*

6–205 When referring to the identified source in a subsequent reference, cite to the particular source by its hereinafter-given name, followed by an *id.* or *id. at* reference as appropriate.

> **Ridgegate** foreclosed on a lien placed on a homeowner's property for delinquent association fees. ***Id. at* 10970.**

Multiple Works by Author

6–206 When multiple works published by one author, editor, or source are included within a document, each work must be cited in full the first time it is referenced. Subsequent references to each work must be clearly identified. Keyboard a complete citation for each work in the usual manner; then keyboard within brackets the word *hereinafter*, followed by the word(s) to be used to refer to that source.

> Teresa Snodgrass. <u>Minor's Right of Privacy: By-pass Procedures to Notification Statutes</u>, 10 J. Juv. Law. 239 (1989) **[hereinafter Minor's Right].**

> Teresa Snodgrass. <u>Parental Immunity Doctrine</u>, 10 J. Juv. Law. 251 (1989) **[hereinafter Parental Immunity].**

Subsequent Case History

6–207 When a document includes a discussion of or reference to the original or earlier court case and decision and its subsequent proceedings, the cases must be clearly identified. The party names in a case may remain the same, but the case will have different reporter citation references. The respective citations for each proceeding must be provided and clearly identified as separate actions and references. Keyboard a complete citation for each case in the usual manner. Then keyboard within brackets the word *hereinafter*, followed by the word(s) to be used to refer to that source.

> *Bellotti v. Baird*, 428 U.S. 132 (1976)
> **[hereinafter *Bellotti I*].**
>
> *Bellotti v. Baird*, 443 U.S. 622 (1979)
> **[hereinafter *Bellotti II*].**

When referring to either source in a subsequent reference, cite to the particular source by its hereinafter-given name, followed by an *id.* or *id. at* reference as appropriate.

> *Bellotti II*, *id. at* 649.

Citation Signals

6–208 Citation signals are abbreviations used to identify the priority and/or significance of cited materials within a legal document. (See Table 6.1.) One or more signals following a statement, proposition, or citation to an authority may identify additional cases, statutes, or other authorities.

6–209 Keyboard a signal at an appropriate point within a sentence or after quoted or paraphrased material. A signal may also appear in parentheses. A comma follows the signal to introduce the cited reference. If the signal appears within the sentence, keyboard a comma after it; when the signal ends the entire sentence, keyboard a period after the entire statement. Include in parentheses a brief statement of the significance or relevance of a citation appearing with a signal.

> ***See, e.g.***, *Lynch v. Donnelly*, 465 U.S. 668, 674, 104 S. Ct. 1355, 1359, 79 L. Ed. 2d 604, 610 (1984).
>
> In *United States v. Sciarrino*, 884 F.2d 95, 97 (3d Cir. 1989), the Court stated that due process does not necessarily require application of a different rule regarding hearsay evidence. ***See also***, *United States v. Torres*, 926 F.2d 321, 324 (3d Cir. 1991). **[At time of sentencing, Court allowed into admission evidence that had been suppressed at trial]**

> Signal within sentence: The Court has remanded a case, ***e.g.***, *United States v. Baylin*, 696 F.2d 1030 (3d Cir. 1982), for sentencing "when the sentencing court had inferred the defendant's involvement in a crime solely from the fact that the government had promised not to prosecute another crime." *United States v. Paulino*, 996 F.2d 1541, 1547 (3d Cir. 1993).

Sequence of Signals

6–210 A series of signals—referred to as *string cites*—should appear in a logical sequence to lead the reader through the various aspects of the discussion or issue. When string-citing, use signals in the sequence listed in Table 6.1.

TABLE 6.1 Citation Signals

Citation signals are abbreviations used to indicate the priority and/or significance of subsequent references following a statement or other authority. When a series of signals is used, cite them in the order shown.

Signal	Definition and Use
No signal	Indicates that the authority cited is the direct source of the statement, proposition, or theory; that the authority asserts the proposition or theory.
e.g. ("for example")	Indicates that the additional authority cited is one of several authorities that supports or states the proposition or theory.
Accord	Indicates that the additional authority or authorities cited agree with the first authority cited in support of the proposition or theory.
See	Indicates that the cited authority—by inference—supports the proposition or theory, although it does not specifically state the proposition or theory.
See also	Indicates that an additional authority or authorities support the proposition or theory. State the relevance of the additional authority in parentheses.
Cf. ("compare")	Indicates that the authority differs from the main proposition or theory but is sufficiently analogous to be compared with the one cited. State the nature and the relevance of the comparison between authorities in parentheses.
Contra	Indicates an authority that is directly opposite to the proposition or theory stated.
But see	Indicates an authority that supports an opposing proposition.
But cf.	Indicates an authority that supports a proposition analogous to the contrary view of the proposition or theory. State the nature and the relevance of the analogy in parentheses.
See generally	Indicates an authority that presents useful background information related to the proposition or theory. Explain the background information in parentheses.

6–211 When using signals that support, compare, contradict, or provide background information, string such signals and their authorities as a single citation in one sentence. When using different types of signals, arrange them as separate citations in separate sentences.

Parenthetical Information

6–212 Additional information within parentheses may be provided after citations to help the reader interpret the reference. (See 6–209.)

Concurring or Dissenting Opinion

6–213 When quoted or paraphrased material is cited from a court opinion, it is cited from the majority opinion. If information is cited from either a concurring opinion or a dissenting opinion, indicate that fact in parentheses after the citation. Include the surname of the justice, followed by *J.* (for "Justice") and a comma. Indicate whether the citation is from the dissenting or the concurring portion of the court opinion.

```
(Ginsberg, J., dissenting)

(Souter, J., concurring)
```

Emphasis Added

6–214 Information appearing in published works will often include words or text that is underscored or italicized by the writer for special emphasis. When citing such material, retain the original style of text so the reader is aware of the emphasis. Keyboard the words *emphasis added* in parentheses immediately after the citation.

```
In a disciplinary action, the Court inferred from the
Petitioner's argument that "pro bono clients deserve
less diligent service than paying clients. . . ." Segal
v. State Bar, 245 Cal. Rptr. 404, 407-408, 44 Cal. 3d
1077, 1084, 751 P.2d 463 (1988). (emphasis added)
```

6–215 If quoted material contains words or text already emphasized by underscoring or italicizing and your document emphasizes *other* words or text, identify the additional emphasis. Keyboard in parentheses the words *first emphasis added* or *second emphasis added*, as appropriate, immediately after the citation.

"Citations Omitted"

6–216 Information in a quotation or paraphrased text may be supported by several citations or references. Including the string of citations interferes with the flow of the sentence, so only the first citation is included. When citations have been omitted, include the words *citations omitted* in parentheses after the first citation.

```
Although a will is frequently contested both on the
ground of lack of mental competency of the testator
and on the ground of undue influence, . . . they are
essentially different grounds of contest, related only
to the extent that the trier of fact may consider the
```

> decedent's state of mind as bearing on his or her abil-
> ity to resist importunity.
>
> *In re Estate of Stoddart*, 174 Cal. 606, 163 P. 1010
> (1917) **(citations omitted)**

"Quoting ..." or "Citing ..."

6–217 When quoted or paraphrased information contains quoted material from another case or source, include the source of the quoted text in the usual form. Then in parentheses, state the full citation from which the quoted material appears, preceded by the notation *quoting (name of source)*.

> The Court stated that "[t]he long-term effects of sur-
> rogacy contracts are unknown, but feared." *Doe v. Att'y
> Gen.*, 487 N.W.2d 484 at 487 (Mich. App. 1992) (**citing** *In
> Re Baby M*, 109 N.J. 396, 441, 537 A.2d 1227 [1988]).

FOOTNOTE REFERENCES

6–218 The purpose of a footnote is to give complete credit to the source of any quoted or paraphrased material and to provide the reader with the information needed to locate the original source if necessary.

6–219 The elements to be included in a footnote depend on the type of reference cited: a court opinion, Constitution, statute or code, treatise, periodical, public document, and so on. Once a particular work has been cited in its complete form in a document, subsequent references to that work appear in shortened form. (See 6–182 • 6–205.)

Placement and Numbering

6–220 Footnotes are generally numbered consecutively throughout a document. However, if the document is divided into separate chapters or if there are a large number of notes, the notes in each chapter or unit may begin with *1* and run consecutively.

6–221 Footnote numbers appearing within the text of a document are identified by *superscripts* (numbers printed slightly above the text line). Complete reference or source information generally appears as a footnote at the bottom of the page on which the superscript appears. (See also 6–271 • 6–272.) The superscripts are placed immediately after the closing quotation mark (for quoted material) or after the last word of paraphrased text. Spacing after the superscript follows the normal spacing after words or marks of punctuation. For example, since two spaces follow a period, two spaces would be keyboarded after a superscript placed at the end of a sentence.

> Attorneys, as well as judges, are using computers in
> the courtroom. Court reporters' notes entered into a

court reporting machine are "read" by scanners,[1] which
"translate" or transcribe notes into readable form.[2]
The notes are electronically input into a computer and
displayed on the screen. The use of high-tech equipment is a step toward paperwork reduction!

———————

[1]Footnote number appearing after comma, followed by
one space.

[2]Footnote number after period, followed by one or two
spaces.

6–222 Word processing programs have a footnote feature that automatically
numbers footnotes sequentially within the document as they are created.
Footnote numbers are automatically changed—renumbered—when text
is edited and references are added or deleted. The footnote feature also
automatically positions footnote references or source information at the
bottom of the page or on a separate Notes page.

If footnote numbers are printed on the line, keyboard a period and a
space before the reference source.

Formatting

6–223 Footnotes that appear at the bottom of a page or that appear at the end of
the report (called Notes, see 6–271 • 6–272) contain the same elements
and are formatted in the same way. Footnote numbers in the body of the
report appear as superscripts; the numbers preceding the footnote references at the bottom of the page may be superscripts or regular keyboarded
numbers followed by a period and two spaces.

1. Frey, Martin A. Alternative Methods of Dispute
Resolution. (New York: Delmar Learning, 2003) at
206-207. **[footnote number on line]**

[1]Frey, Martin A. Alternative Methods of Dispute
Resolution. (New York: Delmar Learning, 2003) at
206-207. **[raised footnote number]**

Follow these guidelines for incorporating footnotes:

1. Keyboard a two-inch footnote-separating line a single space
   below the last line of text; double-space after the line. Word
   processing programs may incorporate the line automatically.
2. Keyboard the footnotes within the margin settings used for the
   document.
3. Precede each reference with an arabic number, followed by a
   period and one or two spaces. The reference number can also be
   keyboarded as a superscript with no space following it.

4. Capitalize the first letter of important words in the titles of books, magazines, journals, and newspapers and underscore the entire title. Titles may be printed in italics instead of underscored.

5. Follow the capitalization, abbreviation, and spacing rules for citations of cases and secondary authorities.

6. Single-space the footnote and double-space between footnotes.

Footnote Elements

6–224 Footnotes generally consist of the following elements:

Name of author, editor, compiler, or translator

Title of work

Volume or series number

Edition number

Name of publisher, if appropriate

Date of publication

6–225 The wording and the form of footnote elements are similar to those for citing both primary and secondary authority discussed elsewhere. The name of the *original* publisher is generally not included; however, the name of any subsequent publisher should be included.

Abbreviations in Names

6–226 The words *Company, Corporation*, and *Ltd.* that appear in footnote references to publishers and in listings of multiple authors' names are omitted. Use the *ampersand* (&) for *and*. Abbreviate *United States* as *U.S.* (except in case citations), and abbreviate geographic words.

Primary Authority

6–227 To cite footnotes to primary authority—case law, constitutions, statutes, legislative materials, administrative and executive materials—see 6–7 • 6–152. Subsequent references to such authority may be shortened as described in 6–193 • 6–195.

Case Law

6–228 To cite footnotes to case law, see 6–82 • 6–152. Subsequent references to such authority may be shortened as described in 6–186 • 6–192.

Secondary Authority

6–229 To cite footnotes to secondary authority—annotations, dictionaries and thesauruses, encyclopedias, legal periodicals, restatements, textbooks and treatises, or uniform laws and model codes—see 6–153 • 6–168. Subsequent references to such authority may be shortened as described in 6–196 • 6–207.

Books

6–230 The first time a book is cited, the notation must include the following elements: the name(s) of the author and/or editor, compiler, and translator; the complete title of the work; the edition (if not the first); the facts of publication (place and publisher); the page number(s); and the name of the publisher, if appropriate.

> 1. **Warner Fara**, <u>The Power of the Pure</u> (Upper Saddle River, NJ: Prentice-Hall, 2006).

Author's Name

6–231 The author's name as it appears on the title page of the book is keyboarded one space after the footnote number. The name is listed in normal order—first name or initial, middle name or initial, and surname—and is followed by a comma.

> 2. **Clarice Feinman,** <u>Women in the Criminal Justice System</u>, 3d ed. (Westport, CT: Praeger Publishers, 1994).

If an institution or organization is the author of the work, cite its name first, followed by the title of the work in the usual form. If the institution or organization is the publisher, its name is not repeated in the publication data.

> 3. **Federal Judicial Center**, <u>Reference Manual on Scientific Evidence</u>, 2d ed. (Washington, D.C., 2000).

Multiple Authors

6–232 If a book has *two* authors, list the authors' names in the order in which they appear on the title page. Abbreviate *and* with the ampersand (&).

> 4. **Paul Craig Roberts & Lawrence M. Stratton**, <u>The Tyranny of Good Intentions</u> (Roseville, CA: Prima Publishing, 2000).

If a book has more than two authors, list only the name of the first author, followed by the Latin abbreviation et al. (meaning "and others"). Be sure to include the period after the abbreviation, but do not underscore or italicize the abbreviation.

> 5. Roy J. Lewicki, et al., <u>Negotiation: Readings, Exercises, and Cases</u>, 2d ed. (Homewood, IL: Richard D. Irwin, Inc., 1993).

Unknown Author

6–233 When the author's name is unknown, begin with the title of the work, followed by the publisher name, the year of publication, and the page reference if appropriate.

> 6. **George Washington's Rules of Civility & Decent Behavior** (Bedford, MA: Applewood Books, 1988).

Editor's Name

6–234 Several kinds of books include an editor's name on the title page: anthologies; collected works; compilations; statutes, codes, and administrative materials; and collected documents.

Anthologies

6–235 An anthology is a compilation of writings drawn from various sources. When citing the title of an article, story, or essay from an anthology, begin the footnote with the author(s) and the title of the work quoted in the document. Place the title of the article within quotation marks. Follow the title by the word *in*, the name of the editor(s), and the title of the anthology and edition, if appropriate. List the name(s) of the editor(s), followed by the abbreviation *ed.* (or *eds.*) in parentheses.

> 7. Brian E. Gray, "National Parks Service Act (1916)," **in** 3 <u>Major Acts of Congress</u> (Brian K. Landsberg, ed.) (New York: Macmillan Reference USA, 2004) at 42-45.

If the reference is to the entire anthology, keyboard the book title followed by the editor's name in parentheses.

> 8. <u>Major Acts of Congress</u> (Brian K. Landsberg, ed.) (New York: Macmillan Reference USA, 2004).

Collected Works

6–236 Collected works consist of all the works by one author, usually with introductions and comments by the editor. In citing collected works, begin the footnote with the author's name (even though it may be repeated in the title), the title of the selection, and the book title. Then include the editor's name followed by *ed.* (in parentheses) and the publication data.

> 9. Phillis Wheatley, "On Friendship," **in** <u>The Collected Works of Phillis Wheatley</u> (John C. Shields, ed.) (New York: Oxford University Press, 1988) at 136.

Compilations

6–237 Compilations contain information on one subject from different sources, reorganized into a coherent book by the editor. Keyboard the title, followed by the editor's name and the publication data.

When a compiled work has been edited or translated, include the complete name of the editor or translator. Include this information even if the work has an author(s).

Editor(s) or Translator(s) Name(s) Only

6–238 If a work does not have an author name, cite the title of the work. In parentheses, cite the name of the editor or translator, followed by either the abbreviation *ed.* or *trans.* In separate parentheses, cite the place of publication, the name of the publisher, and the year of publication. If there are two editors or translators, cite both names, followed by the abbreviation *eds.* or *trans.*; if more than two editors or translators, cite only the name of the first editor or translator followed by *et al.*

> 10. <u>Phantom Risk: Scientific Inference & the Law</u> (D. Bernstein et al., **eds.**) (Cambridge, MA: M.I.T. Press, 1992).
>
> 11. <u>From Our Shoes: Growing Up with a Brother or Sister with Special Needs</u> (Donald Meyer, **ed.**) (Bethesda, MD: Woodbine House, 1997).
>
> 12. <u>Congressional Quarterly's Guide to the U.S. Supreme Court</u> (Elder Witt, **ed.**) (Washington, DC: Congressional Quarterly, Inc., 1990).

Author Name(s) with Editor/Translator Name

6–239 If a work has an author, cite the full name of the author first, followed by the title of the work. In parentheses, cite the name(s) of the editor(s) or translator(s) as indicated above, followed in separate parentheses by the place of publication, the publisher, and the year of publication.

> 13. Federico Garcia Lorca, <u>A Season on Granada</u> (Christopher Maurer, **trans.**) (London: Anvil Press Poetry, 1998).
>
> 14. **Anonymous,** <u>A Woman in Berlin, A Diary</u> (Philip Boehm, **trans.**) (New York: Henry Holt & Company, 2000).

Statutes, Codes, and Administrative Materials

6–240 See 6–3 • 6–73 for citing compilations of statutes, codes, and administrative materials.

Collected Documents

6–241 See 6–236.

Title of Work

6–242 When a book is cited in a footnote for the first time, the complete title should be listed, including any subtitle. Underscore (or italicize) the complete book title.

6–243 If a book is part of a series, the series title and the number are written immediately after the book title. Underscore only the title of the book.

> 15. M. Peterson et al., <u>Punitive Damages: Empirical Findings</u> **15** (Rand Institute for Civil Justice, 1987).

Chapter Title

6–244 If the chapter title from a book is to be included in the reference, list the chapter title after the author's name. Enclose the chapter title in quotation marks and follow it by the word *in*. Then keyboard the book or series title.

16. George M. Reider, Jr., **"Future Insurance Regulation— 'It Will Be What It Will Be'"** in Patricia A. McCoy, <u>Financial Modernization After Gramm-Leach-Bliley</u> (Matthew Bender & Company, Inc., 2002), at 231-232.

17. Paul Craig Roberts & Lawrence M. Tralton, **"Crimes Without Intent"** in <u>The Tyranny of Good Intentions</u> (Roseville, CA: Prima Publishing, 2000) at 45-66.

Edition

6–245 The first edition of a book does not need to be numbered. Subsequent editions, however, must be identified. The edition number is stated on the title or copyright page. Keyboard the edition number in ordinal form after the book (or series) title. A second edition would be identified as 2nd or 2d; a third edition, 3d; and so on.

18. Alan Meisel & Kathy L. Cerminara, <u>The Right to Die: The Law of End-of-Life Decisionmaking</u>, **3d ed.** (New York: Aspen Publishers, 2006).

19. <u>The Bluebook: A Uniform System of Citation</u>, **18th ed.** (Cambridge, MA: The Harvard Law Review Assn., 2005).

6–246 Updated information published in primary and secondary sources often appears in *bound supplements* or *pocket parts*. When citing information from updated sources, identify in parentheses the publisher and the date of publication.

Original publication:

20. Thomas Lee Hazen, 2 <u>Law of Sec. Reg.</u> § 13.16 at 208, 2d ed. (St. Paul, MN: West Publishing Co., 1990).

Updated edition in supplement:

21. Thomas Lee Hazen, 2 <u>Law of Sec. Reg.</u> § 13.16 at 208, 2d ed. **(West Supp. 1994).**

Volume Number

6–247 If a work consists of more than one volume, cite the volume number before the name of the work. Although the volume numbers may appear in roman numerals on the title page, use arabic numerals in the footnote.

22. **2** Restatement of the Conflict of Laws 2d § 269 (1971).

23. Daniel E. Brannen & Richard Clay Hanes, **3** <u>Supreme Court Drama: Cases That Changed America</u> (San Francisco: U.X.L., 2001).

24. **3** <u>Encyclopedia of Public Health</u>, "Mass Media Public Health Campaigns--The Right 'Mix'" (Farmington Hills, MI: Macmillan Reference USA, 2002) at 722-724.

6–248 If a work has more than one volume but no specific volume title or number is given, include the total number of volumes in the series in arabic numerals after the title. Use the abbreviation *vols.*

> 25. Daniel E. Brannen & Richard Clay Hanes (Elizabeth Shaw, ed.), <u>Supreme Court Drama: Cases That Changed America</u>, **3 vols.** (San Francisco: U.X.L., 2001).

6–249 If a volume title is given, enclose it in quotation marks. Keyboard the volume number in arabic numbers, followed by the title of the volume and the publication data.

> 26. Richard A. Westin, "Tax Reform Act of 1986," **3** <u>Major Acts of Congress</u> (New York: Macmillan Reference USA, 2004) at 221-223.

Publication Data

6–250 The publication data, if included, consists of the place of publication, the publisher's name, and the copyright date. Keyboard these elements in parentheses as follows: the *city* of publication, a colon, one or two spaces, and the publisher name. If the city is not widely known, include the state abbreviation after the city name. A comma separates the publisher name and the date of publication.

If the city of publication is well known, include only the city name; otherwise, include the standard abbreviated state name. Keyboard a colon and one or two spaces after the place of publication. If more than one place of publication is shown on the title page of the book, cite the first city listed. Keyboard the publisher's name as it appears on the title page, followed by a comma and the copyright date. If more than one date is listed, cite the most recent date.

> 27. Samuel Walker, <u>Civil Liberties in America</u> (**Santa Barbara**, **CA**: ABC-CLIO, 2004).
>
> 28. Lewis H. Lapham, <u>Gag Rule</u> (**New York**: Penguin Press, 2004).

6–251 When the publisher is part of the series title, the publisher's name need not be included in the publication data.

> 29. <u>McGraw-Hill Yearbook of Science & Technology</u> (New York, 2006).

Page Number Reference(s)

6–252 When reference to a specific page or pages is included in the footnote, keyboard it after the year, preceded by the word *at*. Use arabic numbers. If a range of pages is cited, separate them with a hyphen; if nonconsecutive pages, separate them with a comma.

```
(Burr Ridge, IL:  McGraw-Hill—Irwin, 2008) at 340.
(Burr Ridge, IL:  McGraw-Hill—Irwin, 2008) at 377,
380-385.
```

Periodicals

6–253 Periodicals consist of newspapers, magazines, journals, newsletters, and so forth, that are published at regular intervals. The elements of a periodical footnote are the author's name, if any, the title of the article, the name of the periodical, the volume number (if appropriate), the date of publication, and the inclusive page numbers of the article.

```
30. V. Johnson, "The Perils of Homeland Security," The
Chronicle Review, 49 (2003) at B7.
```

Magazines and Journals

6–254 Articles in some magazines are written by author teams. If no author is listed, begin the footnote with the title of the article.

```
31. "Walking a Mile in Someone Else's Shoes:  A Selec-
tion of Excerpts," The Ledger (Boston:  Federal Reserve
Bank, Spring 2006), 7-17.
```

6–255 When a volume number is included in the periodical, keyboard the volume number immediately after the name of the periodical, with no intervening punctuation. Then keyboard the date in parentheses, followed by *at* and the inclusive page numbers of the article.

```
32. "America's River," Audubon 108 (May-June 2006)
at 30-32.
```

If there is no volume number, keyboard a comma after the periodical title. Follow the standard form for citing periodicals.

Newspapers

6–256 Cite newspaper articles or editorials with the author's name, followed by the title, name of the newspaper, date, and page number. Abbreviate geographic names and other publication data.

```
33. Cass R. Sunstein, "The Minimalist," Los Angeles
Times (May 25, 2006) at B11.

34. Dana Greene, "Virtue Not As Easy As 1, 2, 3," The
Atlanta Journal-Constitution (June 3, 2006) at B2.
```

6–257 Such well-known newspapers as *The Wall Street Journal* and the *Christian Science Monitor* do not need a city name for identification. Abbreviate *The Wall Street Journal* as *Wall St. J.*

```
35. Gwendolyn Bounds, "More Than Squeaking By," Wall
St. J. (May 23, 2006) at B1, B4.
```

6–258 For large city newspapers that print several editions each day, include the name of the edition (first edition, city edition, late edition, etc.), since a news item may not appear in all editions. References to large daily newspapers that include various sections usually include the name or number of the section in which the reference appears.

Public Documents

6–259 Public documents include books, magazines, bulletins, and regulations issued by local, state, and federal government offices or agencies. Footnotes for public documents vary, depending on the type of document cited. In general, references include the name of the city, county, state, or other government division issuing the document; the name of the legislative body, executive department, court, bureau, board, commission, or committee; subsidiary divisions; title of the document or collection; report number or other identifying information useful in locating the specific document; publisher (if different from the issuing body); and the date.

> 35. Executive Office of the President of the United States, Office of Management and Budget, <u>Budget of the U.S. Gov't, Fiscal Year 2007.</u> 2006.

Unpublished Materials

6–260 Unpublished materials include theses and dissertations, papers presented at meetings and symposia, lectures, interviews, speeches and addresses, and letters and memorandums. The elements of a footnote for unpublished works are similar to those for a journal article: author's name, title of the work (with or without quotation marks), the date (in parentheses), identification of the nature of the work, the name and location of the sponsoring body.

> 36. Kathleen M. Meehan, "The Biological Ties That Bind" (1995) (Unpublished paper, Southwestern School of Law, Los Angeles).

Lectures or Papers

6–261 A lecture, paper, speech, or address may be presented to an organization as part of a formal conference or meeting. Identify the place and date of the presentation (if known), as well as the organization to whom the paper or lecture was addressed.

> 37. Mark Leicester, "Tax Affecting S Corporations—The Way out of the Quagmire" (**Paper presented at Suffolk University Law School Center for Advanced Legal Studies, Boston**) (May 12, 2005).

> 38. Jay B. Stephens, "Remarks for 'Do the Write Thing Challenge Program,'" **Address to Challenge Program Participants**, Washington, D.C. (July 8, 2002).

Duplicated Materials

6–262 Duplicated materials include photocopied, phototypeset, or other printed materials, generally prepared or compiled for a specific audience. Identify the author and title of the materials, the place of publication or use, and the method of duplication (typescript, photocopy, photo offset, etc.). When an author's name is unknown, begin the citation with the name of the document.

> 39. E.J. Fong, <u>Legal 135A Syllabus, Wills, Trusts,</u> <u>Probate Administration</u> (Pasadena, CA: Pasadena Area Community College District, Rev. Fall 2005) (xerography).

Nonprint Sources

6–263 Nonprint materials include microforms, audio and video recordings, and computer programs.

Microforms

6–264 Documents reproduced on microfilm, microfiche, strips, or text-fiche are generally available in print form. Cite such references in the same way as their print sources as case citations, codes, statutes, etc. If a print reference in a microform would be difficult to identify or obtain, specify the name of the sponsoring organization, if appropriate, followed by the form of publication at the end of the entry.

Commercial firms and government agencies provide microfilming services. In such cases, cite the document, case, or other publication in the usual way, followed by the words *microformed on* and the citation to the microform service and any identifying or code number assigned to the reproduced form.

Audio Recordings

6–265 References to tapes, compact discs, and other commercial recordings are listed under the name of the composer, writer, or other individual responsible for the content. Include the name of the performer, narrator, or author. Identify the recording company and the number of the recording. Additional information may include copyright date, kind of recording (cassette, compact disc, etc.), the number of items in the series, and so on. Such identifying words as disc or cassette may be used to distinguish the type of sound recording. (Discs, cassettes, and tapes also are used to record pictures and computer programs.)

> 40. Yo-Yo Ma & The Silk Road Ensemble. <u>Silk Road</u> <u>Journeys: Beyond the Horizon</u> (Sony BMG Music Entertainment, 2004) (compact disc)

> 41. Dan Brown, <u>The Da Vinci Code, Unabridged</u> (read by Paul Michael) (New York: Random House Audio, 2003). (audio cassette)

Video Recordings

6–266 Video recordings include slides, films, and textual matter from films. General information should include the author's name, the title of the work (underscored or italicized), publication data, and a description of the form of the recording (slides, film, filmstrips, etc.). If a video recording consists of more than one volume, cite the volume number (in arabic numbers) before the name of the work.

> 42. **4127–A/B** Stephen E. Ambrose, <u>Undaunted Courage, Parts 1 and 2</u> (Newport Beach, CA: Books on Tape, Inc., 1996) (video recording).
>
> 43. <u>Harry Potter & the Goblet of Fire</u> (Burbank, CA: Warner Bros. Entertainment, 2006) (DVD-Video)

Computer Programs

6–267 Computer programs, or software, include packages, languages, and systems. Include the title; the version, level, release number, or additional data to identify the specific program; the place of publication (followed by a colon); the name of the individual, company, or organization having proprietary rights to the program; and the year of publication or release.

> 44. <u>Adobe Printshop Elements 3.0</u> (Windows XP) (San Jose, CA: Adobe System Incorporated, August 2005).

Electronic Databases and The Internet

6–268 Two main sources of obtaining law-related information are electronic databases and the World Wide Web (the Internet). Access to databases generally requires a subscription to gain entry into them. Access to Internet sites requires subscription to an Internet service provider (ISP) through which huge computer networks can be accessed. (Refer to Unit 12, Law Office References, for a bibliography of resources.)

Electronic databases, such as Westlaw (*www.westlaw.com*) and LEXIS (*www.lexis.com*), contain legal resources that can be found in a law library. These databases are subscription services that offer a wide range of information on reported cases, statutes, and other helpful research information and tools. Cite to print materials if available rather than to an electronic source.

6–269 Cite database sources according to the appropriate rules for citing print materials. Following the citation, state the name of the database; include the date of the referenced information as provided on the database.

> *Tex. Op. Att'y Gen.*, 1987 **WL** 256451, 4 U.C.C. 2d 939 (1987). **[source located on WESTLAW database]**

Retirement of Husband as Change of Circumstances War-
ranting Modification of Divorce Decree—Early Retirement, 2002 **WL** 31414142, 2002 A.L.R. 5th 22. **[source
located on WESTLAW]**

Tex. Op. Att'y Gen., 1987 **WL** 256451, 4 U.C.C. 2d 939
(1987). **[source located on WESTLAW]**

In re Nathaniel Cooper, 541 U.S. 986, 158 L. Ed. 2d
523, **2004 US LEXIS 3016**, 124 S. Ct. 2017 (*mandamus
denied*, 2004). **[source located on Lexis database]**

Internet Resources

6–270 The World Wide Web (Internet) provides access to a variety of resources,
many of which also appear in traditional print form. Cite to an Internet
Web site only when a print form is not available or cannot be located on a
database.

Cite online sources according to the appropriate rules for citing print
materials. Following the citation, keyboard the Uniform Resource Locator
(URL) (http://www.). Keyboard the characters and/or numerals of the site
address carefully, including any punctuation and slashes (/); distinguish
between a hyphen (-) and an underscore (_). Some addresses are case-
sensitive, so keyboard the address as required. In parentheses, include the
date the information was last updated or modified or the date the site was
accessed, if appropriate.

Tennessee Valley Authority, "From the New Deal to a New
Century: A Short History of TVA," available at http://
www.tva.gov/abouttva/history.htm (accessed June 11, 2006).

Notes

6–271 Reference or source information may be listed on a separate NOTES page
placed at the end of an article, chapter, or other major section or unit of a
lengthy work. Superscripts, which appear within the body of the document
and are numbered in sequence, identify quoted or paraphrased information. (See also 6–218, Footnote References.)

6–272 Keyboard and center the heading NOTES beginning 2 inches from the
top of the page (for unbound and leftbound documents) or beginning
two and one-half inches from the top (for topbound documents). Entries
on the Notes page are arranged numerically according to the sequence
of superscript numbers presented within the text. The numbers may be
keyboarded on the line followed by a period and one space, or they may
appear as superscripts. Entries are single-spaced with double-spacing
between them.

TABLE 6.2 Abbreviations Used in Citing State Case Reporters

States, State Courts, Names of Reporters

Appellate court opinions within the jurisdictions of the United States are reported in state reporters and also in regional reporters. If a state does not have an official reporter or its reporter has been discontinued, cite to the regional reporter. If only a state name appears as the reporter name, it is assumed that the case was decided by the state's highest court.

State Name and Abbreviation	Name of Court and Abbreviation	State Reporter and Abbreviation	Region and Regional Reporter Abbreviation
Alabama (Ala.)	Supreme Court (Ala.)	Ala. (to 1976) So., So. 2d	Southern So., So. 2d
	Court of Civil Appeals (Ala. Civ. App.)	Ala. App. (to 1976) So., So. 2d	
	Court of Criminal Appeals (Ala. Crim. App.)	Ala. App. (to 1969) So., So. 2d	
Alaska (Alaska)	Supreme Court (Alaska)	None. Cite to P.2d, P.3d (from 1960)	Pacific P.2d, P.3d
	Court of Appeals (Alaska Ct. App.)	None. Cite to P.2d (from 1980), P.3d	
Arizona (Ariz.)	Supreme Court (Ariz.)	Ariz.	Pacific P., P.2d, P.3d
	Court of Appeals (Ariz. Ct. App.)	Ariz. (from 1976); Ariz. App. (to 1976); P.2d, P.3d	
Arkansas (Ark.)	Supreme Court (Ark.)	Ark.	South Western S.W., S.W.2d, S.W.3d
	Court of Appeals (Ark. Ct. App.)	Ark. (to 1981) Ark. App.	
California (Cal.)	Supreme Court (Cal.)	Cal., Cal. 2d, Cal. 3d, Cal. 4th; West's Cal. Rptr., Cal. Rptr. 2d (from 1959)	Pacific P., P.2d, P.3d
	Court of Appeal (Cal. Ct. App.)	Cal. App., Cal. Ap. 2d, Cal. App. 3d,	

TABLE 6.2 Abbreviations Used in Citing State Case Reporters *(continued)*

State Name and Abbreviation	Name of Court and Abbreviation	State Reporter and Abbreviation	Region and Regional Reporter Abbreviation
California (Cal.)		Cal App. 4th; P.2d (to 1959); West's Cal. Rptr. (from 1959)	
	Appellate Departments of the Superior Court (Cal. App. Dep't Super. Ct.)	Cal. App., Cal. App. 2d, Cal. App. 3d, Cal App. 4th; P.2d (to 1959); West's Cal. Rptr. (from 1959)	
Colorado (Colo.)	Supreme Court (Colo.)	Colo. (to 1980); P., P.2d, P.3d	Pacific P., P.2d, P.3d
	Court of Appeal (Colo. Ct. App.)	Colo. App. (to 1980); P.2d (from 1970), P.3d	
Connecticut (Conn.)	Supreme Court (Conn.)	Conn.	Atlantic A., A.2d
	Appellate Court (Conn. App. Ct.)	Conn. App. (from 1983)	
	Superior Court (Conn. Super. Ct.	Conn. Supp. (from 1935)	
	Court of Common Pleas (Conn. C.P.)	Conn. Supp. (from 1935)	
Delaware (Del.)	Supreme Court (Del.)	Del. (to 1966)	Atlantic A., A.2d
	Court of Chancery (Del. Ch.)	Del. Ch. (to 1968); A., A.2d	
	Superior Court (Del. Super. Ct.)	None. Cite to A.2d	
District of Columbia (D.C.)	Court of Appeals (D.C.)	None. Cite to A.2d	Atlantic A.2d
	United States Court of Appeals for the District of Columbia Circuit	F., F.2d, F.3d; U.S. App. D.C. (from 1941)	

TABLE 6.2 Abbreviations Used in Citing State Case Reporters *(continued)*

State Name and Abbreviation	Name of Court and Abbreviation	State Reporter and Abbreviation	Region and Regional Reporter Abbreviation
Florida (Fla.)	Supreme Court (Fla.)	Fla. (to 1948) So., So. 2d	Southern So., So. 2d
	District Court of Appeal (Fla. Dist. Ct. App.)	None. Cite to So. 2d (from 1957)	
	Circuit Court (Fla. Cir. Ct.)	Fla. Supp., Fla. Supp. 2d (1948–1992)	
Georgia (Ga.)	Supreme Court (Ga.)	Ga.	South Eastern S.E., S.E.2d
	Court of Appeals (Ga. Ct. App.)	Ga. App.	
Hawaii (Haw.)	Supreme Court (Haw.)	Haw. (to 1994); P.2d, P.3d (from 1959); West's Haw. Rep. (from 1994)	Pacific P.2d, P.3d
	Intermediate Court of Appeals (Haw. Ct. App.)	Haw. App. (1980–1994); P.2d, P.3d (from 1980); West's Haw. Rep. (from 1994)	
Idaho (Idaho)	Supreme Court (Idaho)	Idaho	Pacific P., P.2d, P.3d
	Court of Appeals (Idaho Ct. App.)	Idaho Ct. App.; Idaho (from 1982)	
Illinois (Ill.)	Supreme Court (Ill.)	Ill., Ill. 2d	North Eastern N.E., N.E.2d
	Appellate Court (Ill. App. Ct.)	Ill. App., Ill. App. 2d, Ill. App. 3d	
	Court of Claims (Ill. Ct. Cl.)	Ill. Ct. Cl.	
Indiana (Ind.)	Supreme Court (Ind.)	Ind. (to 1981) N.E., N.E.2d	North Eastern N.E., N.E.2d
	Court of Appeals (Ind. Ct. App.)	Ind. App. (to 1979); N.E., N.E.2d	

TABLE 6.2 Abbreviations Used in Citing State Case Reporters *(continued)*

State Name and Abbreviation	Name of Court and Abbreviation	State Reporter and Abbreviation	Region and Regional Reporter Abbreviation
Iowa (Iowa)	Supreme Court (Iowa)	Iowa (to 1968) N.W., N.W.2d	North Western N.W., N.W.2d
	Court of Appeals (Iowa Ct. App.)	None. Cite to N.W.2d (from 1977)	
Kansas (Kan.)	Supreme Court (Kan.)	Kan.	Pacific P., P.2d, P.3d
	Court of Appeals (Kan. Ct. App.)	Kan. App. (to 1901); Kan. App. 2d (from 1977)	
Kentucky (Ky.)	Supreme Court (Ky.)	Ky. (to 1951); S.W., S.W.2d, S.W.3d	South Western S.W., S.W.2d, S.W.3d
	Court of Appeals (Ky. Ct. App.)	None. Cite to S.W.2d (from 1976); S.W.3d	
Louisiana (La.)	Supreme Court (La.)	La. (to 1972); So., So. 2d	Southern So., So. 2d
	Court of Appeal (La. Ct. App.)	La. App. (to 1932); So., So. 2d (from 1928)	
Maine (Me.)	Supreme Judicial Court (Me.)	Me. (to 1965); A., A.2d	Atlantic A., A.2d
Maryland (Md.)	Court of Appeals (Md.)	Md.	Atlantic A., A.2d
	Court of Special Appeals (Md. Ct. Spec. App.)	Md. App. (from 1967)	
Massachusetts (Mass.)	Supreme Judicial Court (Mass.)	Mass.	North Eastern N.E., N.E.2d
	Appeals Court (Mass. App. Ct.)	Mass. App. Ct. (from 1972)	
	District Court (Mass. Dist. Ct.)	Mass. App. Div. (from 1980; Mass. Supp. (1980–1983); Mass. App. Dec. (1941–1977)	

TABLE 6.2 Abbreviations Used in Citing State Case Reporters *(continued)*

State Name and Abbreviation	Name of Court and Abbreviation	State Reporter and Abbreviation	Region and Regional Reporter Abbreviation
Michigan (Mich.)	Supreme Court (Mich.)	Mich.	North Western N.W., N.W.2d
	Court of Appeals (Mich. Ct. App.)	Mich. App. (from 1965)	
	Court of Claims (Mich. Ct. Cl.)	Mich. Ct. Cl. (to 1942)	
Minnesota (Minn.)	Supreme Court (Minn.)	Minn. (to 1977); N.W., N.W.2d	North Western N.W., N.W.2d
	Court of Appeals (Minn. Ct. App.)	None. Cite to N.W.2d (from 1983)	
Mississippi (Miss.)	Supreme Court (Miss.)	Miss. (to 1966); So. 2d (from 1998)	Southern So., So. 2d
Missouri (Mo.)	Supreme Court (Mo.)	Mo. (to 1956); S.W., S.W.2d, S.W.3d,	South Western S.W., S.W.2d, S.W.3d
	Court of Appeals (Mo. Ct. App.)	Mo. App. (to 1952); S.W., S.W.2d, S.W.3d	
Montana (Mont.)	Supreme Court (Mont.)	Mont.; State Rptr. (from 1945); P., P.2d, P.3d	Pacific P., P.2d, P.3d
Nebraska (Neb.)	Supreme Court (Neb.)	Neb.; N.W., N.W.2d	North Western N.W., N.W.2d
	Court of Appeals (Neb. Ct. App.)	N.W.2d (from 1992); Neb. App. (from 1992)	
Nevada (Nev.)	Supreme Court (Nev.)	Nev.	Pacific P., P.2d, P.3d
New Hampshire (N.H.)	Supreme Court (N.H.)	N.H.	Atlantic A., A.2d
New Jersey (N.J.)	Supreme Court (N.J.)	N.J.	Atlantic A., A.2d
	Superior Court (N.J. Super. Ct., App. Div.)	N.J. Super. (from 1948)	

TABLE 6.2 Abbreviations Used in Citing State Case Reporters *(continued)*

State Name and Abbreviation	Name of Court and Abbreviation	State Reporter and Abbreviation	Region and Regional Reporter Abbreviation
New Mexico (N.M.)	Supreme Court (N.M.)	N.M.	Pacific P., P.2d, P.3d
	Court of Appeals (N.M. Ct. App.)	N.M. (from 1967)	
New York (N.Y.)	Court of Appeals (N.Y.)	N.Y., N.Y.2d; N.Y.S.2d (from 1956)	North Eastern N.E., N.E.2d
	Supreme Court, Appellate Division (N.Y. App. Div.)	A.D., A.D.2d; N.Y.S., N.Y.S. 2d	
North Carolina (N.C.)	Supreme Court (N.C.)	N.C.	South Eastern S.E., S.E.2d
	Court of Appeals (N.C. Ct. App.)	N.C. App (from 1968)	
North Dakota (N.D.)	Supreme Court (N.D.)	N.D. (to 1953); N.W., N.W.2d	North Western N.W., N.W.2d
	Court of Appeals of North Dakota (N.D. Ct. App.)	None. Cite to N.W.2d (from 1987)	
Ohio (Ohio)	Supreme Court (Ohio)	Ohio St., Ohio St. 2d, Ohio St. 3d	North Eastern N.E., N.E.2d
	Court of Appeals (Ohio Ct. App.)	Ohio App., Ohio App. 2d, Ohio App. 3d	
Oklahoma (Okla.)	Supreme Court (Okla.)	Okla. (to 1953) P., P.2d, P.3d	Pacific P., P.2d, P.3d
	Court of Civil Appeals (Okla. Civ. App.)	None. Cite to P.2d, P.3d (from 1971)	
	Court of Criminal Appeals (Okla. Crim. App.)	Okla. Crim (to 1953); P., P.2d, P.3d (from 1908)	
Oregon (Or.)	Supreme Court (Or.)	Or.	Pacific P., P.2d, P.3d
	Court of Appeals (Or. Ct. App.)	Or. App. (from 1969)	

TABLE 6.2 Abbreviations Used in Citing State Case Reporters *(continued)*

State Name and Abbreviation	Name of Court and Abbreviation	State Reporter and Abbreviation	Region and Regional Reporter Abbreviation
Pennsylvania (Pa.)	Supreme Court (Pa.)	Pa.	Atlantic A., A.2d
	Superior Court (Pa. Super. Ct.)	Pa. Super. (to 1997); A., A.2d (from 1931)	
	Commonwealth Court (Pa. Commw. Ct.)	Pa. Commw. (1970–1994); A.2d (from 1970)	
Rhode Island (R.I.)	Supreme Court (R.I.)	R.I. (to 1980); A., A.2d	Atlantic A., A.2d.
South Carolina (S.C.)	Supreme Court (S.C.)	S.C.	South Eastern S.E., S.E.2d
	Court of Appeals (S.C. Ct. App.)	S.C. (from 1983); S.E.2d (from 1983)	
South Dakota (S.D.)	Supreme Court (S.D.)	S.D. (to 1976) N.W., N.W.2d	North Western N.W., N.W.2d
Tennessee (Tenn.)	Supreme Court (Tenn.)	Tenn. (to 1972); S.W., S.W.2d, S.W.3d	South Western S.W., S.W.2d, S.W.3d
	Court of Appeals (Tenn. Ct. App.)	Tenn. App. (to 1971); S.W.2d (from 1932)	
	Court of Criminal Appeals (Tenn. Crim. App.)	Tenn. Crim. App. (to 1971); S.W.2d (from 1967)	
Texas (Tex.)	Supreme Court (Tex.)	Tex. (to 1962); S.W., S.W.2d, S.W.3d	South Western S.W., S.W.2d, S.W.3d
	Courts of Appeals (Tex. App.)	Tex. Civ. App. (to 1911); S.W., S.W.2d, S.W.3d	
	Court of Criminal Appeals (Tex. Crim. App.)	Tex. Crim. (to 1962); S.W., S.W.2d, S.W.3d	
Utah (Utah)	Supreme Court (Utah)	Utah, Utah 2d (to 1974); P., P.2d, P.3d	Pacific P., P.2d, P.3d
Vermont (Vt.)	Supreme Court (Vt.)	Vt.	Atlantic A., A.2d

TABLE 6.2 Abbreviations Used in Citing State Case Reporters *(concluded)*

State Name and Abbreviation	Name of Court and Abbreviation	State Reporter and Abbreviation	Region and Regional Reporter Abbreviation
Virginia (Va.)	Supreme Court (Va.)	Va.	South Eastern S.E., S.E.2d
	Court of Appeals (Va. Ct. App.)	Va. App. (from 1985)	
Washington (Wash.)	Supreme Court (Wash.)	Wash., Wash. 2d	Pacific P., P.2d, P.3d
	Court of Appeals (Wash. Ct. App.)	Wash. App. (from 1969)	
West Virginia (W. Va.)	Supreme Court (W. Va.)	W. Va.	South Eastern S.E., S.E.2d
Wisconsin (Wis.)	Supreme Court (Wis.)	Wis., Wis. 2d	North Western N.W., N.W.2d
	Court of Appeals (Wis. Ct. App.)	Wis. 2d (from 1978); N.W.2d (from 1978)	
Wyoming (Wyo.)	Supreme Court (Wyo.)	Wyo. (to 1959); P., P.2d, P.3d	Pacific P., P.2d, P.3d

TABLE 6.3 Abbreviations Used in Citing Federal Court Reports
Federal Jurisdiction and Names of Reporters

Opinions of the federal courts are reported in official and unofficial federal reporters. Cite to the official reporter if available; otherwise, cite to or include a parallel citation to the unofficial reporter(s).

Federal Court Jurisdiction	Official Reporter and Abbreviation	Unofficial Reporter and Abbreviation
United States Supreme Court	United States Reports (U.S.)	Supreme Court Reporter (S. Ct.); Lawyers' Edition (L. Ed., L. Ed. 2d)
		United States Law Week (U.S.L.W.)
Court of Appeals (formerly Circuit Courts of Appeals)	None	Federal Reporter (F.) Federal Reporter 2d (F.2d) Federal Reporter 3d (F.3d)

TABLE 6.3 Abbreviations Used in Citing Federal Court Reports *(concluded)*

Federal Court Jurisdiction	Official Reporter and Abbreviation	Unofficial Reporter and Abbreviation
United States Court of Appeals for the Federal Circuit	None	Federal Reporter (F.) Federal Reporter 2d (F.2d) Federal Reporter 3d (F.3d)
District Courts	None	Federal Reporter 2d (F.2d) (to 1932) Federal Supplement (F. Supp.) (from 1932) Federal Supplement 2d (F. Supp. 2d) Federal Rules Decisions (F.R.D.) Federal Rules Service (Fed. R. Serv.) [Callaghan], (Fed. R. Serv. 2d) [Callaghan], (Fed. R. Serv. 3d) [Callaghan]
Bankruptcy Courts	None	Bankruptcy Reporter (B.R.) (from 1979)
Bankruptcy Appellate Panels	None	Bankruptcy Reporter (B.R.) (from 1979)
United States Court of International Trade	Court of International Trade Reports (Ct. Int'l Trade) (from 1980)	Federal Supplement (F. Supp.) (from 1980)
	Customs Bulletin and Decisions (Cust. B. & Dec.) (from 1967)	International Trade Reporter Decisions (I.T.R.D.) (from 1980) (BNA)
	Customs Court Reports (Cust. Ct.) (to 1980)	
United States Court of Appeals for the Armed Forces (C.A.A.F.)	Decisions of the United States Court of Military Appeals (C.M.A.) (to 1975)	Military Justice Reporter (M.J.) (from 1978)
	Court Martial Reports (C.M.R.) (to 1975)	
Tax Court	United States Tax Court Reports (T.C.)	Tax Court Memorandum Decisions (T.C.M.)

TABLE 6.4 Abbreviations of Court Names

Abbreviate names of courts, commissions, or tribunals used in citing cases. The abbreviated name of the court deciding the cited case must be included in parentheses after the citation. The notations in brackets following the court name refer to additional information that must be included in the citation.

Name of Court	Abbreviation
Admiralty [Court, Division]	Adm.
Appellate Court	App. Ct.
Appellate Department	App. Dep't
Appellate Division	App. Div.
Bankruptcy [Court, Judge]	Bankr.
Board of Contract Appeals	B.C.A.
Board of Immigration Appeals	B.I.A.
Board of Tax Appeals	B.T.A.
Chancery [Court, Division]	Ch.
Children's Court	Child. Ct.
Circuit Court [state]	Cir. Ct.
Circuit Court of Appeals (federal)	Cir
Circuit Court of Appeals (state)	Cir. Ct. App.
Claims Court	Cl. Ct.
Commerce Court	Comm. Ct.
Commonwealth Court	Commw. Ct.
County Court	[name] County Ct.
Court of Appeals (federal)	Cir.
Court of Appeal(s) (state)	Ct. App.
Court of Appeals for the Armed Forces	C.A.A.F.
Court of Civil Appeals	Civ. App.
Court of Criminal Appeals	Crim. App.
Court of International Trade	Ct. Int'l Trade
Court of Military Appeals	C.M.A.
Court of Military Review	C.M.R.
Court of [General, Special] Sessions	Ct. [Gen., Spec.] Sess.
Criminal Appeals	Crim. App.
District Court (federal)	D.
District Court (state)	Dist. Ct.
District Court of Appeal(s)	Dist. Ct. App.

TABLE 6.4 Abbreviations of Court Names *(concluded)*

Name of Court	Abbreviation
Domestic Relations Court	Dom. Rel. Ct.
Family Court	Fam. Ct.
Justice of the Peace's Court	J.P. Ct.
Juvenile Court	Juv. Ct.
Law Court	Law Ct.
Law Division	Law Div.
Magistrate's Court	Magis. Ct.
Municipal Court	[city] Mun. Ct.
Probate Court	Prob. Ct.
Public Utilities Commission	P.U.C.
Real Estate Commission	Real Est. Comm'n
Superior Court	Super. Ct.
Supreme Court (federal)	U.S.
Supreme Court (other)	Sup. Ct.
Supreme Court, Appellate Division	App. Div.
Supreme Court, Appellate Term	App. Term
Supreme Judicial Court	Sup. Jud. Ct.
Tax Appeal Court	Tax. App. Ct.
Tax Court	T.C.
Territorial, Territory	Terr.
Tribal Court	[name] Tribal Ct.
Tribunal	Trib.
Workers' Compensation Division	Workers' Comp. Div.
Youth Court	Youth Ct.

TABLE 6.5 Abbreviations of Names and Expressions Used in Citing Cases

Abbreviate names of companies, government entities, individuals, and other expressions when citing case names. For other names and expressions, abbreviate only if the shortened form is clear and properly identifies the case name. The abbreviations used in legal writing may differ from those used for nonlegal writing.

Names and Expressions	Abbreviation
Administrative, administration	Admin.
Administrator	Adm'r
Administratrix	Adm'x

TABLE 6.5 Abbreviations of Names and Expressions Used in Citing Cases *(continued)*

Names and Expressions	Abbreviation
America, American	Am.
Associate	Assoc.
Association	Ass'n
Atlantic	Atl.
Authority	Auth.
Board	Bd.
Center	Ctr.
Central	Cent.
Commission	Comm'n
Commissioner	Comm'r
Committee	Comm.
Company	Co.
Compensation	Comp.
Congress, Congressional	Cong.
Consolidated	Consol.
Construction	Constr.
Cooperative	Coop.
Corporation	Corp.
Department	Dep't
Development	Dev.
Distributor, Distributing	Distrib.
District	Dist.
Division	Div.
East, Eastern	E.
Education, Educational	Educ.
Electric, Electrical, Electricity, Electronic	Elec.
Enterprise	Enter.
Environment	Env't
Environmental	Envtl.
Equipment	Equip.
Exchange	Exch.
Executor	Ex'r
Executrix	Ex' x
Federal	Fed.

TABLE 6.5 Abbreviations of Names and Expressions Used in Citing Cases *(continued)*

Names and Expressions	Abbreviation
Federation	Fed'n
Finance, Financial, Financing	Fin.
Foundation	Found.
General	Gen.
Government	Gov't
Hospital	Hosp.
Importer, Importation	Imp.
Incorporated	Inc.
Indemnity	Indem.
Independent	Indep.
Industry, Industries, Industrial	Indus.
Institute, Institution	Inst.
Insurance	Ins.
International	Int'l
Investment	Inv.
Liability	Liab.
Limited	Ltd.
Machine, Machinery	Mach.
Manufacturer	Mfr.
Manufacturing	Mfg.
Market	Mkt.
Marketing	Mktg.
Medical, Medicine	Med.
Merchant, Merchandise, Merchandising	Merch.
Metropolitan	Metro.
Municipal	Mun.
Mutual	Mut.
National	Nat'l
North, Northern	N.
Organization, Organizing	Org.
Pacific	Pac.
Partnership	P'ship
Product, Production	Prod.
Public	Pub.

TABLE 6.5 Abbreviations of Names and Expressions Used in Citing Cases *(concluded)*

Names and Expressions	Abbreviation
Railroad	R.R.
Railway	Ry.
Rehabilitation	Rehab.
Reproduction, Reproductive	Reprod.
Road	Rd.
Savings	Sav.
School, Schools	Sch.
Science	Sci.
Security, Securities	Sec.
Service	Serv.
Society	Soc'y
South, Southern	S.
Southeast, Southeastern	Se.
Southwest, Southwestern	Sw.
Street	St.
Surety	Sur.
System, Systems	Sys.
Technology	Tech.
Telecommunication	Telecomm.
Telephone, Telegraph	Tel.
Transport, Transportation	Transp.
University	Univ.
Utility	Util.
West, Western	W.

TABLE 6.6 Regional Reporters

Regional reporters consist of a series of seven reporters covering seven geographic areas of the United States. These reporters are components of the National Reporter System published by West Publishing Company. Each regional reporter contains cases of the state supreme courts and their intermediate courts.

Region	Abbreviation	States Included
Atlantic	A., A.2d	Connecticut (Conn.)
		Delaware (Del.)

TABLE 6.6   Regional Reporters *(continued)*

Region	Abbreviation	States Included
Atlantic		District of Columbia (D.C.)
		Maine (Me.)
		Maryland (Md.)
		New Hampshire (N.H.)
		New Jersey (N.J.)
		Pennsylvania (Pa.)
		Rhode Island (R.I.)
		Vermont (Vt.)
North Eastern	N.E., N.E.2d	Illinois (Ill.)
		Indiana (Ind.)
		Massachusetts (Mass.)
		New York (N.Y.)
		Ohio (Ohio)
North Western	N.W., N.W.2d	Iowa (Iowa)
		Michigan (Mich.)
		Minnesota (Minn.)
		Nebraska (Neb.)
		North Dakota (N.D.)
		South Dakota (S.D.)
		Wisconsin (Wis.)
Pacific	P., P.2d, P.3d	Alaska (Alaska)
		Arizona (Ariz.)
		California (Cal.)
		Colorado (Colo.)
		Hawaii (Haw.)
		Idaho (Idaho)
		Kansas (Kan.)
		Montana (Mont.)
		Nevada (Nev.)
		New Mexico (N.M.)
		Oklahoma (Okla.)
		Oregon (Or.)
		Utah (Utah)

TABLE 6.6 Regional Reporters *(concluded)*

Region	Abbreviation	States Included
Pacific		Washington (Wash.)
		Wyoming (Wyo.)
Southern	So., So. 2d	Alabama (Ala.)
		Florida (Fla.)
		Louisiana (La.)
		Mississippi (Miss.)
South Eastern	S.E., S.E.2d	Georgia (Ga.)
		North Carolina (N.C.)
		South Carolina (S.C.)
		Virginia (Va.)
		West Virginia (W. Va.)
South Western	S.W., S.W.2d, S.W.3d	Arkansas (Ark.)
		Kentucky (Ky.)
		Missouri (Mo.)
		Tennessee (Tenn.)
		Texas (Texas)

FIGURE 6.1 Geographic Boundaries of United States Courts of Appeals and United States District Courts

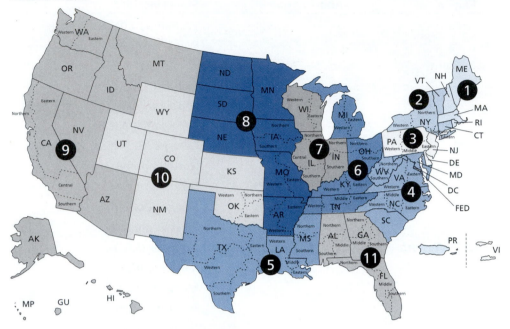

Unit 7

Law Office Correspondence

LAW OFFICE CORRESPONDENCE

7–1 Letters and memorandums are common forms of business communication. Accuracy, neatness, and efficiency in producing these communications are important skills. Since letters and memorandums may also be sent via facsimile (fax) and electronic mail (e-mail), extra care should be taken in creating such communications for distribution or transmission. See 11–38 • 11–58 for faxes and e-mails.

Checklist for Effective Letters and Memorandums

7–2 A well-written letter or memorandum should serve a specific objective, whether short term or long term. All correspondence should also build goodwill and create a favorable impression of the writer and the firm. Use the following checklist to prepare effective correspondence.

- *Organization.* What is the purpose of the letter or memorandum? Is it to inform? To elicit information? To advocate a position or course of action? To defend a point of view? To advise? If writing to elicit information, organize ideas in a way to make it easy for the reader to respond. If writing to persuade, organize ideas in a logical sequence: chronologically (going from the past to the present or vice versa), step by step, event by event, geographically, party by party, or other sequence to make it easy for the reader to follow your thinking process and analysis. Knowing why correspondence is being written helps the writer organize ideas and helps the reader follow the writer's train of thought.
- *Grammar.* Is grammar usage correct? Is sentence structure correct? Do subjects and verbs agree? Are pronouns properly used? Are plural noun forms correctly written? Is word usage appropriate for the meaning of the sentence? Incorrect grammar not only detracts from the message, but it also shows the writer's lack of writing skill.
- *Conciseness.* Have the most effective words and expressions been used? Are only the essential facts included? Irrelevant information and wordiness may decrease the reader's understanding of the message.
- *Clarity.* Will the purpose of the letter or memorandum be clear to the reader? Does the choice of words help the reader understand what is being said? Are the ideas presented in a logical sequence—words within sentences, sentences within paragraphs, paragraphs within the entire letter?
- *Completeness.* Are all the facts and figures (the "what"), dates (the "when"), names (the "who"), and addresses and places (the "where") included? Is only relevant information included? Are the reader's

possible questions (or objections) anticipated and answered? Stating the facts completely helps the reader understand the entire message. It also reduces the need for additional correspondence or other communication.

- *Correctness.* Are the facts, dates, names, numbers and figures, and amounts correct? Incorrect information will confuse the reader and require clarifying communications.
- *Tone.* Is the tone of the letter or memorandum appropriate for the objective of the communication? A friendly tone should be used to inform a client or to elicit information from a client or other individual; a firmer tone may be used to inform or to persuade an adversary.
- *Spelling and word usage.* Are words correctly spelled, capitalized, and divided? Are appropriate words used to express the writer's meaning? Are numbers properly used and correctly written?
- *Punctuation and capitalization.* Is punctuation applied correctly to clarify, separate, and emphasize ideas? Are abbreviations properly used, correctly punctuated, and correctly written?

Types of Letters

7–3 Letters are classified by their objective and their intended reader: whether a client or prospective client, a company or other organization, an opposing counsel, or other individual. Letters may be categorized into four groups: cover letters, general informational letters, demand letters, and opinion letters. Each type of letter serves a specific purpose and must be properly planned and written to satisfy the ultimate purpose of the communication.

Cover Letters

7–4 *Cover letters* are short letters used to transmit and accompany a document or a letter to a client, another attorney, or other individual or organization. Include the following in a cover letter.

- *Requested action.* Identify the document(s) enclosed and state what action the reader is to take: whether to read, initial, sign, sign and return, and so on. State the request courteously and directly.
- *Statement of purpose.* State the purpose of the enclosed document(s) in relation to the requested action. If the reader understands the rationale for the request, he or she is more likely to act or respond promptly.
- *Closing.* Close the letter pleasantly. If appropriate, set a date for return of the document(s) and specify a preferred method for the return—whether by fax, courier delivery, mail, and so on. (If the date of return is critical, include the date in the opening paragraph.)

General Informational Letters

7–5   *General informational letters* convey information of a general nature: informing someone of a decision, updating the status of proceedings, or requesting information or documents. Use a direct approach when providing information or asking for information. Use words and expressions that the reader will understand; avoid legal or technical language unless the reader is familiar with such terms. Include the following in a general informational letter.

- *Introduction.*   Indicate the purpose of the letter: to provide information, to update, to elicit a response, to verify or confirm information.
- *Statement of purpose.*   If appropriate, explain the rationale for any requested information and how it relates to your objective in the matter. Review past or recent developments if necessary to provide a broad context in which the reader can act or make a decision.
- *Closing.*   Summarize briefly.

Demand Letters

7–6   A *demand letter* is written on behalf of a client to demand action of or payment from an individual or company. Since the purpose of such a letter is to obtain action or payment, write persuasively. Include the following in a demand letter.

- *The demand.*   State clearly and concisely your demand. Be specific about the action or payments sought. If appropriate, use a listing when the action requires several steps or involves a period of time.
- *Consequences.*   State clearly what course(s) of action will be taken if the reader does not act as requested. State the date by which such action is expected. Be sure you are in a position to carry through with the stated consequences upon noncompliance.
- *Closing.*   Restate firmly the action to be taken; specify a due date for compliance.

Opinion Letters

7–7   An *opinion letter* offers legal advice or a legal opinion to a client who has requested such information in order to decide whether to proceed further in the matter. Often such legal advice or opinion will be provided to the client's representative, such as an accountant or other financial advisor. Include the following in an opinion letter:

- *Statement of purpose.*   State the purpose of the correspondence. The statement of purpose identifies the scope of research completed on the legal issue or question raised by the client.

- *Statement of facts.*   State the relevant facts of the issue or question. This allows the client to clarify and verify the facts as they were presented. List the facts when appropriate to itemize details and to aid the reader in following the sequence of ideas or events.
- *Conclusion.*   Apply the relevant laws or statutes or other authorities to the stated facts. Summarize the authorities clearly and concisely; use language that the client will understand. Offer a conclusion based on the objective of the requested opinion or advice.
- *Recommendation.*   Make a recommendation concerning what action you believe the client should take. Be objective but forthright. (Note: The recommendation may be placed in the first part of the letter since the client may want to know the recommended course of action before reading the facts and the rationale.)
- *Client follow-up action.*   Depending on the recommendations, state what action the client should take next. State the action clearly and the date by which any decision should be made. State the consequences or other outcome of such action or inaction.

Letter Categories

Business letters fit into one of the following three categories: the guide letter, the form letter, or the individual (personalized) letter.

Guide Letters

7–8

A guide letter is composed of prepared paragraphs that meet the most common situations in daily correspondence. Guide letters are practical when a firm must respond to many similar situations with routine but varied responses.

The text for guide letters usually includes opening and closing paragraphs written in general terms to apply to routine situations. Other paragraphs are more specific and designed to answer a variety of common questions or problems. These paragraphs often have blanks where dates, amounts, numbers, names, addresses, and other variable information may be inserted. The paragraphs are used individually or in different combinations for the body of each guide letter. Figure 7.1 illustrates guide document paragraphs for acknowledgments and responses to customer correspondence.

7–9

Each guide paragraph is assigned a number and stored in a word processor or computer. To prepare a letter, the writer selects the appropriate paragraphs and lists their numbers in the desired sequence. The numbered paragraphs are retrieved and formatted into a letter or other document, which is then printed. This process is called *document assembly.* Figure 7.2 illustrates how relevant paragraphs are incorporated to produce a finished document.

1. OPENING

I am concerned to learn of your recent experience in connection with your trip to (<u>destination</u>). We appreciate your bringing this matter to our attention.

2. OPENING

Thank you for taking the time and effort to write us in detail about your recent experience with us. You are owed an apology, of course, and I want to be prompt in extending it.

3. APOLOGY—POOR SERVICE

Your comments indicate that you did not receive the kind of service as a passenger you expect from us. Please accept our apologies. Your experience has been brought to our flight service manager's attention, and (<u>he/she</u>) will review the matter with the flight crew concerned. Appropriate measures will be taken to ensure better performance and service in the future.

4. RESPONSE TO COMPLAINT ABOUT EMPLOYEE

Thank you for taking the time to write to us about (<u>employee name</u>), (<u>employee position</u>). We appreciate your letting us know when our service has not been up to the high standard you have been accustomed to. We will contact the employee to discuss this matter with (<u>him/her</u>), and appropriate measures will be taken to ensure better performance and service in the future.

5. EXPLANATION—REFUSE CLAIM FOR LATE ARRIVAL OF FLIGHT

We strive for on-time performance on all our flights. However, since no transportation company can guarantee its schedules because of unexpected weather and traffic situations, we must decline reimbursement for any extra expenses as a result of the late arrival of your flight.

6. EXPLANATION—REFUSE CLAIM FOR EXCESS BAGGAGE ALLOWANCE

I am very sorry about your experience with the excess baggage allowance, and I can understand your disappointment. Under a set of standard rules that must be adhered to, the excess baggage receipt accepted by the traveler at check-in must be considered the correct record of the weight of the baggage presented at the time. An adjustment of an excess baggage charge can be made only when a computation error has been made and is brought to the attendant's attention at that time. Although it is difficult to account for the differences in weight you mentioned, there is little we can do in an after-the-fact investigation.

7. EXPLANATION—REFUSED CLAIM—BUILD GOODWILL

We look forward to having another opportunity to demonstrate that we can provide the kind of service you expect.

8. RESPONSE TO COMMENDATION

Thank you for taking the time to commend (<u>employee name</u>), (<u>employee position</u>). It is always reassuring to learn that our employees have done an especially fine job. (<u>Employee name</u>), I am sure, was pleased to be of assistance and joins us in looking forward to serving you again soon.

If there is anything we can do to assist you on your future trips, (<u>Name of passenger</u>), please let us know.

9. CLOSING

We look forward to serving your transportation needs in the future.

10. CLOSING—RESERVATIONS INFORMATION

Reservations can be made at (800) 555-0000 or online at <u>www.bestflight.com</u>.

FIGURE 7.1 Sample Guide Letter Paragraphs

```
Dear

Thank your for taking the time and effort to write us in detail about your re-
cent experience with us. You are owed an apology, of course, and I want to be
prompt in extending it.

I am very sorry about your experience with the excess baggage allowance, and
I can understand your disappointment. Under a set of standard rules that must
be adhered to, the excess baggage receipt accepted by the traveler at check-in
must be considered the correct record of the weight of the baggage presented
at the time. An adjustment of an excess baggage charge can be made only when a
computation error has been made and is brought to the attendant's attention at
that time. Although it is difficult to account for the differences in weight you
mentioned, there is little we can do in an after-the-fact investigation.

We look forward to serving your transportation needs in the future. Reservations can
be made at (800) 555-0000 or online at www.bestflight.com.

                                          Sincerely yours,
                                          BESTFLIGHT
```

FIGURE 7.2   **Final Letter Using Guide Paragraphs (Paragraphs 2, 6, 9, and 10)**

Form Letters/Documents

7–10   A form letter or form document is prepared for large volumes of routine use. Form documents (often called "boilerplates") are tailored to fit a
number of circumstances that occur frequently.

   As in guide letters, such variable information as dates, amounts,
numbers, names, and addresses can be inserted at predefined places in a
document. The form letter or document is retrieved, merged with a database or datafile containing the variable information (created and stored in
a secondary file), and then printed. The resulting letters and documents
appear to be individually prepared. See figure 7.3.

```
                J. C. WEBB COLLECTION ASSOCIATES
                        SERVICE AGREEMENT
                       Terms and Conditions

THIS AGREEMENT is made this date between J. C. WEBB COLLECTION ASSOCIATES
(hereinafter referred to as "Agent") and _____ (hereinafter referred to
as "Client"), whose business address is _____, for the collection of
Client's delinquent accounts by Agent or its network of attorneys and collection
specialists on behalf of Client.

It shall be the intent of Client to retain the services of J. C. WEBB COLLECTION
ASSOCIATES for the purpose of providing debt collection services. In the
interest and spirit of maintaining the highest level of ethical and professional
standards, the parties agree to conduct their business according to the Fair
Debt Collection Practices Act (FDCPA) and the Fair Credit Reporting Act (FCRA).
In addition, all collection activities shall be conducted according to the
standards set forth in the Operative Guidelines of the Commercial Law League of
America (CCLA).
```

FIGURE 7.3   **Form Document**

1. By placing a claim for collection with Agent, Client grants to Agent full discretion and authority to proceed with all collection efforts deemed necessary, including the referral of claims to attorneys for the filing of suit, obtaining judgments, and postjudgment enforcement. Lawsuits will be initiated only upon authorization of Client.

2. Agent is granted discretion and authority to act as it deems appropriate in the collection of claims and is authorized to accept partial payments. Agent shall have the right to endorse for deposit and collection any checks made payable to Client. Client will authorize and consent to any compromise or settlement of any claim.

3. Upon receipt of all payments collected on behalf of Client, Agent will remit said payments to Client within _____ (_____) days of collection; Agent will provide an accounting for such collections.

4. Agent will provide Client with weekly/monthly/quarterly accountings of all activities pursued in collecting accounts on behalf of Client. Such reports will be provided to Client within three (3) days following the end of the week/month/quarter.

5. In accordance with FDCPA, all communication with the Client's debtor(s) will be conducted by and through the offices of the Agent. Client agrees to cease all communications with the debtor(s) or to have the claim handled by any other institution, collection agent, or representative. Client agrees to inform Agent immediately as to the nature and content of any contacts that debtor(s) makes or attempts to make directly with Client as well as other matters germane to the collection of the claim(s). Claims that are compromised by the Client and/or settled directly with the debtor(s) are subject to fees pursuant to Article 6 of this Agreement. Any claims paid directly by the debtor(s) to the Client shall be subject to fees pursuant to Article 6 of this Agreement as well.

6. Fees for collection will be as follows: Any claim placed with Agent that is more than one (1) year outstanding will be billed at a rate of _____ percent (_____%). Any claim placed with Agent that is less than one (1) year will be billed at a rate of _____ percent (_____%). Any claim placed with Agent for return of material goods or services by debtor(s) to Client will be billed at a rate of _____ percent (_____%) of its value. Any claim placed with Agent that is ultimately forwarded to an outside attorney for litigation will be billed at a rate of _____ percent (_____%).

7. In the event Client's claim(s) are withdrawn or the services of Agent are terminated without cause, it is agreed that Agent shall be entitled to fees on such claim(s) and shall be reimbursed and shall recover from Client any advanced court costs, attorney fees, and due diligence expenses incurred on behalf of Client. These fees will be equal to full commission of the principal amounts of the claim. Any claim(s) withdrawn due to Client's error in account placement in collection or are discovered to have been previously paid shall be billed at a rate of ten percent (10%) as an administrative fee. Once legal proceedings have been initiated on behalf of Client, whether pre- or postjudgment, the withdrawal or cancellation of the claim(s) is permissible only after all fees, court costs, and due diligence expenses have been paid Agent.

8. The jurisdiction for resolving any dispute arising under this Agreement shall be in _____ County, State of _____, United States of America.

Dated: _____   _____
                                                     Client Signature

                                     _____
                                     For J. C. Webb Collection Associates, Agent

FIGURE 7.3   **Form Document** *(concluded)*

Individual (Personalized) Letters

7–11   An individual or personalized letter is one that is created to meet a specific situation. Neither a form letter nor a guide letter can be used to respond to the particular circumstance. The individual letter can be keyboarded, dictated to an assistant or to a machine for transcription, handwritten for later keyboarding, or communicated as a rough idea to another person who will compose the actual letter. Such letters can also be created using voice-recognition software as well as handwriting-recognition software. (See 9–43 • 9–48.)

Letter Formats

7–12 Business letters are usually written in these formats: block style (Figure 7.4), modified block style with blocked paragraphs (Figure 7.5), or modified block style with indented paragraphs (Figure 7.6).

Letterhead	**M** The Main Event Planners
	e Richfield Arts Building
	300 Main Street
	ρ Englewood Cliffs, NJ 07632-3309
	(201) 555-0873
Date	November 15, 20--
Inside address	Mr. Christopher S. Lee
	Attorney-at-Law
	19078 Edgerley Road
	Boston, MA 02115-4980
Salutation	Dear Mr. Lee
Subject line	SUBJECT: Topic, reference or file number, or case name or number
	This is an illustration of a letter prepared in the block style. Every line of the letter begins at the left margin.
	The block style is frequently used because it is easy to set up, and letters can be keyboarded efficiently. This form is preferred by many executives because the production rate of secretaries and clerks is increased.
Body	
	To further increase the efficiency in preparing letters, open punctuation may be used with the block style letter. There is no punctuation after the salutation nor after the complimentary closing.
	Because of its simplicity and distinctiveness, the block style has become one of the more popular letter styles.
Complimentary closing	Cordially yours
Company name	THE MAIN EVENT PLANNERS
Signature line	*T. Louise Peebles*
	(Mrs.) T. Louise Peebles
Official title	Human Resources Administrator
Reference initials	pp

FIGURE 7.4 **Block Style Letter, Open Punctuation, Right-Justified Margin**

Letterhead   **Jasper, Keene, Kobayashi & Wu**
                                    A Professional Corporation
                                    190 North Michigan Avenue
                                        Suite 1219
                                    Chicago, IL 60601-7149
                                        ——

                                    Telephone: (630) 450-9372
                                    Fax: (630) 456-7311

Reference lines   Re:
                                                            Our File:
                                                            Your Reference:

Date   December 3, 20--

Inside address   Ms. Arthika Chandramohan
                    Ms. Lorene Endoso
                    American Insurance Corp.
                    1140 Arapaho Drive
                    Tucson, AZ 85001-2230

Salutation   Dear Ms. Chandramohan and Ms. Endoso

Subject line   SUBJECT: Modified-Block Style Letter

                    This letter is keyboarded in the modified-block style with open
                    punctuation.

Body   The date and the signature lines begin at the center of the page.
                    This letter also illustrates the use of a subject line, which
                    relates to the body of the letter. Type the subject line a double
                    space below the salutation and a double space above the body.
                    Precede the subject line by Subject or SUBJECT, followed by a
                    colon and one or two spaces. The subject line in a block style
                    letter must be keyboarded beginning at the left margin; the
                    subject line in the modified-block may be keyboarded either
                    beginning at the left margin or centered.

                    The modified-block style letter is popular because it is easy to
                    set up and gives a balanced appearance.

Complimentary   Sincerely yours
closing

Signature line   JASPER, KEENE, KOBAYASHI & WU

                                            By _____

Reference
Initials   chd

Postscript   Either mixed/standard or open punctuation may be used with this
                     letter style.

FIGURE 7.5   Modified-Block Style Letter, Open Punctuation, Subject Line, and Postscript
292

Letterhead

Superior Steel Corporation
260 South Broad Street
Philadelphia, PA 19102-5166

Phone: 215 233-0156
Fax: 215 233-0157

Date

May 28, 20--
TRANSMITTED BY FAX

Inside address

Hutchinson, Woods, and Kellogg
14078 Alemany Boulevard
Battle Creek, MI 49014-5183

Attention line

Attention: Jennifer Orsini

Salutation

Ladies and Gentlemen:

Body

Please note the arrangement of information in the inside address of this letter, which is prepared in the modified-block style with five space (or one-half inch) paragraph indentations. The letter is addressed to a company but is directed to the attention of an individual, Ms. Orsini.

The attention line may be keyboarded as the second line of the inside address or at the left margin a double space below the inside address and a double space above the salutation (as shown above). An attention line may contain the name of an individual, as shown here, or the name of a particular department or section of the company. The trend today is to omit the attention line and address the letter directly to the named individual.

Notice that the salutation of this letter is "Ladies and Gentlemen," referring to the company to whom the letter is addressed.

The indented paragraphs of this letter style provide balance to the page; however, it is sometimes difficult to remember to indent the first line of each paragraph during keyboarding.

A sheet describing this and other letter styles is enclosed.

Complimentary closing

Cordially yours,

Signature line

Stephanie Michelle Lang

Stephanie Michelle Lang
Human Resources Administrator

Reference initials

pdl

Enclosure notation

Enclosure

File name notation

c:\lang\incorp\jannings.ltr

FIGURE 7.6 **Modified-Block Style Letter with Indented Paragraphs, Mixed Punctuation, Justified Right Margin; Computer File Name Notation**

293

Letter Margins

7–13

Regardless of the format used, the letter must be attractively displayed on the page—arranged with appropriate margins at the top, bottom, and sides of the page. Table 7.1 gives guidelines for margins and spacing of business letters.

Word processing programs have preset (default) margin settings that accommodate most correspondence prepared on standard stationery measuring 8½″ by 11″. (See Table 7.2.)

Average-length letters can be prepared using these default settings. For shorter letters, insert extra line spaces at the top of the page before the return address (on plain paper), between the letterhead or typed return address and date, or between the date and the inside address.

For longer letters, leave fewer lines between these letter parts or continue the letter on another page.

TABLE 7.1   Letter Placement Guide (Standard-Size Stationery)

		12-point font	10-point font
Letter Length	Number of Words	Line length (inches)	Line length (inches)
Short	under 100	1.5	1.75
Average	up to 200	1.5	1.75
Long	200+	1.0	1.25

TABLE 7.2   Preset (Default) Page and Margin Settings

	Microsoft Word	WordPerfect
Top margin	1 inch	1 inch
Side margins	1.25 inches	1 inch
Bottom margin	1 inch	1 inch
Line length	6 inches	6.5 inches
Page length (in inches)	9 inches	9 inches
Page length (in number of lines)	54	54

Punctuation Styles

7–14

There are two common forms of punctuation: (1) mixed or standard and (2) open. The difference between the two styles lies in the punctuation after the salutation and the complimentary closing.

Mixed or Standard Punctuation

7–15

With mixed or standard punctuation, a colon follows the salutation and a comma follows the complimentary closing. (See Figure 7.6.)

Open Punctuation

7–16 With open punctuation, no punctuation follows either the salutation or the complimentary closing. (See Figures 7.4 and 7.5.)

Letter Elements

7–17 Each part of a business letter has a specific purpose in order to convey the desired message clearly. The standard letter contains nine parts: (1) letterhead or return address, (2) date, (3) inside address, (4) salutation, (5) body, (6) complimentary closing, (7) signature line, (8) official title, and (9) reference initials. A letter may also contain such special parts as postal and addressee notations, an attention line, a subject line, typed firm or organization name, enclosure notation, copy notation, computer file name notation, and postscript.

Letterhead

A business letter is prepared on letterhead stationery that should be carefully designed to make the appropriate impression on and promote a professional image of the company to those who receive such correspondence.

Using Letterhead Stationery

7–18 "Letterhead" refers to the high-quality paper imprinted with the firm name, address, and telephone number. The names of the firm's partners and associates are generally printed on the stationery as well. Additional information includes the firm's cable address or a facsimile (fax) telephone number. If the firm has offices elsewhere in the country or the world, those addresses may also be included on the letterhead. Several letterheads are illustrated in Figures 7.4 through 7.6.

Date

7–19 The current date is keyboarded at the left margin (in the block style letter) or beginning at the center point of the page (in the modified-block style). In some cases, to match the arrangement and design of a company letterhead, the date may be centered horizontally.

The date is keyboarded three to five lines below the last line of a printed letterhead. If the letter is prepared on plain paper, keyboard the date approximately 2 inches from the top of the page or immediately after a return address that appears at the top of the page.

Business Style Dates

7–20 In a business letter, the month is always spelled out in the date line. Write the day of the month and the year in figures, separated by a comma.

```
December 27, 20--
```

Military Style Dates

7–21 The military services prefer the inverted method of writing dates: day, month, year. No punctuation is used between the parts of the date.

```
27 December 20--
```

Note: Dates in business letters should not be keyboarded in figures, such as 10/2, because the figures may be misread. In the military, for example, "10/2" would be read as February 10 rather than as October 2.

Postal and Addressee Notations

7–22 Postal delivery notations (such as REGISTERED MAIL, CERTIFIED MAIL, and SPECIAL DELIVERY) or addressee notations (such as PERSONAL and CONFIDENTIAL) alert the Postal Service or mail processors within an organization of the need for special handling. Include these notations on the letter as well as on the envelope. Keyboard these notations in capital letters a double space above the inside address.

If correspondence is being sent or transmitted by other than the U.S. Postal Service, indicate the method of transmittal on the letter itself. Special handling notations include HAND DELIVERY, VIA FACSIMILE, TRANSMITTED BY FACSIMILE, and COURIER DELIVERY SERVICE.

```
COURIER DELIVERY SERVICE

Petit, Henneberger & Rupp
A Professional Law Corporation
3181 Marvin Road
Dayton, OH 45431-9073
```

Inside Address

7–23 The inside address is the complete name and address of the recipient. A complete inside address includes the addressee's complete name, title and/or department (where appropriate), company name (where appropriate), complete street address, city, two-letter state abbreviation, and ZIP code. Keyboard the ZIP code one space after the state abbreviation. (See 5–17 • 5–18.)

```
Jones, Katz & Bloom
3181 Marvin Road
Dayton, OH 45431-9073
```

Some given names, as well as foreign names, may be either a masculine or feminine name (for example, Pat, Leslie, or Jesse). When an individual's gender is not known, omit the personal title in the inside address. Keyboard the inside address at the left margin four to eight lines below the date.

When a window envelope is used, the inside address also serves as the envelope address. The inside address must, therefore, be properly placed on the stationery to be visible through the envelope window. (See Figure 7.12.)

7–24 The following are examples of a complete inside address for a letter written to an individual. An appropriate personal or professional title, such as *Miss*, *Mr.*, *Mrs.*, or *Ms.*, should precede the individual's name. If you do not know and cannot find out the gender of the person, omit the courtesy title in the inside address and the salutation. Use the person's first and last name in the salutation.

<u>Addressee name and complete address</u>

```
Ms. Sally N. Clark
99330 Rosewood Circle
Tucson, AZ 85710
```

<u>Addressee name, title, and complete business name and address</u>

```
Carol D. Kellogg, Esq.
Kellogg & Kellogg, LLP
Suite 201
1000 West Verdugo Road
Glendale, CA 91505-1245
```

7–25 Examples of a complete inside address for a letter written to a company follow.

```
Barrick, Johnson, and Smithwick
The Bank of Norwalk
59-61 North Collins Road
Suite 230
Norwalk, CT 06840-1284
```

```
International Biscuits Corp.
Legal Department
201 North Main Street
Baton Rouge, LA 70807-6004
```

Long Company/Organization Names

7–26 A long company or organization name may be keyboarded on two lines. Indent the second line of a company name two spaces. Try to balance the two-line name.

```
Byron Hayes, Esq.
Fong, Ortell, Hutchinson,
  Hayes & Sarkisian
```

Short Addresses

7–27 In some cases, a street address may not be necessary, as with letters addressed to a large organization or an individual in a small community. Use a two-line inside address.

```
Amana Refrigeration Co.
Amana, IA 52204-6889
```

Post Office Box Addresses

7–28   Some companies and individuals have their mail delivered to a post office box rather than to their places of business. The post office box number is keyboarded in place of the street address in the inside address.

```
Direct Mail Services
P.O. Box 246
Colorado Springs, CO 80901-8246
```

Post Office Box Address and Street Address

7–29   Some companies include both the street address and the post office box number in their mailing addresses. When both addresses are included, the U.S. Postal Service will deliver to whichever address appears on the line above the city, state, and ZIP code.

For delivery to the post office box:

```
Direct Mail Services
9053 Aurora Avenue
P.O. Box 246
Colorado Springs, CO 80901-8246
```

For delivery to the street address:

```
Direct Mail Services
P.O. Box 246
9053 Aurora Avenue
Colorado Springs, CO 80901-8246
```

International Addresses

7–30   The elements of an international address are arranged differently from an address in the United States. The city, state/province, and country names may appear on one line, followed by the delivery or country code on the same or the next line. The country name is generally keyboarded in all capital letters on the last line.

```
Ms. Monalee Luth
OrthoMed Specialties
10711 80th Street
Edmonton, Alberta
T6E T87
CANADA
```

```
Ms. Doris Brougham
Overseas Radio & Television, Inc.
P.O. Box 37-3 Taipei, Taiwan 104
REPUBLIC OF CHINA
```

Attention Line

7–31   An attention line is used to direct the letter to a specific individual or department for processing when the letter is addressed to a company or an organization. The attention line is considered part of the inside address. It is keyboarded either as the second line of the inside address or at the left margin a double space below the inside address. The word *Attention* is followed by a colon.

```
Consolidated Technologies, Inc.
Suite 1401
24605 Bundy Drive West
Albuquerque, NM 87101-5182

Attention: Mr. Martin Isozaki

Consolidated Technologies, Inc.
Attention: Mr. Martin Isozaki
Suite 1401
24605 Bundy Drive West
Albuquerque, NM 87101-5182
```

The attention line can be omitted by addressing the letter directly to that person or department.

```
Mr. Martin Isozaki
Consolidated Technologies, Inc.
24605 Bundy Drive West
Suite 1401
Albuquerque, NM 87101-5182
```

Salutation

7–32

The salutation, or greeting, is keyboarded at the left margin a double space below the inside address or the attention line, if used. A formal salutation includes the person's personal or professional title and surname. An informal salutation consists of the person's first name. Some given names or foreign names may be either masculine or feminine (for example, Leslie, Tracy, Lynn, or Marion), or individuals may use only their first or middle initials. When the individual's gender is not known, omit the personal title in the salutation. (Note: If possible, phone the individual to determine the appropriate title.)

If the letter is prepared using mixed/standard punctuation, a colon follows the salutation. If open punctuation is used, no punctuation follows the salutation.

```
Mrs. Janet K. LaCroix
1427 North Broadway
Lincoln, NE 68529

Dear Mrs. LaCroix:
```

```
Leslie P. Jacobson, Esq.
1430 East Colorado Boulevard
Pasadena, CA 91106
Dear Leslie P. Jacobson

J. J. Rasmussen
General Counsel
Standard Enterprises, Inc.
34 Bramhall
Portland, ME 04102

Dear J. J. Rasmussen
```

7–33 The following salutations meet the majority of letter-writing needs. See 7–82 • 7–85 for other forms of address.

Company or Organization
```
Ladies and Gentlemen
Dear Human Resources Department
Dear Galaxy Electrical Corporation
Dear Customer (or other appropriate salutation)
```
Individual(s) Informal
```
Dear Chadwick
Dear Libby and Floyd
```
Individual (Formal)
```
Dear Mr. González
Dear Ms. Jablonski
Dear Miss Rice
Dear Mrs. Swenson
```
Individual (Gender Unknown)
```
Dear Terry Jackson
Dear W. V. Goldmann
Dear Chu-Li Huang
```
Man and Woman
```
Dear Mr. and Mrs. Mar
Dear Ms. Lee and Mr. Palladino
```
Two Men
```
Dear Messrs. Lopez
Dear Mr. Jackson and Mr. Ruiz or
 Dear Messrs. Jackson and Ruiz
```
Two Women
```
Dear Mses. Kelley
Dear Misses Russell
Dear Mesdames Fargo
Dear Ms. Jablonski and Ms. Fargo or
 Dear Mses. Jablonski and Fargo
Dear Miss Russell and Miss Fargo or
 Dear Misses Russell and Fargo
Dear Mrs. Swenson and Mrs. Swinney or
 Dear Mesdames Swenson and Swinney
```

7–34 When a letter contains an attention line, use a general salutation that matches the name of the company or organization rather than the person or department named in the attention line.

```
Consolidated Technologies, Inc.
24605 Bundy Drive, Suite 1401
Albuquerque, NM 87101-5182

Attention: Mr. Martin Isozaki
```

Dear Consolidated Technologies:

Subject Line

7–35 The subject line sets forth the topic of the letter and is considered part of the body. The subject line generally includes a particular transaction, an account number, or a brief description of the purpose of the letter.

Keyboard the subject line a double space below the salutation and a double space above the body of the letter. The subject line may be positioned at the left margin or centered on the page for letters keyboarded in the modified-block style; the subject line must be positioned at the left margin in block style letters. The word *SUBJECT, IN RE,* or *RE* is keyboarded in all capital letters at the beginning of the line and is followed by a colon.

<u>Prelitigation Phase:</u>

```
RE:  Your Insured, John Q. Client
     Policy No. 95-984036
     Date of Accident, January 30, 20--
```

<u>Pending Litigation Phase:</u>

```
SUBJECT:  John Q. Client v. Defendant Name
          Case No. 95-12345
          Our File No. 95-984
```

Body

7–36 The body of the letter contains the message. The body is single-spaced with a double space between paragraphs. One-paragraph letters may be double-spaced.

In block style letters, the first line of each paragraph is blocked. In modified-block style letters, the first line of each paragraph is either blocked or indented one-half inch (or five or six spaces) from the left margin. (See Figures 7.4 through 7.6.)

Word processing software programs have a justification feature. With right-margin justification on (also called "full" justification), all lines in the document end at the same point at the right margin. (See Figure 7.6.) When right-margin justification is off (the default setting), the lines at the right margin will be ragged or uneven (or "unjustified"). (See Figure 7.5.) Whichever format is selected, it should be used consistently throughout the document.

Lists

7–37 Letters often include lists or enumerations to emphasize information or present key ideas in an easy-to-read form. Items in the list may be introduced by arabic numbers (*1, 2, 3*), letters (*a, b, c* or *A, B, C*), bullets (•), or asterisks (*).

An introductory sentence preceding the list must be a complete sentence. No punctuation is used after the enumerated items unless they are complete sentences.

> The following MCLE courses will be offered in your city.
> • Civil procedures for personal injury cases
> • Issues in family law
> • Mediating the litigated case

7–38 Keyboard the list in the same format as the letter—with either blocked or indented paragraphs. Use blocked paragraphs within a block style letter or a modified-block style letter with blocked paragraphs. Begin each numbered item at the left margin.

The second and succeeding lines of a list may either continue at the left margin or align with the first word in the item. When the block style letter is used, succeeding lines must be continued at the left margin. When the modified-block style letter is used, succeeding lines may either be continued at the left margin or aligned with the first word. Single-space the individual items and double-space between items.

> <u>Succeeding lines at left margin:</u>
> 1. Become acquainted with the law office staff and the working style and preferences of each member.
> 2. Develop effective communications skills with the attorneys, other office support personnel, and clients.
> 3. Understand the importance of meeting deadlines in a law firm; know how to prioritize work.
> <u>Succeeding lines aligned with first word:</u>
> 1. Become acquainted with the law office staff and the working style and preferences of each member.
> 2. Develop effective communications skills with the attorneys, other office support personnel, and clients.
> 3. Understand the importance of meeting deadlines in a law firm; know how to prioritize work.

7–39 In a modified-block style letter with indented paragraphs, indent the first line of each numbered item. Subsequent lines may begin at the left margin or under the first word in the item (see examples in 7–38) or at the paragraph indention as shown below.

```
    A. Become acquainted with the law office staff and
the working style and preferences of each member.
    B. Develop effective communications skills with the
attorneys, other office support personnel, and clients.
```

7–40 Short lists may be keyboarded as a series within a sentence. Separate the items by commas or semicolons if the items contain commas or are long. The introductory statement must lead naturally into each item, and the wording of all items must be consistent.

```
    A list may be used to (a) draw the reader's attention
    to important information, (b) present key ideas in con-
    densed form, or (c) indicate the correct sequence of
    steps in a procedure.
```

Quoted or Graphic Materials and Tables

7–41 Letters often incorporate within their body quoted material, graphics, and/or tables to illustrate the related text. Such information may also be attached to or enclosed with the letter but should specifically be referred to within the letter to alert the reader of this additional explanatory information.

Quoted Material

7–42 Keyboard the quoted material within the margins set for the letter. A short quotation consisting of fewer than 50 words is keyboarded within the paragraph and enclosed in quotation marks. Where appropriate, include the source of the quoted material.

A long quotation consisting of more than 50 words is keyboarded as a separate paragraph, single-spaced, and indented one-half to one inch from the right and left margins. No quotation marks are necessary before or after the text since its position and spacing indicate it is a direct quotation. Where appropriate, include the source of such quoted material. (See 6–169 • 6–175)

Continuation Pages

7–43 The second and subsequent pages of letters are prepared on plain paper of the same quality as the letterhead. A header (heading) is keyboarded at the top of each additional page. The header consists of the addressee's name, the date, and the page number. A header created with word processing software is printed automatically on all or designated pages.

On the second and subsequent pages, continue the body of the letter three or four lines below the heading. Follow the same format (margins, paragraphing, spacing, etc.) as on the first page.

7–44 Follow these guidelines for letters of more than one page:

1. Include at least two lines of a paragraph at the bottom of a page.
2. Do not end a page with a divided word.

3. Leave at least a one-inch margin at the bottom of a page. A larger margin is acceptable to avoid splitting a paragraph inappropriately.

4. Carry over at least the last two lines of a paragraph to the top of the next page.

Block Style Headings

7–45 A three- or four-line block style heading is keyboarded at the left margin approximately one inch from the top of the page. The heading consists of the addressee's name, the date, and the page number. All lines begin at the left margin. A four-line heading would be used when the letter is addressed to a company and contains an attention line to an individual or a department. Single-space the lines of the heading.

```
Ms. Kathryn Ceppi
December 5, 20--
Page 2


Claussen, Wu & Fong
Attention: Richard Fong, Esq.
December 5, 20--
Page 2
```

Horizontal Style Headings

7–46 A one- or two-line horizontal style heading is keyboarded across the top of additional pages of a letter. The addressee's name begins at the left margin, the page number is centered, and the date ends flush at the right margin.

```
Mrs. Kathryn Ceppi    2              December 5, 20--

Claussen, Wu & Fong   2              December 5, 20--
Attention: Richard Fong, Esq.
```

Complimentary Closing

7–47 The complimentary closing is the formal end of the letter. Keyboard the closing a double space below the last line of the body of the letter. The closing may begin at the left margin (for block letters) or at the center of the page (for modified-block letters).

If mixed/standard punctuation is used, a comma follows the closing. If open punctuation is used, no punctuation follows the complimentary closing.

7–48 The following complimentary closings are used in business correspondence.

```
Cordially              Very sincerely yours
Cordially yours        Very truly yours
Respectfully           Yours sincerely
Respectfully yours     Yours truly
Sincerely              Yours very truly
Sincerely yours
```

More personal closings such as the following may be used at the writer's discretion.

As always	Regards
As ever	Warmest regards
Best wishes	With regards
Kindest regards	

Company Name

7–49 Although the company name appears in the letterhead, some companies like to highlight the name by also including it in the closing. Keyboard the name in all capital letters as it appears in the letterhead, a double space below the complimentary closing.

Sincerely yours,

CENTER FOR CONFLICT RESOLUTION

Signature Line

7–50 Leave enough space below the complimentary closing or company name for the writer's signature. Three to four blank lines are usually adequate, depending on the size of the writer's handwriting.

Sincerely yours,

CENTER FOR CONFLICT RESOLUTION

W. Timothy Pownall

W. Timothy Pownall, Executive Director

Sincerely yours,

W. Timothy Pownall

W. Timothy Pownall, Executive Director

By Line

7–51 A *by* line may appear below the complimentary closing to indicate that the person signing the correspondence is signing on behalf of the firm. Keyboard the word *By* followed by a colon or a space and a solid underscore: the signer's name may be keyboarded below the line.

Sincerely yours,

JOAN M. LAURICELLA AND ASSOCIATES

By _____

    Jeffrey Winter, Attorney-at-Law

7–52 Keyboard the writer's full name (first name or initial, middle initial or name, and surname) on all business correspondence, regardless of how the letter is signed. Titles such as *Miss, Mrs.,* and *Ms.,* may appear in parentheses before the keyboarded name. Personal designations such as *Jr., Sr., II, III,* and *2d* should be keyboarded as part of the writer's name.

305

Professional titles or degrees may be keyboarded after the writer's name but are not written as part of the signature.

Yours sincerely,

Stanley A. Hutchinson

Stanley A. Hutchinson, Esq.

Very truly yours

Darlene Wills

(Mrs.) Darlene A. Wills
Attorney-at-Law

Respectfully yours

G. S. Woods

Gary S. Woods, Esq.

Signing for Author

7–53 Often a secretary or other individual signs correspondence in the absence of, or on behalf of, the writer. When this happens, the signer's initials should follow the signature.

Sincerely,

Elizabeth L. Johnson (pp)

Elizabeth L. Johnson

Writing on Another's Behalf

7–54 When a secretary or other authorized person writes a letter on another's behalf, the writer's name is keyboarded on the signature line. Her or his capacity is indicated on the next line as an official title.

Very truly yours,

Patricia Pastis

Patricia Pastis
For Sigrid Johnson, Office Manager

Sincerely

Dustin Aaron Wong

Dustin Aaron Wong
Administrative Assistant to Anne Grussu

Unknown Title/Gender

7–55 If the writer's name does not clearly identify that the writer is a man or a woman, include in the typed signature line an appropriate personal title (in parentheses). This will inform the recipient of correspondence about the correct form of personal title to use in return correspondence. Generally, if no personal title is included, the writer may be assumed to be a man; clarify wherever appropriate.

Sincerely,

(Ms.) Sydnie Harrington

Woman's Title

7–56 A woman's personal title may be included in the signature line. The title *Miss*, *Mrs.*, or *Ms.* may be keyboarded in parentheses before the woman's name, or it may appear in parentheses as part of the handwritten signature, but not both.

Yours sincerely,

Betty Lou Collier
(Ms.) Betty Lou Collier

Sincerely,

(Ms.) Betty Lou Collier
Betty Lou Collier

7–57 For social correspondence, a woman may wish to be addressed by her husband's first name. The signature line would include her husband's full name preceded by the title *Mrs.*

Best wishes

Mrs. Alfred L. Lee
Mrs. Alfred L. Lee

7–58 A widow may use her full name (first name, middle name or initial, and surname) in business and social correspondence. A widow should use her husband's full name only for social correspondence.

Sincerely,   Best wishes,

Rose Hom   *Mrs. George Hom*
Mrs. George Hom   **Mrs. George Hom**

7–59 A married woman who may or may not have taken her husband's surname may use her maiden name and should precede her name with *Ms.* for business purposes.

Sincerely,

Sandra Rittman
(Ms.) Sandra Rittman

A married woman may use both her maiden name and her husband's name for business and social correspondence. The two names may be hyphenated or written separately.

Sincerely,

Anna Li Powers
(Ms.) Anna **Li Powers**

Sincerely,

Anna Li-Powers
(Ms.) Anna **Li-Powers**

Writer's Official Title

7–60 The writer's title or official capacity should follow the keyboarded signature, either on the same line or on the next depending on the length of the name and the title. When both name and title appear on one line, a comma separates them. If the writer's name and title appear in the letterhead, the title need not be included in the signature line.

> Cindy M. Chavez
> **Legal Assistant**

> Chau Banh, **Law Librarian**

Long Titles

7–61 A long title may be written on two lines. Divide the title at an appropriate point and indent two spaces before continuing the title on the second line.

> Martha E. Bellinger
> **Commissioner, Superior Court**
> **Department 231**

Professional Degrees and Official Titles

7–62 When both a professional degree and an official title are included in the signature lines, keyboard only the degree on the same line as the name. When a degree is included, other designations such as *Dr.*, *Ms.*, *Miss*, or *Mrs.* are not used.

> Judy K. Snyder, **PLS, CLAS**
> **Word Processing Supervisor**

Department/Section Names

7–63 When a department or section name is included in the closing lines, keyboard it on a separate line below the writer's official title.

> Ann Armstrong, **PLS**
> **Litigation Secretary**

> Carolann Hughes, **PLS, CCLS**
> **Real Estate Division**

Reference Initials

7–64 Reference initials identify the person who wrote the letter and/or the person who keyboarded it. Reference initials are keyboarded at the left margin a double space below the last line of the signature block. Use capital letters, separating the two elements by a colon. When writing only the keyboarder's initials, use lowercase letters. The writer's initials may be omitted if her or his name appears in the signature line.

> Doris McElwee, M.S.W.
> Psychiatric Social Worker
> Office of the Medical Examiner
>
> **DME: lld**

```
Doris McElwee, M.S.W.
Office of the Medical Examiner
lld
```

If a letter is written by one person for another person's signature, the writer's initials are used in the reference initials line.

```
Margaret M. Straub, CRM
Entertainment Division
CCA:SML
```

Computer File Name Reference Notation

7–65 Correspondence and documents stored on the computer are saved under unique file names to identify the client (surname or firm/company name), the type of document (letter, memorandum, pleading, etc.), the creator of the document, and/or the date of creation.

If desired, a computer file name notation may be included at the bottom of letters; if the document needs to be retrieved, edited, or printed, the file name reference appearing on the hard copy itself directs the user to the appropriate disk file. Such notations are for internal reference purposes only and should appear only on file copies of printed documents—not on the original letter printed for the recipient or for other distribution. Keyboard the file reference notation either a single space below the writer's reference initials or as the last reference line (see Figure 7.6).

```
KCE:iti
c:\powers\trust\endoso.doc
```

Enclosure Notation

7–66 When other documents are to be enclosed with or attached to the letter, an enclosure notation is keyboarded to indicate to the reader that such additional pages are (or should have been) included. Keyboard the enclosure notation at the left margin a single space below the reference initials.

```
CCA:SML              CCA:SML
Enclosure            Attachments
CCA:SML
Enc.
```

Enclosures may be itemized for the reader's convenience. When there is more than one enclosure, the number of items may be indicated.

```
Enclosure:  Release Form Contract
Enclosures  2
Enclosures  (2)
```

Copy/Courtesy Copy Notation

7–67 When a copy of a letter is prepared and distributed to one or more persons, this fact should be noted on all copies as a courtesy to the recipient of the letter. The copy notation appears at the left margin a single space below the last reference line. Keyboard the word *Copy* or *Copies* or the letter *c* or the letters *cc* (for *courtesy copy* or *copies*), followed by the name or names of individuals receiving the copies.

When copies are to be distributed to two or more persons, list the recipients' names in alphabetical order. Some offices prefer to list names in order of seniority or importance within the firm, beginning with the highest-ranking individual.

> **Copy to**   Judy Meredith
>
> **c** Judy Meredith
>
> **Copies to**   Shari Aram
>   Tom Joyce
>   Karen Luchsinger

7–68 The complete address of the copy recipient may be indicated on the letter if appropriate.

> Copy to Shari Aram
>   P.O. Box 916
>   Englewood Cliffs, NJ 07632

If a copy of a letter is being sent to an individual within the organization, that person's internal mailing address should be included in the notation.

> Copy to Stephanie Wu
>   **Tulsa Office**
>
> c Annik Gevorkian
>   **International Law Division**

Blind Copy Notation

7–69 If the addressee is not to know that a copy of a letter is being sent to another person, use a *blind copy notation*. The blind copy notation does not appear on the original letter. The notation does appear on the file copy, the blind copy, and other appropriate copies. Keyboard the blind copy notation at the left margin a single space below the last reference line. Use the abbreviation *bc* or spell out the words.

> **bc** Pereppa Kirk
>
> **Blind copy to** Pereppa Kirk
>
> **Blind copies to Pereppa Kirk**
>   **Judy Meredith**

7–70 Keyboard and print the original letter in the usual way. Return to the document on screen and keyboard the blind copy notation. Save the final document. Print the blind copy, the file copy, and other copies as needed.

Distribution of Copies

7–71 When one or more copies of a letter are to be sent to the individuals listed, each copy must be marked to show the intended recipient of that copy. Place a check mark or underscore the recipient's name on each respective copy of the letter; a highlighter pen may also be used.

```
        Copies to    Shari Aram
                   ✓ Tom Joyce
                     Karen Luchsinger
```

Postscript

7–72 A postscript is an afterthought, sometimes used for emphasis at the very end of a letter. Keyboard the postscript a double space below the last reference or notation line. Use the same style for the postscript as for the body of the letter—either blocked or indented paragraphs.

The position of the postscript at the end of the letter identifies it as an afterthought; therefore, the letters *P.S.* may be omitted.

```
csm
```

Please call me Tuesday to arrange a date and time for the deposition of your client.

ENVELOPES

Return Address

7–73 Most firms use envelopes printed with their return addresses. The return address often matches the design of their letterhead stationery. (See Figure 7.7.) If envelopes are not printed with the company's return address, keyboard it in the upper left corner. (See Figure 7.8.) A return address enables the U.S. Postal Service to return mail to the writer if necessary.

Address Block

7–74 The envelope address should be identical to the inside address of the letter. Envelopes can be addressed and printed using the Envelopes feature of the word processing program. The placement of the address block is set by default according to the envelope size selected on the Envelope menu. The recipient's address can be printed on the envelope by highlighting the inside address of the letter so no additional keyboarding is required. Most word processing programs allow a maximum of six lines in the address block.

The U.S. Postal Service provides guidelines for envelope addresses for various sizes of envelopes. On a No. 10 envelope (See Figure 7.7), begin the address 4¼ inches from the left edge and about 2 inches from the top edge. On a No. 6¾ envelope, begin the address 2½ inches from the left edge and about 2 inches from the top edge. (See Table 7.3 for other envelope sizes).

```
Mr. Thomas F. Joyce
Permalife Insurance Company
1382 East Brookline Street
Rockwood, PA 15557-6812
```

Short Addresses

7–75 Occasionally a street address is not necessary for delivery of mail, as with letters to a large organization in a small community. Use a two-line address.

```
UNIVERSITY OF CALIFORNIA AT LOS ANGELES
LOS ANGELES CA 90024
```

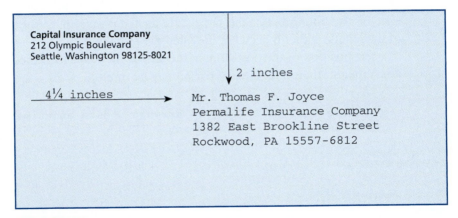

FIGURE 7.7   **Envelope with Preprinted Return Address**

```
R. J. Groppi, President
Arcata Industries
1434 Casa Linda Avenue
Beverly Hills, CA 90210-5387




                              Ms. Joanne Kim
                              Law Librarian
                              819 North Central Avenue
                              Denver, CO 80203-7257
```

FIGURE 7.8   **Envelope with Keyboarded Return Address**

To ensure proper delivery to a large institution or facility, indicate a specific department, building, or facility if known.

```
UNIVERSITY OF CALIFORNIA AT LOS ANGELES
SCHOOL OF LAW
LOS ANGELES CA 90024
```

OCR Address Style

7–76 The U.S. Postal Service uses electronic scanning equipment, called optical character readers (OCR), to speed the processing and delivery of mail. The address block must fit into a rectangle called the OCR read area, illustrated in Figure 7.9. OCR scanning requires a sharp contrast between the ink color and the paper color of the envelope.

Follow these guidelines when addressing envelopes in OCR style:

1. Use single spacing and a block format.
2. Start keyboarding the address at the horizontal and vertical center of the envelope.
3. Keyboard the post office (city), state, and ZIP code on the last line.
4. Do not place any information below or to the side of the address block.
5. Use a simple block typeface. Do not use italic or script type.

Postal Notations

7–77 Postal notations include *AIRMAIL, CERTIFIED MAIL, REGISTERED MAIL, PRIORITY MAIL, RETURN RECEIPT REQUESTED,* and *SPECIAL DELIVERY.* Keyboard postal notations in all capital letters in the upper right corner of the envelope below the postage stamp area. (See Figure 7.10.) See Unit 11 for additional information on postal services.

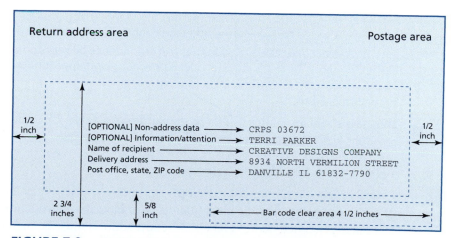

FIGURE 7.9   **OCR Address Format for No. 10 Envelope**

Capital Insurance Company
212 Olympic Boulevard
Seattle, Washington 98125-8021

CONFIDENTIAL   SPECIAL DELIVERY

                              CAROL MITZNER, ESQ.
                              955 BARNES DRIVE
                              PROVO UT 84601

FIGURE 7.10   Envelope with Addressee and Postal Notations

Addressee Notations

7–78 Addressee notations alert the recipient to special handling instructions. Keyboard addressee notations in all capital letters in the upper left corner of the envelope, below the return address. (See Figure 7.10.) The following are common addressee notations.

ATTENTION:	Directs correspondence to the attention of a specific person or department of an organization
CONFIDENTIAL:	Indicates that correspondence contains privileged information and is to be received, opened, and handled only by the addressee
HOLD FOR ARRIVAL:	Instructs that the correspondence is to be held for the addressee's arrival at the particular address; the arrival date is included in the notation
PERSONAL:	Denotes correspondence that is intended only for the addressee and/or is of a personal nature
PLEASE FORWARD:	Asks that correspondence be sent to the addressee's new address if appropriate

Envelope Size

7–79 Business stationery comes in three standard sizes. Table 7.3 indicates the envelope sizes that are appropriate for each stationery size.

Addressing Manila Envelopes

7–80 Letter- or legal-sized manila envelopes and other special types and sizes of envelopes must either be hand-addressed or have the address printed on computer-generated address labels. A return address must be included on all envelopes. See Figure 7.11.

TABLE 7.3 Envelope Sizes for Letters and Memorandums

Size of Stationery	Envelope Size	When to Use
Half Sheet or Baronial ($5\frac{1}{2}$" by $8\frac{1}{2}$")	No. $6\frac{3}{4}$ ($6\frac{1}{2}$" by $3\frac{5}{8}$")	1- or 2-page letter or memorandum
Standard ($8\frac{1}{2}$" by 11")	No. $6\frac{5}{8}$ ($6\frac{1}{2}$" by $3\frac{5}{8}$")	1-page letter or memorandum
	No. 10 ($9\frac{1}{2}$" by $4\frac{1}{8}$")	1-page letter or memorandum with enclosures
		2-page or longer letter or memorandum
	Manila (9" by 12"; 10" by 13")	1- or 2-page letter (unfolded) with many enclosures; multipage letters
Executive or Monarch ($7\frac{1}{4}$" by $10\frac{1}{2}$")	No. 7 ($7\frac{1}{2}$" by $3\frac{7}{8}$")	1- or 2-page letter

Return Address:

Law Offices of L. Edmund Kellogg
1733 Grand Avenue, 5th Floor
Des Moines, IA 50309

Address:

Ninth Circuit Court of Appeals
Law Library
125 South Grand Avenue
Pasadena, CA 91105

FIGURE 7.11 Computer-Generated Address Label on 9″ × 12″ or 10″ × 13″ Manila Envelope

Individual labels on sheets or strips of labels can be prepared using word processing or database programs. The placement of addresses on the labels is predetermined based on the type and size of label selected from the Envelopes and Labels menu option. Companies often use preprinted mailing labels containing the company's complete address with a space for the addressee information; such labels would be printed on continuous sheets or in strips and keyboarded appropriately.

Place the address or mailing label at the approximate center of the manila or other nonstandard-sized envelope. The envelope flap should be to the right.

Folding and Inserting Correspondence

7-81 Methods of folding and inserting correspondence into the appropriate envelopes are illustrated in Figures 7.12 through 7.15. Folding correspondence as shown distributes the thickness evenly throughout the envelope and results in a neatly folded document.

When manila envelopes are used for correspondence and any enclosures or attachments, all documents are inserted into the envelope flat. Papers may be held by a rubber band, but clamps and paper clips should not be used.

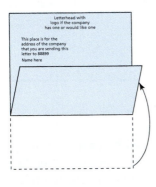
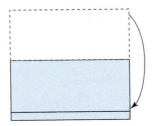
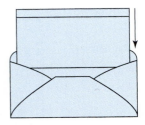

1. Fold up the bottom one-third of the letter; crease.
2. Fold down the top of the letter to about one-half inch from the bottom; crease.
3. Insert the letter into the envelope with last crease first.

FIGURE 7.12   **Folding Half-Sheet Stationery for No. 6¾ Envelope**

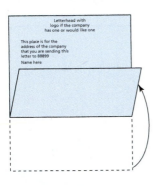
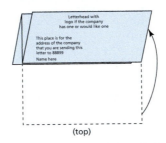

1. Keyboard the inside address on correspondence so it can be properly aligned with the window.
2. Fold up the bottom one-third of the letter; crease.
3. Fold the top edge backward and down to about one-half inch from the bottom fold; crease.
4. Check the placement of the address in the window.

FIGURE 7.13   **Folding Half-Sheet and Standard-Size Stationery for Window Envelope**

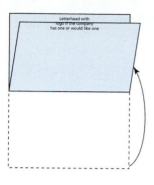
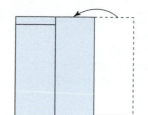
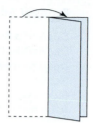

1. Fold up the bottom to within one-half inch of the top of the letter; crease.
2. Fold the right side of the letter about one-third to the left; crease.
3. Fold the left side over to about one-half inch from the right fold; crease. Start with the left side if you are left-handed.

FIGURE 7.14   Folding Standard-Size Stationery for No. 6¾ Envelope

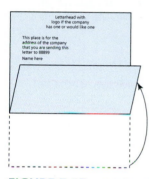
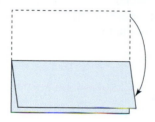

1. Fold up the bottom one-third of the letter; crease.
2. Fold down the top of the letter to approximately one-half inch from the bottom fold; crease.

FIGURE 7.15   Folding Standard-, Executive-, or Monarch-Size Stationery for Monarch and No. 10 Envelopes

FORMS OF ADDRESS

7–82 Correspondence written to certain public officials, foreign religious dignitaries, and other high-ranking or distinguished individuals requires a formal address and salutation. The following lists indicate the proper forms of addresses and salutations for such individuals as religious leaders, political and government officials, military personnel, foreign dignitaries, and academic personnel. *Sincerely yours* is an acceptable complimentary closing, although others may also be used. (See 7.48.)

Academic Officials

7–83

Forms of Address	Salutation
Dean of a School Dean (full name) School of (name) (school/college/university name) (address) (city, state, ZIP code)	Dear Dean (surname) Dear Dr. (surname)

Forms of Address	Salutation
Dean of a School Dr./Mr./Ms. (full name) Dean of (name of school) (school/college/university name) (address) (city, state, ZIP code)	
President of a College or University President (full name) (college/university name) (address) (city, state, ZIP code)	Dear President (surname) Dear Dr. (surname)
Professor of a College or University Professor (full name) (school/division/department) (college/university name) (address) (city, state, ZIP code)	Dear Professor (surname) Dear Dr./Mr./Ms. (surname)
Dr./Mr./Ms. (full name) (title) (school/division/department) (college/university name) (address) (city, state, ZIP code)	Dear Dr./Mr./Ms. (surname)

Government Officials

7–84

Forms of Address	Salutation
Alderman The Honorable (full name) Alderman, City of (name) (address) (city, state, ZIP code)	Dear Alderman (surname) Dear Mr./Ms. (surname)
Ambassador The Honorable (full name) The Ambassador of the United States (foreign address of U.S. Embassy) (city) (country)	Dear Mr./Madam Ambassador
Associate Justice of the U.S. **Supreme Court** Justice (surname) The Supreme Court of the United States Washington, DC 20543	Dear Mr./Madam Justice

Forms of Address	Salutation
Cabinet Member	
The Honorable (full name) Secretary of (department) Washington, DC 20520	Dear Mr./Madam Secretary
Chief Justice of the United States	
The Chief Justice of the United States The Supreme Court of the United States Washington, DC 20543	Dear Mr./Madam Chief Justice
City Attorney	
Honorable (full name) City Attorney of (city) (address) (city, state, ZIP code)	Dear Mr./Ms. (surname)
Mr./Ms. (full name) City Attorney City of (name) (address) (city, state, ZIP code)	Dear Mr./Ms. (surname)

**Commissioner/Director/
   Chief of Government Bureau/
   Department/Agency**	

The Honorable (full name) (title) (name of government bureau) (address) (city, state, ZIP code)	Dear Mr./Ms. (surname)
Consul	
Mr./Ms. (full name) United States Consul (address) (city, country)	Dear Mr./Ms. (surname)
Council Members	
Councilman/Councilwoman (full name) City of (name) (address) (city, state, ZIP code)	Dear Councilman/ Councilwoman (surname)
The Honorable (full name) Councilman/Councilwoman City of (name) (address) (city, state, ZIP code)	

Forms of Address	Salutation
County Officials Honorable (full name) Supervisor (county name) (address) (city, state, ZIP code)	Dear Mr./Ms. (surname) Dear Supervisor (surname)
District Attorney The Honorable (full name) District Attorney (county name) Courthouse (address) (city, state, ZIP code)	Dear Mr./Ms. (surname)
Foreign Officials His/Her Excellency (full name) Ambassador of (country) (address) Washington, DC (ZIP code)	Excellency Dear Mr./Madam Ambassador
His/Her Excellency Mr./Ms. (full name) Minister of (country) (address) Washington, DC (ZIP code)	
Former President of the United States Honorable (full name) Former President of the United States (address) (city, state, ZIP code)	Dear Mr./Mrs. (surname)
Governor The Honorable (full name) Governor of (state) (state capitol) (address) (city, state, ZIP code)	Dear Governor (surname)

Judge (or Commissioner of Court)
The Honorable (full name)
Judge (or Commissioner) of the
  (name of court)
Department (the name or number)
(address)
(city, state, ZIP code)
	Dear Judge/Commissioner
	  (surname)

Lieutenant Governor The Honorable (full name) Lieutenant Governor of (state) (state capitol) (address) (city, state, ZIP code)	Dear Lieutenant Governor (surname)

Forms of Address	Salutation
Mayor The Honorable (full name) Mayor of (city name) City Hall (address) (city, state, ZIP code)	Dear Mayor (surname) Dear Mr./Madam Mayor
Military Personnel (rank) (full name) (branch of service) (address) (city, state, ZIP code)	Dear (rank) (surname)
President of the United States The President The White House Washington, DC 20500	Dear Mr./Madam President
The President of the United States Washington, DC 20500	Mr./Madam President

Secretary General of the United Nations
His/Her Excellency (full name)
Secretary General of the
   United Nations
United Nations Plaza
New York, NY 10017
	Dear Mr./Madam Secretary
	   General
	Excellency

Speaker of the House The Honorable (full name) Speaker of the House of Representatives Washington, DC 20515	Dear Mr./Madam Speaker
Spouse of the United States President Mrs./Mr. (full name) The White House Washington, DC 20500	Dear Mrs./Mr. (surname)
State Legislators The Honorable (full name) The State Senate (state capitol) (address) (city, state, ZIP code)	Dear Mr./Ms. (surname) Dear Senator
The Honorable (full name) The House of Representatives (state capitol) (address) (city, state, ZIP code)	Dear Mr./Ms. (surname) Dear Representative

Forms of Address	Salutation
State Legislators The Honorable (full name) The State Assembly (state capitol) (address) (city, state, ZIP code)	Dear Assemblyman/ Assemblywoman
State Officials The Honorable (full name) Secretary of the State of (name) (state capitol) (address) (city, state, ZIP code)	Dear Mr./Madam Secretary Dear Mr./Ms. (surname)
State Senator Honorable (full name) (name of state) State Senate (address) (city, state, ZIP code)	Dear Senator (surname)
United States Attorney General The Honorable (full name) The Attorney General Department of Justice Washington, DC 20530	Dear Mr./Madam Attorney General
United States Representative The Honorable (full name) The House of Representatives Washington, DC 20515	Dear Representative (surname) Dear Mr./Ms. (surname)
The Honorable (full name) Representative in Congress (local address) (city, state, ZIP code)	
United States Senator The Honorable (full name) The United States Senate Washington, DC 20510	Dear Senator (surname) Dear Mr./Ms. (surname)
The Honorable (full name) United States Senator (local address) (city, state, ZIP code)	
Vice President of the United States The Vice President United States Senate Washington, DC 20510	Dear Mr./Madam Vice President
The Honorable (full name) Vice President of the United States United States Senate Washington, DC 20510	Dear (Mr./Madam) Vice President

Religious Dignitaries

Forms of Address	Salutation
Archbishop	
The Most Reverend (full name)	Your Excellency
Archbishop of (diocese)	Dear Archbishop (surname)
(address)	
(city, state, ZIP code)	
Bishop (Catholic)	
The Most Reverend (full name)	Your Excellency
Bishop of (diocese)	Dear Bishop (surname)
(address)	
(city, state, ZIP code)	
Bishop (Protestant)	
The Reverend (full name)	Reverend Sir/Madam
[or The Right Reverend (full name)]	Dear Bishop (surname)
Bishop of (diocese)	
(address)	
(city, state, ZIP code)	
Cardinal (Catholic)	
His Eminence (given name)	Your Eminence
Cardinal (surname)	Dear Cardinal (surname)
Archbishop of (diocese)	
(address)	
(city, state, ZIP code)	
Chaplain	
Chaplain (full name)	Dear Chaplain (surname)
(full rank, branch of service)	
(P.O. Box address and station)	
(address)	
(city, state, ZIP code/country)	
Minister	
The Reverend (full name)	Dear Reverend (surname)
(name of church)	
(address)	
(city, state, ZIP code)	
Pope	
His Holiness Pope (name)	Your Holiness
Bishop of Rome	Most Holy Father
Vatican City	
00187 Rome	
ITALY	
Priest	
The Reverend (full name) and	Reverend Father
initials of the order	Dear Father (surname)
(name of church)	
(address)	
(city, state, ZIP code)	

Forms of Address	Salutation
Rabbi	
Rabbi (full name)	Dear Rabbi (surname)
(name of synagogue)	
(address)	
(city, state, ZIP code)	
Sheik (Muslim)	
Sheik (full name)	Dear Sheik (name)
(address)	
(city, state, ZIP Code) OR	
(city)	
(country)	
Sister	
Sister (full name or religious name	Dear Sister (full name or
and initials of the order)	religious name)
(name of church)	
(addresss)	
(city, state, ZIP code)	

MEMORANDUMS

7–86 Interoffice memorandums ("memos" for short) are internal communications used to convey information among company employees and are seldom seen by outsiders. There are two types of memorandums: general internal memorandum and memorandum of law. Memorandums of Law are discussed in Reports and Legal Writing, (see 8–16 • 8–19).

Internal Memorandum

7–87 An internal memorandum is a routine form of office communication that conveys general ideas, suggestions, facts, and requests for information. A general informational memorandum is written in narrative form using informal language. (See Figure 7.16 for a typical memorandum format.) See also Checklist for Effective Letters and Memorandums, 7–2.

7–88 Formal memorandums are keyboarded on preprinted memorandum or interoffice stationery. Preprinted memorandum forms come in a standard size of 8½" by 11".

Memos may be prepared on standard-size plain paper or on preprinted memorandum stationery. To simplify the preparation of memos, create a template ("skeleton" form) containing the double-spaced lines of the heading: TO:, FROM:, DATE:, and SUBJECT:. Save the template under its distinctive file name. When a memo is to be prepared, retrieve the template. Insert the appropriate information in the heading, and keyboard the body of the memo. Save the final prepared memo under its own document file name without affecting the "master" memo template.

Label

MEMORANDUM

Heading

TO: Phyllis Brzozowski

FROM: Wei-Ling Ho, Legal Department

DATE: December 19, 20--

SUBJECT: VALIDITY OF LEASE AGREEMENT FOR PREINCORPO-
           RATED BUSINESS ENTERED INTO BY NONCORPORATE
           REPRESENTATIVE (CLIENT: MRS. PEGGY ALLISON)

This memorandum illustrates the block style of keyboarding both the heading and the body of this interoffice communication. Interoffice memorandums-- or memos--are written between individuals within an organization.

All information begins at the left margin. Although the words DATE, TO, FROM, and SUBJECT in the printed heading end at different points, the keyboarded information (addressee, writer, date, and subject line) begins at a tab stop. This style of heading gives a more balanced appearance.

Body

The subject line aids the reader in focusing his or her attention on the topic of the communication and is a valuable aid in filing and retrieving correspondence. The subject line may be keyboarded in all capital letters, as shown, or the first letter of important words may be capitalized.

Memorandums are single-spaced, with double-spacing between paragraphs. Short memorandums may be double-spaced. The most efficient memorandum style is one with no paragraph indentations.

Reference initials indicate the person who keyboarded the document and are placed two lines below the last line of the body. Other notations, such as enclosure or copy, are placed a single space below each other.

Because memorandums are informal correspondence, they are not signed; however, the writer may initial the memorandum either next to the keyboarded name or at the end of the communication.

Reference initials

dm

Copy notation

Copies to Duc Loi
          Armine Mankerian

FIGURE 7.16 **Block Style Memorandum**

Writing Effective Business Memorandums

7–89 Carefully prepared memos project a positive impression to people within the company and help build goodwill among employees at all levels. Thus, memos require careful attention. In addition to the Checklist for Effective Letters and Memorandums (see 7–2), consider the following guidelines to prepare effective memos:

1. Is a memorandum necessary? Can a telephone call, a handwritten note, or a short e-mail message serve the purpose? Is a permanent record of the message required?

2. How important is the message in terms of content and urgency of transmittal? Can information be conveyed—or information obtained—by telephone or via e-mail? An e-mail message can be sent across the country and around the world rapidly.

3. Is the message of a confidential or personal nature? Memorandums that are retained are stored in office files and generally accessible to all personnel. E-mails can be seen and read by many people and saved on network servers, forwarded to others, and transmitted long distances and over time.

Margin Settings

7–90 The margin settings for memos depend on the format and alignment of the heading. If printed memo forms are used, the left margin for the memo may be set where the printed heading begins or two spaces after the colon following the guide words. Use a 1-inch right margin and a bottom margin of $1–1\frac{1}{2}$ inches. Use the default settings of the word processing program. (See Table 7.1.)

Memorandum Elements

Memorandum Stationery

7–91 Memos may be prepared on standard-size plain paper, on preprinted memorandum stationery, or on standard letterhead stationery. The printed memo form may be labeled INTEROFFICE MEMORANDUM or MEM-ORANDUM. If plain paper or letterhead stationery is used, space down 3–4 lines before keyboarding either word, centered on the page.

Heading

7–92 The heading for a memorandum consists of the guide words *TO* (or *MEMO TO*), *FROM*, *DATE*, and *SUBJECT*. The subject line may be introduced by the word *RE* instead of *SUBJECT*. Headings may be arranged in different ways. (See Figure 7.16.) Set a tab stop after the longest guide word so that the information to be keyboarded after the guide words begins at the same point.

If preparing memos on plain paper, keyboard the first line of the heading approximately 1–1½ inches below the words *INTEROFFICE MEMORANDUM*. Double- or triple-space between the heading words.

Date

7–93 Spell out the month in the date.

```
DATE:   November 30, 20--
```

Addressee/Writer Names

7–94 Keyboard the addressee's name, title (if space allows), and department name or number or mail code after the guide word *TO* (or *MEMO TO*). Keyboard the same information for the writer after the guide word *FROM*. Do not use personal titles. Such words as *Department*, *Section*, *Building*, and *Number* may be abbreviated.

```
TO:     Catherine Lee, Senior Partner

FROM:   Olga Gonzalez, Paralegal
```

7–95 If the memo is to be sent to two individuals, keyboard each name and department name or mail code number on a separate line. When a memo is to be sent to several individuals, keyboard their names either after the guide word *TO* or at the bottom of the memo.

```
TO:  Hoa Luu, Administration
     Sharon Outzen, Office Services
```

If the memo is to be sent to a specific group of individuals, address the memo to the group (for example, *Department Managers* or *Administrative Assistants*). At the bottom of the memo, keyboard the heading *Distribution List:* and list all individuals' names alphabetically below.

```
TO:  Litigation Secretaries
```

If the memo is to be sent to a number of individuals, address the memo to *Distribution List Below*. At the bottom of the memo, list the individuals' names and departments or mail codes in alphabetical order under the heading *Distribution List*.

```
TO:  Distribution List Below

Distribution List:
Kevin Cheng, Human Resources
Michelle Corral, Accounting
Anna Marie Fernandez, Payroll
Michael Schwartz, Employee Benefits
```

Individuals' names may also be listed according to their rank or position. List names from the higher-ranking position or title to the lower-ranking position or title. Individuals having the same position or title should then be listed alphabetically.

```
Distribution List:

Jean DeGrignon, Managing Partner

Rosaura Juarez, Senior Partner

Wendy McCord, Senior Partner
```

Subject

7–96   On the subject line, enter the topic of the memorandum. Often the subject will be the caption under which correspondence is filed, such as a client or case name; or it may be a statement of an issue, a point of law, or reference to a statute or code. The subject line should be brief but complete enough to identify the subject matter of the communication. Keyboard the subject in either initial or all capital letters. If a case name has been assigned or if a case is being cited, underscore or italicize the case name.

```
SUBJECT:  KASABIAN BANKRUPTCY

SUBJECT:  Simms v. Amalgamated Chemical

SUBJECT:  The Erie Doctrine Applied to a Nonresident
          Bringing Action in a State Court
```

Body

7–97   The body of the memo contains the message. Begin the body three to four lines below the last line of the heading. The body is single-spaced with blocked paragraphs. Double-space between paragraphs. A short one-paragraph memo may be double-spaced.

Second and Subsequent Pages

7–98   The second and subsequent pages of a memo are keyboarded on plain paper of the same quality as the first page. A block or horizontal style heading (similar to that for a letter) is keyboarded at the left margin one inch from the top of each additional page. The header lists the addressee's name and department, the page number, and the date.

```
Blocked Heading:
Maxine K. Wilson
Accounting Department
Page 2
February 13, 20--

Horizontal Heading:

Maxine K. Wilson
Accounting Department            2           February 13, 20--
```

7–99 Continue the body of the memo on the second and subsequent pages three to four lines below the heading. Use the same form as on the first page.

Reference Initials

7–100 Reference initials identify the person who wrote the memo and/or the person who keyboarded it. Keyboard reference initials at the left margin a double space below the last line of the body of the memo. Use capital letters for the writer's and keyboarder's initials. Separate the two elements with a colon. Use lowercase letters for the keyboarder's initials.

> **LRN:** ITC
>
> itc

If a memo is written by one person on behalf of the person whose name appears in the heading as the sender, use the writer's initials in the reference initials.

7–101 The reference initials line may include the file name of the document. If the document needs to be retrieved, edited, or printed, the document name appearing on the hard copy itself directs the user to the appropriate disk file. Such reference notation appears on the file copies only and is keyboarded a double space below the last line of the memo. Save the document under a descriptive file name reference for easy retrieval. The file name may include the client or case name, subject matter, the writer's name or initials, or an abbreviated department name or code.

> LRN: itc
>
> **C:\reynard\adoption\cisneros.doc**

Signature

7–102 A complimentary closing is not used in memos because they are informal and internal communications. Memos are not generally signed. Instead, the writer initials the document, either next to her or his name in the heading or at the end of the memo. If the writer's signature is required, it is placed at the bottom of the memo.

Enclosure or Attachment Notation

7–103 When one or more documents are to be enclosed with or attached to the memo, an enclosure notation should be keyboarded to indicate to the reader that such additional pages are (or should have been) included. Keyboard the enclosure notation at the left margin a single space below the reference initials.

> CFT: ST
>
> **Enclosure**
>
> **Attachments**

329

Enclosures or attachments may be itemized for the reader's convenience. Also, when there is more than one enclosure or attachment, the number of items may be indicated.

```
Enclosures:  ACV Letter, December 10, 20--
             Escrow Instructions
             Deposit Receipt
Enclosures 3
Attachments 4
```

Interoffice Envelopes

7–104   Many firms use interoffice envelopes to distribute memos. (See Figure 7.17.) These envelopes, generally of manila stock, are usually 9″ by 12″ or 10″ by 12″; they may also be standard No. 10 size. Interoffice envelopes, as well as incoming envelopes, can be used repeatedly; the last name is crossed off and the current addressee's name is added.

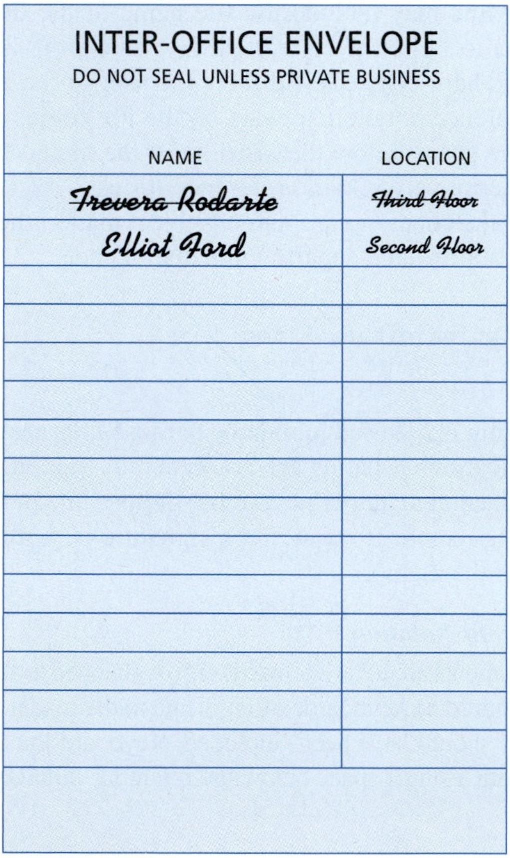

FIGURE 7.17   **Interoffice Envelope**

Unit 8

Reports and
Legal Writing

REPORTS AND LEGAL WRITING

8–1 Writing in a law office requires greater precision, accuracy, complete-ness, and organization than other types of writing. Legal writing includes legal briefs, memorandums of law, appellate briefs, and a variety of court documents. Most legal writing requires research of the law and citations to various authorities. The results of such research and writing will be con-veyed to a court, other attorneys, or institutions.

8–2 To determine the effectiveness of legal writing, use the following checklist:

Checklist for Effective Legal Writing

- *Purpose.* What is the purpose of the document? Who is the intended reader? What is the situation or dispute to be resolved? Is information to be conveyed to others to persuade, to argue, to explain, or to inform?
- *Scope.* What is the scope of the document? What factors, if any, will determine the writer's approach to the subject? Is an in-depth discus-sion or analysis required? Is information being presented? Will a sum-mary of ideas be sufficient?
- *Form and organization.* Is the format of the document appropriate for the scope and type of document? Have various court rules regard-ing form documents been followed?
- *Completeness.* Does the document include all pertinent facts, figures, dates, parties, events, and supporting details? Has the appropriate point of view been presented, and have other points of view been con-sidered in light of the intended objectives and the reader?
- *Clarity.* Is the purpose of the document clear to the reader? If stating "conditional" terms ("if," "when," "what if," "whether"), simplify the wording and the length of the statements. Avoid ambiguous wording and sentence structure.
- *Conciseness.* Is all information presented as briefly as possible? Have words been used effectively to convey the writer's thoughts? Are only the essential facts and information included? Unnecessary information and wordiness may decrease the reader's understanding of the commu-nication and may raise inappropriate issues or questions.
- *Correctness.* Are the facts, dates, names, numbers and figures, and amounts correct? Are the appropriate authorities cited, and are they written properly?
- *Tone.* Is the tone of the document consistent with the purpose of the document and the reader?

- *Spelling, word usage, and number usage.* Are words correctly spelled, capitalized, and divided? Are appropriate words used to express the intended meaning, tone, and objective? Are numbers and abbreviations used properly and punctuated correctly?
- *Punctuation, capitalization, and spacing.* Is punctuation applied correctly to help clarify, separate, and emphasize ideas? Are punctuation, capitalization, and spacing used properly in citations and abbreviations?

OUTLINES

8–3 The outline is an organization plan or map for a letter, report, memorandum, brief, or court document. The writer can use one to structure the complete document or portions of it before starting to write. The outline helps organize ideas into levels of importance in a clear and logical manner. It indicates the major points of the document, the secondary topics to be discussed, and supporting information.

Outline Form

8–4 An outline may be arranged in either standard or decimal form. In standard outlines (see Figure 8.1), roman and arabic numerals and letters of the alphabet are combined to identify different heading divisions. In decimal outlines (see Figure 8.2), arabic numerals are used with decimal points to represent each division.

```
    I.  Purpose of Study
        A.  Scope
        B.  Limitations
            1.  Time
            2.  Money
            3.  Personnel
                a.  Existing employees
                    (1)  Full-time
                    (2)  Part-time
                b.  Outside consultants
   II.  Definition of Study
```

FIGURE 8.1   **Standard Outline**

```
1.  Purpose of Study
    1.1  Scope
    1.2  Limitations
         1.2.1  Time
         1.2.2  Money
         1.2.3  Personnel
                1.2.3.1  Existing employees
                         1.2.3.1.1  Full-time
                         1.2.3.1.2  Part-time
                1.2.3.2  Outside consultants
2.  Definition of Study
```

FIGURE 8.2 **Decimal Outline**

8–5 An outline may contain up to six divisions, depending on the length and detail of the topic. In a standard outline, for example, each division is identified by the following (in order): roman numerals, capital letters, arabic numbers, lowercase letters, arabic numbers in parentheses, and lowercase letters in parentheses.

```
  I.  Major division (first item)
      A.  Second division (first item)
      B.  Second division (second item)
          1.  Third division (first item)
              a.  Fourth division (first item)
              b.  Fourth division (second item)
                  (1)  Fifth division (first item)
                  (2)  Fifth division (second item)
                       (a)  Sixth division (first item)
                       (b)  Sixth division (second item)
          2.  Third division (second item)
 II.  Major division (second item)
```

Regardless of the number of levels or the length or brevity of the outline, there must be at least two items within each division. If there is an *A*, there must also be a *B*; if there is a *1*, there must be a *2*.

8–6 Word processing programs contain an outline feature. This feature automatically inserts the appropriate number or letter for the particular level of the outline (see 8–10).

Outline Styles

8–7   An outline may be prepared in one of three styles: topic, descriptive, or full caption. As a guide for preparing correspondence or documents, an outline can consist of brief notes and ideas, or it can be written to include specific details and sentences that will be incorporated in the final document.

Topic Outline

8–8   In a topic outline, nouns and short phrases may be combined in the various levels. In major divisions, capitalize the first letter of each important word. In lesser divisions, capitalize only the first letter of the first word.

```
[noun]              I.   Purpose
[verb phrase]            A.   Solve problem
[verb phrase]            B.   Seek information
[noun]             II.   Definition
[verb phrase]            A.   Determine scope
[verb phrase]            B.   Determine limitation
[noun]                       1.   Time
[noun]                       2.   Money
```

Descriptive Outline

8–9   In a descriptive outline, the levels are written in phrases or clauses (known also as "talking captions") to provide more details about the information in each division. In major divisions, the first letter of each important word is capitalized. In lesser divisions, only the first letter of the first word and the first letters of proper names are capitalized.

```
[all noun phrases]   I.   Purpose of the Study
                          A.   Attempt to solve a problem
                          B.   Attempt to seek information
                    II.   Definition of the Study
                          A.   Scope of the study
                          B.   Limitations of the study
                               1.   Time not essential
                               2.   Money critical factor
```

Full Caption Outline

8–10   A full caption outline may be written in complete sentences (see Figure 8.3); it may combine sentences, noun phrases, and nouns; or it may combine sentences and verb phrases.

KEYBOARDING AN OUTLINE

I. Placement

   A. Center the outline attractively on the page.
   B. Set margins.
      1. Use a 6-inch line (or 1-inch side margins)
         for most outlines.
      2. Begin the outline 2-2½ inches from the top
         of the first page.
      3. Continue the outline 1 inch down on
         succeeding pages.
      4. Allow approximately 1 inch for a bottom
         margin on all pages.

II. Capitalization

   A. Center the title in all capital letters.
   B. Capitalize the first letter of each important
      word in all major (roman numeral) headings.
   C. Capitalize only the first letter of the first word
      and any proper names in lower-level divisions.

III. Spacing and Punctuation

   A. Follow these rules for line spacing:
      1. Triple-space after the title.
      2. Double-space before and after main divisions.
      3. Single-space all subdivision items.
      4. Double-space very short outlines.
   B. Follow these rules for indentions:
      1. Align roman numerals at the right.
      2. Use four-space indentions for each
         division in the outline.
      3. Begin the second line of an item directly
         under the first letter of the first line.
   C. Follow these rules for punctuation:
      1. Use a period after numerals and letters.
      2. Space twice after the period.
      3. Use a period after an item if a complete
         thought is expressed.
      4. Use no punctuation after single words or
         phrases.
      5. Use parentheses around numerals and
         letters beginning with the fifth division.

IV. Continuation Pages

   A. Use the same margin setting, spacing, and tab
      stops.
   B. Complete an entire section at the bottom of
      a page, if possible. Begin the second or

FIGURE 8.3 Full Caption Outline

subsequent page with a secondary division (identified by a capital letter) if possible. If not,
start the new page with items beginning with
arabic numerals (the third division).

C. Do not start a new page with items beginning
with lowercase letters (fourth division) or
arabic numerals in parentheses (fifth division).

D. Do not keyboard only the first line of a division
at the bottom of the page (called an "orphan").

E. Do not keyboard only the last line of any
division at the top of the next page (called a
"widow").

FIGURE 8.3 Full Caption Outline *(concluded)*

[noun phrase]   I. Purpose of the Study

[sentence (question)]   A. Is it to solve a problem?

[sentence (question)]   B. Is it to obtain information?

[noun phrase]   II. Definition of the Study

[sentence (question)]   A. What is the scope of the study?

[sentence (question)]   B. What limitations are there?

[noun]   1. Time?

[noun]   2. Money?

An outline may be created using the outline feature of word processing
software. Based on the level of the outline being keyboarded, pressing
the ENTER key moves the cursor to the next line at the same level. Pressing the TAB key moves and indents the cursor to the next lower level(s)
of the outline. Moving to the higher level(s) of the outline requires pressing the ENTER key and then the backspace key. Follow the instructions of
the word processing software for keyboarding the outline.

Outline Format

8–11 An outline should follow a consistent format, including appropriate capitalization, spacing after punctuation, and spacing between divisions and
individual entries. (See Figures 8.3 and 8.4)

Keyboarding an Outline

8–12 An outline may be created using the outline feature of word processing
software or using a computer or word processor without an outline feature.

337

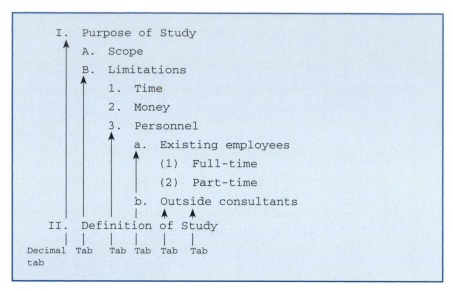

FIGURE 8.4   Outline Tabs

8–13 If using word processing software with an outline feature, follow the instructions accompanying the word processing program to create the format of the outline and define the number of levels or divisions.

CASE BRIEFS

8–14 A *brief* is a written summary of essential elements of a case that was appealed to a higher court with that higher court's decision ("opinion") being published in case reporters (see 6–74). Briefing cases is a note-taking device, which eliminates the need to reread lengthy opinions. Knowing how to summarize case law is an essential skill in legal research.

8–15 A case brief contains the following elements:

- *Names of parties* (plaintiff and defendant or other designation and their respective capacities, if appropriate)
- *Case citation* (official and/or unofficial reporter where the case is reported, including year of decision and court, if appropriate)
- *Facts* (relevant details that affected the legal issues and outcome of the original action or dispute). Include essential parties, places, dates, and events in narrative form. Identify relationships between and among persons and events if appropriate. State the action the plaintiff/appellant took.
- *Proceedings/procedural history* (a statement as to the outcome of the original action or dispute (who the successful party was), what subsequent action(s) (appeals) were taken and by whom)

- *Issue* (the legal question(s) presented in the case—the questions the parties asked the court to decide; questions in dispute that the parties needed resolved by the court)
- *Holding/disposition* (the court's decision or action in response to the legal question(s) raised in the action/dispute; the procedural result of the appellate court's action)
- *Rule of law* (the general legal principle the court applied—a statement of the applicable law or statute)
- *Policy, if applicable* (underlying purpose(s) of the legal rule applied in broader or narrower scope to serve the interests of society and all citizens, where applicable)
- *Concurring opinion, if applicable* (a separate opinion by the judge(s) who agreed with the majority opinion but for other reasons)
- *Dissenting opinion, if applicable* (a separate opinion by the judge(s) who did not concur with the majority opinion)

LEGAL MEMORANDUMS

Memorandum Reports (Memorandums of Law)

8–16 Informal reports written in a law office generally take the form of a memorandum of law. An internal *memorandum of law* is the result of legal research based on a fact pattern posed by a client or a potential client and contains an objective presentation and analysis of issues related to a specific situation. The objective of a memorandum of law is to evaluate the client's position and that of the law firm in terms of whether or how to proceed with a case. A memorandum of law may also be prepared for presentation outside the office, such as to a judge or to an administrative agency.

The memorandum of law follows the same format as other memorandums (see 7–86 • 7–103; Figure 7.16).

Heading

8–17 The memorandum is addressed TO the person(s) within the organization requesting or authorizing it. The report may also be addressed to those who will take action based on the findings.

The FROM heading should include the name, title, and/or department name or number of the person preparing or submitting the report.

The SUBJECT line should briefly identify the topic of the report or study or state its full title. The subject line may also contain the issue or question raised within the report. Keyboard the title in all capital letters or capitalize the first letter of each important word.

339

Body

8–18 The body of the memorandum contains the text. Single-space the body and double-space between paragraphs. If side headings are used, keyboard them at the left margin and underscore them. Triple-space before and double-space after each side heading. Capitalize the first letter of each important word. No punctuation follows the heading.

Elements of an Internal Memorandum of Law

8–19 An internal memorandum of law, which should be informative, includes the following elements:

- *Statement of legal issues.*   State specifically and objectively the issue(s) to be discussed or the question(s) to be answered. If several issues are being addressed, discuss each separately. Each issue may be numbered; or each can be separated into sections, identified by headings, with the issues underscored or boldfaced.

- *Statement of facts.*   State the relevant facts in a narrative, based on information obtained from the client, review of facts or documents provided, or other sources. State the facts thoroughly and objectively, relaying all sides of the situation. Be concise.

- *The answers.*   Respond briefly to each legal issue or question raised. State a brief rationale for the answer.

- *Citations and authorities.*   If desired, include any applicable citations to case law, statutes, and other authorities. Such authorities may be cited verbatim or paraphrased, following proper citation form (see *The Bluebook: A Uniform System of Citation,* also called the *Harvard Bluebook*). Consider the use and appropriateness of primary and secondary authorities in light of the issues or questions raised and the likelihood of pursuing legal proceedings in the matter. (Note: The citations and authorities may be incorporated into appropriate points in the analysis or discussion that follows.) See Unit 6, Legal Citations.

- *Analysis or discussion.*   Provide a thorough analysis of each issue or question raised. Cite relevant cases, statutes, and other authorities to support all points of view. Analyze and discuss the relationship of such authorities to both sides of the issue(s). Make comparisons, state how the current situation can be distinguished from the cited cases, or draw similarities.

- *Conclusion.*   State a conclusion that relates the facts and the analysis or discussion. If a conclusion about a definitive action cannot be reached, state that fact along with a rationale. If additional facts, information, or research is required in order to arrive at a conclusion, state them as recommendations.

APPELLATE BRIEF

8–20 An *appellate brief* is a formal written document submitted to a higher court to challenge or to defend the decision of the trial court—either to argue that the trial court committed an error that affected the outcome of the case (appellant's side) or to argue that no error was made to prejudice the outcome of the case (prevailing party at trial). Such a brief presents various authorities, cases, statutes, and other supporting legal sources for and against one's advocacy position.

Write the memorandum as an advocate for your client, so the content and approach focus on the strengths of your client's position. Write persuasively. Follow the form and content requirements of the court rules of the appropriate jurisdiction.

Elements of an Appellate Brief

8–21
- *Cover Page* (name and jurisdiction of the court; names of parties; case number; name of lower court; party submitting the brief; name(s) of attorney)
- *Table of Contents*
- *Table or Index of Authorities* (listing of cases, statutes, regulations, constitution, secondary authorities cited)
- *Statement of the Issue/Question*
- *Statement of Facts* (narrative of prior proceeding; lower court's opinion and rationale)
- *Argument* (discussion of the issues together with reasoned and logical persuasion)
- *Conclusion* (summary of the party's position and arguments)
- *Relief* (statement of the remedy sought from the appellate court)
- *Appendices* (relevant documents of lower-court proceedings, pleadings, judgments, orders, decisions; relevant portions of the lower court records)

FORMAL REPORTS

8–22 A comprehensive formal report is prepared to convey information of a lengthy or technical nature. This report is generally the result of a study or investigation of all aspects of a particular topic.

Report Elements

8–23 Formal reports usually contain the following elements, assembled in the sequence shown.

Introductory pages (see 8–39 • 8–48)

    Cover

    Title page

    Preface or foreword

    Acknowledgments

    Table of contents

    List of illustrations

    Abstract

Body of the report (see 8–49 • 8–59)

    Introduction

    Discussion

    Summary

    Conclusions

    Recommendations

Supplementary pages (see 8–60 • 8–64)

    Appendix

    Notes

    Bibliography

    Index

Report Format

8–24 The neat and attractive appearance of a well-written report helps convey the intended message effectively. The use of proper spacing and margin settings and the arrangement of section headings and the elements of the report contribute to an impressive presentation.

Margins

8–25 Margin settings depend on whether the pages will remain unbound (loose) or be leftbound. In general, the top margin on the first page of reports is 2 inches; the top margin on subsequent pages is 1 inch. Side and bottom margins should be at least 1 inch. (See Table 8.1).

Leftbound Reports

8–26 Pages of a leftbound report will be stapled or bound at the left side. Leave a 1½-inch left margin to allow for the stapling or binding.

Unbound Reports

8–27 Since the pages of an unbound report will be loose, default margin settings can be used. Wider side margins (shorter line length) may be used for short reports.

TABLE 8.1 Report Margins

	Type of Binding	
	Unbound	Leftbound
Top margin, first page	2 inches	2 inches
Top margin, succeeding pages	1 inch	1 inch
Left margin	1 inch	1½ inches
Right margin	1 inch	1 inch
Bottom margin	1 inch	1 inch

Spacing

8–28 Double-space the text of the report, and indent the first line of each para-graph five spaces (or ½ inch). Lengthy quotations and lists should be single-spaced so they stand out (see 8–55 • 8–58).

Page Numbers

8–29 Word processing software provides automatic numbering—and renum-bering—of pages in both roman numeral and arabic numeral styles. (See Table 8.1.) Number every page of the report consecutively except the cover and the title page. If a report is lengthy or is divided into units or chapters, each unit or chapter may begin with a new number, such as Page 2-1 (for Unit or Chapter 2, page 1).

Introductory Pages

8–30 The introductory pages (see 8–39) are numbered in lowercase roman numerals (*ii*, *iii*, etc.). The title page is not numbered but is assumed to be roman numeral *i*. The first page of the report after the title page should be numbered with roman numeral *ii*. Continue with lowercase roman numer-als on all introductory pages. Center the page numbers and keyboard them approximately ½ inch from the bottom of the page.

Report Pages

8–31 Use arabic numerals for all page numbers within the body of the report, beginning with page 1. (See 8–23.) The number on the first page of each new division, section, or chapter is centered approximately ½ inch from the bottom edge.

    Page numbers can be inserted at the top right or top left corner of each page, at the bottom right or bottom left of each page, or centered at the top or bottom of each page. Page numbers are inserted within the top and bot-tom margins (as a header or footer, respectively) of each page so they do not occupy a line of text space on the page. (See Table 8.2.)

TABLE 8.2 Report Page Numbers

	Leftbound
Page 1	Center—½″ from bottom
Other pages	Top right—½–1″ from top

Supplementary Pages

8–32 Number supplementary pages (see 8–23) consecutively, starting with the next number after that on the last page of the body of the report.

Headings

8–33 The headings within the report usually correspond to the major and secondary headings in the outline. Headings help the reader locate and read the information. Three levels of headings may be used within the report to show the major divisions and the subtopics or subdivisions. (See Figure 8.5.). The placement of a heading shows the relative importance of a particular topic to the overall report.

The "traditional" spacing between report elements shows a triple space (two blank lines) before and after the main headings and before side headings. This may not be easy to accomplish with word processing software since line spacing is set as a standard for the entire document. It may be necessary to use different line spacing—either double- spacing or quadruple- spacing (3 blank lines). Be consistent, however, in whatever line spacing is used.

Report Title

8–34 Center the title and keyboard it in all capital letters 2 to 2½ inches from the top of the first page. A larger size font may be used, in which case the title may be in upper/lowercase. The title may be keyboarded in one or more lines, with each line centered on the page. The lines in the title may be single- or double-spaced. Triple-space after the title before beginning the body of the report.

```
THE RATIONALE FOR EMPLOYEE BENEFIT PLANS
```

Subtitle

8–35 A larger font size may be used for the subtitle, but the size should be smaller than that used for the report title. Center the subtitle a double space below the report title. Capitalize only the first letter of important words. If larger font sizes are available, the subtitle may be a larger size but smaller than the report title.

```
THE RATIONALE FOR EMPLOYEE BENEFIT PLANS
           A Cost-Benefit Analysis
```

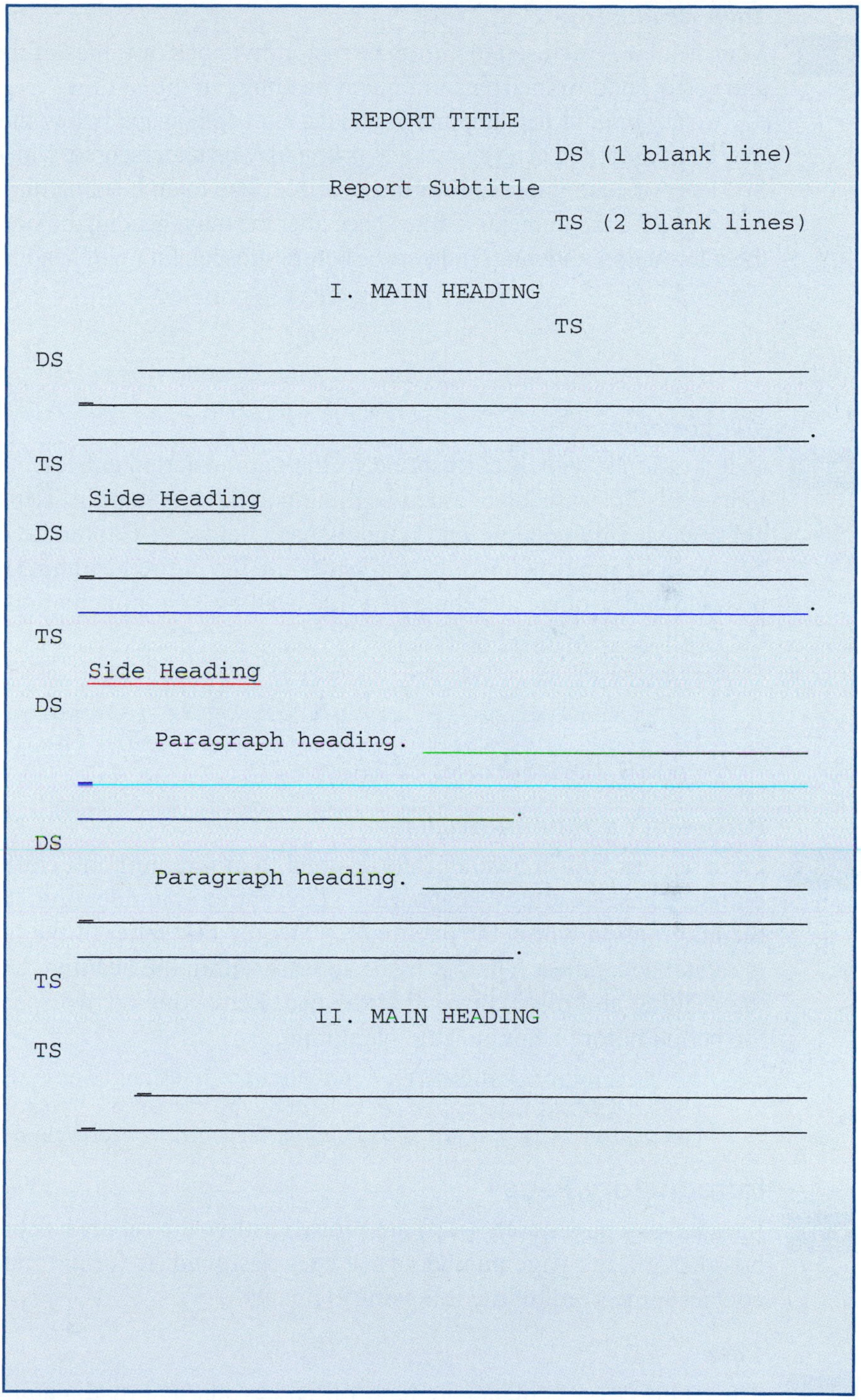

```
                         REPORT TITLE
                                    DS (1 blank line)
                      Report Subtitle
                                    TS (2 blank lines)


                      I. MAIN HEADING
                                    TS
DS        _____
     _____
     _____.

TS
     Side Heading
DS        _____
     _____
     _____.

TS
     Side Heading
DS
              Paragraph heading. _____
     _____
     _____.

DS
              Paragraph heading. _____
     _____
     _____.

TS
                      II. MAIN HEADING
TS
          _____
          _____
```

FIGURE 8.5 **Report Heading Position and Spacing**

Main Headings

8–36 Main headings are used to introduce major divisions or topics of the report and correspond to the roman numeral headings in the outline.

Center a main heading and keyboard it a triple-space below the title. It may be keyboarded in all capital letters or it may be underscored, with only the first letter of each important word capitalized. The main heading may be preceded by a roman numeral. Triple-space after the main heading before starting the information under it. Triple-space before subsequent main headings.

```
             I. SCOPE OF THE REPORT

                       or

             Scope of the Report
```

Side Headings

8–37 Side headings, which correspond to the capital-letter entries in an outline (*A*, *B*, etc.), are keyboarded beginning at the left margin. Triple-space above each side heading and double-space below it. Capitalize only the first letter of important words, and underline the entire heading. (It is also possible to capitalize all letters in a side heading.) No punctuation follows the heading. (See also Figure 8.5.)

```
    Side Heading

       Side headings are keyboarded at the left margin to
    introduce subdivisions relating to the main heading
    within each section of the report.
```

Paragraph (or Run-in) Headings

8–38 Paragraph or run-in headings correspond to arabic numeral entries in an outline. These headings, keyboarded at the paragraph indention, introduce the information within the paragraph. Only the first letter of the first word is capitalized, unless a proper name appears within the heading. Underline the heading and place a period at the end. Leave one or two spaces after the period before beginning the paragraph.

```
       Paragraph heading. A paragraph heading introduces
    the information typed within the paragraph. This heading
    begins at the paragraph indention and is underscored.
```

Introductory Pages

8–39 Introductory pages (see 8–23) are prepared after the report has been keyboarded and the page numbers have been assigned. A formal report may contain some or all of the following elements.

Cover

8–40 The report cover contains the report title, keyboarded in all capital letters and centered. If larger fonts are available, the title may be keyboarded in a larger font in upper/lowercase. Double- or triple-space a title of two or more lines. The report cover is keyboarded or printed on paper of the same quality as the report itself.

Title Page

8–41 The title page contains the report title; the writer's name, title, and/or department; and the date the report is submitted. Each piece of information is centered horizontally on the page, and all information is positioned on the page vertically to provide a balanced appearance.

Writer's Name

8–42 The name of the person who prepared—or who is transmitting—the report is centered and keyboarded about midway between the report title and the bottom of the page. An official title and department or company name may be added a single- or double-space below the writer's name.

```
                    Amelia Fong
          Managing Partner, Audit Division
```

If the report is prepared by an outside consultant, the name and address of the consulting firm is keyboarded on the title page.

```
            LUCAS-JOHNS INVESTIGATORS
            3470 West Adams Boulevard
        Sacramento, California 95822-7186
```

Date

8–43 The month, day, and year the report is prepared or transmitted is centered and keyboarded on a separate line near the bottom of the page.

Preface or Foreword

8–44 The preface or foreword is the introduction to the report. It describes the recipient's original request for the information and may include brief statements about the content of the report.

Acknowledgments

8–45 An acknowledgments page gives credit to individuals or organizations that assisted in the preparation of the report. Center and keyboard the word ACKNOWLEDGMENTS in all capital letters at the top of the page. The acknowledgments may consist of a listing of credits, or they may be written in narrative form.

Table of Contents

8–46 A table of contents should be included for lengthy reports. The contents page lists each main heading and subheading in the report with its corresponding page number. It should also list significant introductory or supplementary pages. The table of contents feature of a word processing program automatically incorporates appropriate page numbers for the keyboarded or highlighted entries. Keyboard and center the heading of the table of contents, CONTENTS, on a separate page. Follow the instructions of the word processing program for creating a table of contents.

List of Illustrations

8–47 When tables, charts, or other illustrations are contained in the report, include an illustrations list at the end of the table of contents or on a separate page. Title the list of illustrations LIST OF TABLES AND CHARTS. Keyboard the list of illustrations in the same format as the table of contents.

Number each illustration by its order of presentation within the report. In the list of illustrations, identify each one by number and title. If there are numerous tables and charts, each type may be listed separately.

Abstract

8–48 An abstract, or synopsis, summarizes the entire report and highlights the major facts, results, recommendations, and conclusions. The abstract should cover the substance of the report as concisely as possible.

Body of the Report

8–49 The body of the report includes the introduction, discussion, summary, conclusions, and recommendations. The introduction and discussion sections of the body of a lengthy report may be divided into separate chapters to help the reader interpret or focus on specific concepts. The presentation of information follows the sequence indicated in the report outline.

Introduction

8–50 The introduction provides background information to help the reader focus on the topic. This section may include the following information:

1. Authorization—Who authorized the report and when?
2. Purpose—What are the objectives?
3. Scope—What are the boundaries of the study?
4. Limitations—What conditions or problems existed before or during the investigation?
5. Organization of data—How is information presented?
6. History or background—What events generated the report?
7. Method of investigation—How was the research conducted? By whom?
8. Sources of information—What authorities were consulted?
9. Definition of terms—How are certain words used in the report?

Discussion

8–51 The discussion contains the facts, the analyses, and the findings. The report is written in formal language (third person) and should present the information objectively and factually. The discussion may contain the following:

1. Strengths and weaknesses of existing situation
2. Details of the methods or functions of existing situation
3. Facts and their substantiating data, including illustrations
4. Narrative or chronology of events, a process, or a problem
5. Proposed procedure(s) or recommendation(s)
6. Comparison of procedures and data
7. Alternate methods or routes
8. Advantages and disadvantages of alternatives

Summary

8–52 The summary is a compilation of all the major facts and findings contained in the report. It reviews the purpose of the report, the main points discussed, and the results of the study or investigation.

Conclusions

8–53 The conclusions are statements or deductions based on the writer's interpretation of the facts of the study. Conclusions should be logical extensions of these facts. They may be presented in narrative form or listed in order of importance.

Recommendations

8–54 Recommendations are suggested methods to be followed or actions to be taken as a result of the data presented in the report and the conclusions drawn. Recommendations must be directly related to the original purpose of the study and be fully substantiated by the facts. Alternate methods or actions also may be included. Recommendations may be presented as an enumerated listing based on their order of importance, or each recommendation may be presented in narrative form in a separate paragraph.

Quoted Material

8–55 When information is taken from another source or when a direct quotation is included in a report, credit must be given to the source of the material. Reworded or paraphrased information taken from any published source must also be credited. Refer to Unit 6, Legal Citations, for citing quoted and paraphrased material.

Enumerated Information

8–56   Itemized, or enumerated, lists may be used to emphasize important ideas or details. Use arabic numbers or lowercase letters in parentheses for itemized lists that appear within a sentence. Separate each enumerated item with a comma.

> The tragic outcome in the Baby Jessica case is the result of two pieces in the tragic puzzle of third-party child custody cases: (1) state parental rights termination statutes that allow involuntary termination <u>only</u> where the parent is found to be "unfit" generally disregard the prospective effect on the children involved; (2) the United States Supreme Court decided in *Santosky v. Kramer*, 455 U.S. 745 (1982), that a parent's interest in his or her child is paramount to any interest of the child, exacerbating the negative impact of the parental rights termination statutes.

Itemized Listing

8–57   Enumerated items may also be set off as separate paragraphs. Indent the first line of each item the same as the first lines of other paragraphs of the document. Use arabic numerals or capital letters followed by a period and two spaces to introduce each numbered paragraph. No punctuation follows the items unless they are complete sentences.

> Five causes of action against each of the Defendants are asserted:
>
> 1. Negligence
> 2. False imprisonment
> 3. False light
> 4. Defamation
> 5. Violation of civil rights

Lists within Paragraphs

8–58   If itemized or enumerated information has been quoted, keyboard the enumerated items as written. Credit must be given to the source of any quoted or paraphrased information. Include an appropriate citation either within the paragraph or following the information.

> The <u>Doe</u> Court identified three grounds on which a statute may be challenged for being vague: "(1) it does not provide fair notice of the conduct proscribed; (2) it confers on the trier of fact unstructured and unlimited discretion to determine whether an offense has been committed; and (3) its coverage is overly broad and impinges on First Amendment freedoms." *Doe v. Attorney General*, 487 N.W.2d 484, 488 (Mich. App. 1992).

Statistical Data

8–59 Statistical data are often included in reports in the form of tables, graphs, and charts. Such information may be created on a spreadsheet or accounting program and merged into the report at appropriate points. (See Unit 10 for information on preparing tables, graphs, and charts.)

Follow these guidelines for incorporating statistical data in the body of a report:

1. Arrange information in a logical, easy-to-read format.
2. Keep all headings simple and self-explanatory.
3. Create graphics that are well designed and self-explanatory. Within the report itself, refer to and summarize the contents of the table, graph, or chart.
4. Leave sufficient space above and below a graphic presentation within the text.
5. Cite all sources from which statistical data were obtained, using superscript numbers to identify the data. The footnote reference or explanation or credit line should appear at the bottom of each graphic.
6. Place each table, graph, or chart within the text or on a separate page following its related text.

Supplementary Pages

8–60 Supplementary report pages consist of the appendix, notes, bibliography, and index. The decision to include these pages depends on the length and detail of the report. These pages are prepared after the report is completed and page numbers have been assigned.

Appendix

8–61 An appendix consists of additional written or illustrative material that verifies or expands on a fact or idea presented in the report. Supporting documents may include a copy of a questionnaire or survey used to obtain the report data, summary tables, and reference materials. An appendix should be included in the report if it is necessary or desirable for the reader to refer to additional data to interpret the report. Appendix pages also may be referred to as *Exhibits.*

Materials included in the appendix may be combined into one section and labeled *APPENDIX.* Each item can also be given a title and labeled individually, such as *Appendix 1, 2, 3* (or *Exhibit A, B, C*). When documents are labeled separately, the table of contents should list each item.

```
APPENDIX 1. Sample Questionnaire  . . . . . . . . . . 87
APPENDIX 2. Summary Tabulations  . . . . . . . . . . 89
```

Notes

8–62 The reference or source information for materials quoted or paraphrased in the report may be presented on a separate page, rather than at the bottom of report pages. Superscript numbers still appear within the body of the report and are numbered in sequence.

In a long report, notes may also be placed at the end of a major section or unit to provide the reader easy access to references or explanatory information.

Keyboard and center the heading NOTES beginning 2 inches from the top of the page (for unbound and leftbound reports) and beginning 2½ inches from the top for topbound reports. Entries on the Notes page are arranged numerically according to the sequence of superscript numbers presented within the report. See also 8–65.

Bibliography

8–63 A bibliography is an alphabetical listing of those references cited in the report and those used to prepare the report. The bibliography appears as a separate section of the report and is placed after the last page of text. (See Bibliographies, 8–66 • 8–79.)

Index

8–64 An index is an alphabetical listing of all topics and subtopics in the report. Each entry in the index is followed by the page number(s) on which the topic is mentioned or discussed. Placed at the end of the report, an index is a valuable aid in helping the reader locate specific information, particularly in long reports. For most reports, a table of contents is sufficient.

Some word processing programs have a feature that can generate an index.

Reference Notes

8–65 Refer to 6–218, Footnotes, in Legal Citations.

BIBLIOGRAPHIES

8–66 For business report purposes, a bibliography is a list of all sources cited in the report and all other works used by the writer to prepare the report. The bibliography appears as a separate section of the report and is placed after the last page of text.

Bibliography Style

Sectional Division

8–67 A lengthy bibliography may be divided into sections by the types of references cited (books, periodicals, etc.), by an author's works, or by importance. References are listed alphabetically within each section.

```
By type of work:        books

                        periodicals

                        government publications

                        unpublished works

By an author's works:   subjects (all the works on a
                        given subject grouped together)

                        dates (all the works pub-
                        lished in a given year or period
                        grouped together)

By importance:          primary sources

                        secondary sources
```

Annotated Bibliography

8–68 An annotated bibliography includes a brief comment for each entry listed in the bibliography. (See Unit 12.) Comments relate to the content of a particular work or why or to whom a work might be of interest. Be consistent in wording each annotation so that all entries are written either in complete sentences or in phrases.

```
Kraemer, Sandy F. Solar Law. Colorado Springs:
Shepard's, Inc., 1978.

Discusses the interrelationship of solar law with the
fields of law, politics, economics, physics, engineer-
ing, architecture, and astronomy.
```

Bibliography Format

8–69 Reference sources in a bibliography are generally listed in alphabetical order according to the first element in the entry, which is usually the last name of the author.

The heading *BIBLIOGRAPHY* or *ANNOTATED BIBLIOGRAPHY* is centered and keyboarded in all capital letters beginning 2 inches from the top of the page for leftbound and unbound reports and 2½ inches for topbound reports. The singular form is used although there are multiple entries and/or several pages. Follow these guidelines:

1. Use the same margin settings that were used for the report.
2. Begin the first line of each entry at the left margin. Indent ½ inch (five spaces) for the succeeding lines of each entry.

> Patterson, Susan, and Seabolt. <u>Essentials of Alternative Dispute Resolution</u>. Dallas: Pearson, 1997.
>
> Warner, Fara. <u>The Power of the Purse</u>. Upper Saddle River, NJ: Pearson Education, Inc., 2006.

3. Single-space each entry and double-space between entries.
4. For an annotated bibliography, begin the annotation a double space below the bibliography entry. Begin the annotation at the left margin (see 8–68).
5. For a divided bibliography, keyboard the division heading in all capital letters and center it on the page. Triple-space before and after each division heading.

> PERIODICALS
>
> Shellenbarger, Sue. "The Juggling Act," <u>The Wall Street Journal</u>, June 6, 2004.
>
> Shreeve, James. "The Greatest Journey," <u>National Geographic</u>, March 2006, pp. 61–73.

Bibliography Elements

8–70 The elements of each bibliography entry correspond to the information contained in a footnote. However, the arrangement of the information in each bibliographic entry differs slightly from that of its corresponding footnote. (See also 6–230 • 6–270.)

> McLaren, Hamar Foster, and Chet Orloff, eds. <u>Laws for the Elephant, Laws for the Beaver</u>. Pasadena: 9th Judicial Circuit Historical Society, 1992.
>
> Rokes, Beverly. <u>Embracing Diversity</u>. New York: South-Western Educational Publishing, 2001.

Author's Name

8–71 The author's name appears in inverted order: surname first, followed by the author's first name or initial, and then the middle name or initial. Separate the surname from the rest of the name with a comma. Place a period after the entire name.

Multiple Authors/Editors

8–72 When a work has two authors or editors, invert only the first author's name. Separate the authors' names with commas and place a period after the last author's name.

> Hirsch, Alan, and Diane Sheehey. <u>Awarding Attorneys' Fees & Managing Fee Litigation</u>, 2d ed. Federal Judicial Center, 2005.

> Valdes, Francisco, Jerome McCristal Culp, and Angela P.
> Harris, eds. <u>Crossroads, Directions and a New Criti-
> cal Race Theory</u>. Temple University Press, 2002.

Unknown Author

8–73 When a work does not have an author or the author is unknown, list the work in alphabetical order according to the first word in the title, excluding any definite or indefinite articles.

> "The Gavel Falls on Small Business," <u>Fortune Small
> Business</u>, April 2006, pp. 14–16.

Multiple Works

8–74 If more than one work by the same author is listed, do not repeat the author's name in subsequent entries. Keyboard eight underscores at the beginning of the line, followed by a period and two spaces. The author's works may be listed chronologically from the earlier work(s) to the more recent work(s) or vice versa.

> Grisham, John. <u>The King of Torts</u>. New York: Doubleday,
> 2003.
>
> _____. <u>The Last Juror</u>. New York: Doubleday, 2004.

Titles

Book Titles

8–75 Titles of books in bibliographic entries are either underscored or italicized. Add a period after the title.

> Kestner, Prudence Bowman, and Larry Ray. <u>The Conflict
> Resolution Training Program</u>. San Francisco: Jossey-
> Bass, 2002.

Chapter and Article Titles

8–76 The titles of chapters from books and articles from magazines are keyboarded within quotation marks and precede the title of the book or magazine.

> Grow, Brian. "Gender Watch: Who Wears the Wallet in the
> Family?" <u>BusinessWeek</u>, August 16, 2004.
>
> Lithwick, Dahlia. "Putting a Lid on Legalese," <u>U.S.
> News & World Report</u>, April 11, 2005, pp. 58–59.

Volume

8–77 Volume numbers are included for periodicals when appropriate. For books published in more than one volume, cite only the volume or volumes used in preparing the report.

> Mueller, Tom. "Provence," <u>National Geographic Traveler</u>,
> **Vol. 23,** No. 3 (April 2006), pp. 62–75. [This article

> appeared in the third issue of the publisher's 23d
> year of publication.]

"America's River," <u>Audubon</u> **108** (May–June 2006),
pp. 30–32. [In lieu of volume number, a month and
year of the publication are cited.]

Gray, Brian E. "National Parks Service Act (1916)" in
3 <u>Major Acts of Congress</u> (Brian K. Landsberg, ed.).
New York: Macmillan Reference USA, 2004), pp. 42–45.
[The third volume of the work is cited.]

Nonprint Sources

8–78 Bibliography entries for microforms, audio and video recordings, and computer programs are similar to those for books. Keyboard the author's name, the title of the work, the publication data, and an identification of the type of material.

> Adobe Printshop Elements 3.0 (Windows XP). San Jose,
> CA: Adobe System Incorporated, August 2005.

Scientific Bibliographies

8–79 Entries for references in scientific reports contain the same elements as other bibliographies, but the format and arrangement of elements may differ slightly. Refer to style manuals and guides recommended by professional scientific societies or universities.

The following bibliographic entry illustrates one form in which the date is keyboarded following the authors' names. Note also that the title of the article is not enclosed in quotation marks and only the first letter of each important word in the title of the work is capitalized.

> Heathcote, P., et al., 2002. Reaction centers: the
> structure and evolution of biological solar power.
> <u>Trends Biochem. Sci</u>. 27:79–87.

> Sternlight, M.D., and Z. Werb, 2001. How matrix metallo
> proteinases regular cell behavior. <u>Annu. Rev. Cell
> Dev. Biol.</u> 17:463–516.

Unit 9

Law Office Management

Law office personnel can increase their productivity by creating and using office procedures to help them *(a)* establish priorities, *(b)* handle calendars and appointments, *(c)* prepare for appointments and conferences, *(d)* plan meetings, *(e)* make travel arrangements, *(f)* handle the various forms of information processing and software, *(g)* create and use form documents, *(h)* edit and proofread work, *(i)* file, *(j)* process incoming mail, and *(k)* make photocopies.

ESTABLISHING PRIORITIES

 Setting priorities means determining the importance of tasks to be done and deciding the order in which those tasks are to be completed. When establishing priorities, keep the following in mind:

1. *Deadline*—when the job or task must be completed.
2. *Turnaround time*—the amount of time it takes to complete a task (or a portion of a task) and return it to the originator or the person responsible for the next phase.
3. *Completion time*—the amount of time required to complete a specific task or job.
4. *Individuals involved*—whether other office staff, outside individuals or companies, or clients—and the amount of turnaround or completion time.
5. *Type of work*—whether the task is routine, creative, or administrative. Creative and administrative work require more concentration and time.

 Make a list of the tasks that need to be done, including longer-range tasks. Divide the tasks into several categories. For example, use the following categories: *high priority*—urgent or must do; *medium priority*—do soon, after the high-priority items; and *low-priority*—do when time permits. High-priority work should always be done first. Schedule other tasks with lower priorities so as to meet deadlines.

There are no concrete guidelines for separating tasks into categories. The size of the law firm, the nature of the practice, and the individuals who perform various tasks will dictate decisions concerning categories of work.

HANDLING CALENDARS AND APPOINTMENTS

 Law office calendars (both paper and electronic) should be kept on a periodic basis—daily, weekly, and monthly. They are essential in planning future events and in documenting events and activities of the past. All calendars should be updated daily. Follow these guidelines when maintaining a law office calendar.

Master Calendaring/Docket Control

9–4 Maintain a master office calendar or docket control system (also known as a tickler or follow-up system) on which all appointments for everyone are recorded. A master calendar provides a permanent record of all appointments in and out of the office: dates of hearings, conferences, and trial dates; amount of time and work performed for clients; court appearances and proceedings; statutes of limitations and other deadlines, renewal, or expiration dates; and so forth. Each attorney or group of attorneys and assistants also should maintain individual master calendars for their appointments.

9–5 Follow these guidelines in maintaining a master office calendar.

1. Include information such as the time and place of appointments, name of the client or title of the matter, nature of the activity (initial consultation, hearing, settlement conference, pretrial activity, mediation, arbitration, court appearance, etc.), and name(s) or initials of office personnel involved.

2. Refer to correspondence, telephone messages, legal papers, and other documents that have been prepared for or received by the firm from opposing counsel or outside firms. Note any specific dates and events mentioned in the correspondence or papers.

3. Note the dates on which papers were served on a party or on which notices were served on your client or firm.

4. Calculate the statutory or court-imposed dates for action, responses, motions, etc.

5. Calculate the time limits for other actions that must be taken and where such activities must take place. Plan for any intermediary steps or proceedings.

6. For litigation practices, note the time period within which an appeal must be filed after a case has been lost.

Monthly Calendaring

9–6 Use a monthly calendar to show the month's activities. A monthly calendar provides an overview of all court dates; appointments with clients, other attorneys, or court personnel; deadlines, filing dates for documents; days away from the office; and meetings, reports, and other documents that require extra preparation. Set "midterm" or intermediate goals for long, involved projects or cases, and mark those goals on the calendar.

Weekly Calendaring

9–7 Keep a detailed weekly calendar to plan for the week's activities. The weekly calendar is useful when scheduling appointments and conferences to avoid conflicts with other activities.

Daily Calendaring

9–8 On a daily calendar, estimate and block off the time an appointment, conference, or other activity is expected to take. Other appointments can then be scheduled around these activities. Use a daily calendar as a reminder to follow up on unfinished matters and to prepare for the next day's work.

Paper Calendars

9–9 Desktop and wall calendars are available in a variety of sizes and forms to meet individual needs and preferences. Pocket calendars and organizers designed to be carried with the individual are also available. Write appointments and other notations in pencil so they can be easily changed as needed. Transfer any appointments—even tentative ones—or notations to the office calendars as appropriate.

Electronic Calendars

9–10 An electronic calendar system allows users to enter, change, and delete appointments through the computer. A weekly meeting can be entered once and automatically added to the calendar for the next several weeks or months. Daily, weekly, and monthly calendars can be viewed or printed.

9–11 Hand-held electronic organizers are available with the same capabilities as paper organizers—keeping track of appointments; names, addresses, and phone numbers; reminders; projects; notes; etc. A password may be assigned for confidentiality purposes. Organizers can be linked to a computer to transfer, store, print, and/or update information. Become familiar with the electronic organizers and their capabilities to obtain the maximum benefit for their use.

Network Calendars

9–12 If the calendaring system is on a computer network, schedules can be viewed and revised from any terminal on the network. With the proper passwords, other employees' schedules can be accessed and, when appropriate, notices and appointments added or updated.

Tickler Files

9–13 A tickler file can be a card file that serves as a reminder of activities and events for each day. As an appointment, meeting, or court date is scheduled—whether on a paper or an electronic calendaring system—prepare a 6- by 4-inch index card, noting the (1) due or deadline date, (2) case or client name, (3) nature of action required, and (4) office personnel involved. Check the tickler file daily. (See 9–148 • 9–150.)

Scheduling Meetings

9–14 Calendar software can be used to search the electronic calendars of those people needed for a meeting and to list the time slots when everyone is available. Once the meeting has been set up, the software can add the date and time to everyone's schedule. This procedure is only effective, however, if all the electronic calendars are current.

Calendar software is often used to schedule the use of conference rooms. Anyone on the network can check the availability of any meeting room. Only authorized users can reserve the room.

Scheduling Appointments

9–15 Schedule appointments, keeping in mind the activities of others who may be involved such as other attorneys, clients, and court personnel. Some attorneys prefer to meet with clients on certain days or at certain times; others prefer to conduct certain types of meetings and conferences on certain days. Learn the preferences of each attorney to avoid conflicts in scheduling.

Steps for Scheduling Appointments and Conferences

9–16 Follow these steps when scheduling appointments.

1. Determine who is requesting the appointment. Is the person a senior partner, associate, or other staff member? A peer? A client? A prospective client?
2. Determine the purpose of the appointment. Is a face-to-face meeting necessary or could the matter be handled in a telephone call? Can the legal assistant take care of the matter?
3. Estimate how much time should be scheduled. Consider the nature, location, and travel distance of the meeting or conference and the participants. Allow for delays in court and anticipate the possibility of lengthy proceedings.
4. Determine which other people will be attending the meeting so that schedules can be coordinated.
5. Make a tentative appointment and confirm it later, after clearing it with the attorney or legal assistant.
6. Record the caller's phone number on the calendar or in the appointment book in case it is necessary to reconfirm, change, or cancel before the appointment. Enter the new date and time in all appropriate calendars.
7. Before ending the call, repeat the time, date, and place of the appointment for the caller.
8. Immediately after making the appointment, write it on all appropriate office calendars. (See Figure 9.1.)

```
┌─────────────────────────────────────────┐
│  August                                 │
│                              Tuesday    │
│  9                                      │
│  ─────────────────────────────────────  │
│   7:00                                  │
│   7:30                                  │
│   8:00                                  │
│   8:30                                  │
│   9:00   R. Kennedy (746-1218)          │
│   9:30   (dissolution/marriage)         │
│  10:00   ////////////////////////       │
│  10:30                                  │
│  11:00   A. Yamada (468-2005)           │
│  11:30   (incorporation docs)           │
│  12:00   ////////////////////////       │
│  12:30   ////////////////////////       │
│   1:00   ////////////////////////       │
│   1:30                                  │
│   2:00   Pinchuk Settlement             │
│   2:30   Van Nuys Court - Dept B        │
│   3:00                                  │
│   3:30                                  │
│   4:00                                  │
│   4:30                                  │
│   5:00   Landau Depo (755-3871)         │
└─────────────────────────────────────────┘
```

FIGURE 9.1   Recording Appointments

Confirming Appointments

9–17 Missed appointments waste individuals' time, particularly when other attorneys, clients, witnesses, and/or court reporters are involved. Missed court dates may result in delays in proceedings or in sanctions. Costs will still be incurred for court reporters or other individuals whose presence at a meeting was required.

1. Consider most appointments confirmed at the time they are made, unless the conversation indicates otherwise.
2. Confirm appointments when they involve client and court conferences, meetings out of the city or state, and meetings arranged several weeks or months in advance.
3. When an appointment must be canceled, notify the meeting participants immediately to give everyone adequate notice. When appropriate, explain the reason for the cancellation. Offer to reschedule the appointment.
4. When a meeting, conference, or court appearance must be rescheduled, notify all the individuals involved and check their calendars for possible dates and times. Confirm the new time, date, and place with all those attending.

5. If there is any confusion about an appointment, call the person(s) involved to verify the date and time.

PREPARING FOR APPOINTMENTS AND CONFERENCES

9–18 In-house meetings and conferences provide an opportunity for individuals within the firm to exchange ideas and information; to keep everyone up to date on the firm's activities; to make or share decisions about prospective clients and cases; to report on the status of any pending litigation; and to establish procedures, strategies, or policies.

9–19 Meetings and conferences outside the office provide an opportunity for individuals to discuss, inform, determine guidelines or timelines, mediate or negotiate, settle, or determine the status of prospective or current cases or other activities.

Follow these suggestions to help the attorney with appointments and meetings.

1. At the end of the day, remind the attorneys and other appropriate staff of the next day's scheduled meetings, conferences, or court appearances. Check the calendar or the tickler card file for the next day to anticipate and prepare for that day's work.
2. Ask whether you will be needed either at the meeting or at your desk to handle any tasks before the meeting ends.
3. Before each meeting participant arrives, give the attorney or other staff any correspondences, files, notes, or other materials that may be needed.
4. Before a meeting, distribute copies of the agenda, plus any other documents that will be discussed or reviewed at the meeting.

Greeting Visitors

9–20 Acknowledge the visitor with a smile, a pleasant greeting such as "Good morning," or "Hello," and an offer to help. If you are on the telephone, make eye contact with the visitor and smile to acknowledge her or his presence. Greet a visitor by name if you know it. It is not necessary to shake hands unless the visitor extends his or her hand.

Keeping a Record of Visitors

9–21 Many firms maintain a register or log of all visitors. The record may be used for security purposes or to document activities of visitors for billing purposes. A sign-in sheet should have places for the date and time, visitor's name and company, other helpful information, and the name of the person or department visited. The visitor should sign in on arrival and when departing.

If the visitor offers a business card, take it and make notes about the visitor and the purpose of the visit that would be helpful later. Date the business card to indicate how current the information is. Keep a business card file, arranging the cards alphabetically by the visitor's name or organization.

Handling Delays

9–22 If appointments are running behind schedule, tell the visitor immediately. If possible, give the visitor an idea of how long the delay will be. Ask the visitor if he or she prefers to wait or to reschedule the appointment.

Occasionally, a visitor will stay longer than the time allotted, delaying the next appointment. When this happens, use the telephone or interrupt the meeting to hand the attorney a reminder of the time and of the next scheduled appointment. If appropriate, include the name of the next visitor. This information will help the attorney decide whether to end the appointment, to ask the next visitor to wait, or to reschedule the next appointment.

If a delay occurs early in the day and is likely to cause delayed appointments throughout the day, contact those with later appointments and inform them of the delay.

PLANNING MEETINGS

9–23 Meetings—routine activities at most law firms—provide an opportunity to exchange ideas and information, to make decisions, and to establish policies. Meetings range from the very informal and spontaneous to extremely formal meetings that follow strict parliamentary procedure.

Arranging a Meeting Place

9–24 You may need to reserve a room for the meeting, arrange to have the room set up (tables and chairs, podium, etc.), and arrange for delivery and set up of audiovisual equipment. Other items that are sometimes requested include pitchers of water and glasses, refreshments, writing materials, and handout materials. Be sure to reserve a room large enough to accommodate the number of attendees. (See also sections 9–14, 9–18 • 9–19.)

Preparing the Agenda

9–25 An *agenda* is a list (in semioutline format) of the order of business for a meeting. The person calling the meeting is responsible for preparing the agenda. If an agenda is required, it should be distributed to the participants before the meeting begins. If detailed or technical matters are involved, participants should receive the agenda well in advance of the meeting. Other pertinent materials may be sent with the agenda.

An agenda contains the following information:

- Name of organization, department, or committee
- Date, time, and location of the prospective meeting
- The heading AGENDA
- CALL TO ORDER (name of presiding individual)
- APPROVAL OF MINUTES (vote of approval for previous meeting)
- OFFICERS' REPORTS (list of officers in sequence)
- COMMITTEE REPORTS (list of committee chairs in sequence)
- NEW BUSINESS (list of new topics to be discussed)
- OLD BUSINESS (list of unfinished/undecided topics previously discussed)
- ANNOUNCEMENTS
- ADJOURNMENT

Taking Minutes/Recording Notes

9–26 *Minutes* are an official record of the business that was transacted at a meeting. An unofficial record may be headed *Notes* and may be less formal. Both follow the sequence of topics and discussion items listed on the agenda (see 9–25). Taking minutes or notes involves listening, concentrating on the business taking place during the meeting, and taking accurate notes.

Minutes should be prepared as soon after the meeting as possible, while the information is fresh in the preparer's mind. Minutes are usually sent to the participants soon after the meeting. Distributing the minutes ahead of the next meeting saves time because people can read them prior to the meeting. Additional copies of the minutes should also be available at the next meeting.

Recording Minutes or Notes

9–27 Notes recorded at a meeting or conference may be done informally or officially. A legal assistant or secretary may be present at the conference to take notes of the meeting informally; this procedure allows the attorney to focus on the proceedings without having to take copious notes. It may be helpful to tape-record the meeting in case there are questions later about the notes.

9–28 If a certified court reporter is to be present to record the official proceedings of the conference or meeting, provide an appropriate area for him or her to work. The reporter should be seated in the room so everyone can be seen and heard clearly.

The notes recorded by a court reporter are transcribed into a written form called a *transcript* of the proceedings. A transcript may be prepared only for the individual party requesting it, or it may be distributed to all participants.

9–29 Follow these guidelines in taking minutes or in preparing to record notes:

1. Before the meeting, review the agenda and any other materials that will be covered. The agenda will serve as an outline for taking the minutes or notes.
2. Before the meeting begins, jot down names and seating positions of unfamiliar participants. It may be helpful to devise a code to identify each speaker quickly in the notes.
3. During the meeting, take notes on the important information discussed. Record word for word any motions that are made; note who made the motion, who seconded it, and whether it passed. The discussion about the motion itself may be summarized.
4. If necessary, interrupt politely to ask for a restatement of any motion or to determine names needed for the minutes.

Resolutions

9–30 A *resolution* is a statement expressing a group opinion made by those at a meeting. Resolutions are often issued to express sympathy for the loss of a member or colleague, to show appreciation to an individual for the work contributed to the organization, and to recognize an outstanding person in the group. The language in a resolution is very formal. Each paragraph except the last starts with *Whereas*; the last paragraph(s) begins with *Therefore Be It Resolved.*

Planning Events

9–31 An event may be a conference or a seminar for a large group of individuals. Refer to 9–23 • 9–24 on planning meetings. Consider the following:

- The meeting schedule (dates and times)
- The intended audience, proposed topics, etc.
- Location (whether a conference/convention facility, hotel room, etc.)
- Site requirements (meeting rooms, equipment, etc.)
- Prospective speakers or presenters (honorarium, if any; topics; schedules of presentations; etc.)
- Accommodations (hotels for participants, speakers, staff, etc.)
- Coordination of staff with site personnel
- Hospitality (food and beverage service, meal service, breaks, etc.)
- Logistics and transportation

- Security
- Registration (conference and hotels)
- Thank you mementos

MAKING TRAVEL ARRANGEMENTS

9–32 Travel arrangements may involve air and ground transportation, overnight accommodations, and documents for travel out of the country. They may also involve coordinating meetings, meals, and reservations for other activities at other locations. Large organizations often have a travel department to handle such arrangements. One advantage of having an in-house travel department is that, if there are a significant number of the firm's employees traveling, special travel packages or discount rates can often be obtained, particularly with hotels.

9–33 In most organizations, travel arrangements are made through a commercial travel agent. Have the following information ready when making travel arrangements:

1. Complete names of traveler(s) (travelers' names must match those on fare ticketing documents)
2. Departure day(s), date(s), and time(s) if several destinations are involved
3. Return date
4. Destination(s) and length(s) of stay
5. Requirements for passport and/or visa(s) (travelers' names on forms of identification must match those on passports and visas)
6. Purpose of the trip
7. Travel preferences (airlines, times, routing, etc.)
8. Appointments and meeting schedules
9. Need for overnight accommodations, rental cars, etc.
10. Company guidelines and restrictions on travel

9–34 A commercial travel agency has direct online communication with airlines, hotels, and car rental agencies. As a result, it has a wide selection of services to choose from. The travel agency can coordinate all travel arrangements for the travelers and can often expedite arrangements.

Select a reputable travel agency and work with the same travel agent so that person learns the preferences of travelers. Travel agencies often have frequent travelers complete "profiles" that include the traveler's preferences for airlines, hotels, auto rental companies, etc.; membership in frequent flyer programs; and credit cards. Travel agencies also often prepare itineraries.

367

Air Travel

9–35 When making an airline reservation, keep in mind that flights can be non-stop (no stops), direct (one or more stops but passengers do not change planes), or connecting (passengers change planes). Flight times are given in local times, so keep the time zone of the destination in mind. For connecting flights, schedule adequate time between flights to allow for travel between airport terminals and gates.

Check the refund policy before making a reservation. Some airline reservations carry restrictions on changes and refunds. Some are fully refundable, some impose penalties, and some are nonrefundable.

Ground Transportation

9–36 Most travelers require ground transportation of some sort from the airport to their destination. The ground transportation may include bus, train, limousine, taxi, or airport shuttle service. Check with a travel agent for available services at the traveler's destination.

Travelers may choose to drive to their destination or may require a car upon reaching the destination. Rental cars are available in a number of sizes and with a variety of mileage plans. Some companies may arrange special rates with certain car rental agencies. Reserve rental cars or limousine services ahead of arrival to ensure their availability upon arrival at the destination. Obtain schedules for public transportation if possible. General information is often available on Internet Web sites for major destination cities.

Overnight Lodging

9–37 Major hotel chains have toll-free telephone numbers for making reservations. Travel agents can also make hotel reservations, but accommodations worldwide can also be made directly via Internet Web sites.

The following information will be needed when making a lodging reservation: name and address of guest, number of guests, dates of arrival and departure, number of nights, and number of rooms needed. The traveler may also have special requests such as the number and size of beds (queen, king) or a smoking or nonsmoking environment.

Generally, the reservations must be guaranteed by the number of a major credit card. Lodging can sometimes be charged directly to the traveler's company if such arrangements are made in advance.

A reservation guaranteed for late arrival means that the room will be held beyond 6 p.m., and the traveler will be charged for it whether he or she uses it. Always ask for a written confirmation or a confirmation number. If it is necessary to cancel a reservation, call before 6 p.m. and get a cancellation number. Keep a written record of the date and time you canceled the reservation along with the cancellation number. In some resort areas, cancellations must be made 24 to 48 hours in advance to avoid a charge.

International Travel

9–38

International travel requires additional planning. A travel agent who is experienced with international travel and the embassy or consulate of the country to be visited can provide detailed information and requirements. Additional considerations include:

1. **Travel documents.**   International travelers will need passports and visas as well as at least one form of identification containing a photograph. Names on all documents must be consistent.

2. **Health immunizations.**   An international certificate of vaccination for such diseases as smallpox may be required. Contact a local health center or the Center for Disease Control (CDC) to determine health requirements. If vaccinations are required, allow sufficient time prior to departure to complete the series of inoculations if more than one is required for complete immunization.

3. **Currency.**   Know the currency of the destination country and its value relative to the U.S. dollar. Exchange U.S. dollars for some currency of the destination country before leaving. The traveler will thus have money available upon arrival for such expenses as ground transportation and tips.

4. **Travel.**   All travelers should take into account baggage restrictions (number and size), check-in requirements, security precautions and procedures, and customs at the departure and arrival airports. If necessary, register certain articles (such as foreign currency, jewelry, equipment, literature, merchandise, or component parts) as owned before leaving on the trip; doing so will avoid having to pay duty on them when returning. Check with the U.S. Customs Service for registration requirements.

5. **Business hours.**   The international traveler should be aware of any differences in business hours. In some countries, businesses close in the middle of the day, with some businesses reopening later. Financial institutions are generally closed on weekends, although automated teller machines are generally available.

6. **Foreign customs and protocol.**   These might include such things as the current political and economic climate in the destination country: time differences and normal business hours; the protocol for meeting people and conducting business; an awareness of what eye contact, body language, and common expressions mean; etiquette and appropriate dress for meals and social functions; tipping; and a working knowledge of the metric system (see 10–25 • 10–26).

Preparing an Itinerary

9–39 An *itinerary* is a chronological schedule of events for a traveler. It may be set up in several different formats. The itinerary should include:

1. Days, dates, times, and cities of departure and arrivals
2. Airport, airline, numbers, and local time for all flights and, perhaps, meals provided on flights
3. Ground transportation (car, bus, taxi, limousine, etc.) or rental car information if applicable (agency, type of car, rate, confirmation number)
4. Name, address, and telephone number of all hotels, as well as confirmation numbers
5. Day, date, time, and location of all appointments and meetings and the names of all persons involved.
6. Days, dates, times, and locations of any business-related meals or other social functions, together with the names of the host or hostess. If the traveler is hosting such an event, include a prospective guest list with telephone numbers.

Copies of the itinerary should go to the traveler, the traveler's family, the traveler's associate(s), and/or assistant.

Travel Expenses and Reimbursement

9–40 Most business travelers must pay for their travel expenses out of pocket and then file for reimbursement. Other business travelers must requisition advances of cash prior to their travel. Companies usually have a written policy on travel expenses and what expenses are eligible for reimbursement and when cash advances are provided. Cash advances and reimbursements may also be affected by Internal Revenue Service (IRS) regulations on travel expenses.

When travel is in connection with work being performed for a particular client, travel expenses should be recorded as billable time. Separate travel expenses should be maintained for such client-related work, supported by receipts.

Most companies have a policy requiring the traveler to prepare and submit a travel reimbursement form promptly after the travel is completed. The traveler should keep notes, as well as receipts, regarding expenses— including expenses paid in cash for tips, meals, and ground transportation. Many travelers keep notes directly on their copies of the itinerary.

INFORMATION PROCESSING

9–41 Information processing combines various computer technologies, procedures, systems, and personnel to convert data (input) into a usable end product (output). The computer is used for information processing, document creation and processing, litigation support, recordkeeping, accounting, and scheduling and calendaring.

There are five steps in the information processing cycle: (1) input, (2) processing, (3) output, (4) distribution, and (5) storage.

Input

9–42

The first step in the information processing cycle is input. Input is the information to be processed. The term *inputting* refers to the process of inserting information into a system. Inputting methods include (1) machine dictation, (2) voice activation or speech recognition, (3) handwriting recognition, (4) handwritten notes, (5) composing at a computer keyboard, and (6) stenography.

Input devices include scanners that convert existing print material and photos and graphics into computer-readable form; digital cameras that transfer photographs to a computer or a printer; a light pen often used with special monitors on which selected objects or icons are displayed; a pen-type device used to write or draw on a pen-Tablet computer screen (see 9–47, Handwriting Recognition); and a stylus used with mobile computers and other mobile devices (PDAs and smart phones). A microphone is another device, providing input access for physically challenged or visually impaired individuals.

Machine Dictation

9–43

An originator or dictator using machine dictation speaks into hand-held, desktop, or centralized dictation equipment to record information onto a magnetic disk or cassette. This is the fastest input method because the originator can dictate as fast as he or she can talk.

Stenography

9–44

Highly skilled and certified court reporters, as well as some paralegals, use a court reporting machine (stenograph) to record verbatim courtroom testimony, depositions, and other statements that require a word-for-word record, or transcript. Reporters key information using a specialized set of abbreviations and symbols recorded on a continuous roll of paper tape. The recorded information is transcribed either manually or electronically. Special computer software "translates" the specialized keystrokes and technical language, with text displayed on the computer screen for formatting, printing, and distribution. This process enables the quick turnaround of final printed transcripts that law office personnel and the courts require.

Dictation Pointers

9–45

Follow these guidelines to dictate more effectively:

1. Organize dictation by preparing an outline or notes of the content of the message. (The transcriber could also use these notes during transcription.)

371

2. At the start of the dictation, identify yourself by name, title, and department.

3. Indicate what is being dictated—letter, memo, report, statistical material, or court papers.

4. Mention any special instructions, such as special mailing services, urgency or confidentiality, additional copies required, or enclosures to be included.

5. Spell out names and addresses and repeat dates, amounts, and figures.

6. When dictating, indicate the start of new paragraphs and any special or unusual punctuation.

7. Attach appropriate notes, correspondence, or file for reference.

Voice Activation/Speech Recognition

9–46

Speech recognition software allows real-time dictation of communications directly into the computer. Programming frequently used words, sentences, technical terms, and entire paragraphs eliminates the need to keyboard such repetitive text.

These preprogrammed words and phrases are first keyboarded and stored as "macros," identified by key words or phrases. When these macros are spoken, the prerecorded text is automatically input into the system and displayed on the screen and can then be edited, formatted, printed, and stored using word processing software.

Using speech recognition software lowers transcription costs and provides greater accuracy when technical language must be keyboarded. The user must be proficient in English grammar, spelling, punctuation, sentence structure, and technical vocabulary.

Advantages of this software are as follows:

1. It runs concurrently with popular word processing programs used in law offices and the courts.

2. The voice commands used are similar to the functions and keyboard keys used in word processing programs: select, move right or left, delete, caps ON/OFF, space, backspace, save, etc. All standard punctuation marks and common symbols are also recognized.

3. Individuals can speak—and therefore write—in a more conversational tone. Using such software can improve written communications overall. Redundancies can be avoided, overly long or short sentences can be eliminated, sentence fragments or run-on sentences can be more easily identified. Most office workers can speak faster than they can keyboard.

4. The tendency for individuals to suffer from carpal tunnel syndrome or repetitive stress injuries is reduced because of the decreased need for constant keyboarding.

Follow these guidelines in using speech recognition software. Also follow the general guidelines for writing effective letters, memorandums, and e-mails (see 7–2); use effective words (see Table 4.2; 4–219, 4–220.)

1. Become familiar with the software and all its features and capabilities. This will require time and trial and error—and patience.

2. Keyboard, assign, and store as macros the key words and phrases that will represent the recognizable phrases and sentences to be input into the system.

3. Position the microphone (attached to a headset) close to your mouth so speech is directed into the microphone. If using a stand-alone microphone, position yourself within speaking range at about 2 feet.

4. Establish your personal speech profile, which is essentially a voice database of your unique speaking style: tone, volume, pace, mannerism, accent, and breathing.

5. Enunciate words, text, commands, and numbers clearly. Pause where appropriate to distinguish dictated text and punctuation from commands. Pronounce words correctly; say whole words rather than syllables; speak in complete sentences rather than word by word. Do not run words together or slur the pronunciation.

6. Spell out technical terms and names as necessary. Add frequently used technical terms to the dictionary to ease future dictation.

7. Know the names of symbols and characters used by the software and pronounce them correctly so they are recognized; for example, "dollar sign" ($), "copyright" (©), "trademark sign" (™), "caret" (^), "number sign" or "pound sign" (#), "ampersand" (&), "right bracket" (]), "tilde" (~), etc.

8. Speak precisely; for example, "Roman 6" is translated into "VI"; "apostrophe s" is translated into "'s"; and "3 point 6," as "3.6."

9. Speak at a normal volume and speed; breathe naturally. Be careful not to strain your vocal cords.

10. Think before you speak!

Once text has been dictated and displayed on the screen, follow the text-editing procedures of the word processing program to draft the finished document.

Handwriting Recognition

9–47 Handwriting recognition software enables text to be input on a pen-Tablet computer. This computer looks like a regular notebook computer, but the screen is hinged so it can be rotated to provide a flat writing surface. Legible printing or cursive writing is used to enter text by writing directly on the screen (called a "slate") using a digital pen. The digital pen is tapped or tapped and dragged to perform the same functions that are performed by clicking or clicking and dragging a mouse.

As text is input, it immediately appears in keyboarded form on the slate. Text can then be edited and formatted within the program itself or on a word processor. Handwriting recognition software can also be combined with speech recognition software and the Internet.

Using a computer and handwriting recognition software is convenient for taking notes at meetings, inputting reminders and short documents, and copying information during legal research. Most people with word processing skills, however, generally find it faster to key information directly into the computer because they can keyboard faster than they can write by hand.

Handwritten Notes

9–48　Originators may draft or write out their correspondence and other documents in longhand for an assistant to input. This is a frequent method of input even though it is the slowest and sometimes the most difficult to transcribe because of illegible handwriting.

Follow these guidelines when writing in longhand.

1. Write legibly.
2. Use every other line to make editing easier.
3. Use only abbreviations that the transcriber will know.
4. Attach appropriate notes, correspondence, or files for reference for the transcriber.

Composing at the Keyboard

9–49　Originators save time by composing routine correspondence and documents directly at the computer keyboard. A draft of the document can be written and stored on disk; the document can then be retrieved by an assistant to format and finalize.

Follow these guidelines when composing at the keyboard.

1. Learn the keyboarding commands and shortcuts of the software being used to make composing, formatting, and editing the document easier.
2. Decide on the purpose and the points to be covered in the document. Make and organize brief notes if necessary.
3. Keyboard ideas as they occur, getting ideas out onto the screen. Do not be concerned about exact wording or organization at this point.
4. Compose and keyboard the message simultaneously. Do not write the message in longhand first.
5. Edit the message as necessary. Rearrange words, sentences, and paragraphs to express the desired meaning. See also 9–87 • 9–96.

Processing

9–50

Processing involves taking the input and producing a final document (output). By using the appropriate commands or instructions of word processing or other applications software, the data can be sorted, merged, moved, calculated, etc. Information can be saved for later retrieval and further processing. Processing methods include (1) machine transcription, (2) longhand transcription, and (3) typewriting.

Machine Transcription

9–51

Machine-dictated information is keyboarded or transcribed by a transcriber. The transcriber uses a transcription machine or computer equipped with earphones to play the recorded disk or tape to produce correspondence or documents using word processing software.

Follow these guidelines to process dictation efficiently.

1. If necessary, listen to the recorded dictation before transcribing. Listen especially for any changes, special notations, or instructions that may be given within the dictated material.
2. Store used recording media separately from unused ones. Immediately after the information has been transcribed, file the media in appropriate storage equipment that is designed to protect them. Many law offices store media with their related correspondence or case files for a period of time.
3. Set up a special correspondence folder for each dictator. Store in this folder dictation media that require further processing and any related correspondence and notes.
4. Divide dictation work into folders marked WORK TO BE DONE and ITEMS TO BE SIGNED.

Longhand Transcription

9–52

Follow these guidelines when transcribing handwritten notes:

1. Learn the originator's handwriting style. It may be helpful to compare old handwritten notes with the corresponding keyboarded copy until the handwriting can be read easily.
2. Insert punctuation marks and paragraphs if they are not included or clear.
3. Read through the entire written document before beginning to transcribe it. Ask the originator to clarify indistinct words, spellings, amounts, dates, figures, etc.

Typewriting

9–53

The typewriter as a method of inputting and processing information has declined with the use of computers and software programs. However, the typewriter still has its uses and benefits for the law office: to complete preprinted forms for the courts and other agencies or entities; to address individual envelopes or file or mailing labels; to jot a quick note or short memo; to prepare a brief cover letter or memo for an enclosure, attachment, or a faxed document. Electronic typewriters offer such basic word processing features as underscoring, boldfacing, font styles and sizes, limited internal memory, and a special character set.

Output

9–54 Output is the end product of information processing. Output may be in the form of hard copy (paper) such as letters, reports, memos, court documents, graphs, and facsimiles that can be duplicated and distributed.

Output devices include monitors that display on-screen processed information; printers to produce hard copies of text and graphics; photo printers that convert electronic photographs stored on media cards into hard copies; and audio output devices (speakers).

Both hard and soft copy may be stored in the computer's memory, on microforms, or on electronic media.

Distribution

9–55 Output from an information processing system is distributed to the appropriate people. Information can be distributed internally through interoffice mail or electronic mail. Correspondence, legal documents, electronic mail, and facsimiles can be distributed to individuals and firms outside the office. Output documents can also be distributed as attachments to electronic mail and linked to an Internet Web site. Communication services are discussed in Unit 11.

Determine the most effective and appropriate method for distributing processed information. Consider the urgency of the communication or document, its importance to the recipient and the related transaction, the nature of the information to be conveyed, the level of confidentiality or privacy required, and the geographic distances and time differences between the sender and the recipient.

Storage

9–56 Information may be stored after it is output or after it is distributed. Information may be stored on (1) hard copy, (2) microforms, and/or (3) electronic media, either internally on the computer's memory or externally on disk. Information stored on electronic media may be retrieved later for viewing, further processing, printing, or distribution. Select and use the proper electronic media based on the type of information to be retained, the length of time information is to be stored (whether short term or archival), and the integrity and quality of information to be retrieved at a later time.

Secondary storage devices include 3½ inch floppy disks; zip disks that provide greater storage capacities than floppy disks and are often used to back up data stored on the computer's internal hard drive; various forms of optical disks (CD-ROMs, CD-R and CD-RW, DVD-ROMs, DVD-R and DVD-RAMs); memory cards and sticks used with digital cameras; and portable USB flash drives.

The output should be stored in a records management system that is organized to find and retrieve the information when needed. (See 9–97 • 9–108 for information on filing systems.)

Microforms

9–57 Microforms are used to store documents in greatly reduced photographic form, thereby saving space. Microforms include microfilm, microfiche, and ultrafiche. Special equipment is required to photograph, read, and print the image on film. Computer-processed information can be output directly onto microforms; the document can be printed later if a hard copy is needed.

INFORMATION PROCESSING SOFTWARE

9–58 Information processing software includes word processing, database management, spreadsheets, presentation, and desktop publishing. Because of the specific functions performed by each software package, keep operating manuals for the software available for reference.

Caring for Electronic Storage Media

9–59 Follow these guidelines to ensure proper care of electronic storage media:

1. Keep all disks away from magnets and magnetic and electrical equipment.
2. Do not place heavy objects on top of disks.
3. Keep disks away from heat and direct sunlight and from smoke and dust.
4. Use only felt tip pens to write on CDs, or print and affix labels on them to identify their content.
5. Remove old labels from disks carefully so layers of labels do not accumulate on disks.
6. Always store media in their protective cases or holders.

Storing Electronic Media

9–60 Determine a records storage system for filing electronic media to protect and safeguard original documents and correspondence. Media may be stored with their respective client or case files. They may be stored in a central location within the office, properly labeled by date, content, client or case name, or staff member responsible. (See 9–97.)

A records management system should be developed for all media stored in a central storage location; this ensures consistency in how media are stored, provides a record of all media and the types retained, provides for uniform storage devices, and aids in efficient access and retrieval of media when needed. Backup files should also be securely stored and labeled as such.

Word Processing

9–61 Word processing involves the creation and editing of text. It can be done on a computer with word processing software or in conjunction with either voice/speech recognition software and/or handwriting recognition software. Once the text is keyboarded or otherwise input into the system, it can be formatted and edited quickly and easily using various text-editing functions without rekeying the entire document. The text may then be printed, stored in the computer's memory, and/or stored on magnetic media.

Text Editing

9–62 Text editing involves changing the text after it has been keyboarded by inserting, deleting, moving, or copying text. Text editing is done through special software commands, with the function keys on the keyboard, and/or by manipulating the on-screen menus and icons with a mouse device. Text that has been input using voice/speech recognition software or handwriting recognition software can be edited by manipulating the on-screen menus and icons with a mouse, digital pen, or voice command.

Proofreading is a major part of text editing. See Sections 9–89 • 9–91 and Figure 9.4 for additional information on proofreading. The Checklist for Effective Letters and Memorandums (Section 7–2) also provides helpful guidelines for the text-editing process.

Text Formatting

9–63 Text formatting involves setting the margins, line spacing, indentions, columns, and other features that determine how the document will look when it is printed. (See also Letter Formats, Section 7–12, and Figures 7.3 to 7.5.)

The default (or preset) format settings on word processing programs can accommodate most documents. For example, the default settings on most word processing programs format documents for single spacing, one-inch top and side margins, and on 8½-by-11-inch paper. These defaults can be changed at any time.

9–64 Many word processing programs offer the user a choice of type fonts and type sizes. A *font* is a complete set of characters in a particular typeface; for example, Times Roman 12 point. A particular typeface also includes boldface and italic characters.

Pitch refers to the number of characters of a particular typeface that fit within an inch. Most documents are printed in 10-pitch (10 characters per inch or 10 cpi) and 12-pitch (12 cpi) type because they are easy to read. The fine print in some documents is often printed in 8 or 10 cpi; the title of a report or special headings may be printed in larger sizes.

Word Processing Software

9–65 Basic word processing functions include the ability to underline, italicize, or boldface type; center copy horizontally; insert text or type over existing text; mark, move, copy, or delete blocks of text; find and replace copy; check the spelling in a document; move quickly around in the document; and print all or designated pages of a document.

Other features available include a grammar checker; a thesaurus; the ability to merge documents; macros; a math mode to calculate subtotals, totals, and grand totals; a setup for newspaper and parallel columns; the ability to sort text in alphabetical or numerical order; a footnote/endnote function; an outline feature; a table feature; a format for headers and footers; widow and orphan line protection; line draw; graphics; splitting the screen into two editing windows; and switching between documents.

Data from a database or a spreadsheet or a presentation program can be incorporated—imported—into a document created or edited in a word processing program.

Using Word Processing Software

9–66 Follow these guidelines to process information efficiently:

1. Review and clarify the originator's instructions.
2. Keep a dictionary, reference manual, and related materials available for reference. If the software has a spell checker, grammar checker, and/or thesaurus, learn to use these features.
3. Run the electronic dictionary through the document before proofreading, saving, and printing it.
4. Double-check the suggested grammar and spellings. Be sure the suggested grammatical usage correctly conveys the intended meaning and emphasis. Be aware of similar sounding words ("to," "too," and "two"; "there," "their," and "they're") and similarly spelled words ("loss," "lost," and "lose"), as the spell-checking programs may consider them correctly spelled although not properly used for the context.
5. If appropriate, send a draft copy to the originator to review before printing the final copy.
6. To facilitate retrieval of documents, save them under descriptive file names. Include in the file names initials of the originator/dictator,

department or section, type of document, etc. If acceptable, keyboard the file name of the document at the bottom of correspondence as a way of easily identifying the stored file; however, such information should appear only on office copies of correspondence and documents.

Database Management

9–67 A database is a collection of related information that can be retrieved, rearranged, and updated. Database management software enables the user to collect, organize, and store information in a structured way. A database may contain names and addresses of clients and local attorneys, names and addresses of specialty attorneys and related professionals (accountants, forensics people, psychologists, investigators, etc.), names and addresses of court houses and presiding officers, case names and attorney information, library holdings and publisher information.

Once the data are entered, they can be sorted or rearranged in any order the user desires. Information can be added or deleted, and the structure of the database itself can be changed. Some or all of the records can be retrieved at any time, and the computer can be instructed to search for records that meet certain parameters.

Database Format

9–68 Information in a database is placed in fields, records, and files. A *field* is a unit of information. For example, in a client database, "Last Name" would be one field. Other fields might include first name, address, city/state, ZIP code, phone, fax, nature of service, and date. All fields relating to one client make up one *record*. Each record must have the same fields, although some fields may be left blank. For example, the record in Figure 9.2 has 11 fields. All related records make up a *file*.

FIGURE 9.2   **Database Structure**

A database management program includes commands to define the structure of a file and to enter, add, modify, update, and delete records. Once data have been entered, records can be displayed, sorted, indexed, edited, searched, and printed. Files can be linked to create various types of reports. Records stored in a database can also be merged into primary documents within a word processing program to create form letters and documents.

Guidelines for Creating a Database

9–69 Information in a database is stored in a very structured manner. It is best to give some thought to how the data will be used before the file is set up.

1. Plan the database. Decide what information will be maintained in the database and how the information will be used.
2. Determine the number of fields that are needed. This step is probably best done on paper.
3. Use self-descriptive field names (first name, last name, city, ZIP code, state, etc.). Determine field type (character, numeric, etc.), field length or width (maximum number of characters in the field), and validity checks (signal an error when data entered are outside a designated number range). Create separate fields for greater flexibility in retrieving and sorting data by smaller categories.
4. Enter the file characteristics into the database program.
5. Enter data for each record consistently, following the format and the parameters created for the database.

Spreadsheets

9–70 A spreadsheet is an electronic worksheet. Spreadsheets are commonly used to calculate interest, percentages, discounts, and prices. Spreadsheets are particularly useful for answering "what if" questions. When variables in the spreadsheet are changed, the software recalculates the results automatically and instantly.

Spreadsheets can be used to prepare budgets, financial statements, income forecasts, loan repayment schedules, and profit or loss ratios. Spreadsheets can also be used to maintain accounting information for billable client or project hours for research, conferences, travel, document preparation, office expenses for clerical assistance, photocopying, delivery or courier services, office space, utilities, etc.

Spreadsheet Format

9–71 A spreadsheet is a grid made up of rows, columns, and cells. (See Figure 9.3.) *Rows* run horizontally (left to right) on the spreadsheet. *Columns* run vertically (top to bottom). *Cells* are the individual squares on the grid, the points where the rows and columns intersect.

381

	A	B	C	D
1	Cell A1	Cell B1	Cell C1	Cell D1
2	Cell A2	Cell B2	Cell C2	Cell D2
3	Cell A3	Cell B3	Cell C3	Cell D3
4	Cell A4	Cell B4	Cell C4	Cell D4
5	Cell A5	Cell B5	Cell C5	Cell D5
6	Cell A6	Cell B6	Cell C6	Cell D6

FIGURE 9.3 Spreadsheet

This spreadsheet has a border that identifies rows 1 through 6 and columns A through D. The cell addresses (A1 through D6) are the working area of the spreadsheet.

Both rows and columns are labeled. Spreadsheet programs label the rows with numbers (1, 2, 3, etc.) and the columns with letters (A, B, C, etc.). A cell then has its own unique address. Cell A4, for example, would be the cell at the intersection of column A and row 4.

The size of the spreadsheet depends on the software program. A spreadsheet of 64 columns and 256 rows is considered minimal. Many programs provide for hundreds of columns and thousands of rows. The formats and widths of the cells may be changed.

The user inserts labels, values (numbers), or hidden formulas in the cells of a worksheet. The formulas direct the program to perform calculations in specified cells. While some formulas contain constant numbers, such as 2 + 2, the most useful formulas contain cell references, such as A1 + C16. The indicated calculations are carried out automatically on the data in the specified cells.

Spreadsheet Software

9–72

Basic features of spreadsheet programs include the ability to add, subtract, multiply, and divide figures in a specified range of contiguous cells. The programs contain built-in functions to perform such computations as percentages, averages, amortizations, and standard deviation.

Other features include the ability to create templates for frequently used applications; to protect cells to prevent information from being accidentally deleted; to display different parts of the spreadsheet on the screen at the same time in separate windows or screens; to merge a spreadsheet with a database file; to link spreadsheets (or a spreadsheet and a graphic); and to use macros. Some spreadsheet programs are customized; for example, a spreadsheet for attorneys keeps track of client billing and one for churches keeps track of contributions and budgets.

Spreadsheet programs have a graphics feature that converts the numeric data in the spreadsheet into a pie chart, bar graph, and/or line graph. Graphs are visual forms of the data in spreadsheets. (See also 10–92 • 10–98.)

Guidelines for Creating a Spreadsheet

9–73 Follow these guidelines to create useful spreadsheets:

1. Before beginning, decide what the purpose of the spreadsheet is, what calculations are to be performed, what data are needed for the calculations, and how the results should be displayed.
2. Label the rows and columns to identify what the numbers represent. (See Figure 9.3.)
3. Determine the appropriate formulas to be used for the various calculations to obtain the desired results. Follow the mathematical protocol for entering formulas to perform calculations.
4. Be certain that the data entered are accurate and the formulas are correctly stated.
5. Apply formulas to the correct range of cells.
6. Protect cells that contain formulas or data that should not be changed.
7. Wherever possible, copy formulas rather than retype them to lessen the possibility of error.
8. Test a spreadsheet before putting it into use.

Desktop Publishing

9–74 Desktop publishing refers to the creation and production of documents of typeset quality by using page layout software, a powerful computer, and a laser printer. Text, headlines, and graphics can be created and arranged on the same page and then manipulated to produce the desired visual presentation. With a scanner, photographs and drawings can be inserted into the document. Word processing software can also be used for desktop publishing, although it does not provide the full range of capabilities and functions for the types of documents desired.

Desktop Publishing Software

9–75 Brochures, manuals, charts, stationery, business cards, and newsletters can be easily prepared. Desktop publishing programs include the ability to create simple illustrations using shapes and lines; importing and placing graphics in the publication; sizing and/or cropping graphics; choosing fonts, sizes, and styles (italic, bold, etc.) of text; placing text in columns and/or boxes; wrapping text around graphics and illustrations; justifying text both horizontally and vertically; adding special textures, lines, and patterns; and WYSIWYG (what you see is what you get) displays that show on the screen what the page will look like when it is printed.

Guidelines for Creating a Desktop Publishing Publication

9–76 Follow these guidelines to produce professional-looking publications:

1. Determine the nature of the document or publication and its intended audience.
2. Make a rough sketch of the document or publication before laying it out on the computer. Consider the overall format, text, graphics, font sizes and styles, etc.
3. Keep the layout simple and uncluttered. Leave white space between text, graphics, and columns.
4. Use a maximum of two typefaces in any publication. Too many fonts become distracting.
5. Make graphics, if used, relevant to the accompanying text.
6. Use rules, borders, boxes, and shading sparingly.

CREATING AND USING FORM DOCUMENTS

9–77 Most law offices prepare the same general types of documents frequently, and many letters contain similar or identical language. Instead of creating a personalized and individualized letter or document for each situation, repetitive types of documents can be prepared by (1) creating form letters and documents and storing them in the computer or on a floppy disk, (2) using the *macro* feature of the word processing program, and (3) merging a form document with a data file.

Creating Form Letters and Documents

9–78 Form letters and documents, also referred to as "boilerplates," are prepared forms of documents—complete letters or forms, partial letters or documents containing standard wording or paragraphs—created for frequently recurring situations requiring a similar type of communication; for example, transmittal letters requesting client signatures, complaints or responses related to certain types of actions, notices for appearance at deposition, and form interrogatories. (See 7–10, Form Letters/Documents.)

Creating a Template ("Skeleton Form")

9–79 Create templates ("skeleton forms") for form letters and documents, and store them on the computer. When needed, the appropriate template can be retrieved and the specific details inserted as needed. For example, a template may be created with the caption or heading on pleadings (jurisdiction and venue, case title, title of the pleading, the brackets or parentheses) or the attorney's name, complete address, bar license number, "Attorney(s) for _____." The completed new document or form is saved under its own file name; the original template remains stored in its original form for future use.

Creating Macros

9–80 A *macro* is a preprogrammed command used to create shortcuts for entering frequently used keystrokes (such as words or phrases) or for performing repetitive operations on the computer. For example, macros may be created to produce a verification form, the jurat, or the signature line at the end of a pleading or letter.

9–81 Once created and stored on the word processor, macros can be used repeatedly. Temporary macros can also be created for use during the current working session only; when the computer is turned off, all temporary macros are deleted. For example, when keyboarding a client or other party or firm name throughout a document, create a temporary macro that will play back that name automatically each time it is needed. (Refer to the software operating manual for creating, using, and storing macros.)

Macros are also used in voice/speech- and handwriting-recognition software programs to store frequently used words, phrases, sentences, and technical terms. (See 9–46 • 9–47.)

Merging a Form Document with a Data File

9–82 The merge feature of a word processing program is used to combine data from two documents to create a third document. Merge operations consist of creating two separate files or documents—a primary file and a secondary file.

Primary File

9–83 A *primary file* is a document that contains all the information that will remain the same for all documents; a primary file is also referred to as a *master document* or *form letter* or *document*. Certain merge codes are placed throughout the document to indicate the points at which variable data (data that will change as the document is printed) are to be inserted.

Secondary File

9–84 A *secondary file* contains all the variable information (information that will change with each printed document) that will be inserted into designated positions within the primary file during printing. This file is essentially a data file or information from a database.

Merged Documents

9–85 In the merging process, data from the secondary file are merged into specified coded positions in the primary document; the result is a new document.

(Refer to the software operating manual for creating, using, and merging primary documents and secondary files.) The resulting merged documents do not need to be stored unless a copy needs to be saved.

9–86 Follow these guidelines in creating form letters and documents:

1. Determine the specific words and phrases, paragraphs, headings or captions, or other text that is keyboarded frequently. Create macros for them. Assign logical names, numbers, or abbreviations for the macros. Create each macro so only a few keystrokes are needed to play it back.

2. Determine the letters and documents that are prepared frequently. Create form documents and letters for the standard paragraphs, even if the final document may require some personalization or alteration.

3. Combine related sets of documents to form a "packet" of forms that can be used in a particular type of legal matter.

4. Store form documents and letters on a separate disk or subdirectory of the computer's hard drive.

5. Print out a set of all macros and form letters and documents. Compile them into a notebook, and index them for easy reference. Identify each by its file name so it can be retrieved easily.

EDITING AND PROOFREADING

9–87 *Editing* is the process of revising a document to make it clear, logical, and complete. *Proofreading* refers to the process of checking a document to detect and correct errors to ensure that the document is error-free.

Editing and proofreading in a law office are critical to avoid costly errors in statements of fact or law; figures, amounts, and dates; names of parties, witnesses, or other individuals; geographic locations and compass directions; etc. Legal work requires concentration and attention to detail.

Editing

9–88 After a rough draft of any document has been written and before the final copy is prepared, the document should be edited. Thoughtful and precise editing will make the document clearer, more concise, correct, courteous, and complete. Check for sense, logical order, errors, consistency, wordiness, redundancies, and the use of trite expressions and jargon. The checklist in Unit 7 (see Section 7–2) provides a good basis for the editing process. It may be necessary to rewrite portions of the document.

Proofreading

9–89 Proofreading is the process of *proving* that the text is correct. Proofreading should be done at each step in processing a document: keyboarding, or other inputting, editing, saving, and printing. Four steps are required because it is nearly impossible to find everything in one pass. In the four passes, check for:

1. **Overall format and appearance.**   Scan the document for its form: is it in correct form for the type of document? Check the appearance: is the information attractively and appropriately arranged on the page(s)? (See also 7–12 • 7–72 for correct format for correspondence; 8–22 • 8–64 for formal reports; and 6–1 • 6–6 for legal citation form.)

2. **Obvious errors.**   Scan the document for obvious errors such as word division and hyphenation, spelling, abbreviations, spacing and punctuation, underscoring or italicizing, and number usage.

3. **Content.**   Read the entire document for its content: organization, logic, correctness, cohesiveness, and completeness. Check for grammatical errors, punctuation, word usage, errors in facts or information, and citation forms. Make sure words are not omitted, duplicated, or transposed.

4. **Numbers, names, and amounts.**   In a separate step, check each number, name, and amount; citations and their elements; spellings of names and geographic locations; amounts spelled out and in figures.

Editing and Proofreading Techniques

9–90 Proofreaders' marks are standardized symbols used to indicate corrections, additions, or deletions to a document. Use a contrasting color of ink, such as red or green, when editing a document and marking corrections with proofreaders' marks. A contrasting color is easier to see and less apt to be missed. It may be helpful to place a paper clip or stick-on note on the page to indicate that there is a correction.

Figure 9.4 shows how the standard proofreaders' marks are used to indicate changes in copy.

9–91 The following techniques may prove helpful when proofreading:

1. Run the electronic dictionary or spell checker of the word processing program first.

2. Proofread the document on the screen before printing a copy; the text can be moved into view one line at a time to aid the proofreader in slowing down and finding errors.

3. Find a quiet place, free of constant interruptions, to concentrate on the document being proofread. Read the entire document slowly, paying attention to small details.

Symbol	Meaning	Example	Result
#	space	add a space	add a space
⌒	close up	some thing	something
℘	delete	extra extra word	extra word
ℛ	delete and close up	pronoun usage	pronoun usage
~	transpose	recieve / to quickly check	receive / to check quickly
∧ ∨	insert	the profits (company)	the company profits
⊙	insert period	end of sentence ⊙	end of sentence.
∨	insert apostrophe	companys	company's
∧	insert comma	2341 miles	2,341 miles
∧	insert semicolon	result that is	result; that is,
⊙	insert colon	the following ⊙	the following:
⌄ ⌄	insert quotation marks	Computers on the Job	"Computers on the Job"
?	insert question mark	Why not ?	Why not?
⟨ ⟩	insert parentheses	see Figure 3	(see Figure 3)
=	insert hyphen	clear cut	clear-cut
.... (stet)	leave as is; do not make correction	Leave originals as written.	Leave originals as written.
(sp)	spell out	Dr. Zimmer	Doctor Zimmer
¶	begin new paragraph	numerous meetings. The result will	numerous meetings. / The results will
no ¶	run together; no new paragraph	numerous meetings. / no ¶ The results will	numerous meetings. The results will
≡	capitalize	personnel department	Personnel Department
/ (lc)	set in lowercase letters	Secretary of State	secretary of state
		PERSONNEL	personnel
———	underline or italicize	the novel Moby Dick	the novel *Moby Dick*
		the novel Moby Dick	the novel Moby Dick

FIGURE 9.4   Proofreaders' Marks

388

Symbol	Meaning	Example	Result
∼∼∼	use boldface	for emphasis	for **emphasis**
(rom)	use roman type	No *italics* needed. (rom)	No italics needed.
⊏	move left	⊏ This is too far.	This is too far.
⊐	move right	⊐ For a new paragraph,	For a new paragraph,
⟋	move as shown	The year when sales . . . (2006)	The year 2006 when sales
⊐ ⊏	center	⊐ Contents ⊏	Contents
‖	align vertically	$35.00 ‖ 25.00	$35.00 25.00
=	align horizontally	Total $150.00	Total $150.00
(SS)	single space	The meeting was held on Friday. (SS)	The meeting was held on Friday.
(DS)	double space	Status Meeting 10:30 a.m. (DS)	Status Meeting 10:30 a.m.
(TS)	triple space	(TS) PROGRESS REPORT Ping-Ying Project	PROGRESS REPORT Ping-Ying Project

FIGURE 9.4 *(concluded)*

4. Always verify the spelling of proper names and the accuracy of numbers and amounts. Proofread this information as a separate step to focus attention on one specific type of potential error.

5. If possible, proofread with another person to check (*a*) statistical material, (*b*) legal descriptions, (*c*) citations, (*d*) quoted material, especially if lengthy or technical, (*e*) measurements, and (*f*) other technical information. Check any footnotes and their citations for consistency and correctness. The person who prepared the document should read from the original material while the second person proofreads the final document. It is always easier to find someone else's errors.

6. If proofreading alone, place the original material and the final document side by side. Proofread using two hands—one on the original copy and the other following the final document. Use a ruler to help you keep your place in the original.

7. Place corrections in the margin of the document where they are easier to see and easier to write out, particularly if the document is single-spaced.

Place a paper clip or a stick-on note at the edge of the page close to the error or notation.

Electronic Dictionaries

9–92   Use an electronic dictionary, or spell checker, to compare every word in a document to the list of words in its dictionary. Spell checker programs are available for legal, medical, and technical/scientific vocabularies. Any word not in the electronic dictionary will be highlighted as a "potential error." Alternative words or spellings are displayed. The user then decides if the word is correct or should be replaced, either with one of the alternatives or with another word.

The electronic dictionary can be used to check a word, a page, or an entire document. Some programs require that the cursor be at the beginning of the document in order to check the entire document. If the cursor is in the middle of the document, the dictionary starts to check the spelling from the cursor position forward.

9–93   Most electronic dictionaries allow the user to add words to the dictionary. Adding frequently used words such as the name of the firm, the names of partners and associates, the firm's various locations (especially international), and words peculiar to the nature of the practice will save time. These words will be highlighted only if they are misspelled.

The electronic dictionary can also be used like a regular dictionary. The user can key in a word, run the spell checker, and find out instantly whether it is spelled correctly.

9–94   Electronic dictionaries do *not* eliminate the need to proofread. Some of the types of errors an electronic dictionary will not find are: (1) a correctly spelled but misused word, such as *to* for *two* or *from* for *form;* (2) omitted or added words; and (3) incorrect grammar.

Electronic Thesauruses

9–95   The electronic thesaurus included in word processing packages provides a list of *synonyms* (words with the same or very similar meaning) for many words. It may also include *antonyms* (words with the opposite meaning). The thesaurus is especially helpful to users who wish to add variety to their writing.

Electronic Grammar Checkers

9–96   Electronic grammar checkers check writing style, grammar, and punctuation; some even evaluate the reading level of the document.

Some of the types of errors grammar checkers will highlight include wordiness, negative words, punctuation errors, clichés, passive verbs, long sentences, subject-verb agreement, misused articles, and misused possessives. Some grammar checkers will display the grammatical rule as well as comments and suggestions.

Grammar checkers might not identify all errors or may highlight items that are not wrong. The user must still be proficient in grammar, punctuation, and other language usage areas to know what correction, if any, needs to be made. Grammar checkers may not be appropriate for some law offices because of particularly technical vocabulary or type of writing that may be involved; for example, a citation to a court decision or other reference source appearing as a complete sentence after quoted or paraphrased text may be highlighted as an "incomplete sentence."

FILING PROCEDURES

9–97 The ability to store and retrieve information is critical in a law office. The type and complexity of the filing system depends on the size of the office and the nature of the practice. Determine how files are to be stored— alphabetically, alphanumerically, numerically, or by subject. (See 9–110 • 9–147.) More than one system may be used to store the different types of records in the law office.

General Guidelines for Filing

9–98 The following general guidelines apply to all filing tasks:

1. To prevent lost or misplaced documents, set up a TO BE FILED basket or box.
2. When possible, work with only one file folder for a client or case at a time. Keep all other folders in the drawers or cabinets.
3. Do not allow items to accumulate from day to day. Use spare moments during the day to sort and file documents. Material that is not filed may be lost or misplaced. Unfiled materials may not be available to individuals when needed.
4. Arrange all folders in sequence before placing the folders in their drawers or cabinets. Prearranging the folders allows for more systematic filing. Drawers in file cabinets need not be opened and closed randomly. Presorting folders also enables several people to file simultaneously.
5. Do not keep file folders in desk drawers. For safety and more efficient retrieval, keep all folders in their appropriate places. For safety and security, return all folders to their appropriate places at the end of each business day.
6. Use hanging folders to prevent individual file folders from slipping down in the file drawer.
7. Maintain and adhere to a charge-out system for borrowing file folders from the drawers or cabinets. The charge-out sheet should list who

has the folder and when it was removed. When individual papers are removed from a folder, substitute a charge-out sheet for the removed papers. When an entire file folder must be removed from the drawer or cabinet, replace it with a special charge-out card to mark the location within the drawer or cabinet of the borrowed folder. Encourage individuals to use the folders at a nearby desk rather than remove them from the file room.

8. Follow the established system for managing records. Doing so ensures consistency and accuracy in filing records that need to be retained and enables efficient access and retrieval.

9. Back up documents stored on the computer hard drive. Do so daily or several times during the day, depending on the quantity of work generated. Store the backup in a safe and secure location.

Setting Up Client Files

9–99 Create a standard client information or intake form for each client (or prospective client) or matter. The top of the form should include the client's name, address, telephone numbers, fax number; date of initial contact; nature of services provided; status of the matter; name of the department or staff involved. Such information may also be preprinted on the top front of file folders or large envelopes.

9–100 Prepare a check sheet, status report form, litigation record, or other form as appropriate on which to record activities, summaries of telephone conversations, actions, etc., to update the file and serve as a reminder of tasks completed and yet to be completed. Note deadline dates and other critical dates in red. Staple the check sheet to the inside front cover of the client's main folder.

9–101 Depending on the nature of the practice and type of services provided, a client folder may be divided into two sections: (1) correspondence and (2) court papers and legal agreements.

9–102 If the law practice provides an extensive range of services and/or as a client's main file expands with papers, split the file into separate units so each folder contains a specific type of record; for example, correspondence, court papers, memorandums and attorney notes, and legal agreements. Label each with the appropriate client name or case name, followed by a description of the contents:

PEEBLES, Byron—Correspondence

PEEBLES, Byron—Engagement Contracts

PEEBLES, Byron—Trust Documents

Setting Up General Office Files

9–103 A law office must maintain a large number of different types of records. The nature and extent of files vary with the size and type of practice. The following are guidelines for establishing a records management system for a law office:

1. Client files (see 9–104 • 9–139)
2. Attorney's personal files (for nonlegal matters and correspondence, memberships, etc.)
3. General correspondence (miscellaneous items unrelated to any particular client or legal matter; may contain information regarding a prospective client, etc.)
4. Electronic media (videotapes, tape recordings, DVDs, computer disks, back-up computer disks, etc.)
5. Professional law materials (Bar Association information, bulletins; seminars, continuing legal education course announcements, etc.)
6. Office management files (personnel/human resources, payroll, general office contracts, equipment inventories, publisher information, etc.)
7. Forms files (preprinted legal forms, legal backs, preprinted stationery and envelopes, etc.)
8. Library file (publishers' names and addresses, subscription information, etc.)

Preparing File Folders

9–104 Follow these suggestions when preparing file folders:

1. When typing or printing a label for a folder, use a consistent style for the caption such as initial caps, a two-space left margin, the same typeface, etc.
2. Place the label as close to the top of the tab as possible and press it firmly against the divider tab.
3. Use dividers of a sturdy material to help support files in file drawers. A general guideline is to have a divider for every 10 to 20 folders. Divider labels should also be prepared in a consistent style so users can tell at a glance they are dividers rather than file folders.
4. Develop a color-coding system to identify *(a)* different types of cases (e.g., real estate, trust and probate, bankruptcy, etc.); or *(b)* attorneys. Labels are available on sheets or rolls with gummed backings, in permanent self-adhesive backing, or removable self-adhesive backing.
5. Use a commercial filing system to help standardize all files; a variety of systems are available and adaptable to any size records management system.

Filing Documents in a Folder

9–105 Follow these guidelines for consistency and to ensure that documents can be found easily:

1. File the document in its appropriate section within the file folder. Within that section, file the most recent document at the front of the folder.
2. When the folder accumulates 40 or more sheets of paper, crease it along the first score mark at the bottom of the folder. The score marks allow the folder to expand to accommodate approximately 50 sheets more per score.
3. When any one section of the folder becomes too unwieldy, divide the client file into separate folders (correspondence, court papers, legal agreements, etc.) as appropriate for the particular client.
4. Before storing a document in a multifolder file, write on the document the client name and in which client file the document will be filed; this ensures that the document will be returned to the proper folder if it should be removed from its folder.

Finding Misplaced Documents

9–106 Documents should be returned to their file folders immediately after they have served their purpose. The longer a document is out of a file, the greater the chance there is of its being misplaced or lost.

Follow these steps to locate a missing item:

1. Look through each section of the folder to see if the document may be in the folder but out of sequence. Look in other folders maintained for the client or case.
2. Look on your desk and ask others who may have handled the document recently to check their work areas.
3. Look for the document in the folders immediately in front of and behind the correct folder.
4. Look under other parties' or individuals' names in the files. Also look under any other word that may have been on the file folder label for these other files.
5. Look under names or subjects that might be related to the missing document, such as cross-references.
6. In numeric systems, look for out-of-sequence numbered files. Also, look under every possible numeric arrangement; for example, File No. 687 may be misfiled as 678, 867, or 876.
7. If searching for electronic media (computer disks, videotapes, DVDs, etc.), look in the appropriate hardware devices to see if they were left there.
8. In color-coded systems, look for color-coded folders that are out of place.

Retaining Files

9–107 Most organizations have a records management plan that indicates what types of documents should be saved, how long to keep each category of records, when records should be removed to inactive storage, and when and how to destroy obsolete records. Federal and state laws determine how long some records must be kept.

Types of Filing Systems

9–108 The most common filing systems used in law offices are the alphabetic, numeric, alphanumeric, and subject filing systems. Paper records, microforms, computer tapes and disks, etc., can be filed under any of these systems. The appropriate system to use depends on the volume of each type of information to be stored and how information will be retrieved by users. Most offices will use a combination of systems to store different types of records.

Alphabetic Filing Systems

9–109 The alphabetic filing system is based on the letters of the alphabet and is used in most offices. Names and subjects are filed in alphabetical order behind dividers for each letter of the alphabet. Most organizations use the filing rules published by the Association of Records Managers and Administrators (ARMA).

Alphabetic Filing Rules

9–110 Alphabetic filing rules are followed when records are filed alphabetically. The alphabetic filing rules apply to personal and business names, names of governmental agencies and bodies, and names of institutions.

9–111 Records are compared and filed according to the filing units in a name. A *filing unit* in an alphabetic system is a letter, a number (whether written in figures or spelled out), an abbreviation, or a word. (A filing unit in a numeric system is a digit or a group of digits separated by hyphens.)

9–112 The filing units in names are compared until a difference is found. This difference in filing units determines the sequence in which documents are filed or stored. Documents for each correspondent are arranged within folders in chronologic order with the most recent item in front of the folder.

The Association of Records Managers and Administrators (ARMA) has developed a set of standardized guidelines for alphabetic filing.[1] Using these rules assures consistency in storing and retrieving records. These rules

---

[1] *Alphabetic Filing Rules* (Prairie Village, KS: Association of Records Managers and Administrators, Inc.).

apply to both manual filing systems and computerized records management systems. The information that follows is a summary of manual filing guidelines used to store various types of records within an alphabetic system.

Filing Unit by Unit

9–113 Arrange file names in unit-by-unit order. Compare each unit letter by letter until a difference is found. The difference determines which name will be filed before the other name(s).

	Name as Filed		
Name as Written	**Unit 1**	**Unit 2**	**Unit 3**
American Bankers Association	American	Bankers	Association
American Bar Association	American	Bar	Association

Filing Personal Names

9–114 In arranging names of individuals, transpose the name so the surname (last name) is the first filing unit, followed by the first name or initial, and then the middle name or initial.

	Name as Filed		
Name as Written	**Unit 1**	**Unit 2**	**Unit 3**
Genio L. Americo	Americo	Genio	L
Theresa Isabella Americo	Americo	Theresa	Isabella

Filing Nothing before Something

9–115 File initials or single letters before names beginning with the same initial or letter. File a name containing a single filing unit before a name containing that same filing unit plus other filing units. In other words, "nothing comes before something."

	Name as Filed		
Name as Written	**Unit 1**	**Unit 2**	**Unit 3**
J. L. Palladino	Palladino	J	L
Jaime L. Palladino	Palladino	Jaime	L
Jaime Lee Palladino	Palladino	Jaime	Lee

Filing Married Women's Names

9–116 A married woman's legal name consists of her given name; her middle name, middle initial, or maiden name; and her husband's surname. A married woman may also use her professional name. Transpose the name and follow the guidelines for filing personal names.

Name as Written	Name as Filed		
	Unit 1	Unit 2	Unit 3
Ms. Carol Kellogg	Kellogg	Carol	Ms
Ms. Carol Kellogg Toogood	Toogood	Carol	Kellogg
Mrs. Charles Toogood	Toogood	Charles	Mrs
	(SEE Ms. Carol Kellogg) OR		
	(SEE Ms. Carol Kellogg Toogood)		

Filing Abbreviated Personal Names

9–117 When personal names are abbreviated (such as *Ed.,* or *Edw.* for Edward or Edwin, *Chas.* for Charles, *Geo.* for George, or *Thos.* for Thomas), arrange the names as written.

Name as Written	Name as Filed		
	Unit 1	Unit 2	Unit 3
Charlton P. Weiss	Weiss	Charlton	
Chas. Weiss	Weiss	Chas	P

Filing Shortened Names

9–118 File shortened names, nicknames, or one-word names as written unless the individual's full name is known. Include cross-references to files stored under different names, if necessary.

Name as Written	Name as Filed		
	Unit 1	Unit 2	Unit 3
Bono	Bono		
Cher	Cher		
Madonna	Madonna		

Filing Prefixes

9–119 A prefix in a personal name is considered part of the surname. Common prefixes include: *Da, de, De la, Del, Di, Du, El, Fitz, La, Las, Le, Los, Mac, Mc, O, Saint, San, Santa, St., Ste., Te, Van, Van de, Van der, Von,* and *Von der.* Index the entire surname as one filing unit.

397

	Name as Filed		
Name as Written	**Unit 1**	**Unit 2**	**Unit 3**
Elizabeth Delacruz	Delacruz	Elizabeth	
Elizabeth M. De La Cruz	DeLaCruz	Elizabeth	M
Jan Van de Boer	VandeBoer	Jan	
Sandra L. Vanowen	Vanowen	Sandra	L

Filing Identical Names/Identifying Elements

9–120 If all filing units of two or more names are identical, use as *identifying elements* the individuals' city, state, and street addresses to distinguish the names from one another. If street names are identical, file by house or building number in ascending order—from the lowest to the highest numbers. If a street address is not given, file by the building name as written. Decide whether to include state names as identifying elements and whether to file by the states' full names or by their two-letter postal abbreviations. Be consistent in following the chosen methods.

	Name as Filed							
Name as Written	**Unit 1**	**Unit 2**	**Unit 3**	**Unit 4**	**Unit 5**	**Unit 6**	**Unit 7**	**Unit 8**
Ms. Kate Meehan, Santa Barbara, California	Meehan	Kate	Ms	Santa	Barbara	California		
Ms. Kate Meehan, 13486 Remington Road, Studio City, California	Meehan	Kate	Ms	Studio	City	California	Remington Road	13486
Ms. Kate Meehan, 13566 Remington Road, Studio City, California	Meehan	Kate	Ms	Studio	City	California	Remington Road	13566

Filing Professional Titles and Degrees

9–121 Personal titles include *Miss*, *Ms.*, *Mrs.*; and professional or courtesy titles such as *Doctor*, *Professor*, *Reverend*. Professional degrees and the abbreviations of professional designations include *M.D.*, *D.D.S.*, *CPA*, *Ph.D.*, *J.D.* Disregard such titles and abbreviations unless they are needed as identifying elements to distinguish identical names.

Name as Written	Name as Filed		
	Unit 1	Unit 2	Unit 3
Darlene Wills, J.D.	Wills	Darlene	JD
Dennis Wills, C.P.A.	Wills	Dennis	CPA
Gloria Winscott, CFP	Winscott	Gloria	CFP
Gloria Winscott, J.D.	Winscott	Gloria	JD

Filing Personal Titles

9–122   Disregard the seniority titles *Jr.* and *Sr.* unless needed as an identifying element to distinguish identical names. Arrange titles *Jr.* and *Sr.* in alphabetic sequence; arrange *2d*, *3d*, and *III* in numeric sequence, with arabic numerals preceding roman numerals and numerals preceding alphabetic designations.

Name as Written	Name as Filed		
	Unit 1	Unit 2	Unit 3
Richard Fong, Jr.	Fong	Richard	Jr
Richard Fong, Sr.	Fong	Richard	Sr
David Pastrana III	Pastrana	David	III
David Pastrana, Jr.	Pastrana	David	Jr

Filing Foreign and Unusual Names

9–123   File foreign names as any other personal name. If the surname and the given name cannot be distinguished, file the names as written; cross-reference under other possible names.

Name as Written	Name as Filed		
	Unit 1	Unit 2	Unit 3
Chakrit Homsuwan	Chakrit	Homsuwan	
	(SEE Homsuwan, Chakrit)		
Kringthong Sayavong	Kringthong	Sayavong	
	(SEE Sayavong, Kringthong)		

Filing Religious and Royalty Titles

9–124 Names of religious persons and royalty are often preceded by only a given name or a surname. File such names as written.

	Name as Filed		
Name as Written	**Unit 1**	**Unit 2**	**Unit 3**
Crown Princess Masako	Crown	Princess	Masako
Mother Teresa	Mother	Teresa	
Pope Benedict XVI	Pope	Benedict	XVI
Prince William	Prince	William	
Queen Sofia of Spain	Queen	Sophia	of Spain

Business and Organization Names

9–125 Business and organization names are generally filed as written, with each word considered a separate filing unit. Each word is a filing unit, including the prepositions *of*, *on*, and *in*; the conjunctions *and*, *but*, and *or*; and the articles *a*, *an*, and *the*. If the article *The* appears as the first word in a name, consider it the last filing unit.

If a name includes the full name of an individual, file the entire business or organization name as written.

	Name as Filed			
Name as Written	**Unit 1**	**Unit 2**	**Unit 3**	**Unit 4**
AI Systems	AI	Systems		
Artificial Intelligencia, Ltd.	Artificial	Intelligencia	Ltd	
Dan Raddon Office Systems	Dan	Raddon	Office	Systems
The Daryl Taylor Group	Daryl	Taylor	Group	The
The Pasadena Playhouse	Pasadena	Playhouse	The	
The Pasadenian	Pasadenian	The		
Raddon Associates, LLP	Raddon	Associates	LLP	

Filing Abbreviations and Acronyms

9–126 Consider abbreviations, acronyms, and radio and television station call letters as one filing unit; file such names as written. (An *acronym* is a pronounced word formed from the first letters of the words in a name or phrase.) If single letters are separated by spaces, consider each letter as an individual unit.

| | Name as Filed | | | | |
Name as Written	Unit 1	Unit 2	Unit 3	Unit 4	Unit 5
A Byte in Time CyberCafe	A	Byte	in	Time	CyberCafe
FAQ Checkers Inc.	FAQ	Checkers	Inc		
Fort Knox Financial Services	Fort	Knox	Financial	Services	
Ft. Meyers Motor Lodge	Ft	Meyers	Motor	Lodge	
KPCC Radio	KPCC	Radio			
KUSC-FM	KUSC-FM				
KW Events Galore	KW	Events	Galore		

Filing Symbols, Punctuation, and Possessives

9–127   Spell out all symbols such as & (and), # (number or pound), $ (dollar or dollars), ¢ (cent or cents), and % (percent or percentage); consider the words as individual filing units and file them as written. Disregard punctuation marks that appear within names, such as commas, apostrophes, hyphens, periods, and diagonals; consider as one indexing unit any names containing such punctuation.

| | Name as Filed | | | | |
Name as Written	Unit 1	Unit 2	Unit 3	Unit 4	Unit 5
A&M Electronics	A&M	Electronics			
B.C. Networks	BC	Networks			
Betty's Fruit Baskets	Bettys	Fruit	Baskets		
Books 'n' Tapes	Books'n'	Tapes			
Cornish's Corner Coffee	Cornishs	Corner	Coffee		
The Cornishes' Coffee Corner	Cornishes	Coffee	Corner	The	
Dial-A-Number Paging Service	DialANumber	Paging	Service		
Fong, Long & Wong, LLP	Fong	Long	and	Wong	LLP
Photographic-Lee Productions	Photographic-Lee/	Productions			
Yasmin's 99¢ Sweet Shop	Yasmins	99	cents	Sweet	Shop

Filing Numbers in Names

9–128   File names that begin with arabic and roman numerals before names beginning with words. Names beginning with arabic numerals are filed before

401

names beginning with roman numerals. Disregard ordinals (2d, 5th) except those spelled out, and consider only the numerals. If a number appears within the business name, file the name with the number before a similar name not having a number; all such names are filed in numeric order.

Name as Written	Name as Filed			
	Unit 1	Unit 2	Unit 3	Unit 4
1-Hour Digital Photos	1	Hour	Digital	Photos
2nd Street Mach Hydraulics	2	Street	Mach	Hydraulics
12th Hour Productions	12	Hour	Productions	
100% Resolution Solutions	100	Percent	Resolution	Solutions
Bistro 451	Bistro	451		
Mach II Garage	Mach	II	Garage	
Twelfth Avenue Theatreworks	Twelfth	Avenue	Theatreworks	

Filing Geographic Names and Compass Points

9–129 Business names that include countries, states, cities or towns, or street names are generally filed as written. Names beginning with such foreign prefixes as *La*, *Las*, *Los*, and *San*, *Santa* are filed as one unit. (See 9–130 for filing government agency names.)

Compass points may be written as one word, as two words, or as hyphenated words. Hyphenated words are filed as one unit; other words are filed as written.

Name as Written	Name as Filed			
	Unit 1	Unit 2	Unit 3	Unit 4
East End Refinery	East	End	Refinery	
Eastern Refinery	Eastern	Refinery		
Los Alamitos Place Mortuary	LosAlamitos	Place	Mortuary	
Los Angeles Party Rentals	LosAngeles	Party	Rentals	
Losano's Cantina & Grill	Losanos	Cantina	and	Grill
North-East News Press	NorthEast	News	Press	
Northeast Nurseries	Northeast	Nurseries		
The Norweigian Fish Shanty	Norweigian	Fish	Shanty	The

Government Names

9–130 Government names include those of federal government agencies, state and local governments, and foreign governments. File departments or agencies of the federal government under the filing units *United States Government.* Then file by the name of the department or agency and then by the office or bureau name.

Distinguish between government agency names and names of businesses or organizations whose names include the words "United States" or "U.S." Do not assume that the letters "U.S." in a name refers to the United States government; file such names as written.

Name as Written	Name as Filed
United States Gems & Jewelry	United States Gems and Jewelry
U.S. Farmers Home Administration (FHA)	United States Government Farmers Home Administration (FHA)
U.S. Food and Drug Administration	United States Government Food and Drug Administration

Bureau of Indian Affairs, Department of Interior	United States Government
	    Interior Department
	    Indian Affairs, Bureau of

Department of Treasury, Internal Revenue Service, US Government	United States Government
	    Treasury Department
	    Internal Revenue Service

U.S. Creative Artists Agency	US Creative Artists Agency

State and Local Government Names

9–131 File first by the name of the government entity—state, city, county, commonwealth, etc. Include as the last units the subdivision designation

Name as Written	Name as Filed
California Department of Motor Vehicles	California State Motor Vehicles Department (of)
Massachusetts Registry of Motor Vehicles	Massachusetts State Motor Vehicles Registry (of)
New Hampshire Athletic Club	New Hampshire Athletic Club
Department of Transportation of New York City	New York City (of) Transportation Department (of)
New York Designer Factory	New York Designer Factory
Ohio Bureau of Employment Services	Ohio State Employment Services Bureau
Commonwealth of Pennsylvania Department of Education	Pennsylvania Commonwealth (of) Education Department (of)

as "Office of," "Department of," or "Bureau of." File the names accordingly. Distinguish between government entities and business or organizations whose names include cities, counties, provinces, or towns.

Foreign Government Names

9–132 Names of foreign governments are filed by their specific name, followed by their identification as "Republic of," "Kingdom of," "Commonwealth of," etc. Then file by the branch, department, or agency name as written.

Name as Written	Name as Filed
Commonwealth of Australia	Australia Commonwealth of

People's Republic of China
Ministry of Education
	China
	    People's Republic of
	    Education Ministry (of

Institution and Organization Names

9–133 Institutions include schools, colleges, and universities; churches, synagogues, temples, and cathedrals; hospitals, sanitariums, and convalescent homes; and financial institutions. Generally, file such names by the distinctive words in the names. If an institution name contains the complete name of an individual, file the entire name of the institution as written.

If several organizations or institutions have the same name, use the city and state names as identifying elements and file accordingly. If the word "The" appears in a name, add it at the end of the name.

9–134 ### School Names

Name as Written	Name as Filed
John Adams Intermediate School	John <u>A</u>dams Intermediate School

John Marshall Fundamental School, Pasadena, California	John <u>M</u>arshall Fundamental School
	    Pasadena
	    California

John Marshall High School, Los Angeles, California	John Marshall High School
	    Los Angeles
	    California

The New England Conservatory of Music	New England Conservatory of Music (The)

Patrick Henry High School, Portland, Maine	Patrick Henry High School
	    Portland
	    Maine

9–135 Organization Names

Name as Written	Name as Filed
American Institute of Certified Public Accountants	American Institute of Certified Public Accountants
California Bar Association	California Bar Association
Women's Council of KCET	KCET Womens Council
National Association of Paralegals	National Association of Paralegals

Filing College and University Names

9–136 File college and university names as written. When filing names of multicampus institutions, use their city and state names as identifying elements.

Name as Written	Name as Filed
Leland Stanford, Jr., University	Stanford, Leland, Jr., University Palo Alto California
University of California at Davis	California, University (of) Davis California
University of California at Irvine	California, University (of) Irvine California
Merrimack College, Lawrence, Massachusetts	Merrimack College Lawrence Massachusetts
University of Michigan, Central Campus, Ann Arbor, Michigan	Michigan, University (of) Central Campus Ann Arbor Michigan
University of Michigan, North Campus, Ann Arbor, Michigan	Michigan, University (of) North Campus Ann Arbor Michigan

Filing Names of Religious Institutions

9–137 File names of churches, synagogues, temples, and cathedrals as written or by the distinctive words in their names. Include the city and state names as identifying elements if necessary.

Name as Written	Name as Filed
Temple Beth Shalom	Beth Shalom Temple
Iglesia Biblica Berea	Iglesia Biblica Berea
Church of Jesus Christ of Latter-Day Saints	LatterDay Saints, Jesus Christ Church (of)
St. Gregory Armenian Apostolic Church	St.Gregory Armenian Apostolic Church
St. James Episcopal Church	St.James Episcopal Church
St. James United Methodist Church	St.James United Methodist Church
Unitarian Universalist Church	Unitarian Universalist Church

Filing Names of Hospitals

9–138 File names of hospitals, sanitariums, rest homes, and convalescent homes as written or by the distinctive words in their names, followed by their city and state names.

Name as Written	Name as Filed
Hospital of the Good Samaritan, Los Angeles, California	Good Samaritan Hospital (of the) Los Angeles California
Saint Mary Mercy Hospital, Gary, Indiana	Saint Mary Mercy Hospital Gary Indiana
Veterans Hospital, Cincinnati, Ohio	Veterans Hospital Cincinnati Ohio
Veterans Hospital, Cuyahoga Falls	Veterans Hospital Cuyahoga Falls Ohio

Filing Names of Financial Institutions

9–139 Financial institutions include banks, savings and loan institutions, credit unions, trust companies, and insurance companies. File names under their distinctive words, followed by their city and state. If a branch location or other identifying information is included, consider each word as an additional filing unit.

Name as Written	Name as Filed
First National Bank East Capitol Branch Jackson, Mississippi	First National Bank East Capitol Branch Jackson, Mississippi
First National Bank Tombigbee Branch Jackson, Mississippi	First National Bank Tombigbee Branch Jackson, Mississippi
Standard Life Insurance Company, Jackson, Mississippi	Standard Life Insurance Company Jackson, Mississippi

Subject Filing Systems

9–140   A subject filing system is based on the arrangement of records by content, or subject classifications. This system works best when the categories or classifications of information are more important than an individual's or an organization's name. A subject filing system may be used for office management files, general correspondence files, or individual attorney files.

The subject filing system follows alphabetic filing rules, except that the captions on file guides are topic names. Subject folders filed behind the file guides are usually arranged in alphabetical order.

A subject filing system requires a master index that lists all subject headings and subtopics used in the system. Such an index may be kept in a computer file or on index cards. This cross-referencing system allows a user to refer to the index of possible topics before attempting to locate a file.

The subject system can be arranged into either encyclopedic order or dictionary order. In an *encyclopedic subject system*, records are stored first by large, general categories and then subdivided into related topics. In a *dictionary subject file system*, subjects are arranged alphabetically without considering the relationships of types of records. Table 9.1 shows the difference between the two subject systems.

Numeric Filing Systems

9–141   Materials in a numeric filing system are arranged by numbers that are assigned to individuals, organizations, products, subjects, etc. This system permits quick and easy identification of records and eliminates the duplication of files that often occurs in an alphabetical system. Numeric filing systems are used and work best when large volumes of records are stored and/or when the security of stored records is important.

A numerical filing system, however, is an indirect filing system. Before a document or correspondence can be filed or a folder retrieved, the assigned file number for the correspondent must be determined by referring to an alphabetic index, which may be maintained on a computer file

TABLE 9.1   Comparison of Dictionary and Encyclopedic Subject Filing Systems

Dictionary	Encyclopedic
Automobile Insurance	<u>Medical Health Insurance</u>
Buildings—Extended Coverage	Dental Insurance
Dental Insurance	Dread Disease Insurance
Disaster Insurance	Health Insurance
Dread Disease Insurance	Long-Term Health-Care
Earthquake Insurance	Insurance
Fire Insurance	Major Medical Insurance
Flood Insurance	Vision Insurance
Health Insurance	Workers' Compensation
Homeowners Insurance	Insurance
Liability Insurance	<u>Liability Insurance</u>
Long-Term Health-Care Insurance	Malpractice Insurance
Major Medical Insurance	Personal Liability (Umbrella)
Malpractice Insurance	<u>Property Insurance</u>
Personal Liability (Umbrella)	Automobile Insurance
Property Insurance	Buildings—Extended
Umbrella Insurance (see Personal Liab.)	Coverage
Vision Insurance	Disaster Insurance
Workers' Compensation Insurance	Earthquake Insurance
	Flood Insurance
	Fire Insurance
	Homeowners Insurance

or on index cards. As each correspondent is assigned a file number, an entry is made to the master alphabetical index. The assigned file number on the computer file or card contains the name, address, telephone numbers, and other relevant information.

The most common methods of numeric filing are (1) consecutive number filing and (2) terminal-digit filing.

Consecutive Number Filing

9–142   In a consecutive number filing system, numbers are read from left to right. Folders are filed in consecutive number order; new files are assigned the next number. The newer files tend to have the most activity, and those with lower numbers (older files) tend to have less activity.

Each digit in a file number is a filing unit. Compare each number unit by unit (digit by digit) until a difference is found. Then arrange the files in ascending order—from the lower number to the higher number.

    File No. 23110

    File No. 23113

    File No. 24113

Terminal-Digit Filing

9–143 In the terminal-digit filing system, numbers are assigned in consecutive sequence; however, the assigned file numbers are read in numeric groups from right to left.

For example, a folder numbered 112364 would be read as "64 23 11." It would be filed in:

Drawer 64

Section/Divider 23

Folder 11

The next number assigned would be 112365, which is read as "65 23 11." It would be filed in:

Drawer 65

Section/Divider 23

Folder 11

This system is useful when the security or confidentiality of records is important, as in a medical facility. One advantage to this system is that new folders are evenly distributed throughout the files.

Cross-Referencing

9–144 Cross-referencing refers to filing a document under the most logical caption but placing cross-reference sheets at other possible captions. When users look for a file under the alternate caption, the cross-reference sheet will refer them to the caption under which the document is filed.

File records under the most commonly used or recognized name, which is usually the client name. When a file could be identified by another name— such as an opposing party or parties or third parties—use a cross-reference to refer to the file name or number under which records are stored.

Both the subject and the numeric filing systems require a cross-referencing system; that is, a master alphabetical index must be created to enable users to retrieve stored documents from under the appropriate file names.

File Name	Cross-Reference under Name
Derantriassian Family Trust	Derantriassian, Gevork
Federal Express	FedEx
IBM	International Business Machines
Lopez-Miranda v. Machas	Machas v. Lopez Bros.
TAT Industries	Toys and Things Industries

9–145 Use a cross-reference sheet when it is likely that a file will be identified under more than one name. Cross-references are appropriate when:

1. It is difficult to determine which unit of a personal name is the surname (Van Nguyen)
2. A person or company changes names.
3. The parties' names in a case on appeal are changed *(sub nom)*.
4. A person has an unusual nickname (Dizzy Dean, Jay Hanna Dean)
5. A company or organization is equally well known and referred to by its name and its initials or abbreviation (UPS, United Parcel Service; IRS, Internal Revenue Service).
6. A company name consists of two or more names or hyphenated names (Jones and Sahagian Consultants, Sahagian-Jones Consultants) or words (Toys & Tots, Tots 'n' Toys).
7. Several clients or correspondents have identical names that need to be referred to differently.
8. A married woman uses her maiden name or a hyphenated surname or other different form.

9–146 Follow these guidelines when cross-referencing:

1. Label the cross-reference sheet or folder with the alternate caption. Indicate the main caption under which the document or folder is filed.
2. Store all related documents in the main file only.

Cross-Referencing in Numeric Filing Systems

9–147 In numeric filing systems, the alphabetic card index serves as the cross-reference to the main numeric files. By referring to the name in the alphabetic index, the user can determine the assigned file number.

Follow-Up Files

9–148 A *follow-up file* is a reminder file to show what tasks need to be completed or followed up on during a month or year. This file may consist of either or both a tickler card file and a set of special correspondence- or legal-size file folders used only for follow-up purposes. The follow-up file is arranged chronologically with dividers for each month and a subdivision for each day of the month. The day dividers for weekends and holidays should be turned over so reminders will not accidentally be filed for those days when the office is closed. Written reminders or copies of documents to be followed up on are filed behind the appropriate date. If a certain individual in the office is responsible for the follow-up, that person's name should be written on the document itself or on a stick-on note containing instructions or other notations of the follow-up action.

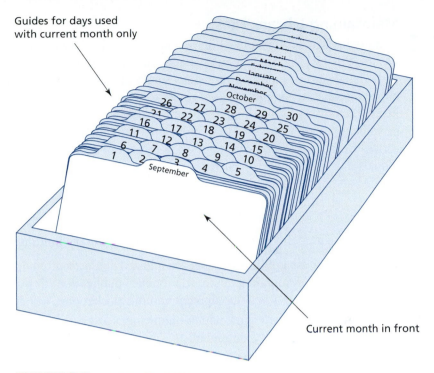

Guides for days used
with current month only

October
September
26
27
28
29
30
21
22
23
24
25
16
17
18
19
20
11
12
13
14
15
6
7
8
9
10
1
2
3
4
5

Current month in front

FIGURE 9.5   Tickler Card File

9–149   A tickler card file or docket system can be maintained on 6" × 4" index cards that are filed in a box or tray. (See Figure 9.5.) If the docketed files are to be maintained for follow-up purposes only, they should be kept in a separate FOLLOW-UP FILES drawer or cabinet and not filed with other stored records until the required action has been taken, if appropriate.

Using a Card Tickler System

9–150   Check the tickler file every day at a set time (usually first thing in the morning) to see the tasks that need attention on that day. At the end of the day, move the divider for that day behind the next month's guide. The current date should always be at the front of the tickler file. In most cases, the reminder card can be thrown away.

When maintaining a tickler or follow-up system for several people, use a color-coded system. Use different colors of metal or plastic clips hooked on the cards or folders to identify individuals. If certain individuals process follow-up files regularly, use a different color folder for each person.

When using calendaring software with a networked computer system, enter information regularly to update everyone's calendars. Electronic calendaring systems enable follow-up notes and reminders to be maintained, with reminder messages displayed on the screen at a designated time on a designated day.

Maintaining Library Files

9–151 If individuals other than a law librarian are responsible for maintaining the library, this task involves regular management of both library materials and related card or indexing files. Law books and periodicals are updated either by separate supplement volumes or by pocket parts to be inserted inside the cover of a hardbound volume. Looseleaf volumes are updated periodically with new pages that replace the same numbered pages in the series. Because the research function is critical in a law office and individuals must have access to current information, law library holdings must be filed and updated regularly.

9–152 Follow these guidelines for maintaining and filing library holdings.

1. Determine those publications that are updated and how often updates are published. Maintain a tickler file for each publication (or publisher) and the type of update—supplement volume, pocket part, or new pages.
2. Prepare a schedule to show which publications are updated weekly, monthly, semiannually, or annually.
3. Set aside a period of time on a weekly basis, if necessary, to update library holdings.
4. Jot notes on the tickler file indicating the dates when updates were received.
5. Immediately after updating the library materials, destroy—if appropriate—the dated publications. If older publications or supplements are to be retained, highlight the publication or issue dates.
6. Legal journals, magazines, bulletins, or other materials that are circulated throughout the firm before they are filed in the library should be stored in the library after final circulation. (See 9–157.)

PROCESSING MAIL

9–153 With the exception of correspondence for others marked *Personal* or *Confidential*, incoming mail should be processed as quickly as possible. Correspondence should be answered within 48 to 72 hours of receipt. Legal papers and documents should be answered as appropriate for the type of document, following either rules of procedure or the courts or other timelines. If an answer cannot be given immediately or if information must be obtained, notify the correspondent by telephone concerning the status of the matter.

Opening Mail

9–154 Follow these guidelines when opening incoming mail:

1. Use a letter opener. If mail often includes checks, money orders, or valuable papers, open three sides of the envelope to be sure everything has been removed.
2. Date stamp all incoming correspondence; either write in the date or use a date/time receiving stamp. Use colored ink and put the notation in the same place on all items (e.g., the upper right corner).
3. If desirable, maintain a mail log to record all incoming mail.
4. Verify the return address on the envelope—especially the ZIP code—with the sender's address on the letter and the address on file in company records. Staple the envelope to the correspondence if there is a discrepancy between the addresses, if there is a major discrepancy between the date of the postmark and the date on the correspondence, or if the envelope is needed for legal purposes.
5. Verify that any enclosures noted in the letter are included. Notify the sender if an enclosure is missing.

Sorting Mail

9–155 Sort mail into categories. Give priority to mail in the following order:

1. Urgent or special mail (express, registered, special delivery, courier delivery)
2. Regular mail (first-class mail, legal documents and papers, and others requiring prompt attention and/or response)
3. Routine mail (interoffice correspondence, correspondence not requiring prompt attention or response)
4. Newspapers, bulletins, and magazines
5. Catalogs and advertising materials

Distributing Mail

9–156 Before placing mail on the recipient's desk, attach any previous correspondence or files that might be needed to process the mail.

When mail must be routed to several departments for processing, the person who originally received the mail and is responsible for further routing should keep a record of the mail. The record should include the following information: name of correspondent, date of letter, subject matter, person or office where routed, and date routed.

Routing Mail

9–157 Routing slips should be used when reports, newspapers, bulletins, circulars, or magazines are regularly circulated to office personnel. A printed routing slip lists the names of the people who are to see the item, either alphabetically, by department, or by section.

Routing slips save time because they indicate to whom the material should next be sent. If an individual does not have time to read the routed material or wants to save a portion of it, the individual should route it to the next person without checking off her or his name on the routing slip.

If library materials or other date-sensitive materials are being circulated, indicate a *due date* by which the item should be circulated and returned to the library or other location.

COPYING

9–158 Copying is the easiest method of making high-quality copies of documents quickly and easily. Copiers offer a wide range of features such as reduction and enlargement, automatic feeding of stacks of original documents, collation and stapling, color-copying, and duplex (front-and-back) copying.

Combination copier-facsimile machines enable copied documents to be sent automatically via facsimile to recipients. Three-in-one machines—printer, copier, facsimile—enable computer-generated correspondence and documents to be printed and/or copied, and sent via facsimile.

9–159 Follow these guidelines in making copies of documents:

1. Determine the number of copies to be prepared—both "original" sets to be signed and conforming copies.
2. Use colored paper to make office file copies or draft/working copies of documents. Standardize the color of paper used for such copies so they can be distinguished as working copies or office files.
3. If only a few copies of a short document are needed, print them from the computer. This may be faster and more cost-effective than copying.
4. Keep a record of the number of photocopies made so their costs can be billed to the appropriate client or case.

Duplicate Originals

9–160 *Duplicate original* and *triplicate original* refer to photocopies of an original document that will also be signed and considered an original and therefore have the legal effect of an original document.

Conforming Copies

9–161 A *conforming copy* of a document is a photocopy of the original; however, the conforming copy or copies made from the original are not signed. Conforming copies should be marked or stamped COPY. These copies are made for the office files, the client, or other individuals who request them.

Unit 10

Numerical Data

MATHEMATICS FOR THE LAW OFFICE

0–1 Mathematical calculations are routinely made in law offices. These calculations include (1) percentages, (2) discounts, and (3) interest. Other math skills that are helpful to an office worker include rounding numbers, estimating answers in multiplication, and proving division.

Rounding

10–2 Rounding an answer to a shorter number is used when precision is not required or when several numbers to the right of the decimal point are unnecessary. Numbers are rounded from right to left. The number in the desired rounding place is rounded to the next higher number when the digit to its right is 5 or higher. The number is not changed when the digit to its right is 4 or lower. Digits to the right of the rounding place are replaced with zeros or, in the case of decimals, dropped. For example,

> 93.68 rounds to 94
>
> 27.29 rounds to 27

Rounding Decimals

0–3 When rounding decimals, determine the number of decimal places desired in the answer. Then carry the calculation one decimal place *beyond* the desired rounding place. For example, if an answer requires two decimal places, carry the calculation to at least three decimal places before rounding. If an answer requires three decimal places, carry the calculation to at least four decimal places, etc.

> Example: Round 1,346.0561
>
> To 3 decimal places = 1,346.056
>
> To 2 decimal places = 1,346.06
>
> To 1 decimal place = 1,346.1
>
> To a whole number = 1,346

Rounding Dollars and Cents

10–4 When a dollars-and-cents amount is desired, an answer having three decimal places or more should be rounded to the nearest cent.

> Round $424.93275 to the nearest cent = $424.93
>
> Round $424.93601 to the nearest cent = $424.94

Estimating Answers

10–5 Often, an estimated or "ballpark" answer is more useful than an exact calculation. It can, for example, serve as a quick check on a calculation. To estimate an answer, round the factors (any number or symbol in mathematics) to numbers that are easy to work with. For example, in a multiplication problem, increase one factor and decrease the other factor.**NT**

Problem: 57 × 32

Estimate: 60   Actual: 57
                × 30   × 32
               ─────   ─────
               1,800   1,824

Problem: 46 + 22 + 19 + 54 = 141 Actual
Estimate: 50 + 20 + 20 + 50 = 140
Problem: 1,824 ÷ 57 = 32 Actual
Estimate: 1,800 ÷ 60 = 30

If a problem involves decimals, drop the decimal before estimating the answer.

Proving Division

10–6 Check the accuracy of a division computation by multiplying the quotient (the answer) by the divisor (the number that is divided into another). The result should match the dividend (the number that is being divided).

$$\begin{array}{r} \$\ 1.34 \\ 18\overline{)\$24.12} \end{array} \ \text{quotient} \atop \text{dividend}$$

$$\begin{array}{r} \$\ 1.34 \\ \times\quad 18 \\ \hline \$24.12 \end{array} \ \begin{array}{l} \\ \text{divisor} \\ \text{dividend} \end{array}$$

↑
divisor

Percentages

10–7 Percentages are used in such calculations as discounts, commissions, and interest. Percentages are used to determine the relationship of one number to another. A percentage is a part of a total amount (100%) expressed in hundredths.

To solve percentage problems, first convert the percent figure to a fraction or decimal.

Converting Percentages to Decimals

10–8 To convert a percentage to its decimal equivalent, drop the percent sign and divide by 100. Dividing by 100 has the effect of moving the decimal point two places to the left.

$$25\% = 100\overline{)25.00}^{\ .25} = 0.25$$

$$37.5\% = 100\overline{)37.500}^{\ .375} = 0.375$$

$$115\% = 100\overline{)115.00}^{\ 1.15} = 1.15$$

Converting Decimals to Percentages

10–9 To convert a decimal to a percentage, move the decimal point two places to the right and add a percent sign.

417

$$0.2\underset{\smile}{5} = 25\%$$

$$0.3\underset{\smile}{75} = 37.5\%$$

$$1.1\underset{\smile}{5} = 115\%$$

Converting Percentages to Fractions

10–10 To convert a percentage to a fraction, first drop the percent sign. Then use the percent as the numerator and 100 (or a multiple of 100) as the denominator of a fraction. Reduce the fraction to its lowest terms by dividing the numerator by the denominator.

$$25\% = \frac{25}{100} = \frac{1}{4}$$

$$37.5\% = \frac{375}{1000} = \frac{3}{8}$$

$$115\% = \frac{115}{100} = 1\frac{3}{20}$$

top number—numerator

bottom number—denominator

Converting Fractions to Percentages

10–11 To convert a fraction to a percentage, follow these s teps:

1. Convert the fraction to its decimal equivalent. Common decimal equivalents appear in Table 10.1. Divide the numerator of the fraction by its denominator, carrying the calculation to four decimal places.

$$\frac{1}{4} = 4\overline{)1.0000} \, .2500 = 0.2500$$

$$\frac{3}{8} = 8\overline{)3.0000} \, .3750 = 0.3750$$

$$1\frac{3}{20} = 20\overline{)3.0000} \, .1500 = 0.1500 + 1 = 1.1500$$

TABLE 10.1 Decimal Equivalents of Common Fractions

1/3 = .3333	1/6 = .1667	1/12 = .0833
2/3 = .6667	2/6 = .3333	2/12 = .1667
1/4 = .25	3/6 = .50	3/12 = .25
2/4 = .50	4/6 = .6667	4/12 = .3333
3/4 = .75	5/6 = .8333	5/12 = .4167
1/5 = .20	1/8 = .125	6/12 = .50
2/5 = .40	2/8 = .25	7/12 = .5833
3/5 = .60	3/8 = .375	8/12 = .6667
4/5 = .80	4/8 = .50	9/12 = .75
	5/8 = .625	10/12 = .8333
	6/8 = .75	11/12 = .9167
	7/8 = .875	

2. Move the decimal point two places to the right and add a percent sign. Drop any unnecessary zeros.

$$0.2500 = 25\%$$
$$0.3750 = 37.5\%$$
$$1.1500 = 115\%$$

Base, Rate, and Portion

10–12 The parts of percentage computations are the base, the rate, and the portion. The *base* represents the total or the whole amount; the *portion* is a part of the base; and the *rate* represents the size of the portion written in a percent figure. When two parts of the calculation are known, the third part can be determined.

10–13 To determine the portion, use the following formula:

Portion = Base × Rate

Example: What is 25% of $800?

Portion = Base × Rate

$$= \$800 \times 25\% = \$800 \times .25$$
$$= \$200$$

10–14 To determine the rate, use the following formula:

Rate = Portion ÷ Base

Example: $3,500 is what percentage of $4,800?

Rate = Portion ÷ Base

$$= \$3,500 \div \$4,800 = .729166 = 72.9166\%$$
$$= 73\% \text{ [rounded to nearest whole percent]}$$

10–15 To determine the base, use the following formula:

Base = Portion ÷ Rate

Example: $570 is 12% of what amount?

Base = Portion ÷ Rate

$$= \$570 \div 12\% = \$570 \div .12$$
$$= \$4,750$$

Discounts

10–16 A discount is a decrease or markdown from an original amount and is usually represented as a percentage. A discount problem may be solved for (1) the discount amount or (2) the net amount. Before making any calculations, convert the discount rate (the percentage) to a fraction or its decimal equivalent. (See Table 10.1.)

Example: What is the price of a $58.95 calculator after it has been discounted by 3%?

Discount Amount

10–17 To calculate the amount of the discount, multiply the original price by the decimal equivalent of the discount rate. Round the answer to the nearest cent.

$$\$58.95 \times 3\% = \$58.95 \times .03 = \$1.7685 = \$1.77 \text{ discount amount}$$

Net Amount

10–18 To calculate the net amount, subtract the discount amount from the original price.

$58.95	original price
− 1.77	discount amount
$57.18	net amount

10–19 When only the net amount must be determined, first subtract the decimal equivalent of the discount rate from 1.00, the decimal equivalent of 100%. The difference is known as the *complement.*

1.00	
− .03	discount rate
.97	complement

To calculate the net amount, multiply the original price by the complement. Round the answer to the nearest cent.

$$\$58.95 \times .97 = \$57.1815 = \$57.18 \text{ net amount}$$

Interest

10–20 Interest is the amount of money charged for borrowing money or the amount of money accrued in a savings or other investment account. Interest is always stated as a percentage of the amount borrowed or on deposit. Interest is calculated on an annual basis using a year of either 360 or 365 days.

Simple Interest

10–21 Simple interest on a loan is calculated by using the following formula:

$$\text{Interest} = \text{Principal} \times \text{Rate} \times \text{Time} \quad (I = PRT)$$

The principal is the amount borrowed. The interest rate must be converted to its decimal equivalent (see Table 10.1). Time is stated in terms of days or months and is usually expressed as a fraction.

Example 1: What is the interest charge for a $7,500 loan at a 15.5% interest rate for 90 days using a 360-day year?

$$\text{Interest} = \text{Principal} \times \text{Rate} \times \text{Time}$$

$$= \$7,500 \times .155 \times \frac{90}{360}$$

$$= \$290.625 = \$290.63$$

Example 2: What is the interest charge for a $5,000 loan at an interest rate of 9.5% for 3 months?

$$\text{Interest} = \text{Principal} \times \text{Rate} \times \text{Time}$$
$$= \$5,000 \times .095 \times \frac{3}{12}$$
$$= \$118.75$$

10–22 The maturity value (the amount that must be repaid on the due date) equals the principal plus the interest. Using example 2 from 10–21,

Maturity Value = $5,000 + $118.75 = $5,118.75

Compound Interest

10–23 Compound interest is the interest on not only the principal but also on any interest paid in the past. For example, 4% interest on $100 compounded and paid quarterly is $1 ($100 × .04 × 3/12). The principal amount for next quarter is $101 ($100 principal + $1 interest) and the interest paid is $1.01 ($101 × .04 × 3/12).

Compound interest may be paid on a daily, monthly, quarterly, semi-annual, or annual basis. Normally compound interest is determined from a table or from a program in a calculator or computer.

UNITS OF MEASUREMENT

10–24 Units of measurement include the metric system of weights and measures and the U.S. customary (or standard) measures. While some items are measured in metrics (such as film size, medicine and drugs, automotive parts, and soft drinks), others follow the standard units of measure. Still other items are measured using a combination of both.

Metric System

10–25 The metric system, now known as the International System of Units, is a decimal system of measurement used by 90 percent of the world's population. Metric system units are based on a scale of 10 within each of the following seven basic units.

Unit	Symbol	Quantity/Measurement
meter	m	length or distance
kilogram	kg	mass weight
degrees Kelvin	°K	temperature
second	s	time
ampere	A	electric current
mole	mol	matter or amount of substance
candela	cd	luminous intensity

421

Metric-U.S. Customary Equivalents

10–26 The most commonly used metric units are the meter (length or distance), the liter (liquid and dry measure), and the gram (weight). The following are metric and customary equivalents for familiar measurements.

1 gram = 0.035 oz	1 ounce = 28.35 g
1 kilogram = 2.2 lbs	1 pound = 0.4536 kg
1 liter = 1.057 qts (liquid)	1 quart = 0.946 ℓ (liquid)
= 0.908 qt (dry)	= 1.101 ℓ (dry)
1 centimeter = 0.3037 in	1 inch = 2.54 cm
1 meter = 1.094 yds	1 yard = 0.9144 m
1 kilometer = 0.621 mi	1 mile = 1.609 km

U.S. Customary Units of Measure

Standard units of measurement include those for length, area, volume, mass, circular and angular measures, quantity, paper quantity, time, and temperature.

Length

10–27 A linear unit measures length or distance from one point to another on a straight line.

    1 inch (in)
    1 foot (ft) = 12 in
    1 yard (yd) = 3 ft
    1 rod (rd) = $5\frac{1}{2}$yd
    1 furlong = 40 rds or $\frac{1}{8}$ mi
    1 mile (mi) = 320 rd or 5,280 ft
    1 league   = 3 mi

Area

10–28 A square unit measures the area of a surface and its length and width. Multiply the length by the width of an area to determine the square unit measurement.

    1 square inch (sq in)
    1 square foot (sq ft) = 144 sq in
    1 square yard (sq yd) = 9 sq ft
    1 square rod (sq rd) = $30\frac{1}{4}$ sq yd
    1 acre (a)   = 160 sq rd
    1 square mile (sq mi) = 640 a

Volume or Capacity

10–29 A cubic unit of measure gives the amount of space in three dimensions: length, width, and depth.

Volume

10–30
1 cubic inch (cu in)
1 cubic foot (cu ft) = 1,728 cu in
1 cubic yard (cu yd) = 27 cu ft

Dry Volume

10–31
1 pint (pt)   = 2 cups
1 quart (qt)   = 2 pt
1 peck (pk)   = 8 qt
1 bushel (bu) = 4 pk
1 barrel (bbl)

Fluid Volume

10–32
1 fluid ounce (fl oz)
1 pint (pt)   = 16 fl oz
1 quart (qt)   = 2 pt
1 gallon (gal) = 4 qt
1 barrel (bbl) = 31.5 gal[1]

Weight or Mass

10–33 A unit of weight measures the quantity of matter within a body.

Avoirdupois Weight

10–34 Avoirdupois measurement is the standard system of weights and measures.

1 grain (gr)
1 dram (dr)   = 27.34 gr
1 ounce (oz)   = 16 dr
1 pound (lb)   = 16 oz
1 hundredweight (cwt) = 100 lb
1 short ton (st)   = 2,000 lb
1 long ton (lt)   = 2,240 lb

Apothecary Weight

10–35 These units are used to measure drugs and medicines.

1 grain (gr)
1 scruple (s ap) = 20 gr

---

[1] Barrel measurements vary from 31 to 42 gallons, depending on the standards for a particular industry.

1 dram (dr ap) = 3 s ap
1 ounce (oz ap) = 8 dr ap
1 pound (lb ap) = 12 oz ap

Troy Weight

10–36 These units are used to measure precious metals and gems.

1 gram (gr)
1 carat (c)   = 3.086 gr
1 pennyweight (dwt) = 24 gr
1 ounce (oz t)   = 20 dwt
1 pound (lb t)   = 12 oz

Circular and Angular Measures

10–37
1 sec (sec or ″)
1 minute (min or ′)   = 60 sec
1 degree (deg or °)   = 60 min
1 quadrant or 1 right angle = 90°
1 circumference or 1 circle = 360°

Quantity

10–38
1 dozen (doz.)   = 12 units
1 gross (gr.)   = 12 doz. = 144 units
1 great gross = 12 gr.   = 1,728 units

Paper Quantity

10–39
1 quire (qr)   = 24–25 sheets
1 ream (rm)   = 500 sheets
1 bundle (bdl or bdle) = 2 rm
1 bale   = 5 bdl or bdle

Time

10–40
1 second (sec)
1 minute (min)   = 60 sec
1 hour (hr)   = 60 min
1 day (d)   = 24 hr
1 week (wk)   = 7 d
1 common year (yr) = 365 d
1 leap year   = 366 d
1 decade   = 10 yr
1 century   = 100 yr
1 millennium   = 1,000 yr

Temperature

10–41 Temperature is a measure of the hotness or coldness of a body or environment. There are two common measures of temperature: the Fahrenheit scale (°F) and the Celsius scale (°C). The following table lists various temperatures on the two scales.

	Fahrenheit Scale	Celsius Scale
Freezing point of water	32°F	0°C
Cool day	50°F	10°C
Mild day	60°F	20°C
Hot day	86°F	30°C
Normal body temperature	98.6°F	37°C
Heat wave conditions	104°F	40°C
Boiling point of water	212°F	100°C

VISUAL PRESENTATION OF DATA

10–42 Tables, charts, and graphs are the most effective and compact ways to illustrate statistical relationships, trends, and comparisons. They may be placed in the body of a letter, memo, or report. They may also be displayed on a separate page and attached to the letter, memo, report, or other document.

Charts and graphs can best be prepared using a spreadsheet program. Spreadsheet programs convert data in a worksheet into a graphic—a pie, bar, or line chart. Integrated software allows data and information to be "imported"—incorporated—into documents created with other software programs. For example, word processing programs can "import" or accept charts and graphs created in a spreadsheet program; graphics from spreadsheet programs can be incorporated into presentation software programs.

Generally, use a word processing program to create tables consisting primarily of text or numbers and amounts that do not require actual calculations to be performed. Use a spreadsheet program when calculations are to be performed using mathematical formulas.

Numbering

10–43 Each table, chart, and graph in a document should be given a number and a title so that it can be easily referred to in the text. Use the label *Table* to identify tables; use *Figure* for both charts and graphs. Tables and figures may be numbered consecutively throughout the document (Figure 1, Figure 2, Figure 3, etc.), or they may be numbered consecutively by chapter or section (Figure 3.1, Figure 3.2, Figure 3.3, etc.).

Placement of Numbers

10–44 The number of an illustration may be placed a double space above the title and the graphic or below the figure, followed by the title on the same line.

> Table 4
>
> Percent of Paralegals and Legal Assistants Pursuing a Law School Education

> Figure 13. Sales Volume (in thousands of dollars), First Quarter 2008

TABLES

10–45 A table presents figures (numbers) and/or words in columns and rows. (See the parts of a table in Figure 10.1). Tables are useful for presenting comparisons involving actual numbers, dates, or amounts. Tables can best be prepared using the table feature of word processing programs.

If calculations are involved with multiple columns or rows of numbers or amounts, use a spreadsheet program, which contains features for performing mathematical functions and entering formulas.

Placement of Tables

10–46 Short tables are usually placed within the text of the document—letter, memo, or report. Longer tables are placed on separate pages and inserted close to (preferably immediately after) the related discussion. If a document has a number of tables, they could all be placed in an appendix at the end of the document.

All tables should be created and labeled so they are self-explanatory and can be understood without reading the related text.

Tables in the Text

10–47 When the table appears within the document, follow these guidelines. (See Figure 10.2.)

1. Format the table within the margin settings of the document.
2. Introduce the table with a brief statement in the text.
3. Single-space the table unless double-spacing is requested or enables easier reading. Consider using 1.5 line spacing as an alternative.
4. Format the table to provide easy reading. Set wider side margins for the table or set narrower column widths. Use the "auto fit" feature of the word processing program to compress column widths to accommodate the length of information within the columns.
5. Leave a double space (one blank line) below the table before continuing the text.

6. Do not split a table between pages if possible; reset margins and column widths (or cells) so the table fits on one page. For lengthy tables that must be continued, repeat the columnar headings on each subsequent page.

7. Place any explanatory comments or sources at the end of the table.

Separate Tables

10–48 When the table appears on a separate page, follow these guidelines.

1. Use plain paper of the same color, quality, and finish as that used for the other pages of the document.

2. Arrange the table attractively on the page. If the table is part of a bound report, allow an extra ½ inch in the top or side margin for the binding.

3. Rule or box the table to give it a more professional look and to make reading easier. The table can also be formatted as an "open" table— without ruled lines.

Parts of a Table

The parts of a comprehensive table are illustrated in Figure 10.1. The boxed table shows all levels and types of headings that may be used when presenting finite categories of information. Whether a table is created using the table feature of a word processing program or using tab settings across the document page, the levels of headings would be the same.

Title

10–49 The title should accurately and specifically identify the content of the table. The title of a table is centered and keyboarded in all capital letters. Titles that are more than one line long should be single-spaced. The title may be printed in a large-size font. Titles and other headings may also be printed in bold type. If there is no subtitle, triple-space after the title.

Subtitle

10–50 A subtitle further identifies the contents of the table. It may be enclosed in parentheses. Keyboard the subtitle a double space below the title. Capitalize only the first letter of important words. Leave a triple space (two blank lines) after the entire heading before beginning the table.

Spanner Headings

10–51 Spanner headings extend over two or more columns of information. These headings (sometimes called braced headings or straddle headings) group different categories or classifications of data and are helpful in lengthy or detailed tables. Spanner headings may be either underlined or keyboarded

Table Number	───→	Table 12
Centered main title	───→	DEMOGRAPHIC DATA
		WESTLAKE COMMUNITY CENTER POPULATION●
Centered subtitle	───→	July–September 20—

	Male		Female		Totals	
Characteristics	No.	Percent	No.	Percent	No.	Percent
Age						
Under 18	9	13.85	13	14.44	22	14.19
19–25	5	7.69	4	4.44	9	5.61
26–40	18	27.69	22	24.45	40	25.81
41–50	18	27.69	18	20.00	36	23.23
51–60	7	10.77	13	14.44	20	12.90
Over 60	<u>8</u>	<u>12.31</u>	<u>20</u>	<u>22.23</u>	<u>28</u>	<u>18.06</u>
Totals	65	100.00	90	100.00	155	100.00
Marital Status						
Married	29	44.62	40	44.44	69	44.81
Divorced, Widowed, Separated	18	27.69	22	24.45	40	25.81
Single	<u>18</u>	<u>27.69</u>	<u>28</u>	<u>31.11</u>	<u>46</u>	<u>29.68</u>
Totals	65	100.00	90	100.00	155	100.00
Education (Years Completed)						
12 (High School)	8	12.31	18	20.00	26	16.77
13	10	15.39	16	17.76	26	16.77
14	20	30.77	26	28.89	46	29.66
15	18	27.69	16	17.78	34	21.94
16	5	7.69	5	5.55	10	6.45
Over 16	<u>4</u>	<u>6.15</u>	<u>9</u>	<u>10.00</u>	<u>13</u>	<u>8.39</u>
Totals	65	100.00	90	100.00	155	100.00

Labels on the left of the figure:
- Table Number
- Centered main title
- Centered subtitle
- Centered spanner heads
- Centered column headings
- Subheadings
- Stub captions
- Caption divisions
- Underlined column totals
- Footnote
- Credit (source) line

● Includes Fairsun Satelline Center
Source: Westin County Records, 20—

FIGURE 10.1   A Comprehensive Boxed Table

with horizontal rulings above and below. A spanner heading is centered and keyboarded a single or double space above the columnar headings to which it refers.

Columnar Headings

10–52 Columnar headings may be (1) left-aligned (started at the beginning of the column), (2) centered across the column, or (3) right-aligned (generally

Larkspur Insurance, LLP

August 30, 20--

Mr. Alfred L. Stack
Mr. Kenneth H. Stack
913 McKensie Avenue
Salem, OR 97201

Dear Messrs. Stack:

This letter illustrates the placement of a table within the body of a letter. The modified-block style should be used so that the tabulated information will appear balanced on the page.

Only a short table should be incorporated within the body of a letter. Lengthy tables should be placed on separate pages, and appropriate references to them should be made in the letter. Identify each table by title and place a table close to its related discussion or explanation. The table must be arranged within the margin settings of the letter. It is preceded and followed by either one or two blank lines, as illustrated.

TERM INSURANCE PREMIUM FOR FIVE-YEAR PERIODS

(Face Value at $30,000)

Age	Annual Premium
25	$ 966
30	1,232
35	1,849
40	2,305
45	2,980

The format of the table follows that used for other tables: triple-space after the entire main heading and double-space after columnar headings, if used. Information within the table may be either single- or double-spaced, depending on the number of columns and the number of entries.

Sincerely yours,

Micah Nguyen

Muong Cai ("Micah") Nguyen
Registered Agent

kc

Golden West Towers   Suite 2204   645 Westhill Ave.   Phoenix, Arizona   85004–3864

FIGURE 10.2   **Table within a Business Letter**

used over columns of numbers). Lengthy column headings should be keyboarded in two or more lines, balanced over the information within the column. Columnar headings may be either underlined or keyboarded with horizontal rulings above and below (unless the table is ruled or boxed).

In a ruled or boxed table, the cells containing columnar headings may be shaded, using the shading feature of the word processing program, to distinguish headings from the column entries. Use light shading so the headings can be easily read.

Column headings may also be printed in boldface. If the cells containing columnar headings are shaded, the boldfaced headings will stand out.

Stub Headings or Captions

10–53 A stub heading is used to separate various categories of data in a complex table. A stub heading is always accompanied by stub captions and caption subdivisions. Stub headings are keyboarded in the same manner as columnar headings.

Stub Headings or Captions

10–54 The information under the stub heading is divided into categories. These stub captions (or line captions) are positioned at the left margin and may be underscored. Single- or double-space between stub captions.

Caption Subdivisions

10–55 Subdivisions below the stub captions may be necessary to create another category of information. These subdivisions are indented two or three spaces.

Table Entries

10–56 Table entries may be single- or double-spaced. Setting line spacing for 1.5 lines would provide more rows of information on a page, especially if the table is incorporated within text.

Formats for Column Entries

10–57 Text, numbers, and dollar amounts within the columns may be keyboarded or edited in left-aligned, right-aligned, or decimal alignment format. Which type(s) of settings to use within a table depends on the type of information presented in each column.

Tab settings on word processing software allow information to be keyboarded across the page at predetermined stops where specific types of tab settings have been identified. When the table feature is used, indentions within the cells must be made by spacing across 2–3 spaces to obtain the desired indention.

10–58   *Left-aligned text.* When text is aligned at the left, all entries in the column begin at the tab stop setting or at the beginning of the column. Use a left-aligned format for columns of words or when all numbers contain the identical number of digits.

Lisbon	4,879
Paris	2,110
Toledo	3,876

10–59   *Right-aligned text.* When text is aligned at the right, all entries in the column end flush at the right. As entries are keyboarded, characters are moved to the left so each entry is aligned at the right. Use right-aligned format for numbers, amounts, and words.

Welcome	Phyllis Brzozowski
Introductions	Carol Mitzner

```
        16,439
         1,265
           897
        10,489

       $21,890
         6,012
           559
        14,300
       $42,761
```

10–60   *Centered text and headings.* Columnar headings are generally centered across the width of the columns. As information is keyboarded, text is distributed within the cell or column to balance the words in the heading. Text within a column may also be centered.

C. Polaski	J. Hernandez	M. Rowe
D. Chien	P. Pastis	L. Samuelson

Representatives	District	Territory
Michael Belmonte	Northwest	Idaho, Oregon, Washington
Elizabeth Polenzani	Southwest	Arizona, California, Nevada

10–61   *Decimal alignment.* Decimal alignment is used for columns of numbers and amounts containing decimal points. All entries are aligned at the decimal point down the column. In columns containing times expressed in *a.m.* or *p.m.*, decimal alignment may be set to align the periods.

10–62 *Dot-leader alignment.* Dot leaders consist of a row of periods appearing between the columns of information to guide—*lead*—the eyes across the table from one column to the next.

```
INTRODUCTION............................. 1
DESCRIPTION OF THE STUDY.................. 3
```

Presenting Figures in Tables

10–63 Columns of information may be arranged using left-aligned, right-aligned, centered, or decimal tab stops. Which type(s) of settings to use within a table depends on the information presented in each column.

Whole Numbers in Tables

10–64 Align columns of whole numbers at the right, using the right-aligned feature. Insert a comma in figures of four or more digits.

```
  905
2,378
   25
```

Negative Numbers in Tables

10–65 Many tables include negative numbers. Keyboard a negative number within parentheses, or place a minus sign (a hyphen) in front of the negative number. Align the digits on the right.

```
3,655              3,655
(286)              -286
 478                478
```

Decimal Numbers in Tables

10–66 Align columns of decimal numbers on the decimal points. All the decimal numbers should have the same number of decimal places. If necessary, add zeros to decimal figures to accommodate the largest decimal figure in the column.

```
  311.5000
3,817.9000
    2.1556
```

Percents in Tables

10–67 Align the percent symbols that appear after the figures in a column. When the entire column consists of percentages, keyboard the percent symbol only after the first entry and after any subtotals and the total. If the column head includes the word *percent*, the percent symbols should still appear with the first figure in the column and again in the total.

```
    100%           Percent of
     12             Increase
     96               100%
     14                12
      2                96
    ────               14
    224%                2
                      ────
                      224%
```

Dollar Signs in Tables

10–68 Align the dollar signs in front of the amounts in a column. When an entire column consists of dollar amounts, keyboard the dollar sign only before the first entry, before subtotals, and before the total. Align the dollar sign with the largest dollar amount (which may be the subtotal or total). If the columns contain only even dollar amounts, omit the decimal point and zeros.

```
$   200.00
  2,535.07
  3,216.45
     21.50
  ─────────
$4,973.02
     24.95
    100.00
  ─────────
$6,097.97
```

Mathematical Symbols in Tables

10–69 Align keyboarded mathematical symbols in front of the figures in a column. The figures themselves should be right-aligned. Generally, all numbers in a column are presumed to be positive numbers unless a minus sign precedes the number or the number is written in parentheses.

59	-13	44
-2	21	15
4	-2	-6

Footnotes

10–70 Footnotes are used to explain the data in the table or to add qualifying information.

Footnote References

10–71 Within the table, keyboard footnote references as superscripts (numbers or letters raised above the line of type) in consecutive sequence. To ensure that the footnote reference stands out within columns of numbers, use lowercase letters (*a, b, c,* etc.) rather than arabic numerals (*1, 2, 3,* etc.), which are used in the text of a report.

Start numbering the footnotes with *a* at the top left. Move from left to right across the table and from top to bottom for additional footnote references. If there is only one footnote, an asterisk (*) may be used instead of a letter.

Separating Line

10–72 If a table is not ruled or boxed, separate the footnotes from the body of the table by keyboarding an underscore line 1½–2 inches long. Leave one blank line (a double space) after the footnote-separating line before keyboarding the footnotes.

Spacing for Footnotes

10–73 Single-space footnotes and leave a double space between them. Begin each footnote at the left margin. Do not leave any extra space between the superscript letter and the note itself. Additional lines of a footnote may begin either at the left margin or even with the first word of the footnote.

Credit Line

10–74 The source of the information in the table is placed at the end of the table. Leave one blank line between the last footnote and the credit line. Keyboard the word *Source*, followed by a colon, before the credit information.

Ruled and Boxed Tables

10–75 Within a table, ruled lines aid the reader in following the information from column to column and down the page. A *ruled table* contains horizontal rulings above and below the columnar headings and above and below the totals. If there are no totals, the rule is placed at the bottom of the table. (See Figure 10.3.)

10–76 A *boxed table* contains both horizontal and vertical rules. (See Figure 10.4.) A boxed table may also be completely enclosed in the rules. The table feature on word processing programs automatically creates ruled and boxed grids (called "cells") for the number of columns and rows desired. Columns are vertical; rows are horizontal.

Formatting Tables

10–77 To look professional, a table should be formatted attractively on the page. The table feature of word processing programs automatically determines the default or preset height and width of each cell in the table, based on the

Table 6			
TANGLEWOOD TOWNEHOMES ASSOCIATION STATEMENT OF DISBURSEMENTS For Month Ended August 31, 20--			
Expenditures	**Monthly Budget**	**Actual for Month**	**Variance**
Alarm system	$ 60.00	$ 31.84	$ 28.16
Common areas	356.00	80.00	276.00
Elevator maintenance	160.00	160.00	–0–
Gardening	250.00	250.00	–0–
Insurance	656.00	677.17	(21.17)
Building maintenance	360.00	160.00	200.00
Office expense	15.00	12.70	2.30
Trash removal	140.00	141.00	(1.00)
Electricity	550.00	574.25	(24.25)
Gas	450.00	356.76	93.24
Water and sewer	250.00	303.36	(53.36)
Total Disbursements	$3,247.00	$2,947.08	$499.92

FIGURE 10.3   Ruled Table

number of columns and rows desired, the line spacing, and the paper size. The table is automatically displayed within the set margins of the document, although a small table can be indented from both margins.

The page preview feature of the word processing program allows you to see the layout of the table on the page before actually printing it. The AutoFit feature of the word processing program can be used to compress the entire table to accommodate the table contents and the column widths.

Table Columns

10–78

The arrangement of information presented up and down the page is formatted in *columns*. The maximum number of columns across the page is determined by the paper size and the margins set for the document.

Columns can be compressed or widened to accommodate the data in the cells to fit the paper size and margins. The column widths can also be widened or narrowed manually by moving the vertical column rulings to the right or the left. Additional columns are difficult to insert because of the standard paper width (8½ by 11 inches) and margin settings for the document. If more columns are desired, change the paper orientation to *landscape* mode (11 × 8½ inches).

Table Rows

10–79

Each line of information presented in a table represents a *row*. The maximum number of rows per page is based on the paper size, although a table

Centered column
headings

Left-aligned text

Table 6			
TANGLEWOOD TOWNEHOMES ASSOCIATION STATEMENT OF DISBURSEMENTS			
For Month Ended August 31, 20--			
Expenditures	**Monthly Budget**	**Actual for Month**	**Variance**
Alarm system	$ 60.00	$ 31.84	$ 28.16
Common areas	356.00	80.00	276.00
Elevator maintenance	160.00	160.00	–0–
Gardening	250.00	250.00	–0–
Insurance	656.00	677.17	(21.17)
Building maintenance	360.00	160.00	200.00
Office expense	15.00	12.70	2.30
Trash removal	140.00	141.00	(1.00)
Electricity	550.00	574.25	(24.25)
Gas	450.00	356.76	93.24
Water and sewer	250.00	303.36	(53.36)
Total Disbursements	$3,247.00	$2,947.08	$499.92

Right-aligned columns
of figures

FIGURE 10.4 Boxed Table

can be continued to subsequent pages. Lengthy text in a column will be wrapped (moved) automatically to a subsequent line within the cell. Additional rows can be inserted easily, and the table may be continued to a new page. If so, repeat the column headings for subsequent pages.

Horizontal Centering

10–80 The table feature of the word processing program automatically determines the column widths and the width of the entire table, based on the number of columns and the width of the paper. Columns can be compressed or widened to accommodate the data in the cells and the paper size.

Formatting Columnar Headings

10–81 Column headings may be (1) left-aligned (blocked), (2) centered over the column, or (3) right-aligned. Lengthy column headings may be split on two or more lines if necessary to maintain a balanced appearance of the columns.

Left-Aligned (Blocked) Column Headings

10–82 Column headings that begin at the left of the column or that begin at the same tab setting as the column entries are *left-aligned* (blocked). This style is the most efficient and can be used for columns of text or numbers and figures. (See 10–81 and Figure 10.4)

Right-Aligned Column Headings

10–83 Column headings that line up at the right of the column are *right-justified* headings. This style can be used for columns of numbers or figures to ensure that decimal points, commas, and dollar signs are aligned consistently within the columns. If other column headings are centered and/or left-aligned, be consistent in following the predominant type of heading based on the types of information contained in the columns.

Centered Column Headings

10–84 Column headings are positioned across the width of the column. A long heading will be moved (wrapped) automatically to a second or subsequent line within the cell.

CHARTS AND GRAPHS

10–85 Charts and graphs present data in a visual form. They are not as detailed as tables, but they do provide concise comparisons and relationships. Three common chart styles are (1) the pie chart or circle graph, (2) the bar chart or bar graph, and (3) the line chart or line graph.

Use the graphics feature of a spreadsheet program to create professional-looking charts. The data must first be entered in table format in a spreadsheet program. The data to be compared are then designated; and titles, labels, and legends are added. The data may be converted into several graphic forms—pie chart, bar chart, or line chart.

Once charts have been created as a worksheet in a spreadsheet program and saved, they can then be imported—incorporated—into documents created with word processing programs. Incorporate charts into the document immediately after the discussion. Charts may also be displayed on separate pages and inserted after the related discussion.

Numbering of Charts

10–86 Charts, referred to as figures, are numbered consecutively throughout the report or within each chapter or section. (See also 10–43.)

Titles and Supplementary Information

10–87 The title and subtitle, footnotes, and credit lines follow the same format regardless of the type of chart or graph.

Title

10–88 The title should accurately identify the chart. The title is centered and keyboarded in all capital letters. Titles that are more than one line should be single-spaced. Use a large-size font and/or boldface type. Leave two blank lines (a triple space) after the title; leave one blank line (a double space) if there is a subtitle.

Titles may also be placed below the chart or graph. In this case, keyboard the figure number and the title in all capital letters on the same line, centered on the page. Continue a lengthy title on additional lines.

FIGURE 6. EMPLOYEE ABSENTEE RATES

Subtitle

10–89 A subtitle is positioned a double space below the title. Center the subtitle, and capitalize the first letter of each important word. Leave a triple space (two blank lines) after the entire heading before the chart or graph.

Footnotes

10–90 Keyboard any footnotes a double space below the chart or graph. Begin the footnotes at the left margin and use lowercase letters (*a*, *b*, *c*, etc.) rather than numbers. It is not necessary to keyboard a footnote-separating line. (See Figure 10.5.)

Credit Line

10–91 A credit line provides information about the source of the data contained in the chart. Keyboard the credit line at the left margin a double space

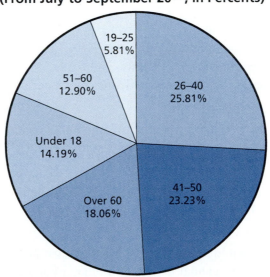

Figure 12
DISTRIBUTION OF AGES OF TOTAL
WESTLAKE COMMUNITY CENTER POPULATION
(From July to September 20- -, in Percents)[a]

19–25
5.81%

51–60
12.90%

26–40
25.81%

Under 18
14.19%

41–50
23.23%

Over 60
18.06%

[a] Includes Fairsun Satellite Center.
Source: Westin County Records.

FIGURE 10.5   Pie Chart

below any footnotes. Keyboard the word *Source*, followed by a colon, before the credit information.

Pie Charts

10–92 A pie chart (or circle graph) is a circle that is divided into sections to show the parts of the whole. (See Figure 10.5.) The entire circle represents 100 percent; each section represents a certain percentage of the whole. A pie chart should contain a maximum of six to seven sections. If there are several small categories, lump them together in a category called "Other" and give the details in the footnote.

Bar Charts

10–93 Bar charts (or bar graphs) are used to compare data at a given time or show changes over a period of time. A horizontal axis and a vertical axis are drawn at right angles to each other to relate the constant data and the variable data being compared. Information on a bar chart may be presented horizontally or vertically.

10–94 Follow these guidelines when creating a bar chart:

1. Use a separate bar for each category of information.
2. Use a different bar format (solid, stripe, color, or other design) to distinguish each type of data. Add a legend to explain which bar format represents which category of information. (See Figure 10.7.)
3. Color-code the bars as a way of distinguishing types of information; however, consider the effects of the colors when the chart is photocopied.

Horizontal Bar Charts

10–95 The horizontal bar chart in Figure 10.6 is read from left to right. The greater quantities are to the right of the chart. The horizontal axis shows the constant information (such as amounts, percentages, dates, or time). The vertical axis shows the variable information being compared. The point at which the horizontal and vertical axes meet should represent the lowest degree on the horizontal scale.

Vertical Bar Chart

10–96 The vertical bar chart in Figure 10.7 contains the same elements as the horizontal bar chart in Figure 10.6, but they are reversed. The constant data are placed along the vertical axis; the variable data are on the horizontal axis. The point at which the horizontal and vertical axes meet should represent the lowest degree on the vertical scale.

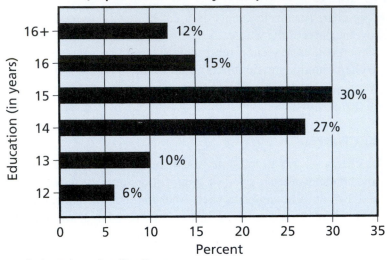

Figure 13
YEARS OF EDUCATION COMPLETED BY
65 MEN AT WESTLAKE COMMUNITY CENTER
(Population from July to September 20- -)[a]

[a] Includes Fairsun Satellite Center.
Source: Westin County Records.

FIGURE 10.6   Horizontal Bar Chart

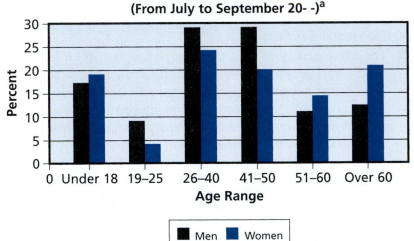

Figure 14
AGE COMPARISION OF
MALE AND FEMALE POPULATION AT
WESTLAKE COMMUNITY CENTER
(From July to September 20- -)[a]

[a] Includes Fairsun Satellite Center.
Source: Westin County Records.

FIGURE 10.7   Vertical Bar Chart

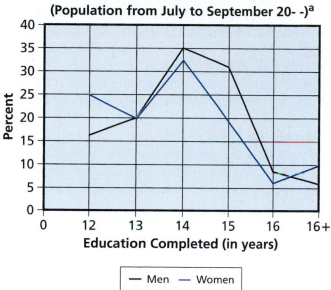

Figure 15
COMPARISON OF YEARS OF EDUCATION COMPLETED BY MEN AND WOMAN AT WESTLAKE COMMUNITY CENTER
(Population from July to September 20- -)[a]

[a] Includes Fairsun Satellite Center.
Source: Westin County Records.

FIGURE 10.8 Line Chart

Line Charts

10–97 A line chart or graph is used to illustrate a trend or movement of data over a period of time—daily, weekly, monthly, annually—or a series of activities. (See Figure 10.8.)

10–98 The horizontal axis represents the variable information (such as time, names, etc.) and the vertical axis represents the constant amounts (such as percentages or other numbers). Up to four separate lines may be shown on one graph to provide comparisons among related items. Designate a separate line for each related item being compared. Use different styles of lines to identify the variable information represented. Add a legend to explain which line format represents which category of information. If using different colors of lines, consider the effects of the line colors when the chart is photocopied.

Incorporating Graphics with Text

10–99 Once data have been entered in a spreadsheet worksheet, they may be converted into various graphic forms (see Figures 10.1, 10.5–10.8). Such graphics may then be included within the body of text-based documents created with word processing programs.

Importing Graphics into Text

10–100 Graphics from a spreadsheet program can be incorporated into a document by (1) copying and pasting or (2) linking. The two methods yield an identical graphic display; however, a graphic that has been *copied and pasted* in a document cannot later be edited or updated without returning to the spreadsheet source document and editing the data. The entire process of converting the worksheet data into a graphic must be repeated before a new document can be reprinted.

A graphic that has been *linked* to a document will automatically be updated each time the spreadsheet source document is updated. Only a reprinting of the text document is required, ensuring that changes in the worksheet will be reflected in the printed document.

Copying and Pasting a Graphic into Text

10–101 Follow these steps to copy and paste a graphic from a spreadsheet into a text document:

1. Access the desired graphic file in the spreadsheet program.
2. Select the desired chart.
3. Highlight (select) the range of the graphic to be included in the body of the text document.
4. Select the *copy* feature to create a duplicate of the selected graphic.
5. Position the cursor in the text document at the point where the graphic is to be imbedded.
6. Select the *edit-paste* feature.
7. When the graphic is displayed, edit or reformat the page as necessary.

Linking a Graphic to Text

10–102 When a chart is incorporated in a text document as a *link*, the graphic will be connected—linked—to its originating data source in the spreadsheet worksheet. If data in the worksheet are changed, the graphic will be updated automatically; this ensures that the latest data are represented in any graphic that may be incorporated within a printed document.

Follow these steps to link a graphic from a spreadsheet to a text document:

1. Follow steps 1–5 outlined above.
2. Select the *Paste Link.*
3. Identify the source file (worksheet) in the spreadsheet program.
4. When the graphic is displayed, edit or reformat the page as necessary.

Unit 11

Communication Services

Getting information from sender to receiver can be accomplished through a variety of services including telephone services, facsimile (fax) services, telecommunications services, the U.S. Postal Service, private mail services, and telegraphic services.

TELEPHONE SERVICES

11–1 The telephone is the most commonly used business communication device. Correct use of the telephone saves time and reduces correspondence and travel costs. Many public and private companies offer a variety of telephone services.

Telephone Courtesy

11–2 A telephone call is frequently the first contact with and the first impression someone has of an organization. Follow these guidelines to make that impression a positive one:

1. Sound interested, pleasant, and helpful. Put a "smile" in your voice by smiling as you talk.
2. Speak directly into the mouthpiece. A voice is carried most clearly when the transmitter is directly in front of, but not touching, the mouth.
3. Speak distinctly. Pronounce words carefully and speak at a moderate rate of speed (not too fast and not too slow).
4. Use a normal tone of voice. A loud voice may irritate the person at the other end of the line and disturb those nearby. A weak voice can cause the listener to strain to hear what is being said and to ask that comments be repeated.
5. Use language that is courteous, appropriate, and grammatically correct.
6. Concentrate on the telephone call by listening carefully, by taking notes, and by repeating details, especially names, telephone numbers, and messages.

Effective Telephone Use

Effective telephone skills include the ability to make calls, receive calls, transfer calls, place calls on hold, screen calls, and take and leave messages.

Making Calls

11–3 Follow these suggestions to be efficient, productive, and courteous when making outgoing calls:

1. Plan the call. Make notes of the items to be discussed. This saves time for both the caller and the person called and creates the impression that the caller is organized.

2. Check the time difference before calling across the nation and around the world. An 8 a.m. call made from the East Coast would be received at 5 a.m. on the West Coast; at 10 p.m. in Tokyo, Japan; at 2 p.m. in Paris, France; and at 11 p.m. in Sydney, Australia. Refer to a telephone directory for time zones in the United States and around the world.

3. Look up numbers in the telephone directory before calling directory assistance. A charge is made for each call to directory assistance (information). To help control telephone costs, keep an up-to-date list of frequently called numbers.

4. Whenever possible, place calls personally instead of having another person place them and then put you on the line.

5. Let the telephone ring for about a minute (10 rings) to give the person called sufficient time to answer.

6. If placing a call for someone else, identify yourself and then the person, department, company, or organization that is calling.

7. If the person called is not available, leave a name, telephone number, and convenient time for a return call—whether you are speaking with someone or leaving a voice-mail message. If appropriate, include a brief message concerning the nature of the call. (See 11–10.)

8. Consider the day, time of the call, and time zone if a return call is requested and especially if an immediate response or action is necessary.

Receiving Calls

11–4 Follow these guidelines for incoming calls:

1. Answer promptly—by the end of the second ring, if possible.

2. Be ready to talk as soon as the receiver is lifted.

3. Identify yourself and your office or department. Greet the caller pleasantly.

4. Take calls for absent coworkers efficiently and courteously. Ask coworkers when they will return so that callers can be told when to call back or when to expect a return call.

5. Keep a notepad handy and jot down messages. Do not trust telephone information to memory. Repeat to the caller—and ask the caller to verify—dates, numbers, amounts, addresses, and messages. Never hesitate to ask the caller to repeat information. (See also 11–8.)

6. Spell out difficult-to-understand information. Clarify letters in the names of persons and companies that sound like other letters (for example, "b as in boy," "d as in dog," "n as in Nancy," "m as in mother").

7. Apologize to a caller for errors or delays; be sincere and natural.

8. Use the hold button when leaving the line for even a few minutes. The telephone is very sensitive and can pick up office noises and conversations.

9. Suggest a time when the caller may call again to reach someone.

10. Do not argue with a caller, especially one who is upset or angry. Allow the caller to "let off steam" by listening before asking questions or trying to solve a problem.

11. Unless authorized to do so in communications with certain clients or other individuals, do not answer questions or offer information related to clients' legal matters.

12. Let the caller hang up. Put the receiver down gently under any circumstance.

Transferring Calls

11–5 When transferring calls, follow these guidelines:

1. Transfer a call only when it is necessary.

2. Be tactful, especially when the caller has reached the incorrect number.

3. Explain *why* the call is being transferred. Give the caller the name and the telephone number of the person to whom the call is being transferred, in case the transfer does not go through or the caller wishes to call directly at a later time.

4. Be sure the caller is willing to be transferred.

5. If a call is being transferred to someone's voice mail, inform the caller of this action so that she or he can anticipate leaving a message.

Placing Calls on Hold

11–6 Follow these guidelines when placing callers on hold:

1. Explain why the caller has to be put on hold and then ask if the caller wishes to hold, leave a message, or call back.

2. Depress the hold button.

3. Check on the caller every 30–45 seconds to see if he or she wishes to continue holding. Some telephone systems have a built-in reminder system: the telephone rings every 30–45 seconds as a reminder that a caller is on hold.

Screening Calls

11–7 Calls may be screened to find out who the caller is before indicating whether the person being called is available. Follow these guidelines when screening calls.

1. Find out from the person whose calls you are screening whether there are any people he or she won't talk to.
2. Be discreet so the caller does not realize you are screening the call.
3. *Before* you ask who is calling, say that the person called—and whose calls you are screening—is unavailable. After finding out who the caller is, follow one of these procedures:
   a. If the caller can be put through, simply say that the person being called is now available and put the call through.
   b. If the caller cannot be put through, ask if you can help or take a message.
   c. If appropriate and you are authorized to do so, transfer the call or refer the caller to another person in the office. Be sure that the referred person is able to assist the caller.
   d. Be firm but polite in explaining that the person called is currently not available.

Taking Messages

11–8 Taking accurate messages is an essential office skill. Use a message form, preferably one on colored paper that will stand out. A message should include (1) the date and time of the call; (2) the name of the person the message is for; (3) the name of the caller; (4) the caller's organization, if appropriate; (5) the caller's telephone number, including any extension and an area code, if appropriate; (6) the message; and (7) the name or initials of the person taking the message.

11–9 Follow these guidelines when taking messages:

1. Be prepared to take a message. Pick up a message form or notepad and a pencil when answering the telephone.
2. Write the message while the caller is still on the line. Repeat the message and any telephone numbers to verify their correctness.
3. Do not give out information to the caller. Simply say that the person is unavailable and offer to take a message.
4. Ask whether the caller wishes to call back, whether the person called should return the call and at what time, or whether a message can be taken. Ask the caller whether she or he wishes to leave a voice-mail message, in which case the call can be transferred to the voice-mail system.
5. Promise to *deliver* the telephone message to the appropriate person; do not promise that the person receiving the message will return the call.

Leaving Messages

11–10 Follow these guidelines for leaving messages with the person answering the telephone, on an answering machine, or on a voice-mail system:

1. If it is not obvious, state the full name of the person for whom the message is intended.

2. Identify yourself, your company or department, and your telephone number with area code and extension if appropriate. If a cellular telephone number is given, indicate that so the caller knows which number is being called. This would suggest that the call may be returned during other than "normal" business hours.

3. If leaving a message on an answering machine or voice-mail system, indicate the information listed in items 1 and 2 as well as the time of the message. Do not leave messages regarding the legal status or nature of the call.

4. If the call is of a general nature—not confidential or related to a legal question or situation—state briefly the nature of the call and what type of response, information, or action is desired. This enables the person called to obtain the appropriate information before returning the call.

5. Give a convenient time—and day, if appropriate—for a return call. It may be desirable to state times when you would not be available to accept a return call.

Answering Machines

11–11 An answering machine, as well as voice-mail systems, after a predetermined number of rings, answers incoming calls with a recorded message. Callers' messages are stored electronically and played back at the recipient's convenience. Both messaging systems are available with such features as remote retrieval of messages from locations other than the "home" base; a day and time "stamp" indicating when messages were received; a display indicating the number of messages recorded; and so on.

Voice-Mail Message Systems

11–12 Voice mail uses the telephone to transmit messages to a computer, where they are stored until retrieved. Incoming calls may be answered by a person or a recorded message. The recording instructs the caller to leave a message. The caller's message is stored in an electronic audio mailbox until the recipient calls the mailbox to retrieve it. The digitized format gives the mailbox holder several options, including (1) sending the same message to several voice mailboxes; (2) erasing, saving, or forwarding the message; and (3) programming the mailbox to send a message or make the call at a set time.

Answering machines, cellular telephones, and networked telephone systems provide voice-mail features. Stored messages can be retrieved at a later time as well as from remote locations. Various calling and telephone messaging features are provided by local telephone companies as well.

Record a brief outgoing message that will be played to callers; include the telephone number and the mailbox holder's name if desired. It may be helpful to indicate whether a message of unlimited length or a short message can be left, since storage capacities of devices and systems vary.

Telephone Services

11–13 Telephone services are provided by local telephone companies and a number of long-distance telephone companies. The services available from individual companies vary.

Local Telephone Exchange Company

11–14 Local telephone companies handle local, nearby, and long-distance calls within the borders of a service area. (Large local companies may have more than one service area.) Local calls are those made between persons within the same city, community, telephone exchange, or other specified geographic area or zone.

Telephone companies may charge a *flat rate* per month for unlimited local calls. With *measured rate service*, a charge may be made for each call or for a specific number of calls per billing cycle.

Toll Calls

11–15 Local toll calls are those made to numbers outside a local area but still within the area serviced by the provider. Rates charged depend on (1) the distance called, (2) the length of the call, and (3) the time of day.

Long-Distance Telephone Companies

11–16 For long-distance service, telephone customers may choose from among several long-distance companies. These companies handle calls between service areas and to other states and countries. Charges vary by company and are based on (1) the distance of the call, (2) the length of the call, (3) the type of call made, and (4) the time of day.

Long-distance calls may be dialed directly, or the operator can assist in placing these calls. In some locales, specially designated telephones allow the caller to make telephone calls and charge the cost of those calls to a personal or corporate credit card. The cost of such calls appears on the caller's monthly credit card statement.

Operator-Assisted Calls

11–17 Operator-assisted calls cost more than other types of calls because an operator is involved in completing the call. The rates charged depend on

(1) the distance called, (2) the length of the call, and (3) the time of day. These include (1) collect calls, (2) calling card calls, (3) prepaid calling card calls, (4) third-number calls, (5) conference calls, and (6) person-to-person calls. In some areas, an operator may be a voice-activated recording directing callers to select options using the phone's number and symbol keys.

Collect Calls

11–18 On a touch-tone telephone, a collect call can be dialed directly by dialing 0, the area code (if necessary), and the number. The operator will intercept and complete the call. The person being called must agree to accept the cost of the call.

Calling Card Calls

11–19 Telephone calling cards, which are similar to credit cards, are issued by the telephone company. These cards are useful for making calls when the caller is away from the office telephone. The cost of these calls is itemized on the caller's regular monthly telephone bill.

On a touch-tone telephone, the call can be dialed directly by entering the calling card number and the number being called; no operator assistance is needed.

Prepaid Calling Cards

11–20 Prepaid calling cards can be purchased for varying amounts, allowing for a specified number of minutes of telephone time. These cards allow a user to make long-distance calls, toll calls, or other calls for which there is a charge without having to pay or be billed for them or to go through an operator. The cost of each call is instantly deducted from the prepaid cash value of the card upon completion of the call. To use the card, the caller must dial a special telephone number to gain access to the telephone network system, enter a special access code number accompanying the card, and then enter the desired telephone number. These cards may have expiration dates and cannot be replaced if they are lost or stolen.

Third-Number Calls

11–21 The charge for this type of call is billed to a third number, which is neither the number of the caller nor the number being called. The operator must call the third number to verify that the charges will be accepted.

Conference Calls

11–22 Persons at three or more different locations can arrange to talk on one line at a predetermined date and time. Some telephones have a conference call option; if so, a conference call can be placed without the assistance of an operator. Check the telephone directory for instructions on setting up a conference call.

Person-to-Person Calls

11–23 A person-to-person call is placed to a specified individual. No charge is made for the call if the operator does not reach that person.

International Calls

11–24 In most parts of the United States and Canada, a caller may dial direct to certain countries in the world. International calls are made by dialing the international access code (011) + the country code + the city code + the local telephone number. Wait approximately 45 seconds for the telephone to connect and ring. The operator can also place the call. Consult your long-distance telephone company and the telephone directory for additional instructions and for a listing of country and city codes.

Other Telephone Services

11–25 Additional telephone services include mobile calls and cellular telephones, videophones, WATS lines, and custom calling services.

Mobile Calls

11–26 Mobile calls provide access to local and long-distance lines through a combination of conventional telephone equipment and radio transmission for cars, trucks, trains, ships, boats, and aircraft. Dial directly or dial 0 and ask for the mobile operator.

Cellular Telephones

11–27 Cellular telephones have nearly taken over telephone communications and have become for many their only telephone service; that is, some people no longer subscribe to the traditional "land-line" telephone services (see 11–31 • 11–37) because of the portability and myriad features offered by cell phones.

Cellular phones can be used anywhere. Cellular towers located throughout the country and around the world transfer radio signals from one microwave base station to another station in another cell area. The strength of telephone reception depends on the proximity to such towers and stations. These mobile telephones are battery operated, so they must be recharged periodically to retain power to both receive and make telephone calls.

A variety of cellular telephone service plans and telephone features are available; however, their capabilities are ever-increasing and ever-changing.

Cellular Telephone Protocol

11–28 Follow these guidelines for using cellular telephones:

1. When receiving a call while driving, pull off the road to take the call if convenient; otherwise, answer the call and tell the caller you will

return the call at a more convenient time. Allow the call to be routed to voice mail so the caller can leave a message.

2. Avoid using a cell phone in public places where a conversation can be overheard by others or be disturbing to others nearby.

3. Do not give out personal information or discuss sensitive or confidential business matters in public; others may be eavesdropping on the conversation.

4. Remember that telephone conversations are not private. The more public the venue for a call, the louder one must speak to be heard by the other party.

5. Silence the cell phone so it does not ring when you are at an event or dining; turn the phone to vibrate or silent mode to avoid the disturbing ring of the phone.

Videophones

11–29 Using regular telephone lines, a videophone transmits color pictures and sound and displays them on a screen that is part of a telephone. This capability is available on many cellular telephones.

WATS Calls

11–30 Wide-Area Telephone Service (WATS) provides long-distance service at reduced rates to and from certain offices, agencies, and organizations. Inward WATS calls, also known as toll-free or 800 service, are made without charge to the caller by dialing 1 + 800 + the telephone number.

Custom Calling Services

11–31 For extra charges, several features can be added to a telephone system without adding extra equipment. For local availability, check with the telephone company. Custom calling features include (1) call waiting, (2) call answering, (3) call forwarding, (4) three-way calling, (5) speed calling, and (6) caller ID.

Call Waiting

11–32 When the telephone is in use, a beep signal lets the user know that another caller is trying to get through. The user can place the first call on hold and answer the second by depressing the receiver button. Both callers may be kept on the line and spoken to alternately by pressing and releasing the receiver button.

Call Answering Message Center

11–33 The call answering message center service operates much like an answering machine or voice mail. When the telephone is in use, a recording prompts the caller to leave a message. The next time the user tries to make a telephone call, he or she hears a beeping sound rather than the dial tone to signal that a message has been left. Messages can be checked from any touch-tone phone; and messages can be retrieved by inserting a personal code number.

Call Forwarding

11–34 Call forwarding permits the user to program a telephone to automatically transfer incoming calls (both local and long distance) to any telephone, including cellular phones and pagers, anywhere in the country that can be reached by direct dialing. The caller is charged for the call to the user's number, as well as for the long-distance forwarding.

A related service, remote access to call forwarding, allows the user to turn the call forwarding feature on or off remotely. This feature also allows the forwarded number to be changed as the user's location changes.

Three-Way Calling

11–35 Three-way calling allows a user to talk with two others in different locations at the same time. This three-way calling service is currently automatically included on all telephones; a user is charged only when the feature is used.

Speed Calling

11–36 With speed dialing, frequently called numbers can be dialed quickly using a preprogrammed one- or two-digit code. Pressing the one- or two-digit code activates the call quickly without having to dial the entire number. Special buttons on the telephone may be programmed for one-touch dialing of frequently called numbers. Most answering machines and cellular telephones include the speed dialing feature. The telephone company offers this optional service for a monthly charge and provides equipment with different number capacities.

Caller ID

11–37 Caller ID allows the user to view on a display screen on the telephone the caller's telephone number and/or name, as well as the time of the call. This feature is used to screen calls to determine whether the telephone should be answered. Even if the caller does not leave a voice-mail message, the caller's identification will still be displayed; this information remains displayed until the next call is received.

ELECTRONIC MAIL AND THE INTERNET

Electronic Mail

11–38 Electronic mail, or e-mail, provides instant computer-to-computer message delivery between offices and individuals in any location worldwide, regardless of time differences or availability of the receiver. Electronic mail requires a computer, a modem, and telecommunications software that allows users to send keyboarded messages to other users or systems. Electronic messages are held until the receiver can access them at his or her terminal through a password, and then respond to the messages through e-mail. E-mail messages can also be stored (saved).

The Internet is an internationally accessible computer-oriented communications network that allows users to contact one another through e-mail, as well as tap into a vast range of information on almost every conceivable topic and interest. (See 11–52, Internet Services.)

Writing Effective Electronic Messages (E-Mail)

11–39 Follow these guidelines for writing effective e-mail messages. (See also 7–2, 8–2.)

1. Store the names and e-mail addresses of frequent correspondents in the electronic address book or contact file. This ensures accuracy of the addresses and saves time in having to key in an address each time. Having names in your address book also enables communications from those correspondents to be "recognized" as approved senders.

2. Keep e-mail messages short. Use e-mail as you would a telephone to convey a quick message, to respond briefly to an inquiry, to serve as a cover document when attaching electronic messages, to express thanks or appreciation, etc.

3. Write a memorandum or a letter when a lengthy or detailed communication is required; when a legal, ethical, or personnel issue is involved; when confidentiality, privacy, or security is indicated; and when a permanent record of the communication is required. Do not use e-mail when face-to-face communication is required—to convey unpleasant news, to relate or discuss personal or personnel matters, or when emotions may otherwise be involved.

4. Remember that electronic messages are not protected or secure. They are saved on network servers and can be retrieved, read, and forwarded to others—intentionally or unintentionally. E-mail communications can be transmitted long distances and over time; communications sent via e-mail are subject to public disclosure. Although e-mail messages

can be printed and stored, they can also be easily deleted from the computer.

5. Become familiar with the user identification extensions following the names of Internet service providers (ISPs). These extensions identify the source of e-mail messages:

.com	a business or other commercial enterprise (*wsj.com*; *nytimes.com*)
.edu	an educational institution (*pasadena.edu*; *ucla.edu*)
.gov	a government agency (*irs.gov*; *whitehouse.gov*)
.mil	a military institution or installation (*www.norad.mil*)
.net	an administrator of a network (*earthlink.net*; *comcast.net*)
.org	other organization, agency, or institution (*pbs.org*)

6. Use your word processing software to compose technical or detailed e-mail messages offline. This method saves time and frees up the network.

7. Before sending an e-mail, proofread the message and run the spell-checker program if available. Spell-check any attachments as well unless they were created by others, in which case they should be transmitted as they are. (See 9–89, Proofreading)

Elements of Electronic Mail (E-Mail) Communications

11–40 Internet service providers (ISPs) and Web browsers provide computer network access to create and receive electronic messages. E-mail options offer features similar to those word processing programs to create, edit, store, and print messages.

An e-mail address book, or contact list, contains the list of names and e-mail addresses of frequent e-mail correspondents. Having such names in the electronic address book provides quick, easy, and accurate access when needed. Addresses may also be created for specific groupings of individuals belonging to a particular department, interest group, or organization. One message can be sent automatically to all addresses listed and stored in that group file.

Parts of an E-Mail Communication

11–41 Regardless of the particular e-mail program or software used for electronic mail communications, all provide similar features and screen displays. The screen contains an area for the heading and a screen for the message. The menus and buttons contain commands to send, reply, print, save, or forward e-mail messages. Certain text-editing and formatting commands are also included.

Addressing E-Mail Messages

11–42 The address box at the top of the screen displays information for the heading similar to that for memorandums: TO, FROM, DATE, and SUBJECT.

TO: Key in the e-mail address of the recipient, or select the recipient's name from the electronic address book. For multiple recipients, keyboard a semicolon to separate the addresses.

FROM: The writer's name and/or e-mail address are generally automatically included on all outgoing e-mail messages and may not be displayed on the screen. Thus the writer's information does not need to be keyboarded.

DATE: The date the message is created and sent is automatically included in all outgoing messages. The date may not appear on the e-mail screen.

SUBJECT or RE: Keyboard a brief but descriptive subject to let the recipient know the content of your communication. (See 7–96.)

11–43 COPY: When a copy of the e-mail message is to be distributed to another person, enter the e-mail address of that person in the COPY block. When courtesy copies are to be sent to several people, either key in the e-mail addresses of the recipients or select the recipients' names from the electronic address book. For multiple recipients, keyboard a semicolon to separate the addresses.

The names and/or e-mail addresses of those receiving copies of the e-mail will appear on the original message to the recipient, as well as those receiving the copies. Send copies only when appropriate or when authorized and only when the recipient would deem it acceptable that others have knowledge of the communication and the content of his or her message.

11–44 BC or BCC: If the addressee of the e-mail is not to know that a copy of the e-mail message is being sent to another person, use the *blind copy notation*. The blind copy notation does not appear on the original message; however, the notation does appear on the copy of the message sent to the person who is receiving the blind copy.

11–45 ATTACHMENTS: If a document is to accompany—be attached to—the e-mail message being sent, the document must be retrieved from its storage location within your computer. The "Attach" or "Attachment" feature will direct you to the appropriate computer directory, from which the desired document can be retrieved and attached to the e-mail message. The name of the stored document will appear at the bottom of the e-mail message. Within the body of the e-mail message, indicate that a document or documents are being attached so the recipient will be aware of the inclusion.

Elements of E-Mail Messages

11–46 The parts of an e-mail message are similar to those of letters and memorandums. Generally, e-mail messages are less formal than letters, but they should be written with correct grammar, spelling, punctuation, and word usage. Use technical and legal terms only if the recipient is familiar with them.

The parts of an e-mail message include a salutation, the body (message itself), and a closing or signature block.

Salutation for an E-Mail Message

11–47 Many individuals consider a formal salutation unnecessary because of the generally informal nature of the communication. However, a salutation provides a courteous opening, whether to a colleague or someone outside the firm.

Dear Rudolfo:

Hi, Casper,

Jennifer,

Body of an E-Mail Message

11–48 Key the body of the message as you would a memorandum or letter. Consider the type of communication being sent and the nature of the contents. See 7–3 • 7–7. Follow the checklist for writing effective communications. (See 7–2.)

Keyboard the message within the margins of the screen, double-spacing between paragraphs to make reading easier. Do not use all uppercase letters for the message, as this is the equivalent of yelling or shouting. Use underscoring, boldfacing, or a color font to highlight important information; however, use these sparingly. Keep in mind that the appearance of an e-mail message on the recipient's screen may be different from that on your computer.

Use a standard 12- or 14-point font to make reading easy. Most people prefer reading messages on-screen rather than printing them out, so an easy-to-read font size aids in readability.

Closing of an E-Mail Message

11–49 As with memorandums, the closing lines included in letters—the complimentary closing and the writer's keyboarded name and title—are omitted in e-mail messages. This is true especially when messages are sent to individuals within the firm. The writer's name may be keyboarded at the end of the message if desired.

Jim

Penelope

Add a cordial closing in e-mail messages sent to individuals outside the firm as a courtesy.

> Best regards,
>
> Sincerely,

Signature Line in E-Mail Messages

11–50 Most e-mail programs provide for a "signature line or block" to be created and incorporated automatically at the bottom of all messages. Such signature lines may or may not appear in the window of an e-mail message. Create a signature block that includes the writer's complete name, mailing address, telephone numbers, a fax number, and other identifying information. Include professional titles or academic degrees as appropriate.

Retrieving and Responding to E-Mail Messages

11–51 Check for e-mail messages at least twice a day—in the morning and the afternoon—to keep abreast of activities and information. Keep in mind time differences across the country or around the world, as such differences will affect the actual time and date of receipt of messages in your electronic mailbox.

Follow these guidelines for processing e-mail messages:

1. Scan messages from the same sender. Read the earlier ones first so the subsequent messages make sense when read. The more recent messages may contain changed information or instructions that could affect previously proposed courses of action or communication.

2. Acknowledge all e-mail messages immediately—if only to say when you will respond or provide the requested information, etc.

3. When responding to a message, do not include the sender's original message. If necessary to include, select only what is relevant to your return message. (Highlight and delete the unwanted text or cut and paste the appropriate portion and incorporate it into your response.)

4. Before forwarding—sending on—an e-mail that has been forwarded to you, delete the listing of other recipients and their e-mail addresses! Having to scroll down the page before reaching the actual message is time-consuming and discourteous to subsequent recipients. (Highlight the listing and delete the unwanted information.)

5. Change the subject line when a different topic or a new subject is discussed.

Internet Services

11–52 The Internet is an extensive worldwide system of interconnected computer networks composed of a large number of host computers. Accessing the worldwide Web requires a telephone line, communications software, a computer with a modem, and a subscription to an *Internet service provider* (ISP). The Internet allows access to and exchange of a vast amount of information online with providers of services, products, and information. Electronic mail (e-mail) capabilities are provided by the Internet service providers or through software provided by communications services.

Use the online resources available via the Internet to obtain reference information (dictionaries, encyclopedias, directories); investment data (stock and bond quotations, historical data on performance, company profiles); government agencies and services; travel planning guides (airline and railway reservations, hotel reservations, general tourism and convention offerings); current news and weather; publications (newspapers, magazines, journals); employment information (job search sites for businesses and government agencies); and so on.

Electronic commerce (e-commerce) provides individuals and companies with the worldwide connections to sell and purchase goods and services through marketplace Web sites.

11–53 Access the worldwide Web by keyboarding the appropriate Uniform Resource Locator URL) address (http://www.) in your computer's browser (such as Microsoft Internet Explorer). Key in the specific address for the desired Web site, including correct punctuation. Become familiar with the user identification extensions following the names of Internet service providers (ISPs). These extensions identify the type of business, organization, or government entity. (See 11–39.)

The Web sites of businesses, organizations, and agencies will differ in their appearance, organization, and format. All should allow easy movement through pages of text, direct connection by way of *links* to specific features or information, and information about how to contact the organization if additional information or assistance is needed.

Searching the Internet

11–54 Internet search "engines" provide access to general and specific information on almost any subject desired. Each search engine categorizes and presents information differently; some will yield pages of links on the subject and/or related topics. The following are some common search engines:

Alta Vista	(www.altavista.com)
Google	(www.google.com)
Infoseek	(www.go.com)
Lycos	(www.lycos.com)
Yahoo!	(www.yahoo.com)

The quality, quantity, and nature of the information produced from the search depends on how narrow or broad the specifications identified in your initial query. Become familiar with the composition of search parameters as well as such conditional operators as AND (all specified elements to be included in the search), OR (either of one or several specified elements), or NOT (excluding a specified element).

Refer to Unit 12 for a listing of selected Internet addresses related to law, business, and government Web sites.

FACSIMILE/FAX SERVICES

11–55 A facsimile (fax) machine, hooked up to a telephone line, scans and sends a copy of handwritten material, graphics, photographs, and print material electronically over the telephone lines via a modem to another fax machine or to a computer. Faxes have become a popular and inexpensive way to transmit documents from point to point. Fax machines can send documents to and receive documents from around the country and around the world 24 hours a day.

Sending Faxes

11–56 Prepare a fax transmittal or cover sheet to be sent as the first page of the transmission. The transmittal is generally prepared on preprinted forms containing the company's identifying information. Typical information contained on the transmittal form includes the following:

- Name and address of the recipient
- The destination fax number
- The sender's complete name, address, telephone and fax numbers, and e-mail address (if not already printed on the transmittal form)
- The number of pages being transmitted—including the cover sheet; for example, Page 1 of 5 (transmittal/cover sheet), 2 of 5, 3 of 5, etc. (The recipient will know that all pages of a document have been properly transmitted.)
- A brief message written or keyboarded on the transmittal if desired

Sending Fax to Fax

11–57 Unless otherwise directed, a fax will automatically be sent to the recipient's fax number. The recipient's incoming fax will automatically print the time and date of receipt on each page of the message.

Sending Fax to Computer

11–58 Faxes may also be sent directly to the recipient's computer, equipped with the appropriate fax software and a modem. These components allow faxed messages and documents to be sent between computers as well as between fax machines and computers. The fax software may include a process or system for managing or tracking fax communications.

There need not be an attendant. A one-page fax can be transmitted in less than a minute. The cost of a fax message is about the same as a telephone call of the same length. Fax/modems installed in computers enable electronic media to be faxed directly from one computer to a receiving fax machine.

PAGING SERVICES

11–59 Paging (or "beeper") services provide local, regional, and nationwide coverage. A variety of pagers are available, including tone and tone/voice pagers, numeric display pagers (display code or telephone numbers), alphanumeric pagers (display complete messages), and those that provide voice-mail services.

TELECOMMUNICATIONS SERVICES

11–60 *Telecommunications* refers to the transmission of information over long distances using combinations of telephone lines, computerized equipment, coaxial cables, microwaves, fiber optics, and satellites. Telecommunications services are used to transmit messages and other data when speed and a written record are essential.

Electronic Mail

11–61 Electronic mail (e-mail) is the most common means of communicating between individuals—whether in the same department or organization, branch offices across the country or around the world, companies across the country or around the world, or government officials and offices around the world. (See 11–38.)

Voice Mail

11–62 Voice mail uses the telephone to transmit messages to an "electronic mailbox," where they are stored until retrieved. Voice mail has almost eliminated the "telephone tag" process that callers have experienced in trying to make and return calls when individuals cannot be reached directly. (See 11–12.)

Telex or TWX

11–63 Teletypewriters, also known as teleprinters or teletypes, are special electronically controlled typewriters connected to a network. Using communications lines, written messages are sent and received between the machines.

Telex and TWX are worldwide direct-dial systems linking a subscriber's teleprinter with others around the world to send written communications at high speed. Telex or TWX terminals can receive messages around the clock and do not need an attendant. Messages are transmitted as fast as they are keyboarded, and two-way "conversations" can take place easily and inexpensively with someone on the other side of the world.

Teleconferencing

11–64 Teleconferencing enables individuals in distant locations to meet and exchange information without having to travel to a central meeting place. Teleconferencing equipment includes telephones, computer hardware and software, and special transmission equipment.

Teleconferencing methods include audio conferencing and video conferencing.

Audio Conferencing

11–65 Audio teleconferencing transmits only sound, using special audio equipment set up in each distant location. Several people may participate at each location since the audio equipment will pick up voices throughout the room. This medium allows conversations to take place among a number of people without the need for each one to use a telephone.

Video Conferencing

11–66 Video teleconferencing transmits both images and sound and is the next best thing to a face-to-face conference. Film or video may be transmitted during the conference; the meeting may also combine dialog and "chalkboard" illustrations. Computer-generated graphics presentations and other visuals may also be transmitted.

Video systems require a special "chalkboard" using special writing implements, a video monitor, and a special conference telephone at each fixed site. Handwriting or drawing images on the board appear on the video monitor at all locations. Individuals at each location can write on the boards—adding or deleting information—enabling everyone to participate actively in the conference. Hard copies of the chalkboard images may be printed using a printer connected to the board.

U.S. POSTAL SERVICES

11–67 The U.S. Postal Service is responsible for mail service within the United States. Updated information on postal laws, regulations, charges, and services is available at any local post office. For detailed information, consult the *Domestic Mail Manual*, available at the post office and from the Superintendent of Documents or at www.usps.com. Using the proper postal services not only speeds up the delivery of mail but also saves on postage costs.

Effective Mail Service Use

11–68 Follow these guidelines to get the most efficient and economical mail service:

1. Type addresses on envelopes or mailing labels.
2. Address the envelope correctly. (See also 7–73 • 7–78.)
3. Use the Envelope and Labels feature of the word processing program to print the letter address on either an envelope or a label. With the cursor positioned in the address block of the letter, the program will automatically insert and print the inside address.
4. Identify special categories of services by using stickers or special envelopes provided by the Postal Service or by printing the class of mail on the envelope.
5. Use postal cards for short, nonconfidential messages. Postal cards are handled as first-class mail, but cost less. The cost of stationery and envelopes is also saved.
6. Use airmail only for first-class international mail. Domestic mail, if going a distance, automatically goes by air.
7. Request a certificate of mailing when proof of mailing is essential.
8. Use the RETURN RECEIPT REQUESTED service (see 11–96) when sending important documents or materials by registered mail (see 11–95) or certified mail (see 11–92) services.
9. Mail early in the day for the most efficient handling.
10. Use bulk-mail services when sending two hundred or more pieces and delivery time is not critical. Bulk mail, however, must be arranged in ZIP code order and properly bundled.

Domestic Mail Classes

11–69 Domestic mail services and rates apply to letters and parcels sent to (1) any place in the United States, (2) Canada and Mexico, and (3) a member of the armed forces with an Army Post Office (APO) or Fleet Post Office (FPO) address.

Express Mail

11–70 Express mail is the fastest, but most expensive, delivery service available from the United States Postal Service. Express mail is available for mail weighing up to 70 pounds and up to 108 inches in combined length and thickness. Letters, merchandise, business records and tapes, etc., may be sent in special envelopes provided by the Postal Service.

11–71 Express mail service is available 7 days a week, 365 days a year. Next-day delivery is guaranteed by 12 noon or 3 p.m. to U.S. addresses, including post office boxes and military addresses (APO/FPO). Express mail provides a signature for proof of delivery upon receipt. Use this service for time-sensitive materials, with guaranteed next-day or second-day delivery. Insurance against loss or damage is provided for up to $100 at no additional charge.

First-Class Mail

11–72 First-class mail, if mailed by the last pickup time listed on the Postal Service drop box or before the last pickup time at the post office, is delivered in one to three days. It is sealed and cannot be opened for postal inspection. First-class mail includes letters, postal cards, postcards, business forms, sealed greeting cards, and other documents.

11–73 The first-class rate applies to mail weighing up to 13 ounces. The minimum rate is charged for the first ounce, with a lower charge for each additional ounce. First-class mail weighing over 13 ounces must be sent priority mail (see 11–75).

11–74 First-class mail must meet the minimum and maximum sizes listed in Table 11.2. Mail that is less than the minimum is not accepted for mailing by the U.S. Postal Service. A surcharge is levied on nonstandard mail— mail over the maximum size or under weight. Such mail must be processed by hand.

Priority Mail

11–75 First-class mail that weighs less than 70 pounds is designated Priority Mail. The size must not exceed 108 inches in length and thickness. Delivery takes two to three days.

Priority Flat Rate

11–76 For a set charge, correspondence, documents, books, and merchandise that can fit inside a special envelope or box can be sent by Priority Mail. The Postal Service provides Flat Rate Envelopes and two sizes of Flat

TABLE 11.2 Standard Sizes of Mail

Dimensions	Minimum	Maximum
Height	3½ inches	6⅛ inches
Length	5 inches	11½ inches
Thickness	0.007 inch	¼ inch

Rate Boxes (11.875 inches × 3.375 inches × 16.625 inches and 11 inches × 8.5 inches × 5.5 inches) at no additional charge.

Parcel Post

11–77 Parcel post is generally used for merchandise, printed matter, catalogs, thick envelopes, and advertising material weighing between 1 and 70 pounds. The size can be no larger than 108 inches in combined length and thickness. Rates are based on the weight, distance, and shape. Delivery is available to all addresses in the United States, including post office boxes and military addresses (APO/FPO). Saturday and Sunday deliveries are available at no additional charge.

Mixed Classes

11–78 A first-class letter may be attached to or enclosed in a package sent by parcel post. If the envelope is attached to the outside of the parcel, use first-class postage on the envelope and fourth-class postage on the parcel. If the letter is enclosed in the parcel, write *FIRST CLASS MAIL ENCLOSED* on the outside and pay postage for both items.

International Mail

11–79 International mail service through the U.S. Postal Service is available to most countries. Mail to Army Post Offices (APOs) and Fleet Post Offices (FPOs), however, is considered domestic mail.

International Priority Airmail

11–80 International Priority Airmail is used for bulk mailings sent airmail for worldwide delivery of business invoices, direct mail advertising, catalogs, small packages of merchandise, and correspondence. A minimum of 11 pounds of mail per mailing is required. Undelivered items are returned directly to the sender's address without additional charge.

Global Airmail Service

11–81 Global airmail service is used to send letters or packages to almost all countries in the world. Global airmail letter-post is used to send letters under 1 ounce to Canada and Mexico.

Global Priority Mail

11–82 Global Priority Mail provides expedited mail service of most types of printed materials, correspondence, and merchandise weighing less than 4 pounds. The service covers deliveries to 51 countries and territories worldwide. Flat-rate envelopes are available at no additional charge.

Global Airmail Parcel Post

11–83 Global Airmail Parcel Post includes letters enclosed in the classic red, white, and blue bordered envelopes.

11–84 Many of the services available for domestic mail are also available for international mail, depending on the service and country of destination. Collect-on-delivery (COD) and certified mail, however, are not available for international mail. The *International Mail Manual*, available at most post offices and from the Superintendent of Documents, contains detailed information about international mail.

For information on addressing envelopes for international mail, see 7–30.

Aerogramme

11–85 An aerogramme is an airmail letter on special lightweight stationery that folds to form an envelope. Aerogrammes can be purchased from the post office and are an economical means of overseas communication. No enclosures are allowed.

Air Parcel Post

11–86 Parcels meeting specific weight and dimension limitations can be sent to overseas destinations using air parcel post. Each country has its own limitations and regulations. Goods sent abroad must be specially packaged for shipment and must meet the customs regulations of both the United States and the destination country. Air rates vary, depending on the destination; check with the Postal Service for current rates and restrictions.

INTELPOST

11–87 International Electronic Post (INTELPOST) is used to transmit facsimile messages between the United States and about 40 other countries. It is available at the main post office of 12 large U.S. cities. The document and a transmittal form are scanned by a facsimile reader and then sent by cable. A black-and-white image is printed at the destination country, and the message is either delivered to the addressee according to the country's means for processing such mail or picked up by the addressee.

11–88 Arrangements can be made to fax a message to a post office offering INTELPOST services. INTELPOST is then used to send the message (1) to someone in another country who does not have a fax machine, (2) to a fax service business in another country, or (3) to a sender who does not want to wait for an available telephone line to another country.

Special Postal Services

11–89 Other services available from the U.S. Postal Service include business reply mail, certificate of mailing, certified mail, collect on delivery, insured mail, post office box rental, postal money orders, registered mail, return receipt, special delivery, and special handling.

FIGURE 11.2 Business Reply Envelope

Business Reply Mail

11–90 Business reply mail makes it easy for the recipient to send a response. The sender obtains a special permit from the post office and guarantees to pay the postage on all replies returned, based on first-class mail rates plus an additional service fee. Preprinted envelopes or postal cards designating business reply mail must state *NO POSTAGE NECESSARY IF MAILED IN THE UNITED STATES. POSTAGE WILL BE PAID BY ADDRESSEE.* The first-class mail permit number and the name, city, and state of the post office issuing the permit must also appear. (See Figure 11.2.)

Certificate of Mailing

11–91 A certificate of mailing provides proof that a letter or package was presented to the post office for mailing on a specific date. The sender completes the form, which is then stamped by the Postal Service for a small fee. A certificate of mailing may be obtained for both domestic and international mail. It does not provide insurance or delivery guarantees nor does the Postal Service keep a record of certificates stamped. The sender must retain the Certificate of Mailing as evidence of proof of mailing.

Certified Mail

11–92 Certified mail, available for first-class and priority mail only, provides both proof of mailing and proof of delivery. It is used for items having no intrinsic value such as records or files. As a result, certified mail cannot be insured. (For valuable items, use insured or registered mail or send

467

by Express Mail; see 11–94 and 11–95.) A return receipt is available for a nominal fee. Delivery may be restricted to a specific person for an additional fee. The delivering post office keeps a record of delivery for two years.

Collect on Delivery (COD)

11–93 First-class mail may be sent on a collect-on-delivery (COD) basis if the letter, merchandise, or parcel was ordered or acceptance agreed to by the addressee. The addressee pays the United States Postal Service for the postage, the COD fee, and the value of the goods in the letter or parcel at the time it is delivered. The amount collected by the mail carrier is sent to the sender by a postal money order.

Insurance up to $100 against loss, damage, and failure to collect payment from the addressee is available. There is a maximum COD amount. This service is not available for international mail or mail addressed to military addresses (APO/FPO).

Insured Mail

11–94 First-, third-, and fourth-class mail may be insured against loss or damage to the contents. The maximum liability is $600, and fees are based on the value of the contents. Return receipt and restricted-delivery services are available at nominal fees.

First-class mail may be insured against loss, rifling, or damage to the contents. The maximum liability is $500, and fees are based on the stated value of the contents. Return receipt and restricted-delivery services are available at additional nominal charges.

Registered Mail

11–95 Registered mail offers protection for irreplaceable papers, stocks, bonds, and other items with a value up to $25,000 (insurance liability is limited to the value declared by the sender). It is the most secure means of sending valuable mail. This service is available for domestic first-class and priority mail. The sender receives a receipt at the time of mailing, and the Postal Service keeps a record of mailing. The Postal Service also keeps track of the item as it moves through the postal system. Return receipt and restricted-delivery services are available at additional nominal fees.

Return Receipt

11–96 A return receipt must be signed by someone at the address when the mail is delivered. A copy of the receipt is returned to the sender as legal proof of the date and place that the item was received. Return receipts for merchandise sent priority, registered mail, insured, COD, and Express Priority are also available. This service is generally purchased with certified mail or both proof of mailing and proof of delivery.

Special Handling

11–97 Special Handling is a service used to mail unusual items (such as small animals) that require extra care. Preferential handling is given, based on the practicality and mode of transportation required. Such mail will be handled as first-class mail from post office to post office, if possible. Special handling does not include items of a fragile nature but is required for live merchandise such as ants and bees. This service is available within the continental United States and mail should be marked SPECIAL HANDLING.

Special handling fees are based on weight and are in addition to the regular postage. Special handling may be combined with special delivery for an additional fee.

Post Office Box Rental

11–98 Individuals and businesses may rent boxes and drawers at most post offices. These boxes provide privacy for the renter and are a convenience when it is not desirable to have mail delivered to a house or business address. Mail is delivered to the post office box number, where it may be picked up by the renter, in some places even when the post office is closed. The cost of box rentals varies according to the classification of the post office and the size of the box. (See also 7–28 • 7–29 for information on addressing correspondence to post office box numbers.)

Postal Money Orders

11–99 Postal money orders provide a safe, convenient, and economical means of sending money through the mail. These negotiable instruments may be purchased and redeemed at any post office or cashed or deposited in the payee's bank account. The maximum amount of a postal money order is $1,000. If the money order is lost, damaged, or stolen, it can be replaced.

Telegraphic Money Order

11–100 Telegraphic money orders are an alternative to postal money orders. Telegraphic money orders are a fast, safe method of sending money to almost any point in the world. The sender pays Western Union the amount to be sent with cash, a cashier's check, or a money order, or the sender charges the amount to a credit card. The recipient is notified by the receiving telegraphic office and is paid the amount of the money order upon showing proper identification.

PRIVATE MAIL SERVICES

11–101 In addition to the U.S. Postal Service, there are a number of private companies that provide delivery systems. Two of the best known are United Parcel Service (UPS) and Federal Express (FedEx). Most of the larger national companies deliver anywhere in the United States and to most foreign countries. Delivery time varies from overnight to several days. Limits on sizes and weights vary among companies.

Packages can be taken to the delivery company or, for an additional fee, picked up at the sender's place of business. Some companies even have conveniently located drop boxes.

Check "Delivery Service" in the Yellow Pages of your telephone directory for the local and long-distance carriers in your area.

Private Delivery Services

11–102 Private courier services are available to pick up and to hand deliver documents and packages within local geographic areas. Generally, as soon as a package is picked up from the sending location, it is immediately hand-delivered to the destination point.

Unit 12

Law Office References

Law office personnel should be familiar with the reference books and source materials discussed in this unit. Each category of reference books is defined and discussed and followed by a bibliography of key titles. Some of the entries are annotated; that is, they include a description of the contents of the book.

The reference books listed in this unit are representative of the many that are available. Specialized reference books exist for almost any subject of interest. The federal government and most state governments publish a variety of reference materials on laws, regulations, agency organizations and services, and so on.

Most reference books are available at the reference department of public libraries. Many resources are also available on the World Wide Web and the Internet.

BIOGRAPHICAL BOOKS

Biographical books supply data about prominent people. Information may include background, age, marital status, parentage, schools attended, occupation or profession, affiliations, achievements, and honors. Professional associations and national and regional organizations also publish biographical books.

Concise Dictionary of American Biography. **New York: Charles Scribner's Sons.**
Contains information on deceased American men and women.

Current Biography. **New York: The H. W. Wilson Co. Monthly and cumulative annually.**
Covers such dignitaries as monarchs, prime ministers, presidents, senators, cabinet members, and Supreme Court justices and celebrities such as radio, television, film, stage, and sports personalities. The annual edition is titled *Current Biography Yearbook.*

The International Who's Who. **London: Routledge.**
Contains up-to-date information on persons of distinction in all fields in all parts of the world, primarily outside the United States.

Webster's New Biographical Dictionary. **Springfield, Massachusetts: Merriam-Webster, Inc.**
Contains biographical sketches that identify people of any nationality from any period of history.

Who's Who. **London: A&C Black. Annual.**
Is an up-to-date source of information on living persons of distinction in all fields in all parts of the world.

Who's Who in America. **Chicago: Marquis Who's Who, Inc. Biennial.**
Contains biographies of best-known living men and women in all fields of achievement.

Who's Who in Finance and Industry. **Chicago: Marquis Who's Who, Inc. Biennial.**
Includes biographical data of outstanding business professionals throughout the world.

> *Who's Who of American Women.* **Chicago: Marquis Who's Who, Inc. Biennial.**
> Contains biographical data on notable living American women.

Other biographical reference books published by Marquis Who's Who, Inc., include:

> *Who's Who in American Politics, Who's Who in American Law,* **etc.**
>
> *Who's Who in the East, Who's Who in the Midwest,* **etc.**
>
> *Who Was Who in America*

DICTIONARIES AND WORD BOOKS

Dictionaries

12–3 The dictionary is the most important general reference book for office workers. Dictionaries are published in various sizes, from small abridged pocket editions to large unabridged multivolume sets. *Abridged* dictionaries contain information about the more common words, while *unabridged* dictionaries give authoritative information about virtually every word in the English language. (See also information on electronic dictionaries, 9–92 • 9–94.)

12–4 Know the contents and organization of dictionaries and how and when to use them. The main entry for each word provides information on spelling, syllables, pronunciation, part of speech (noun, verb, etc.), etymology (origin of the word), meanings (definitions), usage, capitalization, synonyms (words with similar meanings), and certain irregular forms. Most dictionaries also provide useful supplementary information in appendixes.

> *The American College Dictionary.* **New York: Random House, Inc.**
>
> *The American Heritage Dictionary of the English Language.* **Boston: Houghton Mifflin Co.**
>
> *The Oxford English Dictionary* **(20 volumes with supplements). London: Oxford University Press.**
> A complete, unabridged dictionary of the English language, origin of words, etc.
>
> *The Random House Dictionary of the English Language.* **New York: Random House, Inc.**
>
> *Webster's New World Basic Dictionary of American English.* **Springfield, Massachusetts: Webster's New World.**
>
> *Webster's Third New International Dictionary.* **Springfield, Massachusetts: Merriam-Webster, Inc.**
> Since the original publication, there have been two supplements containing 12,000 additional new words.

Specialized Dictionaries

12–5 Dictionaries provide information on spelling, synonyms, pronunciation, etymology, and usage. Most legal dictionaries also include citations to cases that define certain words. Such case citations should be referred to as a secondary source when a word is being defined in a legal document. Specialized legal and medical dictionaries are also available.

> *Attorneys Medical Deskbook 3d.* New York: Clark, Boardman, Callaghan.
>
> *Ballentine's Law Dictionary.* Rochester, New York: Lawyers Co-operative Publishing.
>
> *Black's Law Dictionary.* Eagan, Minnesota: Thomson West.
>
> *Stedman's Medical Dictionary.* Baltimore: Lippincott, Williams & Wilkins Publishing.

Word Books and Thesauruses

12–6 A *thesaurus* is a word book that gives *synonyms* (words with similar meanings) and, in some cases, *antonyms* (words with opposite meanings) of words. (See also 9–95.)

> Burton, W. C. *Legal Thesaurus.* New York: McGraw-Hill.
>
> Gordon, Frank S., Thomas M. S. Hemnes, and Charles E. Weinstein. *The Legal Word Book.* Boston: Houghton Mifflin Co.
>
> *Roget's International Thesaurus.* New York: Thomas Y. Crowell Company.
>
> *Roget's Thesaurus of English Words and Phrases.* London: Penguin Books Ltd.
>
> *Roget's Thesaurus of Phrases.* Cincinnati, Ohio: Writer's Digest Books.
>
> *Webster's New Dictionary of Synonyms.* Springfield, Massachusetts: Merriam-Webster, Inc.

A word book contains an alphabetical listing of words and their syllables for word division. Legal, medical, and technical-scientific word books are available for people who use a specialized vocabulary.

> *20,000+ Words: Spelled and Divided for Quick Reference.* Columbus, Ohio: Glencoe Publishing Company.

DIRECTORIES

12–7 A directory is an alphabetical listing of names and addresses of people within a particular community or a given business, industry, or profession. Directories can be used to verify the spelling of an individual's name; find the address or telephone number of a person or company; or identify a company's officers, products, and/or services.

Directories are available for many specialized areas, such as manufacturing, shipping, hotels and motels, newspapers, attorneys, educational institutions, insurance firms, and sales executives.

***AT&T Toll-free 800 Directory.* Bridgewater, New Jersey: AT&T.**
Lists all published toll-free 800 phone numbers.

***The Bank Directory* (5 volumes). Skokie, Illinois: Accuity/Thomson Financial Publishing. Semiannual.**
This premier five-volume bank reference directory, introduced in 1876, provides information on banks worldwide including national routing codes, industry statistics and rankings, standard settlement instructions, credit ratings, and a Resource Guide featuring suppliers to the marketplace.

City directories. Taylor, Michigan: R. L. Polk and Company. Annual.
Available for over 1,400 cities and suburbs. Each directory has four sections: (1) Buyer's Guide and Classified Business Directory (arranged in alphabetical order by type of business), (2) Alphabetical Directory (includes name, address, occupation, and employer), (3) Street Directory of Householders and Businesses (arranged alphabetically by street name; includes name of occupant, home owner or tenant, phone number, and ZIP code), and (4) Numerical Telephone Directory (telephone numbers arranged in numerical order; lists name of person).

***Corporate Technology Directory* (4 volumes). Wellesley Hills, Massachusetts: Corporate Technology Information Services, Inc. (CorpTech).**
Lists over 95,000 U.S. companies that manufacture or develop high-technology products.

***Dun's Business Rankings.* Parsippany, New Jersey: Dun & Bradstreet, Inc.**
Gives credit and capital ratings of firms, with addresses and type of business.

***Encyclopedia of Associations* (3 volumes). Detroit, Michigan: Thomson Gale.**
Lists over 22,000 national and international organizations. Includes address and phone of an association's headquarters, as well as a brief description of its organization and publications.

***Martindale-Hubbell Law Digest* (3 volumes). Summit, New Jersey: Martindale-Hubbell. Annual.**
Contains a digest of laws of each state and the federal government, plus international and Canadian laws.

***Martindale-Hubbell Law Directory* (25 volumes). Summit, New Jersey: Martindale-Hubbell. Annual.**
Contains a state-by-state list of all lawyers by name and type of practice.

Mergent's manuals (formerly known as Moody's manuals). New York: Mergent, Inc.
Consists of a series of manuals providing detailed financial data on companies in many areas including banking and finance, municipal and

government, OTC industry, and public utility. In addition, Mergent's publishes bond surveys, mutual funds updates, dividend records, and a directory of obsolete investments.

Official Congressional Directory. **Washington, D.C.: Superintendent of Documents, U.S. Government Printing Office.**
Lists the names and addresses of members of Congress and executive personnel.

Standard & Poor's Register of Corporations, Directors and Executives **(3 volumes). New York: Standard & Poor's Corporation. Annual.**
Contains information on firms and executives and directors in the United States and Canada, in various industrial classifications.

Telephone directories.
Compiled and published by telephone companies and distributed to telephone subscribers annually. Lists subscribers, their telephone numbers, and addresses. Also includes information on types of telephone services, rates, etc. The Yellow Pages lists business subscribers by particular product or service. May be ordered for other cities. Directories for most major cities are available in public libraries.

Thomas Register **(book of CD-ROM). New York: Thomas Industrial Network. Annual.**
A comprehensive listing of manufacturing businesses, cross-indexed with products and services, company profiles, and supplier catalogs.

ENCYCLOPEDIAS

12–8 Encyclopedias provide authoritative information on a great number of subjects arranged in alphabetical order and discussed briefly in articles written by specialists. Many encyclopedias are illustrated with pictures, graphs, maps, and charts that help the reader understand the written material. Specialized encyclopedias for a particular field or subject are found in school and public libraries and in the libraries of professional and technological societies or organizations. Some encyclopedias are also available on CD-ROM.

The Concise Columbia Encyclopedia. **New York: Columbia University Press.**

The Encyclopaedia Britannica **(32 volumes, CD-ROM and Online versions). Chicago: Encyclopedia Britannica, Inc.**

The Encyclopedia Americana **(30 volumes). New York: Grolier Incorporated.**

Lincoln Library of Essential Information. **Cleveland, Ohio: The Lincoln Library Press.**

McGraw-Hill Encyclopedia of Science and Technology **(20 volumes). New York: McGraw-Hill.**

LEGAL ENCYCLOPEDIAS

12–9 *American Jurisprudence 2d (Am. Jur. 2d)* **(83 volumes). Rochester, New York: Lawyers Co-operative Publishing.**

Corpus Juris Secundum (C.J.S.) **(162 volumes). St. Paul, Minnesota: West Publishing Co.**

ONLINE RESOURCES

12–10 Many resources are available online via the World Wide Web (www.) and the Internet: by entering known addresses to access a source directly (e.g., www.irs.gov); by using a search engine that accesses categories of information by topics (www.google.com); and by clicking a link within a Web site to be directed to other sites and related topics. Some resources are available by subscription only, some charge a nominal fee per use, and some allow free access. A wealth of resources can be obtained readily on any number of subjects—law, medicine, technical and scientific areas, business, the arts, history, biographies, current news stories, and so on.

12–11 The number and the quality of resources produced during a search depend on the parameters—the scope or limitations—specified. Keying in a word or phrase (such as *Brown)* will yield an unlimited number of results. Including OR indicates that either one or another key word or phrase (such as *Brown* **OR** *Board of Education)* is to be included in the search and must appear in the search result. Including AND in a search (such as *Brown* **AND** *Board of Education*) indicates two or more key words or phrases are to be searched and must appear in the search result. The word NOT indicates what information or key word or phrase is to be excluded from the search. Become familiar with these and other guidelines in conducting online searches to access relevant information efficiently.

12–12 Evaluate the quality and accuracy of information obtained online, using the following criteria: (1) Consider the source of the information and whether the author or organization is a recognized authority on the subject. (2) Determine how current the information is and how often the site is updated. Consider whether the links are current. (3) Determine the scope of information presented and whether there is adequate coverage of the topic. (4) Evaluate the accuracy of the information and whether there are any factual errors. (5) Consider whether information is presented objectively and without bias.

Online Search Tools

12–13 The following is a partial listing of common Web sites, which include search engines, directories, and other research tools. Although many sites provide similar information, some are easier to reference or contain more in-depth information or provide links to related topics.

Directories

12–14 An online directory lists a range of topics of information. At the home page of the directory, click on the link for the desired subject. These links will lead to additional online resources for the search topic entered.

- Excite   (www.excite.com)
- InfoSeek   (www.go.com)
- Yahoo!   (www.yahoo.com)

Search Engines

12–15 A search engine produces more responses than directories; in fact, sometimes too many responses. Use key words or terms to limit the parameters for the search to produce relevant information.

- AltaVista   (www.altavista.com)
- Google   (www.google.com)
- HotBot   (www.hotbot.com)
- Metacrawler   (www.metacrawler.com)

Selected Legal Research and Writing Resources

12–16
- American Bar Association Uniform Citation System
  (www.abanet.org/citation)
- DePaul University
  (www.law.depaul.edu)
- Introduction to Basic Legal Citation by P.W. Martin
  (www.law.cornell.edu/citation)
- Legal Research and Writing
  (www.law.utk.edu/library/research.htm)
- Lexis-Nexis and Shepards
  (www.lexisnexis.com/shepards)
- Uniform System of Citation ("Harvard Bluebook")
  (www.legalbluebook.com)
- University of California at Berkeley
  (www.law.berkeley.edu)
- The University of Memphis Library
  (www.lib.memphis.edu)

Selected Law Directories

12–17
- Martindale-Hubbell Directory
  (www.martindale.com/locator/home.html)
- Parker Directory listing attorneys and law offices as well as all federal courts and districts
  (http://uscourts.com)

Selected Professional Legal Organizations

12–18
- American Accounting Association
  (www.aaahq.org)
- American Association for Paralegal Education (AAFPE)
  (www.aafpe.org)
- American Association of Law Libraries (AALL)
  (www.aallnet.org)
- American Institute of Certified Public Accountants
  (www.aicpa.org)
- Association of Legal Assistants and Paralegals (NALA)
  (www.nala.org)
- American Bar Association (ABA)
  (www.abanet.org)
- American Center for Law and Justice
  (www.aclj.org)
- American Civil Liberties Union
  (www.aclu.org)
- Association of Legal Administrators (ALA)
  (www.alanet.org)
- The Association for Legal Professionals
  (www.nals.org)

Selected Resources for Case Law

12–19
- Cornell Legal Information Institute
  (www.law.cornell.edu)
- FindLaw
  (www.findlaw.com)
- Law Crawler
  (http://lawcrawler.findlaw.com)
- Lexis (by subscription only)
  (www.lexis.com)
- Nolo (varied legal and business resources)
  (www.nolo.com)

- United States Supreme Court
  (www.supremecourt.org)
- United States Supreme Court Decisions
  (www.findlaw.com/casecode/supreme.html)
- Westlaw (by subscription only)
  (www.westlaw.com)

Selected Law School Resources

12–20
- Information from a specific law school
  (www.law.\<name of law school\>.edu)
  (Example: www.law.upenn.edu = University of Pennsylvania School
  of Law)
- Information on specific topics
  (http://law-library.rutgers.edu/ilg/topical.php)

Selected Government Web Sites

12–21
- 50States.com (for state-by-state information)
  (www.50states.com)
- Congressional Proceedings and Materials
  (www.archives.gov/records_of_congress)
- Equal Employment Opportunity Commission (EEOC)
  (www.eeoc.gov)
- Federal Register Information
  (www.archives.gov/federal-register)
- Internal Revenue Service
  (www.irs.gov)
- Library of Congress (for searches of any published book)
  (http://lcweb.loc.gov)
- National Aeronautics and Space Administration (NASA)
  (www.nasa.gov)
- National Archives
  (www.archives.gov)
- National Labor Relations Board (NLRB)
  (www.nlrb.gov)
- Securities and Exchange Commission
  (www.sec.gov)
- Small Business Administration
  (www.sba.gov)
- THOMAS Legislative Information
  (www.thomas.loc.gov)

- United States Code provisions
  (http://uscode.house.gov)
- U.S. Department of Education
  (www.ed.gov)
- U.S. Department of Treasury
  (www.treas.gov)
- U.S. Government Printing Office
  (www.access.gpo.gov)
- U.S. Patent and Trademark Office
  (www.uspto.gov)
- The White House
  (www.whitehouse.gov)

Travel Sites

12–22
- Consumer Reports
  (www.consumerreports.org)
- Expedia.com
  (www.expedia.com)
- MapQuest
  (www.mapquest.com)
- Google Earth
  (www.earth.google.com)
- Librarians' Internet Index
  (www.lii.org)
- Maps.com
  (www.maps.com)
- Rand McNally
  (www.randmcnally.com)
- Travelocity.com
  (www.travelocity.com)
- Yahoo! Travel
  (www.travel.yahoo.com)

Selected Business and Corporate Information Sites

12–23
- American Bar Association
  (www.abanet.org)
- Bankrate.com
  http://bankrate.com
- Better Business Bureau
  (www.bbb.org)

- E•Trade Financial
  (http://us.etrade.com)
- Morningstar.com
  (www.morningstar.com)
- MSN Money
  (www.money.msn.com)
- NASDAQ
  (www.nasdaq.com)
- Tax and Accounting Directory
  (www.taxsites.com)
- Yahoo! Finance
  (http://finance.yahoo.com)

Dictionaries/Encyclopedias

12–24
- TechWeb: The Business Technology Network
  (www.techweb.com/encyclopedia)
- Webopedia (online computer dictionary for computer and Internet terms)
  (www.webopedia.com)

Selected Periodicals

12–25
- *BusinessWeek*
  (www.businessweek.com)
- *Financial Times*
  (www.ft.com)
- *Forbes*
  (www.forbes.com)
- *Fortune*
  (www.fortune.com)
- *Market Watch*
  (www.marketwatch.com)
- *New York Times*
  (www.nytimes.com)
- *Wall Street Journal* (online to subscribers; some free access)
  (www.wsj.com)

Selected Multipurpose Resource Sites

12–26 The following Web sites contain a vast amount of law-related information
and case law as well as general business information.

- Cornell University
  (www.law.cornell.edu)
- FindLaw (for constitutions, statutes, case law, etc.)
  (www.findlaw.com)
- Google.com
  (www.google.com)
- Yahoo!
  (www.yahoo.com/law)

Other Search Sites

Although individual Web sites provide a means of seeking help to clarify a search, there are also other ways to obtain research assistance.

- www.ask.com—This site provides automated "Expert Advice" by using the key words or phrases posed in a query.
- www.clearinghouse.net—This site provides links to virtual libraries, Internet directories, and Internet search tools.
- www.elibrary.com—This site enables searches of the Web for newspaper and magazine articles, books, transcripts of television and radio broadcasts, and maps.

STYLE MANUALS

12–28 Style manuals present information on the arrangement and content of formal papers and reports such as term papers, research papers, theses, dissertations, and manuscripts. Colleges and universities, professional associations, and publishers require that documents be prepared according to certain styles.

The Bluebook: A Uniform System of Citation. Cambridge, Massachusetts: The Harvard Law Review Association.

Campbell, William Giles, Carol Slade, and Stephen Vaughan Ballou. *Form and Style: Theses, Reports, Term Papers.* Boston: Houghton Mifflin Co.

The Chicago Manual of Style. Chicago: The University of Chicago Press.

Dworsky, Alan L., and Jason Geer. *User's Guide to the Bluebook.* Buffalo, New York: William S. Hein & Company, Inc.

MLA Handbook for Writers of Research Papers, Theses, and Dissertations. New York: Modern Language Association.

Wydick, Richard C. *Plain English for Lawyers,* 2d Ed. Durham, North Carolina: Carolina Academic Press.

PROFESSIONAL LAW OFFICE REFERENCES

 Attorneys and other law office personnel are guided by standardized codes of ethical standards and professional responsibility outlined in Model Codes and Rules. Other references provide general information about various aspects of the legal profession, including practices, procedures, and documentation.

> American Bar Association. *Model Code of Professional Responsibility.*
>
> American Bar Association. *Model Rules of Professional Conduct.*
>
> *NALS Code of Ethics and Professional Responsibility with Discussion.* Tulsa, Oklahoma: National Association of Legal Secretaries (International).
>
> *NALS Manual for the Lawyer's Assistant.* St. Paul, Minnesota: West Publishing Company.
>
> National Association of Legal Assistants, Inc. *Code of Ethics and Professional Responsibility.*
>
> National Association of Legal Secretaries (International). *The Career Legal Secretary.* St. Paul, Minnesota: West Publishing Company.
>
> Nemeth, Charles P. *The Paralegal Resource Manual.* New York: McGraw-Hill.

FORM BOOKS

 Form books are published for federal practice and for individual state practices. These books contain forms specifically tailored for a particular jurisdiction and type of law practice. Many of these forms books are available on computer disks.

> *Am. Jur. Legal Forms 2d* (20 volumes). Eagen, Minnesota: Thomson West.
>
> *Am. Jur. Pleading and Practice Forms, Revised* (30 volumes). Eagen, Minnesota: Thomson West.
>
> *Bender's Federal Practice Forms* (15 volumes). New York: Matthew Bender.
>
> *Federal Procedural Forms* (68 volumes). Eagen, Minnesota: Thomson West.
>
> *West's Legal Forms, 2d.* (CD-ROM). Eagen, Minnesota: West Publishing Co.

INDEXES

 Indexes list the contents of books and periodicals and are helpful when information on a particular subject must be located. Indexes list article titles (often grouped by subject), book titles, and sources (name of publisher for books, name and date of periodical or newspaper for articles). Many indexes are also available on CD-ROM.

Electronic databases such as WESTLAW and LEXIS contain information that is also available in print form.

Bell and Howell Newspaper Index. Wooster, Ohio: Bell and Howell.
Indexes articles in major newspapers.

Books in Print. New York: R. R. Bowker Co.
Gives author, title, price, publisher, and year of publication of all books included in publishers' annual trade lists.

Business Periodicals Index. New York: The H. W. Wilson Co. Monthly except July and cumulative annually.
A subject index to periodicals in accounting, advertising, banking, general business, and other fields.

Cumulative Book Index. New York: The H. W. Wilson Co. Monthly and cumulative twice a year.
Indexes all books published in the English language by author, title, and subject.

Current Law Index. Foster City, California: Information Access Corporation.
Contains over 700 permanent legal periodicals arranged by subject, author and title, and other categories.

The Education Index. New York: The H. W. Wilson Co. Cumulative.
Is a periodic index (by subject and author) for magazines, journals, yearbooks, and monographs in the field of education. Lists book reviews by author, giving publisher's address.

Index to Legal Periodicals. Bronx, New York: H. W. Wilson Company. Monthly.
Includes articles published in over 500 periodicals. Is indexed by subject and then by author.

Legal Resource Index. Farmington Hills, Michigan: Gale Group.
Contains the same information as the *Current Law Index* but is published in computerized and microfilmed versions.

The New York Times Index. New York: The New York Times Co. Biweekly with annual cumulation.
Classifies material in the *New York Times* alphabetically and chronologically under subject, title, person, and organization.

Reader's Guide to Periodical Literature. New York: The H. W. Wilson Co. Semimonthly and cumulative annually.
Indexes articles of a popular and general nature by subject and author.

OTHER REFERENCE SOURCES

12–32 A number of other reference books contain useful information on a variety of topics.

Bartlett's Familiar Quotations. Boston: Little, Brown and Co.
A collection of passages, phrases, and proverbs traced to their sources in ancient and modern literature.

Commercial Atlas & Marketing Guide. Chicago: Rand McNally & Co. Annual.
Contains reference maps and general information for the United States, Canada, and the rest of the world.

Consumer's Index to Product Evaluations and Information Sources. Ann Arbor, Michigan: Pierian Press. Online.
Lists magazine articles and government resources that provide information on consumer and health-related topics and on specific products and services.

CRC Handbook of Chemistry and Physics. Cleveland, Ohio: CRC Press. Annual.
Contains mathematical, chemical, and physical data.

Domestic Mail Manual, V. 58. Washington, D.C.: United States Postal Service.

Facts on File. New York: Facts on File, Inc. Online.
A weekly world news digest with cumulative index.

Guide to Reference Material (3 volumes). Westport, Connecticut: Libraries Unlimited.
Lists recent reference books and bibliographies, international in scope, but with emphasis on items published in the United Kingdom.

Guiness World Records. London: Guiness. Annual.
Lists many significant and interesting records.

Leonard's Guide. New York: G. R. Leonard & Co., Inc. Online.
A complete shipper's guide with rates and routings for freight shipments, express, and parcel post. Also includes information concerning Canadian and overseas parcel post.

Rand McNally Cosmopolitan World Atlas. Chicago: Rand McNally & Co.
Contains maps with geographical statistics and population figures for each area.

Robert's Rules of Order Newly Revised. Cambridge, Massachusetts: Da Capo Press, Perseus Books Group.
Covers rules on how to conduct meetings using parliamentary procedure.

U.S. Government Printing Office catalogs (Monthly Catalog, New Books, and U.S. Government Books). Washington, D.C.: Superintendent of Documents, U.S. Government Printing Office.
Catalogs list numerous government publications available for purchase including the title, stock number, and price.

Index

Index

Administrative materials, footnote references to, 6–240

Adverb-adjective compound, 1–157

Adverbial phrase, 1–39

Adverb-participle compound, 1–158

Adverb(s)
  absolute terms, 1–183
  comparison, 1–175 • 1–182, Table 1.7 (p. 42)
  conjunctive, 1–146 • 1–150
  defined, 1–145
  negative, 1–148
  prepositional phrase used as, 1–194
  similar, 1–174 • 1–189, Table 1.6 (p. 41)
  and split infinitives, 1–144
  words ending in -ly, 1–182

adverse/averse, 4–114

advice/advise, 4–115

Advisory opinions, citing, 6–71 • 6–72

Aerogramme, 11–85

affect/effect, 4–116

Afterthought, dash for, 2–82

Agenda, 9–25

Ages, 5–19 • 5–20

aid/aide, 4–117

Airmail, 11–68

Air parcel post, 11–86

Air travel, 9–35

Alderman, 7–84

A.L.I.; *see American Law Institute (A.L.I.)*

Alignment; *see also* Columnar headings
  centered, 10–60
  decimal, 10–61
  dot-leader, 10–62
  left, 10–58
  presenting figures in tables, 10–63
  right, 10–59
  tab settings on word processing software, 10–57

allowed/aloud, 4–123

all ready/already, 4–118

all together/altogether, 4–119

allude/elude, 4–120

allusion/illusion, 4–121

all ways/always, 4–122

almost/most, 1–186

Alphabetic filing
  business and organization names, 9–125 • 9–129
  defined, 9–109
  filing unit by unit, 9–113 • 9–124
  government names, 9–130 • 9–132

institution and organization names, 9–133 • 9–139

numeric filing systems, 9–141 • 9–143, Table 9.1 (p. 408)
  reasons for, 9–110
  rules for, 9–110 • 9–143
  subject filing systems, 9–140

A.L.R.; *see American Law Reports (A.L.R.)*

already/all ready, 4–118

altar/alter, 4–124

Alta Vista, 11–54

altogether/all together, 4–119

always/all ways, 4–122

Ambassador, 7–84

Amendment, 6–15 • 6–17

American Bar Association, 6–168

American Jurisprudence 2d (Am. Jur. 2d), 6–158

American Law Institute (A.L.I.), 6 • 161

American Law Reports (A.L.R.), 6–154

American Standard Code for Information Interchange (ASCII), 5–55

among/between, 1–201, 4–215

amount/number, 4–213

Amounts
  parenthesis to set off, 2–16
  word division, 4–100

Ampersand, in company name, 2–56

a.m./p.m., 5–49 • 5–50, 5–52, 5–54, 5–97 • 5–98, 10–61

-ance/-ant suffixes, 4–13 • 4–14

and/but, 1–214

and/or, 2–87

Angular measure, 10–37

Annotated bibliography, 8–68

Annotations, 6–154 • 6–155

Answering machines, telephone, 11–11

-ant/-ance suffixes, 4–13 • 4–14

Anthology, footnote reference to, 6–235

Antonym, 12–6

anxious/eager, 4–214

any one/anyone, 4–125

any way/anyway, 4–126

APO; *see* Army Post Office (APO)

Apostrophe; *see also* Contractions; Possessives
  abbreviations for feet or minutes, 2–11
  contractions, 2–9
  defined, 1–91, 2–2
  omitted numbers, 2–10
  plurals, 2–13
  possessives, 1–52, 2–2 • 2–8

quotation within quotation, 2–12

Apothecary weight, 10–35

appellant/appellate, 4–127

Appellate brief, 8–20 • 8–21

Appendix
  of appellate brief, 8–21
  of formal report, 8–61

Appointments
  confirming, 9–17
  greeting visitors, 9–20 • 9–21
  handling delays, 9–22
  in-house meetings, 9–18
  off-site, 9–19
  preparing for, 9–18 • 9–22
  recording, Table 9.1 (p. 362)
  scheduling, 9–15 • 9–16

Appositive, 1–28 • 1–29, 2–18, 2–35 • 2–36

appraise/apprise, 4–128

Arabic numbers; *see also* Figures; Numbers
  in body of formal report, 8–31
  lists introduced by, 7–37
  in outlines, 8–4

Archbishop, 7–85

Area code, 5–46

are/hour/our, 4–129

Argument, of appellate brief, 8–21

ARMA; *see Association of Records Managers and Administrators (ARMA)*

Armed forces, capitalization, 3–40

Army Post Office (APO), 11–69, 11–71, 11–77, 11–79, 11–93

Article
  capitalization, 3–13, 3–60
  definite, 1–169, 1–172 • 1–173
  indefinite, 1–169 • 1–171

as, as comparison word, 1–93

as ... as/not so ... as, 1–215

as/as if/as though/like, 1–216

ASCII; see *American Standard Code for Information Interchange (ASCII)*

assistance/assistants, 4–130

Associate Justice of the U.S. Supreme Court, 7–84

Association (Assn.) names; *see also* Organization names
  capitalization, 3–50
  in case name, 6–94

Association of Records Managers and Administrators (ARMA), 9–112

Asterisk, 2–14 • 2–15

Index

Index

Index

L

Labor union, as party in action, 6–95 • 6–97

lake, 3–35

Landscape orientation, 10–78

last/latest, 4–227

later/latter, 4–178

latter/former, 4–223

Law directories, online, 12–17

Law office management
    calendars and appointments, 9–3 • 9–17
    copying, 9–158 • 9–161
    editing, 9–87 • 9–96
    filing procedures, 9–97 • 9–152
    form documents, 9–77 • 9–86
    information processing, 9–41 • 9–57
    information processing software, 9–58 • 9–76
    making travel arrangements, 9–32 • 9–40
    planning meetings, 9–23 • 9–31
    preparing for appointments and conferences, 9–18 • 9–22
    priorities, 9–1 • 9–2
    processing mail, 9–153 • 9–157
    proofreading, 9–87 • 9–96, Figure 9.4 (pp. 388 • 389)

Law office references
    biographical books, 12–2
    dictionaries, 12–3 • 12–4
    directories, 12–7
    encyclopedia, 12–8 • 12–9
    form books, 12–30
    indexes, 12–31
    legal encyclopedias, 12–9
    online references, 12–10 • 12–27
    other reference sources, 12–32
    professional law office references, 12–29
    style manuals, 12–28

Law school resources, online, 12–20

Lawyers Co-operative Publishing Company, 6–106

lay/lie, 4–179

lead/led, 4–180

leased/least, 4–181

Lectures, 6–261 • 6–262

Left-aligned (blocked) column headings, 10–81 • 10–82, Figure 10.4 (p. 436)

Left-aligned text, 10–58

Leftbound report, 8–26

Legal citations; *see also* Footnote references; Primary authority; Secondary authority
    abbreviations, 6–5 • 6–6
    capitalization, 3–43
    defined, 6–2
    spacing, 6–5 • 6–6
    underscore names of parties in, 2–161

Legal documents
    expressing numbers in, 5–3
    numbers and amounts in, 5–31

Legal encyclopedias, 12–9

Legal memorandums; *see* Memorandums

Legal periodicals, 6–160

Legal research and writing resources, online, 12–16

Legal terms, capitalization, 3–45

Legal text, expressing numbers in, 5–3

Legal writing
    appellate brief, 8–20 • 8–21
    bibliographies, 8–66 • 8–79
    case briefs, 8–14 • 8–15
    checklist for, 8–2
    defined, 8–1
    formal reports, 8–22 • 8–65, Table 8.1 (p. 343), Table 8.1 (p. 343), Table 8.2 (p. 344), Table 8.5 (p. 345)
    legal memorandums, 8–16 • 8–19
    outlines, 8–3 • 8–13, Figure 8.3 (pp. 336 • 337), Figure 8.4 (p. 338)

Legislative bodies, capitalization, 3–38

Legislative intent, 6–54

Legislative materials
    committee reports, 6–54, 6–59
    Congressional Record, 6–53
    description of, 6–51
    elements of, 6–56
    federal legislation, 6–52
    House and Senate bills, 6–57 • 6–58
    United States Code Congressional and Administrative News, 6–55 • 6–56

lend/loan, 4–184

lessen/lesson, 4–182

less/fewer, 1–184, 4–221

Letter (correspondence); *see also* Business letters (correspondence); Envelopes; Memorandums; Social correspondence; Unpublished materials

capitalization of parts, 3–27

capitalize nouns with, 3–16 • 3–18

categories of, 7–8 • 7–11, Figure 7.1 (pp. 287 • 288), Figure 7.2 (pp. 287, 289), Figure 7.3 (pp. 289 • 290)

checklist for, 7–2

defined, 7–1

elements of, 7–17 • 7–72, Figure 7.4 (p. 291), Figure 7.5 (p. 292), Figure 7.6 (p. 293), Figure 7.12 (p. 316), Table 7.6 (p. 293)

formats for, 7–12, Figure 7.4 (p. 291), Figure 7.5 (pp. 291 • 292), Figure 7.6 (p. 293)

letter margins, 7–13, Table 7.2 (p. 294)

punctuation styles, 7–14 • 7–16, Figure 7.4 (p. 291), Figure 7.5 (p. 292), Figure 7.6 (p. 293)

table within, Figure 10.2 (p. 429)

types of, 7–3 • 7–7

Letterhead stationery, 7–17 • 7–18, 7–73, Figure 7.4 (p. 291), Figure 7.5 (p. 292), Figure 7.6 (p. 293), Figure 7.7 (p. 312)

Letter margins; *see* Margins

Letter placement guide (standard-size stationery), Table 7.1 (p. 294)

Letters (alphabet)
    abbreviations, 5–65 • 5–66
    broadcasting station call letters, 5–71
    join single, 2–111
    names consisting of series of capital, 6–112
    in outlines, 8–4
    plural word forms of single, 4–68 • 4–69

LEXIS electronic database, 6–268

liable/libel, 4–183

Library files, 9–151 • 9–152

lie/lay, 4–179

Lieutenant Governor, 7–84

Light pen, 9–42

like/as/as if/as though, 1–216

-like/-less suffixes, 4–17

Limited or *Ltd.,* 6–89 • 6–90

Limiting adjectives; *see* Article

Linear unit measure, 10–27

Line chart or graph, 10–85, 10–97 • 10–98, Figure 10.8 (p. 441)

Index

Q

R

Index

Mc Graw Hill **McGraw-Hill Irwin**

The McGraw·Hill Companies

McGraw-Hill Higher Education

ISBN 978-0-07-351183-2
MHID 0-07-351183-8

90000

EAN

9 780073 511832

www.mhhe.com

T3-BIS-686